ST. MARY'S COLLEGE OF MARYLAND
ST. MARY'S CITY, MARYLAND

W9-AFT-732

India and World Civilization

49216

INDIA
AND
WORLD CIVILIZATION

by D. P. Singhal

Volume II

MICHIGAN STATE UNIVERSITY PRESS

1969

Copyright © 1969
Michigan State University Press
Library of Congress Catalog Card Number: 68-29146
Manufactured in the United States of America
Standard Book Number: 87013-143-5

★
 ★
★
 ★
 ★

Contents

India and World Civilization

Chapter 1

THE EASTERN HORIZON
OF BUDDHISM

ONCE BUDDHISM had a firm foothold in Central Asia and China, it was inevitable that it should spread into neighbouring areas, such as Korea, Japan, and Mongolia. These countries had some direct contact with India, although part of the Buddhist influence in Mongolia was the result of contacts with Tibet. Whilst the exact origins of Buddhist penetration into Korea are obscure, there is no doubt that Korea, like China, felt the effect of two great waves of influence: one from the north, originating in Central Asia and travelling to Korea and Japan by way of the Wei Empire; and the other from the south, originating in India and Southeast Asia and travelling through southern China, towards northern China, Korea, and possibly also to Japan.

It was in the latter half of the fourth century that Buddhism reached Korea. At the time Korea was divided into three kingdoms—Koguryu in the north, Pekche in the southwest, and Silla in the southeast. These states were continually engaged in warfare, and their boundaries fluctuated. Although all of these states welcomed Buddhism and the fortunes of Korean Buddhism, like Korean politics, were linked with developments in China, the history of Buddhism in these three regions is not identical.

Buddhism was brought to Koguryu in 372, reputedly by royal invitation, by a Chinese monk, Shun Tao (or Sundo), who came from a small kingdom—China at the time was divided into sixteen states—on the upper borders of Korea. He was followed by another Chinese monk, A Tao, and in 375 the King built two temples, one for each monk. Buddhism came to Pekche in 384 from the south through an Indian or Tibetan monk named Marananda. It is said that the Pekche King came to the outskirts of the capital to receive him. Marananda was soon

1

followed by other monks from China. Temples began to appear and Buddhism became the state religion. Because of its isolated position, Silla was the last kingdom to receive Buddhism, more than thirty years after it had been introduced into Koguryu. According to tradition, a Buddhist priest, Mukocha, having cured the King's daughter of illness by offering prayers to the Buddha, persuaded the King of Silla to send for monks from China.

It is quite possible that Buddhism reached Pekche by sea even before it was introduced into Koguryu, because Pekche had maritime links with South China. Establishing this fact is difficult for very few Buddhist works of art from this period have survived in Pekche, as is also the case in Koguryu. In both kingdoms, art works were destroyed during their dynastic wars with Silla. The absence of definite information is particularly regrettable, since it was Pekche which established contact with Japan and, in the middle of the sixth century, acted as a launching pad for Buddhist doctrine and art into Japan.

In 668 Korea was united under the Silla dynasty which ruled until 935. Many Korean monks went to China to study Buddhist doctrines, and some even went to India. According to I-tsing, five Korean monks visited India during the seventh century. Prajnavarman, a Korean monk, travelled by sea to Fukien in China and then, after learning Sanskrit and studying Buddhism for ten years at the Monastery of Great Faith, proceeded to India in company with a Chinese monk. Of those who went to China to study, Yuan-tso (613–683) of the Fa Sian sect and Yuan-hiao (617–670) and Yi-siang (625–702) of the Huayen sect are best known. An outstanding monk of the period was Wonhyo, who laid the firm foundations of Korean Buddhism, and whose works are highly esteemed, even in China and Japan. However, he did not go to China, which was under the T'ang dynasty at the time, although it was the fashion for scholars to do so. The Huayen doctrine, proclaiming the Buddha-nature of all beings without distinction, was first introduced into Korea in the latter part of the seventh century. As a result of the work of Yui-shih, a Korean monk who had been actively associated with the learned circles of T'ang China, the "consciousness-only" doctrines of Yogacara Buddhism spread in Korea. Korea borrowed profusely from the Chinese civilization, and this tendency helped the development of Buddhism at the time even though Confucianism, its formidable rival, was also introduced in the early eighth century.

Kyongu, the capital of Silla, was a flourishing centre of Buddhist culture and trade, attracting merchants from India, Tibet, and Iran. With the expansion of Buddhism, monasteries, temples, and stupas appeared. Today a number of ruins survive in the vicinity of Kyongu, and some of the early Sillan art is distinctly Indian in style.

The next dynasty, the Koryo which replaced the Sillas in 935, was devoted to Buddhism.[1] Consequently, Buddhist art and learning were extensively practiced, and the eleventh century became the period of greatest prosperity for Buddhism in Korea. It was, however, a time of recurrent pressures and invasions from people beyond the borders. Despite success against these intruders, a feeling of insecurity remained in Korea which may have increased the need to seek solace in religious escape and consolation. At the end of the century, the crown prince became a monk, went to China to study, and upon his return propagated the teaching of T'ien-t'ai Buddhism. On his initiative, numerous Buddhist texts were imported from neighbouring areas and published in Korea. During the Koryo period, Buddhism became the entire basis of Korea's religious life, affecting the ideology, customs, and morals of the people as well as the political and economic life of the state. Festivals were celebrated by the Court with great splendour, and magnificent monasteries were founded. Many Buddhist monks even occupied high positions in the administration. Buddhist participation in politics, however, caused increased opposition which had begun to emerge during the latter part of the Koryo ascendancy.

Buddhism, hitherto the religion of the Korean aristocracy related to the Silla dynasty, became the faith of the common people through the efforts of such eminent monks as Pu-chao, who introduced Korea to Son (Dhyana or Ch'an) Buddhism, and who is famous for his editing of the catalogue of the Chinese Tripitaka, known in Korean as the *Taejang*, published in 1010. Son Buddhism spread widely in Korea and during the twelfth century it became extremely popular as taught by Chinsul. Son Buddhism eventually assumed predominance in Korea, although during the period of Mongol ascendancy in China, Lamaism was introduced into Korea.

After the decline of the Koryo dynasty in 1392, Buddhism was generally suppressed by the state with only occasional periods of respite. Reflecting Chinese Neoconfucianism, the Korean rulers of the Yi Chosun dynasty (1392–1910) encouraged the revival of Confucianist teachings. Confucianism was accorded such enthusiastic royal patronage that the Confucianists became extremely intolerant of other faiths. The feudal lords, who had suffered loss of power and prestige because of the Buddhist emphasis on the equality of man, sided with Confucianism. Despite the state policy of suppression, which became severe under King Taijong (1401–1418), Buddhism continued to flourish as the religion of the masses. A monk, Hanho, published a famous book denouncing the severe persecution. The next king, Sejong, who in fact styled himself as the Buddha's protector, managed to end the persecution. A wise and perceptive ruler, he realized the great literary value of the Buddhist scriptures, which he helped translate. He is also regarded as the inventor of the Korean alphabet, the *Hangul*.

In the fifteenth century, when Korea fell under Chinese domination, the fate of Buddhism in Korea became all the more contingent upon the fluctuations of its counterpart in China. However, with the rise of Japan as a major power, Korea came increasingly under Japanese domination, and in 1910 was annexed by Japan. Taking advantage of the changed political situation, Japanese Buddhists intensified their activities to encourage Buddhism in Korea and recast it on the model of their own. Whilst Korean Buddhism retained its own distinctive personality, it certainly benefited by the efforts of Japanese monks. According to the figures compiled in 1926, Korea had 1,363 temples and 7,188 Buddhist clerics.

Buddhism in Korea is still held in high esteem, and, despite the influence of Confucianist ethics on Korean thought and life, Korea is one of the countries where Buddhists are still actively engaged in public welfare activities, especially education. Modern Korean Buddhism is Zen tinged with a belief in Amitabha Buddha and Maitreya Bodhisattva. Although Korea did not contribute a school of her own to Buddhism, and made no notable developments in its doctrine, she acted as a cultural intermediary between China and Japan, and thus transmitted Buddhism to Japan.

Before the arrival of Buddhism in Korea, the existing local belief was rooted in a form of Shamanism, a combination of cults of the sun, earth, and natural forces, in addition to ancestor worship. In the days of the Three Kingdoms, Koreans believed that the ultimate objective of man was to understand, obey, and worship a heavenly emperor, who was the judge of all human affairs. To this society, Confucianism introduced its ethic and Buddhism its divinities. Buddhism came not only as a well-developed philosophy but also as a mature religion. Soon it permeated all segments of society and began to influence and enrich Korean culture, arts, music, and all branches of scientific learning. It gave Koreans what they lacked most: a sense of security and hope. When Buddhism first entered the peninsula, it absorbed the local deities into the Buddhist pantheon in the same manner as it had in China and Japan, hailed them as previous incarnations of the Buddha, and gave them new names. For instance, the spirit of the Ever-White

4

Mountains, the Virgin in Ever-White Robes, was called Manjusri, whose abode was in the unmelting snows.

Korean Buddhism has frequently been a powerful factor in national affairs, and at times it practically controlled the state. A major reason for this was, apart from its popularity amongst the common men and a certain military nature in its organization, its appeal to the intellectuals and men of learning. Often Buddhists actively participated in patriotic wars against aggression. An important example of this was the resistance movement organized by Sosan, a monk, against invasion by the Japanese war-lord, Hideyoshi. In war and peace Buddhists co-operated with the state by mobilizing labour from their monastic order for works of public welfare. For instance, the Manhan mountain fortress was built by the Buddhist monks under the direction of the monk, Pyogam. As Buddhism came to be associated more and more with secular affairs, the construction of temples and pagodas and the publication of scriptures came to be considered symbols of state protection against enemy powers. Buddhist structures were also built for defence and security, although their primary objective had always been religious advancement.

During the period of the Silla Empire, when Korea was united under one dynasty, Korean culture made great advances in all spheres. This period witnessed, amongst other things, the construction of the magnificent cave temples at Sokkulam, southeast of Kyongu. These caves form a link in the long chain of cave temples extending from India to Korea through Central Asia and from China to Japan. Sokkulam is constructed according to a remarkably symmetrical plan and is decorated with brilliant reliefs and statues. It was probably built in the middle of the eighth century, although some scholars give it an earlier date. The foundations of Korean temple architecture, however, were laid during the period of the Three Kingdoms.

The sites and general environment of Buddhist temples and monasteries in Korea closely resemble those of China and Japan. Usually situated on hills or high mountains, they are walled around by tall and imposing trees, inspiring awe and devotion. An impressive gateway is erected at some distance in front of the temple. On the frieze of the portal, the name of the temple is inscribed, occasionally in Sanskrit letters. The most impressive of the thirty-four Buddhist retreats in the Diamond Mountains is Yu Chom-sa, which features fifty-three diminutive sitting and standing figures of the Buddha placed on the roots of an upturned tree. According to an ancient Buddhist legend, this structure commemorates the foundation of the monastery by fifty-three

Indian monks who came to Korea many centuries earlier, and triumphed over the hostile dragons by placing an image of the Buddha upon each root of the tree.

Another art developed by the Koreans was the casting of bronze bells, impressive and artistic features of every Buddhist temple and important in Buddhist ritual. In Korea, however, they are particularly fine in form, and are embellished with relief decorations of figures and ornaments. The Buddhist art of Silla was taken to China and Japan by many emigrants. For instance, temples in the Shantung province of China were built on the Korean model.

In China, or in those neighbouring countries where Chinese culture penetrated, learning was the prerogative of a few noblemen and officials, who guarded it jealously from the masses. But Buddhism broke these barriers, and whilst the Confucianist classics formed the basis of courtly and aristocratic education in Korea, Buddhism appealed to the intellectuals and to the common people, and formed the basis of popular education. Indeed, by purposely recruiting converts from the humbler classes, Buddhism made a significant contribution in the diffusion of culture. Wherever Buddhists went, religious literature was published in the local languages. Even the statues, pictures, and scrolls carried vernacular explanations.

China gave her language and ideographs to Korea. India contributed Sanskrit and phonetic letters from which syllabaries or alphabets were constructed, not only for vernacular writing and printing, but also as aids to the popularization of Confucianist teachings. The Korean syllabary, called *nido,* was, like the *kana* of the Japanese, a collection of syllables and not a true alphabet. The nido gave a phonetic value to some of the more common Chinese characters, although the idea of having a vernacular system of writing was probably suggested by Sanskrit letters, some of which represented Korean sounds accurately. The Korean alphabet, *unmun* (common language), was invented by a Buddhist monk named Syel-chong (or Sye-chong), one of the ablest scholars in Korean history.[2]

The fourth King of the Yi dynasty, Sejong, encouraged the translation of Buddhist scriptures, and is credited with having made a few translations himself. The real efforts at translation, however, were made by the seventh ruler, Sejo, a devout Buddhist and a great ruler of the dynasty. He created an office for Buddhist affairs and had many Buddhist scriptures translated.

From Korea, Buddhism spread to Japan. Although a small country, Japan has played an extremely important role in history. Despite the limitations of their physiographic environment, the virile and dynamic people of Japan were able not only to maintain their independence at a time when almost all of Asia had succumbed to Western domination, but also to make remarkable progress in modernizing their industry and technology without losing the distinctive character of their traditional culture. A major reason for this unique blending of tradition and modernity is her readiness to receive and adapt alien contributions. Japan has demonstrated that the willingness to borrow and assimilate foreign traits is not a mark of cultural inferiority but evidence of vitality. Japanese culture is a compound of Shinto, Confucianism, and Buddhism. Prince Shotoku Taishi, who laid the foundations of Japanese civilization, likened these three systems to the three parts of the tree of Japanese culture: Shinto being the root embedded in the soil of national traditions and disposition, Confucianism the stem and branches of legal and educational institutions and of ethical codes, and Buddhism the blossoming flowers of religious sentiment and the fruit of spiritual life. The Japanese people may follow Buddhism, Shinto, or Confucianism, or any combination of these. Indeed, at the beginning of the nineteenth century there was a movement called Shingaku (heart learning) advocating such a combination. Whilst proud of their traditional culture, the Japanese have often consciously endeavoured to acquire knowledge from other lands. As early as the seventh century, Japanese leaders would carefully select able and promising young scholars and attach them to their embassies abroad, especially in China, charging them to bring back foreign knowledge. Few parallels can be cited from history to match this Japanese practice of importing knowledge. Even though the Japanese Emperor did not at times agree with the Chinese Emperor on the question of rank, the Japanese desire to acquire all that was useful from China was not diminished.[3] Because the Japanese eagerly sought foreign knowledge and have guarded and enriched it with extreme care, Japan is often justifiably described as a storehouse of East Asian culture. Indeed, this characteristic has made it possible for historians to gain valuable insight into the processes of the evolution of Asian culture itself. The history of Asian music, of the theatre, and of ritual dancing would have been imperfect without the aid of Japanese material. Some cultural forms, extinct in their homelands, still survive in Japan: for example the music-drama of seventh-century India.

Shinto, the indigenous religion of Japan, reflects the life and temperament of the people and is closely connected with national traditions and social institutions.[4] At first, it was an inarticulate religion and preached no fixed doctrines; it was an unorganized worship of the

7

deities and spirits of nature and of the dead, although some authorities deny that Shinto originally included the veneration of ancestors. Whilst the spirit of ancestor worship and the desire to preserve one's house and family possibly existed, there was no clear conception of loyalty or filial piety, now an integral and important part of the moral life of the people. Earlier religion was indistinguished from administration, and this practice enabled the imperial family to become the head household of the nation and for the Emperor to assume divinity.

Chinese thought and religious practice played some part in pre-Buddhist Japan, but these had degenerated into methods of divination. It was only after Japan had been exposed to Confucianist ethics with a metaphysical background, as modified by Buddhist thought, that Chinese ideas made an impact on the Japanese mind. Confucianism gained popularity with the royal court, and was later to exercise a real influence on Japanese legal and educational institutions, and to contribute a systematic method of teaching morality. Taoist thought also had some influence on Japan but it was never very significant. Real advances in Japanese thought and civilization were made only after the advent of Buddhism.

With Buddhism came its rich heritage of learning in arts and sciences, letters and philosophy, which inspired higher ideals and encouraged indigenous art and literature. Buddhism provided a wealth of material for metaphysical speculation, satisfying Japanese yearnings for the unseen. Indeed, it gave them a clear and deep insight into a profound mysticism hitherto unknown to them. It resulted in the development of elaborate methods of spiritual training and the organization of ecclesiastical institutions, and led to the teaching of a system of cosmology and eschatology. The Mahayana form of Buddhism which was introduced into Japan had acquired various ideas and practices on its journey from India across Central Asia, China, and Korea, but Japan was able to impress upon it a distinctive Japanese character.

Whilst there is general agreement that Buddhism first came to Japan from Korea, the records differ as to the exact date of its advent. Buddhist figures have been found on bronze mirrors dating from about 300, but it is not certain whether their real significance was known to the Japanese at the time. The first known prominent Buddhist is Shiba Tachito, who went to Japan as a refugee in 522. Later his family produced more eminent Buddhists, including the first Japanese Buddhist nun and the greatest artist of the seventh century, Tori, who cast the main image of the Horyuji Temple at Nara.

The history of Buddhism in Japan is generally divided into three

8

broad periods: the period of importation lasting from the sixth to the eighth century (known as the Asuka and Nara periods); the period of nationalization from the ninth to the fourteenth century (the Heian and Kamakura periods); and the period of continuation from the fifteenth to the twentieth century (the Muromachi, Momoyama, and Edo periods, and the modern age).

Officially, Buddhism came to Japan for diplomatic reasons with a delegation from the Kingdom of Kudara (Pekche). The delegation was accompanied by Buddhist priests, and they presented to the Japanese Court of Yamato a gold-plated image of the Buddha with some other ceremonial articles, sutras, banners, and a letter praising the doctrine.[5] The Emperor is reported to have been extremely delighted at what he thought was "an exquisite teaching" and a radiant and beautiful figure. The generally accepted date of this event is 552, one hundred and fifty years after the introduction of Confucianism in Japan. Certain militarist factions inside the Court and some conservative sections outside it opposed Buddhism, but the Court supported the administrators and diplomats who favoured a progressive policy. The scales were soon tipped in favour of Buddhism with the growing influx of Buddhist missionaries, artisans, and other immigrants. The introduction of medicine, arts, and sciences, and especially of writing and astronomy, which invariably accompanied the Buddhist missions, helped to further break the conservative opposition.

Emperor Yomei, who came to the throne in 585 for a brief period, was the first Mikado to embrace Buddhism. He commissioned an image of Bhaishajyaguru, the Buddha of Healing, which was completed after his death and later installed in the world-renowned Horyuji Temple where it can still be seen. It was during his reign that for the first time a Japanese, Tasuna, renounced the world to become a Buddhist monk.

Emperor Yomei's son, Prince Shotoku Taishi, ensured the permanence of Buddhism through a variety of ordinances and legal measures. He became regent in 593 during the reign of his aunt, Emperor Suiko (573–628), and was extremely popular with his people.[6] He and other Japanese dignitaries adopted Buddhism because they believed it was the world trend of the time in philosophical thought. In February 594, he issued his first Imperial ordinance as Regent of the Empire, proclaiming Buddhism as the state religion and urging the development of the *Triratna,* the three basic tenets of Buddhism: the Buddha, the Dharma, and the Sangha. They were to be the principal objects of faith and undivided devotion, and were to constitute the fundamental basis of an upright life.

During Prince Shotoku's regency (593–621), the state built the first Buddhist pagodas, seminaries, hospitals, dispensaries, and homes for the aged and destitute. The temple of Kokoji was built in 596 and the temple of Horyuji in 607.[7] At the latter, Prince Shotoku himself gave lectures on the Mahayana sutras, especially on the *Saddharma bundarika* (The Lotus of the True Law), the *Vimalakirtinirdesa,* and the *Srimala devi-simhanada-sutra.* Later the Horyuji Temple became an important centre for the study of Buddhist idealism of the *Vijnapti-matrata,* or Yogacara School.

Officials competed with one another to express their gratitude towards Shotoku for erecting Buddhist temples. These temples and their art were effective means of attracting the people's admiration and reverence for the Buddhist religion. The mural paintings, panel decorations, ceilings, and pillars provided the settings for Buddhist worship and ceremonies, which were performed with musical accompaniment around the statue of the Buddha installed on a dais in the central part of the temple. Thus, all the fine arts were a part of Buddhist worship, which not only captivated the devotees, but also automatically and almost imperceptibly released and refined the aesthetic energies of its followers. The Japanese were fascinated by these temples, and by 624 there were forty-six temples, eight hundred and sixteen priests, and five hundred and sixty-nine nuns in Japan. Japanese temples have always been built to honour emperors and ancestors and, although the temples of all sects have mainly functioned as centres of learning, worship, and the expansion of Buddhism, they have also performed functions connected with funerals and the custody of family graves. Thus, the Japanese worked out a harmony between the family system, the emperor, and Buddhism.

Shotoku sent envoys to China for Buddhist texts, and he himself wrote commentaries and expositions which have survived intact. He did not interpret the Mahayana philosophy literally but according to his understanding of its true meaning. The value of his work for Buddhism in Japan is perhaps as great as Asoka's work in India. He set up direct diplomatic relations with China, introduced reforms in administration, and laid down fundamental principles of state organization in his *Kempo* (known as the Constitution in Seventeen Articles). He thus provided the basis of national unity, guided and inspired the country with the spiritual ideals of Buddhism, and educated the people in arts and sciences.

With the establishment of a new and impressive capital at Nara (literally meaning the "abode of peace") in 710, Buddhism received further impetus, and a new phase in its history was begun. Emperor

Shomu (701–756) played the central part in this progress; he spent the last seven years of his life in monastic robes, having renounced the throne after a rule of twenty-five years. Indeed, many Japanese emperors retired from the burdens and pleasures of secular power to the ascetic and peaceful life of the Buddhist monk. Known as the Era of Heavenly Peace, Shomu's reign marks a climactic period in the development of religion and art, as well as in government administration. He built temples and monasteries throughout the country as centres of religious observance and discipline as well as of social work, especially medical care. He erected the impressive temple, Todaiji, at Nara which houses the imposing image of Roshana (or Vairocana Buddha) cast in a mood of calm reflection and superb dignity. The dedication ceremony of this statue took place in 752, with many Indian monks and visitors in attendance, and it is regarded as the most brilliant event in the history of Japanese Buddhism. Emperor Shomu also constructed the Daibutsu, the great bronze Buddha statue rising forty-nine feet from the ground, which has come to be looked upon as a symbol of a united nation.

In 794, a grandiose new capital was built at Heian, modern Kyoto, a few miles north of Nara. The capital of Japan remained in Kyoto until 1868 when it was moved to Tokyo. With the change of capitals, a new phase in Buddhist activity began and new Buddhist structures were built at Kyoto. It was during the Heian period (794–1191) that the Kana alphabet was invented and widely used. *The Tale of Genji*, perhaps the finest literary masterpiece of Japan, in which the pessimistic views of Buddhism are interwoven with the sensuality of life, was also written during this period in the eleventh century.

As Buddhism began to permeate Japanese society, its adherents began to show preference for one or the other of its several imported varieties, but later Buddhism in Japan began to develop its own distinctive local schools of thought. During the ninth century two new sects were founded: the Tendai by Saicho, and the Shingon by Kukai. Their principal object was to present Buddhist doctrines in Japanese terms, and to discipline the monks. Both sects stressed not only spiritual salvation, but also its fulfilment in this world. It was through the efforts of the monks of these two sects that Buddhism became firmly and popularly nationalized.

Despite its growing success, however, Buddhism still remained too scholarly to be easily comprehended by common men, who were prone to ignore its intellectual content and to respond only to its devotional aspects. Consequently, a new Buddhist movement arose in the tenth century preaching faith in the Amitabha Buddha as the best means of salvation. The believers of this school needed only to recite the name of Amidabutsu (the Japanese form of the Amitabha Buddha), praying to be reborn in Jodo, the Pure Land, and thus obtain *satori* or enlightenment. Various other sects, such as Yuzu-nenbutsu, Jodo-shu, and Ji-shu, similarly emphasizing devotion for the Amitabha Buddha, arose during the Kamakura period (1192–1333). Because these sects made efforts to purify as well as simplify the doctrine and its practice, they were able to command a large following amongst the peasants.

During the Kamakura period, when the devotional sects were gaining popularity and feudalism was growing in strength, two new schools of Buddhist thought emerged in the country. One was the Zen (Ch'an or Dhyana) introduced by Eisai and Dogen, and the other was the Nichiren founded by Nichiren. Whilst these schools shared some of the characteristics of the contemporary sects of the Pure Land, they were based on different principles. Pure Land Buddhism believed in salvation through faith in others, whereas the doctrine of salvation through one's own enlightenment was the basis of the Zen and the Nichiren sects. Zen Buddhism found its adherents mainly amongst the warriors, or *samurai,* and gave rise to *bushido,* the characteristic Japanese ideal of chivalry, which is the most notable cultural development of this period. The samurai attached special value to loyalty, self-denial, temperance, and the power of mind and will. Whilst the growth of these sects was the outcome of the process of adjustment between traditional Japanese thinking and the vast and varied body of past Buddhist experience, the emergence of sectarian differences, in turn, increased religious activity and the acceptance of Buddhism by the masses.

After the Kamakura period no new major sect was founded in Japan. But as a result of the cultural processes having been firmly set into motion, there developed during the fifteenth and sixteenth centuries, literary activities, as represented by the *kyogen* or no plays and the tea cult, which, combined with Zen Buddhism, symbolize the culture of this era.

Later, during the Edo or Tokugawa period (1603–1867), Buddhism was used to combat the influence of Christianity. The Tokugawa shoguns required everyone to belong to a temple, called *danka,* which meant that all Japanese families during this period were at least nominally Buddhist. The Buddhist clergy was also compelled to co-operate with the feudal society of the Shogunate.

After the Meiji (meaning enlightened) Restoration in 1868, Buddhism stood in danger of being deprived of puplic support because of the hostility of nationalistic Shinto, although the new constitution guaranteed freedom of religion. However, loss of state patronage and the challenge of modernization compelled Buddhist scholars to investigate the doctrines of Buddhism scientifically and to find new meaning in the old doctrines. The Meiji government, whilst granting religious freedom to all, reasserted the independence of Shinto from Buddhism and set it up as a state religion. For a thousand years Shinto had more or less been absorbed by Buddhism, and Buddhist priests had moulded Shintoism according to their will. Even the fact that Shinto itself had profited enormously by this long tutelage under Buddhism did not discourage the new rulers from making it independent and supreme. Moreover, as Buddhism was favoured by the defeated Tokugawa shogunate, it was looked upon as a dangerous political adversary. Consequently, Buddhism suffered from 1867 to 1872 under a policy of ruthless oppression; Buddhist temples were reorganized and their economic foundations shaken; large parts of the temple properties were confiscated; and Buddhist statues, scriptures, paintings, carvings, and ceremonial instruments were destroyed in misplaced patriotic zeal. Buddhist monks and nuns were compelled to take up secular work. Debarred from participating in Shinto ceremonies, they were subjected to beatings and threats. Members of the royal family were no longer allowed to continue in Buddhist orders, and Buddhist ceremonies in the Imperial Palace were discontinued. But Buddhism survived this period of hostility and humiliation through the zealous efforts of monks such as Ekido, Nisshu, Tetsujo, Dokuon, Sesso, Unsho, and Mokurai, who realized the need for further reforms in their order to adapt it to the changing times. The state, for its part, realized the futility of repression against a faith which had become an integral part of Japanese culture and life. Even if there were to be no counterrevolution to the anti-Buddhist policy, which seemed unlikely, Shinto-Buddhist bonds could at best be severed in official areas and in the public institutions of the two religions, but never in the homes. The beliefs of the common people were too inextricably a blending of Shinto and Buddhism to allow the continuation of any open policy of Buddhist suppression. In any case, exclusivist policies are alien to the Japanese temperament, and even the official recognition of Shinto as a state religion was abolished after World War II.

The technological progress of Western civilization which deeply impressed the Japanese mind proved another challenge to Buddhism. But it also stirred the Japanese Buddhists to emphasize their own original rationalism and spirit of inquiry, thus bringing their faith in line with the demands of changing times. Simultaneously, the missionary activities of Christian missions, which invariably came with Europeans, gave a strong impetus to Buddhist revival. In fact, the forces of opposition, persecution, rationalism, and evangelism served to fill the Buddhists with a new zeal to modernize and sharpen their doctrine.

Meanwhile, Europe had begun to study Buddhism with scientific scrutiny, some scholars with sympathy and admiration but none with devotion. This movement gave a further helping hand to Japanese Buddhism, although by far the most energy and ability to reform came from within. Eminent Japanese scholars, such as Masaharu Anesaki, Junjiro Takakusu, Bunyo Nanjio, and Bunzaburo Matsumoto, studied in Europe and returned to direct modern Buddhist studies in Japan. Their efforts, despite some opposition from orthodoxy, bore remarkable success, culminating in a movement amongst the clergy, laity, scholars, intelligentsia, artists, and others to advance the new scientific Buddhism.

Few Indian Buddhist monks came to Japan; Buddhism was spread there largely through the efforts of Japanese and Chinese monks. During the reign of Emperor Kotoku (645–654), a scholarly Indian monk, Hodo (Dharmamarga or Dharmapatha), is said to have come to Japan from Rajagrha, India. However, evidence supporting this visit is inconclusive. Japanese chronicles mention Bodhisena as the most prominent amongst a number of early Indian monks who came to Japan. Whilst the details of his life in India are not known, he is much revered in Japan. Having received mystic inspiration from the Bodhisattva Manjusri, he set out from India for China and arrived there in 730. Young in years but mature in wisdom, he was welcomed by both the clergy and laity. Impressed by his integrity and reputation, some Japanese monks and envoys who were on a mission in China at the time persuaded Bodhisena to come to Japan. Accompanied by monks and musicians, including a Vietnamese monk, Fu-che, and a Chinese monk, Tao Hsuan, Bodhisena arrived in Japan on 18 May 736 after a stormy sea journey. By this time Japanese Buddhism was more than two hundred years old and visiting monks were, as would be expected, accorded an honourable reception. Bodhisena settled in Japan and taught Sanskrit and preached Buddhism until he died in 760 at the age of fifty-seven. When the statue of Vairocana Buddha (Daigutsu), the biggest in the world, was cast and installed at Nara, it was Bodhisena who presided over the religious ceremony of dedication. A stupa known as Baramon Sojo (Brahaman Archbishop) was built in his memory.

There are many distinctive features in Japanese Buddhism. For instance, it abolished all discrimination between priestly life and secular life, the prayers of saints and common people are of the same merit, and people are instantaneously saved by Amidabutsu merely by reciting prayers. An important aspect of Japanese Buddhism has been that the worship of Avalokitesvara as Kwannon is not an exclusive characteristic of one sect.

However, today there are thirteen representative Buddhist sects in Japan: the Kegon (the Avatamsaka school), the Ritsu (the Vinaya school), the Hosso (the Dharmalaksana school), the Tendai, the Shingon (Tantric Buddhism), the Jodo, the Jodo-shin, the Yuzunenbutsu, the Ji-shu, the Rinzai, the Soto, the Obaku, and the Nichiren. There were three others—the Sanron (the Three Sastra school of Madhyamika), the Kusha (the Abhidharma-kosa school), and the Jojitsu (the Satyas-siddhisastra school)—but they are more or less extinct and have little independent influence. Most of these sects originated in China. The Kegon, the Ritsu, and the Hosso have retained their Chinese character, whilst the others are Japanese creations. The three Chinese sects were influential in the Nara period but they lost much of this influence afterwards as they were opposed to the new Buddhism. The Hosso sect is a type of Buddhist idealism, derived from the Yogacara School, and regards everything as the manifestation of the fundamental mind-principle. The Kegon sect centres around the worship of the Vairocana Buddha.

The thirteen sects are generally grouped into five major sects—the Tendai, Shingon, Zen, Pure Land or Jodo, and the Nichiren. The Tendai sect, founded in 804 by Saicho (767–822), better known as Dengyo-Daishi, greatly influenced the cultural and spiritual life of the Japanese. Saicho sought to harmonize all beliefs with the teachings of the *Hokke-kyo* (Lotus sutra); he taught that all men can become Buddhas and urged them to attempt to do so. An offshoot of the Chinese T'ien-t'ai, the Tendai sect absorbed the ideas and principles of other doctrines, such as the Tantric, the Dhyana, and the Vinaya Schools. It differs from the Chinese T'ien-t'ai in its practical approach, although both base their teachings essentially on the Mahayana text, the *Saddharmapundarika*, laying stress on the Ekayana theory.

A younger contemporary of Saicho, Kukai (774–835) also known as Kobo Daishi, founded the Shingon sect, which is the third largest religious organization in Japan with approximately twelve thousand temples. An ascetic, a traveller, an accomplished calligrapher and sculptor, Kukai was a versatile and remarkable scholar. In the records and legends of Japanese Buddhism there is no more celebrated name than his.[8] Shingon literally means "true word," the *mantra* or sacred formula, and its doctrine, based mainly upon the *Mahavairocana-sutra*, is essentially magical or mystical. According to this sect, enlightenment can

15

be attained through the recitation of a mantra or *dharani*. It is now the only sect in Japan which retains Tantric ideas, and it has successfully avoided the shortcomings of Indian and Tibetan Tantrism. Like Tendai, Shingon also endeavoured to effect a unification of Buddhism with Shinto.

Pure Land Buddhism embraces the Jodo-shu, Shin-shu, Yuzunenbutsu, and Ji-shu sects. The last two of these are much less important than the others. All these sects believe that salvation can be attained only through undivided faith in the saving power of the Amitabha Buddha, Amidabutsu. The followers of this system recite Nenbutsu, the name of Amitabha, praying to be reborn in his paradise called Jodo (Sukhavati). The emphasis, however, is on faith, not on recitation.

Founded in 1175 during the Heian era by Genku, better known as Honen (1133–1212), the Jodo sect was mainly inspired by the teachings of Shan-tao (613–681) of the Amitabha School in China. Honen selected the *Sukhavativyuha Sutras* and the *Amitayurdhyana Sutra* as his canonical texts. In the thirteenth century Shinran introduced several important reforms in the Jodo sect and its monastic order, seeking to remove the division between the clergy and the laity. According to him, all living beings will be saved because of the vow taken by Amitabha. Hence, the recitation of the name of the Buddha is but the expression of gratitude. The Jodo sect as reformed by Shinran is known as Shin-shu. Being a simple creed, it suited the common man admirably and rapidly became popular. Today it has the largest following in Japan.

As a specific form of Buddhism, Dhyana or Zen was first founded in China by Bodhidharma in the early sixth century, but ultimately it is a variation of the Mahayana School of Buddhism of northern India. Zen Buddhism has three branches in Japan: the Rinzai, the Soto, and the Obaku. Soto-Zen has the largest following, being second only to Shin-shu. Rinzai-Zen was founded by the Japanese monk, Eisai (or Yesai 1141–1215); Soto-Zen by his disciple, Dogen (1200–1253); and Obaku-Zen by a Chinese monk, Igen (or Yin-yuan), in about 1653. Eisai and Dogen had spent several years studying in China. Dogen is known not only for his strict religious discipline but also as one of the most prominent philosophers of Japan. He led a life of stern discipline and devoted himself to discovering persons who could competently spread the teaching of Zen Buddhism. His sermons were collected and published by his disciples after his death. The most important of these, *Sho-bo-gen-zo* (the Essence of the True Doctrine) is considered to be one of the best philosophical works in Japan. He preached: "All human beings have already been enlightened. They are Buddhas by

nature. The practice of meditation is nothing but the Buddha's act itself."

All sects of Buddhism emphasize tranquillity of mind but Zen Buddhism stresses it most strongly. Zen teaches that tranquillity of mind
is the same as the Buddha's ideal. Zen doctrine emphasizes that meditation or contemplation alone can lead one to enlightenment. The essence of Zen Buddhism is: "Look into the mind and you will find Buddhahood." This philosophy found great favour amongst the warriors
who valued tranquillity of mind. Patronized and encouraged by the
Shoguns, Zen Buddhism rapidly spread throughout the country, and
made far-reaching contributions to Japanese culture.

The Nichiren sect was founded in 1253 by Nichiren (1222–1282),
the son of a fisherman who became a patriot and saint of Japan. He
lived at a time when Japan was in danger of invasion by the Mongol
Emperor of China. Nichiren declared: "I will become the loyal pillar
of Japan, the eyes of Japan, the ship of Japan." After wandering about
the country and long years of study of various doctrinal beliefs, he
concluded that the *Saddharma Pundarika* was the final revelation of the
truth, and that the deliverance of the country from suffering could best
be achieved by following its teaching. Perhaps to counteract the influence
of Nenbutsu of the Jodo sect, he introduced the use of the mantra
formula, *namu myoho renge kyo* (homage to the Sutra of the Lotus of
the True Law), the recitation of which could give men the power to
fuse themselves with eternal life. Because of his rudeness and violent
expressions, Nichiren was frequently in trouble with the authorities, and
his story is a long catalogue of persecution, although he always mi-
raculously escaped.

These Buddhist sects were not free from rivalry and conflict, and
disputes between monasteries were at times settled by force of arms.
There was much antagonism between the followers of Nichiren and
those of Shinran in the last half of the fifteenth century, mainly because
Buddhism in Japan was too closely associated with the political and
social affairs of the country. Consequently, during periods of political
upheaval, religious leaders combined religious ambition with the contest for power. Buddhism in Japan has often been a major political
force and, as in the Fujiwara period (858–1068), even threatened the
sovereignty of the state. Buddhist militancy, as reflected both in sectarian disagreements and interference in power-politics, was also conditioned by the prevalent feudal divisions, which became more pronounced
in times of political agitation.

However, it would be wrong to characterize Japanese Bhuddism as

17

militant or aggressive, because if this were true, its missionary activities would have invited military reaction and its highly developed philosophy and intellectual equipment would have crushed many primitive beliefs, mythologies, and superstitious traditions. It never declared a holy war, *jihad* (crusade), although for patriotic reasons, Japanese Buddhism has sanctioned national wars as crusades for peace and goodwill on earth. Because of its spirit of accommodation, Buddhism did not encounter sustained hostility from traditional beliefs, except for brief occasional spells.

Although both Buddhism and Shinto have survived and have interacted on each other, there has been, in marked contrast to China, no persecution of "foreign" Buddhism by the "nationalistic" Shinto. Shinto is a Chinese word (Shen-tao) and means "way of the spirits"; in Japanese it is called *Kami no Michi*. Buddhism adopted a characteristic policy of tolerance and assimilation towards Shinto. It accepted the Shinto cult of ancestor worship, and the Shinto deities or *Kamis*—Kami has a wide meaning, which may signify a natural object, or a god, or the original spirit itself—as the temporal manifestations of Buddhist divinities. To the early Japanese, Kamis were superior to men but, although powerful (chi-haya-baru), they were not omniscient. This made it relatively easy for the Buddhists to designate Kamis as the earthly incarnations of the Buddha. The Buddhist pantheon was generally thought to represent the "Indestructibles" *(Honji)*, whilst the Shinto deities were interpreted as their partial appearances *(suijaku)*. Thus, every Kami was regarded as a manifestation of a certain deity. The chief Shinto deity, the Sun goddess, was identified with the Buddha Vairocana. Buddhists made a practice of reading the Sutras before the altar of the Shinto deities. They worshipped publicly at the Meiji and other Shinto shrines, and incorporated Shinto deities and doctrines into their body of beliefs, including the doctrine, given up since World War II, that the Emperor was the direct descendant of the sun goddess and divinely authorized to rule.

Shinto was mainly a primitive form of nature worship based on a simple feeling of awe at the forces of nature, and anything awe-inspiring was called Kami. It had no moral code, and its prayers and sacrifices did not aim at seeking spiritual blessings. Shinto, like Confucianism, had nothing to say about the state of the dead. Shinto had no educational function; its priests did not preach or teach. The theorists of this simple faith, which in fact has no philosophy, leaned heavily on the well-developed philosophy of Buddhism in attempting to interpret Shinto ideas. Hence, Buddhism so influenced Shinto that it is claimed that without

Buddhist umbrage for more than a thousand years Shinto could hardly have survived as an organized religion; "Buddhism imparted a depth and meaning to the old Shinto mythology and made it philosophically respectable and acceptable to educated men. In others words Buddhism equipped Shinto—a primitive religion—with a worthy doctrinal and ethical content."[9]

Whilst it is true that there has been no sustained and violent hostility between Buddhism and Shinto, it would be wrong to deny the existence of disharmony between the two. Several Neoshinto movements arose in the mediaeval period to emphasize the differences between Shinto and Buddhist thought, and to assert the supremacy of the former. For example, *Yui-itsu Shinto,* prominent at the end of the fifteenth century, was the only school that sought to reverse earlier Buddhist interpretations of Kamis and declared that the Buddhist deities were not the primordial powers, but the temporal manifestations of the Kamis. In the eighteenth century a similar movement, Return to Antiquity Shinto (*Fukko* Shinto), emphasized the divine origins of kingship and exhorted the people to return to pure Shinto. For a brief period after the Meiji Revolution in 1868 it appeared that Buddhism might suffer under the instigation of Shintoist revivalists, but the Constitution guaranteed freedom of religion to all and the fear proved unfounded. Much of the limited and intermittent religious hostility was the result of Buddhist involvement in state politics. It could be said with reasonable justification that it was the politics of the Buddhist order, not the doctrine of Buddhism, that spurred occasional resentment. For example, the resistance exhibited towards Buddhism at the time of its official entry in the sixth century was the undoubted outcome of political rivalry between two warring factions—the militarists and the administrators—at the royal court; the militarists sought to exploit the foreign origin of Buddhism in their favour. This conflict lasted about forty years, and it became menacing enough at one stage to threaten the stability of the state and the life of the sovereign.

Shinto opposition to Buddhism has generally taken the line of an expression of patriotic resentment towards an alien creed. Shintoists tend to glorify the pre-Buddhist culture and belittle Buddhist contributions, but this feud, although real, must not be magnified. After all, the overwhelming majority of the Japanese people are Buddhist; Japan is the leading Buddhist nation today; and Buddhism is inseparably woven into the national fabric of Japan.

As in China, there was considerable Confucianist opposition toward Buddhism in Japan. But Confucianism was also a foreign doctrine, and

19

appears to have kept its antagonism subdued until the seventeenth century, even though Confucianist hostility in China had been active for centuries. These two systems did not come into conflict in Japan until the seventeenth century when Confucianists began to attack Buddhism from motives which were not purely religious. Their censure was not directed against Buddhist thought; rather, they denounced Buddhist political influence upon the nation and the administration. Antagonism between the two came to the surface again during the early Meiji era when some Confucianist scholars aligned themselves with a powerful group of Shintoists to vent their doctrine of *Haibutsuorn*, "Down with Buddhism." But this movement was short-lived.

Approximately two-thirds of Japan's inhabitants profess Buddhism. The various Buddhist sects combined maintain about eighty thousand temples and one hundred and fifty thousand clerics, and there are several colleges and institutes primarily devoted to Buddhist studies. There is no doubt that Buddhism is an integral part of Japanese life and a powerful force in the country. Throughout the country, countless images of the Buddha and the Bodhisattvas, sutras, paintings, and other sacred objects have been preserved, both for the tourist and the devotee. Buddhist festivals not only perform an attractive religious function in keeping the spirit of the religion alive, but lend colour to the cultural life of the country. For example, on 15 July every year Buddhists celebrate *Ulambana*, a principal event in Japanese Buddhist life. It is a service to pacify the souls of the dead, who are believed to return to their old homes on that day. There are also the *higan* periods in spring and autumn, each period comprising seven days spread around the two equinoctial days, called *chunichi*. On higan, Buddhist services recall the memories of the dead. At midnight on the last day of the year bells begin to sound in Buddhist temples. Through the ringing of the bells the worldly passions of the previous year are supposed to be completely eradicated.

Whilst Buddhism provided a bridge between Indian and Chinese civilizations, it also linked Chinese and Japanese culture. Those Indian ideas which found their way to Japan were transmitted through China or Central Asia, although there was some direct contact between India and Japan by sea. According to a scholar of ethnology, there is evidence of the presence of an Indian community in the Shima district in Mie Prefecture.[10] These Indians were called *Tenjiku Ronin,* meaning the "masterless Indian samurai."

Although China and Japan had always been in contact, it was not until Buddhism was firmly entrenched in Chinese life that China was able to influence Japanese culture. Before the arrival of Buddhism, Japan led a fairly isolated, primitive life; writing was unknown, and religious beliefs centred around the worship of natural forces and ancestors. But once Buddhism had become an integral part of Japanese life and thought, Japan appears to have begun to seek and adopt new ideas with amazing aptitude.

The best way of assessing the influence of Buddhist thought and practice on Japanese cultural life, suggests Suzuki, is to wipe out all the Buddhist temples together with their treasures, libraries, gardens, anecdotes, tales, and romances, and see what is left in the history of Japan: "First of all, there would be no painting, sculpture, architecture, or even music and drama. Following this, all the minor branches of art would also disappear—landscape gardening, tea ceremony, flower arrangement, and fencing (which may be classed as art since it is the art of spiritual training and defence of oneself against the enemy, morally as well as physically). The industrial arts would also vanish, the first impetus to which was given by Buddhism."[11]

The advent of Buddhism made Japan India-conscious, eager to know the country and the original texts of its new faith. The Japanese became familiar with Indian culture and studied the Sanskrit language and literature. Even today, outside of India, "there is no country in the world where so many students are learning a rudimentary knowledge of Sanskrit and Pali languages. There are many universities where they are taught these languages. A great many books concerning these languages have appeared in recent times."[12] In some Japanese temples, very ancient manuscripts in Sanskrit are preserved intact. It is significant that many of those manuscripts found in Japan are much older than those preserved in India.

Kukai started the study of Sanskrit letters, known as *Shittan*, a Japanese equivalent of the Sanskrit word *Siddham*, with which ancient Indian inscriptions and works often begin. Before this, during the Nara period, the Vinaya; the *Abhidharmakosa* by Vasubandhu; the *Satyasiddhi* by Harivarman; the works of Nagarjuna and Aryadeva; the *Vijnaptimatrata*, Buddhist idealism; and the *Gandavyuha sutra* had been studied. These are called "the Six Schools of the Ancient Capital."[13] In addition, Buddhist logic had been introduced into Japan in 661 by Dusho. In the seventh century Dusho went to China with Tzu-en (Jion) and, under Hsüan-tsang, studied the system of Buddhist idealism, which was then the newest system of Buddhist logic. Later, in the beginning of the eighth century, further impetus was given the study of logic through the efforts of Genbo. In Japan, Dusho's tradition is called "the teaching

21

at the Southern Temple" and Genbo's "the teaching at the Northern Temple," because they taught at Gango-ji Temple and Konfuku-ji Temple respectively. Since then this system of logic has been studied in the Hosso sect as a discipline subordinate to the study of Buddhist idealism and the *Abhidharmakosa*. The study of logic became very popular and it appears that prior to Western influence, more than two hundred works were composed on Buddhist logic in Japan.[14]

After Kukai, the other prominent name in the history of Japanese Sanskrit studies is Jogon (1639–1702), who edited some Sanskrit *dharanis* (magic verses or syllables) and composed a remarkable Sanskrit work entitled *Shittan-Sanmitsu-Sho*. Jiun (1718–1804) compiled a thesaurus of many extant Sanskrit manuscripts of the kind which consisted of one thousand volumes.

Although common people in Japan do not know Sanskrit, they are to some extent familiar with the Devanagari alphabet. It is not uncommon to find wooden tablets written in Devanagari characters in Japanese cemeteries. Japanese temples contain images of the Buddha, Bodhisattvas, and other divinities with nagari characters inscribed beneath them. These letters are called seeds, (*bija*, a Sanskrit term), with each identifying a single divine being. In mediaeval times some Japanese warriors went into battle wearing helmets with Sanskrit characters for *mangala* (blessing).

Japanese characters are undoubtedly constructed on the lines of Chinese characters. Whereas Chinese characters are ideographic, Japanese characters are phonetic like the Devanagari letters and are arranged in a sentence in the same order as in Sanskrit—subject, object, and verb. Word order is not in itself indicative of family affinity in languages, but there is further evidence suggesting constructional similarities. The Japanese used certain shortened Chinese characters to develop a syllabic alphabet of their own. The older method of using Chinese characters with a similar pronunciation to render certain Japanese words phonetically did not work satisfactorily, because it was neither simple nor well regulated. A Chinese character represents a whole syllable and thus the Japanese did not think of spelling the sounds of their language by separate signs for vowels and consonants until they came into contact with the Indian alphabet, which, regarding the consonants as the most important letters, indicated the vowels by additional signs placed around the consonants. In the Japanese syllabary the vowels are arranged in exactly the same order as in the Indian alphabet: a,i,u,e,o. The groups of consonants then follow accompanied by vowels: for example, ka, ki, ku, ke, ko. A Japanese song, *irohauta*, attributed to Kukai, the supposed inventor of Japanese letters, is made up of all the forty-seven letters, and is nothing but a free translation of a Buddhist poem written in ancient India.[15]

The arrangement of the Japanese syllabary into fifty phonetic sounds is regarded by Japanese scholars as no more than an adaptation of the Sanskrit alphabet. The system is undoubtedly the work of a Buddhist, perhaps Bodhisena. If the Chinese language and script had not penetrated deeply into Japan before the Indian alphabet, there is little doubt that the Japanese would have found it far more convenient to adopt the Indian script rather than Chinese characters.[16]

Unlike Chinese, but like Korean, Japanese has a well-developed verbal system. In their phonetic systems Chinese and Japanese have nothing in common. In Chinese, inflection is unknown and tenses and modes of action are indicated if necessary by isolated words. The idea of a sentence is implicit in Chinese by the syntactic relations of the meaning of characters, and, strictly speaking, it is not possible to differentiate between nouns and verbs.

The development of a simple writing method and the perfection of the Kana syllabary, together with the introduction of Buddhist texts, inevitably influenced Japanese literature and learning. Indeed, a remarkable process of literary activity commenced which was to bloom in the Classical Age of Japanese literature during the Heian period. The first philosophical works ever written by a Japanese, although in Chinese, were Prince Shotoku's commentaries on the three Buddhist scriptures— the *Hokke-kyo* the *Yuima-kyo,* and the *Shoman-kyo.* The first legendary tale, *Taketori Monogatari* (Tale of a Bamboo Cutter), the story of a divine maiden written in the ninth century, drew inspiration from various Buddhist works, such as the Jatakas, and embodies the Buddhist idea of moral causation. The fullest development of the monogatari tale is found in Japan's first novel, the *Genji Monogatari* (the Tale of Genji), written in the early eleventh century and a masterpiece of Japanese classical literature. In the novel, the sensuality of worldly life is interwoven with the pessimistic doctrines of Buddhism. This work, probably the earliest novel of its kind in world-literature, was written by Murasaki Shikibu, a lady-in-waiting at the royal court.

Buddhist influence with its stress on asceticism and didacticism can be seen in the twelfth century collection of about two hundred stories, entitled *Uji Shui Monogatari* (Gleanings at Uji), which includes a number of Buddhist morality tales. The thirteenth-century work, *Jikkinsho* (Selection of Ten Teachings), contains ten stories illustrating Buddhist moral principles.

23

Indian legends also found their way into Japanese literature. An example of this is the legend of *Rishyasringa* in which a rishi who had never seen a woman was seduced by Santa, the daughter of King Lomapada. This is a very famous story in the *Mahabharata*. In the Japanese version the saint is named Ikkaku Sennin, that is Ekasrnga (Unicorn). The Kabuki drama, *Narukami*, was derived from this legend. Many such Indian stories were incorporated into Buddhist literature and conveyed to Japan.

Painting was allied to literature, and received added impetus because of the Buddhist keenness to disseminate knowledge through this medium. One of the most celebrated Buddhist empresses of Japan, Komyo, had a million miniature pagodas made for distribution. Each pagoda contained a print of a short Buddhist *dharani*, or text.[17]

Buddhists also were remarkably successful in preserving the existing knowledge of rival faiths. Buddhist institutions in Japan acted as custodians of Japanese learning, whether Shinto, Confucianist, secular, or religious. Without the protection of the Buddhist order, much of the documentary material of Shinto would not have survived. The increasing power of war-lords in various regions of the country, and the rise of a warring feudal society in the mediaeval period, naturally put a greater premium on martial skill than on intellectual learning. Therefore the Buddhist monasteries rather than the official academies became the repositories and guardians of knowledge and the chief sources of education.

Numerous Buddhist deities were introduced into Japan and many of these are still very popular. Some Hindu gods, who had been incorporated into the Buddhist pantheon, were amongst them. For example, Indra, originally the god of thunder but now also the king of gods, is popular in Japan as Taishakuten (literally the great King Sakra);[18] Ganesa is worshipped as Sho-ten (literally, holy god) in many Buddhist temples, and is believed to confer happiness upon his devotees. A sea-serpent worshipped by sailors is called Ryujin, a Chinese equivalent of the Indian *naga*. Hariti and Dakini are also worshipped, the former as Kishimojin, and the latter by her original name. Bishamon is a Japanese equivalent of the Indian Vaisravana (Kubera), the god of wealth.

Even Shinto adopted Indian gods, despite its desperate efforts after the Meiji Revolution to systematically disengage itself from Buddhism and assert its own independent identity. Indeed, Shinto, before it felt the influence of the Buddhist iconography, did not cast deities into human form but represented them with symbols such as a mirror, a jewel, a sword. The Indian sea god, Varuna, is worshipped in Tokyo as Sui-ten (water god); the Indian goddess of learning, Sarasvati, has become Ben-

24

ten (literally, goddess of speech), with many shrines dedicated to her along sea coasts and beside lakes and ponds. Siva is well known to the Japanese as Daikoku (literally, god of darkness), which is a Chinese and Japanese equivalent of the Indian Mahakala, another name of Siva. Daikoku is a popular god in Japan. At the Kotohira shrine on the island of Shikoku, sailors worship a god called Kompira, which is a corruption of the Sanskrit word for crocodile, *kumbhira*. The divine architect mentioned in the *Rig Veda*, Visvakarma, who designed and constructed the world, was regarded in ancient Japan as the god of carpenters, Bishukatsuma. The Indian Yama, the god of death, is the most dreaded god of Japan, under the name Emma, the king of hell. The idea of rewards and punishments after death was introduced by Buddhism; early Shinto texts do not refer to this subject.[19]

The climbers wearing traditional white dress, who scale the sacred Mount Ontake as a religious observance, sometimes have inscribed on their robe Sanskrit *Siddham* characters of an ancient type. Sometimes they put on white Japanese scarfs (*tenugui*) which carry the Sanskrit character *OM*, the sacred syllable of the Hindus.

The Japanese customs of cremation and ancestor worship were influenced by India. Until the Meiji Revolution all funerals were performed by Buddhist priests, and even now many Japanese who are not Buddhist prefer Buddhist burial rites and ceremonies. To enjoy good incense with a calm mind has become a cultivated art amongst educated Japanese. The varieties of incense popular in Japan and China were partly supplied by India. Specimens of ancient incense from India have been preserved as national treasures in the Imperial Shoso-in repository.

The profundity of Japanese mythology and philosophy has its roots in traditions that have been dominated by Buddhist thought since the days of Shotoku Taishi. Both the individual and national dispositions of the Japanese people have been conditioned by the teachings of Buddhism. Even the common ideas and ideals that inspire and guide the Japanese in their daily life are a reflection of Buddhist ideas. The notion that everyone can attain Buddhahood is common to all Buddhism, but it is particularly popular in Japan. The Japanese faculties of precise observation, concentrated reflection and efficient transmission, humility and perseverance, and the stress on the fulfilment of duties and national obligations, are attributed to Buddhism which is no doubt "the greatest promoter of the culture of the intellect."

An example of Buddhist influence on modern Japanese thought can be seen in the philosophy of Nishida Kitaro (1870–1945), who is regarded as the most stimulating thinker Japan has ever produced. In the latter part of the nineteenth century a movement to blend Buddhist philosophy with Western thought emerged in Japan. This philosophical blending is perhaps best represented in Nishida's doctrine in which he sought "to give to oriental culture its logical foundation," or to see "a form in the formless, hear a voice in the voiceless."[20] In the formulation of his theory he drew upon the Buddhist concept of *sunyata*.

Buddhist influence can also be seen in the Japanese theory of government. Initially, Buddhism was officially recognized in Japan for diplomatic reasons, and the first Japanese constitution, promulgated in 604 by Prince Shotoku Taishi, was inspired by Buddhist ideals. Buddhist monasticism played a significant role in practical politics in the tenth and eleventh centuries. Nichiren, in the thirteenth century, sought to identify religion with the state, and nationalism with Buddhism. Buddhist monasticism in the sixteenth century has been described as the greatest power in Japan at the time. The gallant samurai and *daimyo* classes were influenced deeply by the various schools of Zen Buddhism. Although Zen doctrines had been taught in Japan before the Nara period, it was not until the Kamakura period that the various Zen schools profoundly influenced the government and the military classes. In 1916 the Buddhist Church publicly encouraged and welded the spirit of nationalism, and protected the Imperial family and state. When Japanese militarism was at its peak in 1937, the Buddhist Movement of the Imperial Way became very powerful. Indeed, the Chinese Buddhist Society severely criticized the Japanese Buddhists for co-operating so enthusiastically with Japanese imperialist policies. The demands of religion and the pressures of patriotism are not always easy to reconcile. Japanese Buddhism departed from the principles of the Buddhist Sangha, and adopted the distinct role of lending its support to a totalitarian state ideology.

Japanese education and social service originated in Buddhism. Education began in the Horyuji and other Buddhist temples, and a scheme of general education was designed for the first time by Kukai when he built his school in 829 known as Sogei Shuchi-In. The monks not only taught religion and philosophy but also practical arts and sciences. They even taught the people how to read and write, and initiated the compilation of Japanese histories. Above all, they fostered the love of nature and humanity, and broadened the religious outlook of the people, instilling a compassionate idealism both in their thought and conduct. They founded hospitals, dispensaries, health-resorts, taught the art of healing, built alms houses, conducted free funerals for the poor, and brought widespread relief from famine and pestilence.

Buddhist social welfare programs continue to be exceptionally impressive. Having recovered its balance from the Shinto-Confucianist attack of the nineteenth century, Buddhism applied itself to alleviating some of the damaging consequences of a capitalistic economy on society. Today Buddhism maintains an imposing array of social welfare activities, such as public dispensaries, hospitals, infirmaries, maternity homes, asylums, nurseries, kindergartens, schools, homes for the disabled and the aged, libraries, information bureaus, social education institutions, settlement houses, continuation schools, reform schools, employment offices, and legal offices for the protection of the poor and needy.

Through the journeys of indefatigable Buddhist monks the whole country was opened up, mountains were conquered, harbours were made, roads were built, rivers were bridged, wells were dug, and swamps were drained. These monks promoted agriculture and forestry, planted trees, constructed irrigation canals, and opened up new and extensive tracts of land to a more enlightened industry and agriculture than primitive Japan had ever known. For example, the cultivation of cotton in Japan is traced to an Indian who had drifted to the shore of Aichi Prefecture in 799. To commemorate the event, the Japanese named the village where the shipwrecked Indian had landed Tenjiku; Tenjiku was the Japanese name for India, and means Heaven. The Japanese also erected a shrine in his honour and installed in it his statue cast in Indian costume.

Japanese art, remarkable for its distinctive beauty, dexterity, and dignity, bears some imprints of Indian styles. "The debt of art to Buddhism is even greater in Japan than in China, for on the whole the gift of Buddhism to China was ideas rather than technique, whereas in ancient Japan there was no art worth mentioning. Painting, sculpture, and architecture, as well as engraving, printing, and even writing, were all introduced in connection with Buddhism."[21] Pre-Buddhist Japanese art is important to history and to the understanding of Japanese society of the time, but it is a very remote, almost unrecognizable and poor parent of the rich Japanese art one is most familiar with. Buddhism provided the spiritual inspiration that caused the Japanese to either refine their own traditional art styles, or import Chinese or other styles.

Earlier Japanese paintings, found mostly on the walls of chambers of burial mounds, consisted mainly of totemic symbols and geometric patterns in colour. Of the early Buddhist paintings, the most famous is the one found on the panels of a portable wooden shrine, the *Tamamushi-nozushi* shrine. It was done during the period of the Emperor Suiko (592–628) and is preserved today in the Horyuji Temple. The oil painting shows landscapes and Buddhist figures with slender limbs and

27

faces, which are regarded as the typical features of the Chinese art of the period of Six Dynasties. Much of early Japanese art was produced with the help of Chinese and Korean artisans, but they too were mainly Buddhists who had been inspired by Indian tradition. Architectural development also began to bloom as Buddhist temples were built on a grand scale with elaborate detail. The Horyuji Temple, the oldest wooden building in the world (with the possible exception of the treasury at Nara, the *Shoso-in*), dates from the beginning of the seventh century.

In the eighth century when Buddhism had almost become the national religion, Japanese painting embarked on a fresh and brilliant course of development under the influence of the Indian chiaroscuro style transmitted through T'ang China. A unique illustration of this is found in the fresco painting, closely resembling the Ajanta art, in the Golden Hall of the Horyuji Temple. In contrast to the romantic and transcendental figures of the preceding period, the figures in this painting are rotund and human.[22] During the Nara period, encouraged by royal patronage and enthusiasm for their faith, Buddhists made magnificent contributions in art, architecture, sculpture, painting, and music. The accomplishments of this period were so brilliant that even today Nara is the most impressive site in Japan from an artistic standpoint. Typical of the excellence of the Nara art is the nine foot seated bronze Buddha, attended by the sun and moon.

Japan by this time had matured artistically and had developed indigenous traditions. Furthermore, her contact with China was broken around the end of the ninth century. Japanese art began to assume its own character with the paintings of Kanaoka Kose, who flourished in the ninth century and who is traditionally regarded as Japan's greatest painter. He painted secular scenes as well as Buddhist subjects. Genshin, better known as Eshin Sozu (942–1017), is particularly associated with the beatific vision of the Amitabha Buddha. He was a profound thinker and held the view that the Buddha-nature was inherent in everyone and that by contemplation of the innermost depths of the soul a manifestation of the Buddha's wisdom and power could be realized. This philosophy gradually led him to concentrate on Amida Buddha, and he painted the Pure Land in graceful lines and harmonious colours. Indeed, the surviving pictures of the early period are all Buddhist, although the artists also painted secular themes.

Kamakura painting, which is the most truly national, was deeply inspired by Buddhism. Nobuzane, one of the outstanding masters of the period, is famous for a series of portraits of poets, but his masterpiece is the portrait of the Buddhist saint, Kukai, depicted as a child kneeling upon the lotus. The great bronze Buddha Daibutsu, although an emulation of Nara style, is in fact characteristic of the art of the period, reflecting the mood of Amidism as influenced by the widening of Buddhist consciousness. Temple architecture of the Kamakura period witnessed a variety of styles, some incorporating Nara features and some influenced by the emergence of Zen Buddhism, which became the premier spiritual force in Japanese life during the Muromachi period (1336–1753). Zen Buddhist influence on art can be seen on the ink paintings of the period, including the extensive work done by the Zen monk Sesshu (1420–1506), and the paintings of Arhats or Buddhist saints by Mincho (or Cho Densu) (1341–1427). The Zen emphasis on contemplation reduced the importance of icons in religious worship. Consequently, sculpture declined in importance.

After this period the influence of Buddhism, which had been thoroughly localized in any case, began to decline; or more accurately, it began to lose its Buddhist identity as it assumed a Japanese character. However, a good deal of it can yet be recognized in the works of the Zen monk-painters, such as Hakuin and Sengai, and the poet-painters of the Tokugawa period (1420–1868).

In modern times, when art began to depart from religion and head towards secularism, it was inevitable that Buddhist inspiration should lose much of its force. Still, modern Japanese art bears marks of the Buddhist ideals of simplicity, restraint, and dignity. Buddhist ideals and traditions are reflected perhaps to a greater degree in sculpture and architecture, because of the utilitarian value of those arts in religious life and ritual. The art of the woodcut, which has been brought to a remarkable perfection in Japan, is a by-product of Buddhism, since woodcut engraving was first used for printing Buddhist sutras and pictures. In fact, the earliest specimen of extant printed texts are Buddhist charms enclosed in miniature wooden pagodas distributed amongst the temples of Japan in the eighth century.

Japanese music and dance was in a state of primitive development until the arrival of Buddhism, in whose religious observances music played an important role. Young Japanese musicians went to China and Korea to study. The earliest known music-dance of Japan is Gigaku, a kind of primitive mask-play which was brought to Japan in 612 from Korea by Mimashi. Although Mimashi learned his art in China, the Gigaku was of Indian origin, as is indicated by the masks representing Indian features. More than two hundred of these masks are still preserved in the temples of Nara. The masked dancers were led by *Chido*, a figure, whose function was to clear the way. Even today religious processions in

Japan are headed by a person wearing a long-nosed mask, who is called *Tengu*. Amongst the dancers were characters representing a lion and an eagle, which also suggests links with India, because there were no lions in Japan (or in China) and the term for the eagle character, *Karura*, is a derivative of the Sanskrit *Garuda*.

Whilst most parts of Gigaku have been lost, some fragments of it later merged with the elegant and grateful *Gagaku*. Gagaku is the name for a piece of music, but it brought with it the dance called *Bugaku*. Both were introduced to Japan by Bodhisena. This court dance and music was performed for the first time in 752 in celebration of the opening of the Todaiji Temple at Nara. At this ceremony the Emperor Shomu unveiled the Vairocana Buddha statue, and hundreds of foreign musicians, a number of whom were Indians, performed. Many of the instruments used on that occasion are still in the Shoso-in Treasure House at Nara. Buddhism was a strong inspirational force, and there is little doubt that the orchestras of Japan were first organized to meet Buddhist needs. Although this music-drama is more than twelve hundred years old, it is still preserved in Japan in its original form, not only in records, musical instruments, and masks, which are kept in the Horyuji Temple, but in the dance form itself.

From the beginning, the Japanese aristocracy patronized this dance and music. Consequently, the Gagaku and Bugaku became the music of the court itself, both for ceremonial use and for entertainment. During the eighth century, a Gagaku institute was founded, and was directed on a national scale by professional musicians and officials. Many local variations of the Gagaku resulted, but a clear distinction was made between the local and foreign varieties. Those derived from India and China were called *Saho-no-mai*. In the eighteenth century, it was decided to designate only music of foreign origin as Gagaku, but at present the term embraces both foreign and indigenous dances. The Bugaku is still played in some Buddhist temples and shrines, but the formal stage for this art is found only in the Royal Palace. However, during its long journey from the Nara period Bugaku has influenced the music of Japan in a variety of ways, including the national anthem, as well as the *Kurodabushi*, a popular drinking song. These court dances and music are now extinct in India, their original home.

Japanese dance music is composed of eight, possibly more, pieces: *Bosatsu, Garyobin, Konju, Bairo, Bato, Riowo* (or *Ryo-o*), *Ama Ninomai*, and *Banshuraku*. Some of these names can be easily traced to Indian origins; for example, *Bosatsu* is the Japanese adaptation of Bodhisattva, *Bairo* of Bhairava, *Garyobin* of Kalavinka, a sonorous, sweet-voiced bird. The *Riowo* dance, according to the famous scholar Takakusu, is a part of an ancient Indian opera, *Nagananda* (The Joy of the Snake) written by Emperor Harsha. I-tsing, during his pilgrimage to India, saw a performance of this music-drama and, presumably, it was he who brought it back to China, from where it was later transmitted to Japan.

The *no* plays of Japan were developed during the thirteenth to the fifteenth century from what was called *Dengaku-no-noh,* meaning field-music performance. The no owes its present form to two men: Kanami (1333–1384), who was a priest of the Kasuga Shrine near Nara, and his son Zeami (1363–1443), who was an outstanding actor, author, and composer. The intricate term *yugen,* meaning "what lies beneath the surface," which occurs throughout Zeami's writings, is derived from Zen literature. During the sixteenth century, comic interludes called *kyogen* were incorporated in the traditional no performances. Kyogen was the name of secular entertainments given to relieve the strain of long religious ceremonies and the term implies a prayer to the Buddha that the chatter of the mountebank may be transformed into a hymn of praise.

Certain analogies between Indian drama and the Japanese no play have been pointed out. Just as Indian drama was originally a combination of song and dance performed for inspiration at sacred festivals, so was the Japanese no. Again, the development of Indian drama was from narrative recitation to dialogue, first sung then spoken, just as in Japan the recitative of the "tonsured lutist" was followed by the sung and spoken dialogue of the no. Furthermore, in Indian drama the narrative connection was often preserved by interpreters whose function closely resembled that of the chorus in Japanese no. Both dramas were performed in the open courts of palaces or temples, and artificial scenery was necessarily absent. Neither drama considered it strange that a character should make journeys on stage. Both dramas excluded performance of the vulgar acts of life: actors did not die, eat, sleep, or make love on the stage. Indian dramatists invariably used classical phraseology which was generally incomprehensible to the majority of their audiences, just as no plays were written in the classical language of the period, although the kyogen used the common vernacular of the day.

By the seventeenth century the no play had become essentially an aristocratic art. However, Okuni, a woman dancer from the Buddhist shrine at Izumo, in the beginning of that century became the leader of a movement to expound and popularize Buddhist religious dances to the accompaniment of flute and drum. Through Okuni's originality of interpretation the dance took the form of a simple operetta, which appealed to the people. The new popular form was called *Kabuki*. The Kabuki borrowed extensively from the no plays, and eventually the no play became less exclusive and Kabuki less traditional.

Flowers, symbolizing joy, purity, and good luck, play an important role in Buddhist worship. Incense, light, and flowers are regarded as the best offerings to Buddhist deities, who are said to live surrounded by beautiful flowers; Buddhist images are always placed on a pedestal of lotus flower. The Goddess of Mercy, Kwannon-Bosatzu, always carries flowers in her hand. Various Buddhist ideas are expressed by the different colours of flowers; for example, white flowers denote safety and health, red respect, and yellow wealth. Inspired with religious fervour, the Japanese perfected their art of flower arrangement. This art was, indeed, one of the remarkable outcomes of the period of warriors. Its name, *ikebana* (living flower), explains the fundamental principle underlying the art: the flowers must be so arranged as to convey the idea of life, they should look as if they were growing, and not as though they had been cut. Preserving the living aspect of flowers is derived from the Buddhist injunction against the destruction of life.

The tea ceremony of Japan also has its origin in Buddhism. The ceremonial came from China, but its elaborate conventions and its complexity as practiced in Japan would be utterly alien to China. It became immensely popular during the mediaeval period of militarism. The principles of tea-making were prescribed by the celebrated Buddhist monk, Dogen. The etiquette observed during the tea ceremony ought to become part of daily routine because all outward formalities are merely expressions of the inner spirit. Tea must be offered with reverence, purity, and calmness of mind: an expression of Zen Buddhism. The history of tea in Japan goes back to the time of the Buddhist Emperor Shomu in the eighth century. It is said that tea was offered to the image of the Buddha, and after the service to the monks. Possibly, the use of tea was encouraged to keep the monks from drinking wine, as well as to keep them awake during long ceremonies.

The popular Japanese game of *sunoroku* or *sugoroku* (backgammon), played at the royal court of the Nara rulers and still popular in Japan, is of Indian origin. In Japan the game is played as nard. Nard is generally regarded as an Iranian game, but the ninth century Arab scholar, Al Yaqubi, considered nard an Indian invention used to illustrate man's dependence on chance and destiny. The board stands for the year, and it has twenty-four points for the hours of the day. It is divided into two halves, each of twelve points for the months in a year. The thirty men stand for the days in a month. The two dice are day and night, and the sum of opposite faces of the dice is seven for the days of the week. However, this symbolism was also known to Byzantine Greeks, and this fact disputes the theory of Indian origin. Whatever the paternity of nard, sugoroku came to Japan from India by way of Central Asia and China. *Shwan-liu,* the Chinese name for sugoroku was introduced into China from India in the seventh century, possibly earlier. According to *Wei-Shu,* sugoroku was brought to China in ancient times from Hu country, which at the time meant a country somewhere in the vicinity of India. Again, as Karl Himly has pointed out, the *Hun Tsun Sii,* written during the Sung period (960–1279), states that t'shu-pu, another Chinese name for sugoroku, was invented in western India, that it was known in its original form as *chatushpada,* and that it reached China during the Wei period (220–265).[23]

Because the whole framework of Japanese culture has been provided by Buddhism, it is only natural that the Japanese should take a deep interest in Indian studies. In modern times there are few countries where Indian studies are so widespread as in Japan. In 1881 a regular course in Indian philosophy was formally instituted at the University of Tokyo. In 1904 an independent chair of Indian philosophy was established in Tokyo. Also situated in Tokyo is the Centre for East Asian Cultural Studies under the directorship of the eminent scholar Naoshiro Tsuji. At other national universities, such as Kyushu, Hokkaido, Nagoya, and Osaka, Buddhism and Indian studies are systematically pursued. Consequently, there have emerged from Japan numerous Buddhist works and scholars of world repute.

In the changed political and cultural climate of Indo-Japanese relations after World War II, renewed interest in Indian studies developed in Japan, particularly in the exploration of the socio-political, as well as intellectual, background of early Buddhism. Consequently, Indian society and history are also studied at various universities in Japan. Hajime Nakamura has played a significant role in this renewal of interest in Indian studies.

Japan's industrial and political achievements in this century have inspired the Indians, and Japan is playing an important role in the repatriation of Buddhism in India, as well as in Indian economic advancement. Buddhist studies in India have begun at university level, and much of what Indians now study comprises contributions made to Buddhist thought and literature by the Japanese and other Asians. Courses of Japanese language and literature have been established at Indian universities: for example at the Vishvabharati. The exchange of leading statesmen and scholars in recent years has also helped to reactivate cultural contact. The first president of the Republic of India, Rajendra Prasad, paid his first official visit to a foreign country when he visited Japan in 1958. In the same year, a Japan-India Society was founded in India to further the cultural ties between the two countries. Independent India declined to demand reparations from Japan after World War II, and indeed it offered to return all Japanese property which had been seized by the former British Government of India.

Chapter II

RED INDIANS OR ASIOMERICANS[1]—
INDIAN FOAM ON PACIFIC WAVES

HISTORY IS full of misnomers; one such term is the New World, as applied to the Americas. The landing of Columbus in 1492 undoubtedly created a new life on the continents, but it neither created nor discovered a new world. Many centuries earlier, Asian migrants had come to the western shores in substantial numbers and in successive waves across the Bering Sea, as well as across the Pacific; later, the Europeans landed on the Atlantic coastline. The Norsemen or the Vikings founded a colony in Vinland in the early eleventh century on the eastern coast of America, probably as far south as present-day New England. And, according to the archaeological researches of Paul Norlund, who excavated bodies in Greenland that were clothed in mid-fifteenth century European garments, the contact between Europe and the American region continued until the so-called discovery of America.[2]

The first Maya Empire had been founded in Guatemala at about the beginning of the Christian era. Before the fall of Rome the Mayas were charting accurately the synodical revolutions of Venus, and whilst Europe was still lingering in the Dark Ages the Maya civilization had reached a peak of greatness.

The most significant development of the ancient American or Asiomerican culture took place in the south of the United States, in Mexico, in Central America, and in Peru. The early history of Asiomericans is shrouded in mystery and controversy due to the absence of definitive documentary evidence, which was destroyed by the European conquerors in their misguided religious zeal. However, it appears that after the discovery or introduction of maize into Mexico, Asiomericans no longer had to wander about in search of food. Men in America, as in other parts of the world, settled down to cultivate food, and culture, a by-product of agricultural life, inevitably followed.

Of the Asiomerican civilizations, the best known are the Maya, the Toltec, the Aztec, and the Inca. The Mayas were possibly the earliest people to found a civilization there; they moved from the Mexican plateau into Guatemala. They were later pushed out, presumably by the Toltecs who, in turn, were dislodged by the Aztecs.

The Mayan civilization was certainly in existence in the early seventh century B.C., and there is strong evidence that it had existed prior to that time. According to their calendar, which is extant, the time record of the Mayas began on 6 August 613 B.C. It is an exact date, based upon intricate astronomical calculations, and prolonged observations. To work out this kind of elaborate calendar must have taken well over two thousand years of studying stars, and the Asiomericans must have been remarkably shrewd observers. The Mayan calendar was adopted by other Asiomerican civilizations: amongst them, the Aztecs.

Indeed, one of the most characteristic features of the Asiomerican culture has been the use of this calendar with certain variations in different ages and areas, dividing the year into eighteen months of twenty days with an additional month of only five days to complete the full 365 days of the solar year. The Mayas divided a month into twenty days, possibly because they counted by twenties instead of tens. Each month and day had a name, the days also being numbered progressively from one to thirteen, then starting again from one. The 365 days divided by thirteen left a remainder of one, but each of the thirteen numbers could begin the new year. Hence, it was not until fifty-two years had elapsed that a year could begin with the same day-name and numbers. Thirteen twenty-day months made another wholly arbitrary period of 260 days, which the Aztecs called *tonalamatl*. This system, with no basis in nature or astronomy, was a pure invention, a reckoning device. It ran simultaneously with the other astronomical 365-day calendar as two wheels of time. The two wheels came together again after fifty-two years. The Aztecs adopted this fifty-two year cycle, and called it a "bundle of years" and two such cycles "an age."

Lacking accurate clocks, Asiomericans must have needed long periods of astronomical observations to calculate the mean duration of the day. They became aware of the increasing discrepancy between their calendar and the celestial phenomena, and succeeded in working out the error with remarkable accuracy. The Mayas calculated the length of a year to 365.2420 days; the present corrected Gregorian or New Style Calendar reckons it to 365.2425. Whilst Asiomericans did not interpolate any leap days, they computed the necessary correction at twenty-five days in 104 years or two calendar rounds. They brought the revolutions of the moon into accord with their day count with an error of only one day in three hundred years. In addition to this general division of the year, the Mayas were using a long count, connecting their dates with a zero point of their own, and "position numbers" for each day of a month. This zero date represented some unknown or mythical event or perhaps the day of creation, somewhat similar to the birth of Christ or the supposed date of the creation in 3761 B.C. of the Jewish calendar. Because the Mayas, unlike the Aztecs, did not content themselves with a fifty-two-year period but calculated time by *katuns* of twenty (a *katun* was equal to twenty *tuns* and a tun was equal to 360 days) and cycles of four hundred years, and because the dates of Maya inscriptions are mostly from their eighth, ninth, and tenth cycles, which roughly correspond to the first six centuries of the Christian era, their fixed zero date or the starting point of their first cycle would be the cycle before 3000 B.C. The experts generally place it on or about 12 August 3113 B.C. There is, however, no absolute evidence at present to substantiate that their calculations of time had begun that early.

The calendar did not exhaust the astronomical and mathematical accomplishments of the Mayas. Although they did not know that the earth and Venus revolve about the sun, they had worked out that eight solar years correspond almost exactly with five years or the revolutions of 584 days each of Venus, and that sixty-five years of Venus coincide with 104 solar years. Indeed, in astronomy the Asiomericans, particularly the Mayas, reached the peak of their scientific achievement. They made remarkable accomplishments for a people without astronomical instruments, and without any real contact with other civilizations.

The Mayas of Yucatan were the first people besides the Indians to use a zero sign and represent number values by the position of basic symbols. The similarity between the Indian zero and the Mayan zero is indeed striking. So far as the logical principle is concerned, the two are identical, but the expressions of the principle are dissimilar. Again, whilst the Indian system of notation was decimal, as was the European, the Mayan was vigesimal. Consequently, their 100 stood for 400, 1000 for 8000, 1234 for 8864, and so on. Whilst the place of zero in the respective systems of the Indians and the Mayas is different, the underlying principle and method are the same, and the common origin of the Mayan and Indian zeros appears to be undoubted. But dispute continues amongst scholars in the absence of any conclusive evidence, apart from that of cultural parallels. As chronological evidence stands today, the Mayan zero would appear to be anterior by several centuries to its Hindu counterpart.

The Mayas had a practical knowledge of physics and geometry, were exceptional draughtsmen, and used a form of hieroglyphics. They were also accomplished builders and artists. Their architecture, sculpture, and painting, especially of their peak period from 450 to 600, are skilfully and artistically conceived and executed.

It is significant that the zenith of Maya civilization was reached at a time when India had also attained an unparalleled cultural peak during the Gupta period, and Indian cultural intercourse with Southeast Asia, as well as with Central and East Asia, was exceptionally close. In fact, the Gupta period had begun more than a century before the Mayan classical age in 320 and Buddhism and Hinduism had been well known in neighbouring regions for several centuries. If there was contact between Mayan America and Indianized Southeast Asia, the simultaneous cultural advance would not appear surprising. In marked contrast, this was the darkest period in Europe's history between the sack of Rome and the rise of Charlemagne; China was in a prolonged state of political unrest following the collapse of the Han dynasty.

At the end of the twelfth century the Mayas of Yucatan were overthrown by Quetzalcoatl who came from the Mexican plateau. Thus began the period of the Toltecs or Master Builders' ascendancy in Asiomerican history. The Teotihuacan Toltecs were accomplished architects, carpenters, and mechanics. Their era saw the blossoming of a unified Central American civilization: the Toltecs were so prosperous that their foodstuffs were not even priced. Quetzalcoatl was king, hero, priest, astronomer, and the embodiment of all wisdom and compassion for his people. He is identified with gods, and a vast legend has developed around him. He adopted the Mayan calendar, reducing it to a system of signs and ideographs to make it comprehensible to the diverse peoples of Central America.

The succeeding era in Asiomerican history was a chaotic one, generally referred to as the period of Aztec supremacy, which lasted with varying degrees of authority until the Spanish conquest. Before their decline the Aztecs made some striking cultural advances. They developed a lake civilization based on the island in Lake Texcoco, where they built their remarkable city, Mexico-Tenochtitlan, which was linked to the shores by causeways, and surrounded by the colourful *Chinampas*, floating gardens which were really artificial islands made by scooping up mud from the marshy borders of the lake and holding it in place by a breastwork of reeds. The roots of the trees planted on them cemented the earth together. Thus the Aztecs converted the barren marshy land into a grid of waterways and productive areas. This city was described by Bernal Diaz, the companion of the Spanish commander Cortes, as a dreamland which inspired the Spanish invaders to lyrical adulation and murderous plunder. Diaz wrote that the Mexicans were like the Romans, and that there was nothing in Spain to match the royal palace of Montezuma.[3]

The Asiomericans had an advanced system of medicine and herbal remedies, including digitalis. They had extensive knowledge of the human body, its muscles, skeleton, and nervous system, and the Mayas were particularly skilled in treating eye diseases. The Aztecs had well-organized hospitals, which even their Spanish conquerors admired, and their sanitation system was so far in advance of anything the Spaniards had left behind in Europe that they were unable to operate it.

At the time of the Spanish conquest none of the nations of Europe was much superior to the Mexicans in botanical knowledge, and their botanical gardens were more elaborate than any in Europe. They had, in addition, developed an aesthetic appreciation of plants, and the Valley of Mexico was full of cultivated flowers. Their cultivation of crops was also highly skilled and sophisticated.

By the time of the Spanish conquest in 1519, however, the Aztec Empire had degenerated to the extent that the Spanish triumph and its accompanying ruthless slaughter and destruction appeared less savage than they really were. Past-master of intrigue, betrayal, and wholesale massacre in Cholula, the most important sanctuary in pre-Columbian America, Cortes slaughtered, in less than two hours, six thousand people who had gathered in a temple patio. Destruction of Aztec cities was so complete that almost everything lay in ruins. The élite of the Asiomericans were put to death almost to the last man. After his entry into the conquered capital Tenochtitlan, Cortes wrote that "you could not put down your foot without stepping on an Indian corpse." In addition, his soldiery, as that of Pizarro a few years later in the Inca Empire, driven by their lust for gold, melted down irreplaceable works of art by the ton to get the precious metal. The Aztec civilization thus came to a violent end, but the Aztecs live even now, for without their Asiomerican ancestry and heritage, there would be no Mexican people or civilization today.

If the history of pre-Columbian America is obscure, it is because after the Spanish conquest, the first Bishop of Mexico, Juan de Zumarraga, burned all the records of the Library of Texcoco in Tlatelolco market square as "the work of the devil," and religious fanatics destroyed temples and statues. Zumarraga, gloating over his success, wrote to his superiors in 1531 that he alone had had five hundred temples razed to the ground and twenty thousand idols destroyed. Diego de Landa, the second Bishop of Yucatan, following the pattern, reduced the Maya Library in Yucatan to ashes in 1562. These libraries contained records of ancient history, medicine, astronomy, science, religion, and philosophy. What Emperor Theodosius of Constantinople did to the library at Alexandria to save Christianity from the Greek and Oriental pagan knowledge deposited there, these priests did in Central America with similar motives but larger success. The burning of manuscripts continued for decades. Soldiers were encouraged to ransack palaces, public buildings, and private houses to find manuscripts. Pablo Jose de Arriaga, the head of the Jesuit College in Peru, in almost unparalleled fanaticism, caused the systematic and wholesale destruction of all state archives, customs records, royal and imperial archives, codes of laws, temple archives, and historical records. Less than a score of manuscripts escaped annihilation.

The Spaniards destroyed whatever they could, but they could not, for instance, burn the great Pyramid of the Sun and the remains of Teotihuacan, which speak of the splendid bygone civilization. The memory as well as the material evidence of Asiomerican past greatness was lost in the excitement of the discovery and conquest of the new and rich lands offering prospects for migration. No matter how much historians stretch their imagination, it will never be possible to reconstruct a picture of these advanced civilizations which would do them justice, and yet be held historically acceptable. Thus, today the sources of ancient Mexican history comprise about ten codices or books of pictures written principally in ideographs but also in the partially phonetic representation of Nahuatl, the language of the Aztecs and Toltecs; some folios written by Asiomericans in the Nahuatl language using the Latin alphabet manage to salvage something of their folklore, literature, and archaeological findings.

Beyond Mexico to the south flourished the civilization of the Incas in Peru, which remained stable and prosperous for at least three centuries prior to its subjugation by Spain. The ancient Andean or Peruvian civilization also has an obscure history, although there is enough evidence to support its existence and general nature. The first known Inca chief was Sinchi Roca, who possibly began his rule in 1105. The Incas suffered an even worse fate at the hands of the Spaniards than did their neighbours in Central America. The Spanish assault on the Incas, the Spanish avarice for gold, and the barbarities perpetrated in the wake of victory, including the inhuman tortures publicly inflicted on the Inca King, Atahuallpa, are illustrations of savagery seldom surpassed in history. So complete was the destruction of historical materials pertaining to the Peruvian culture that there are no extant records except those left by the Spaniards; these are, of course, terribly inadequate and partisan. Perhaps the Incas did not have a written language in the generally accepted sense of the term.

Despite the Spanish conquerors, the Inca culture survives today. Inca government, based on a unique village system, was remarkable even by modern standards. The village was not only a community of people but a communion of these people with the soil; there was complete identification between men and land. They were skilled farmers, and it is said that the Incas lived as if they were to die the next day but farmed as if they were to live forever. The soil belonged to the community of the people, but the metals underneath were state property. In criminal law, which was rather severe, the Incas made a distinction between stealing for want or necessity and stealing from malice or avarice. Of the two, the latter was a capital offence, but the former entailed punishment of the offender's village official for allowing his administration to create a situation in which theft became necessary.

The Inca communication and road systems were elaborate. Two main roads ran the length of the kingdom, one along the coast and the other in the highlands, whilst transverse roads connected all the important towns. The coast or Royal Road ran through the Andes south through Ecuador, Peru, Bolivia, Argentina, and Chile. It covered about three and a quarter thousand miles, which makes it longer than the longest Roman road which ran from Hadrian's Wall, separating England from Scotland, to Jerusalem. Baron Von Humboldt claimed that as an engineering feat, the Inca road system surpassed that of the Romans.[4]

Little is known of the pre-Inca Moche and Chimu cultures, except what can be gleaned from archaeological remains. But these speak eloquently of their skills, ingenuity, and accomplishments. The dry desert climate along the coast has preserved surprisingly well the remains of its early inhabitants, including bones, textiles, pottery, and temples. The Moches perhaps developed a means of communication by signs incised on lima beans, and their pottery is particularly interesting. The canals and aqueducts, bringing water from the mountains to irrigate the parched coastal valleys, speak highly of their engineering skill; the aqueduct at Ascope is nearly a mile long and fifty feet high. Their carefully controlled hydraulic system in the fields was, perhaps, even more remarkable. If the water flowed too fast, it could erode the banks; if it flowed too slowly, it could silt up the conduits. By control

41

of the imported water, terracing, and natural fertilizer, the desert was made productive enough to support a population far larger than any living there since.

Why did the Aztecs and the Incas submit to such inhuman and merciless punishment from the Spaniards, and how was it that a handful of mercenaries and adventurers were allowed to wipe out the highly advanced civilization of an entire continent? The Spaniards had four hundred men, fifteen horses, and seven light guns, whilst Montezuma had at his command thousands of brave, experienced warriors with bows and arrows, as well as the macquaitl sword which was so sharp that it could lop off a human head with a single stroke. The Aztecs and the Incas did not offer any resistance at first, allowing the Spaniards to roam the streets, enter the most sacred places, destroy the idols they so fervently worshipped, and even capture King Montezuma in the midst of his own people. It was not fear that kept them submissive, for the Asiomericans did eventually resist. The only explanation that appears somewhat convincing is that the Asiomericans believed that at some period of their prehistory, white men with beards had landed on their shores and had given them all their knowledge. They were the white gods, who had left with a promise to return one day. Hence, the Spaniards were mistaken by Asiomericans for their legendary white gods, who were to be made welcome, and if they inflicted suffering it was to be accepted as a divine judgement. And, by a tragic coincidence, the Spanish conquerors invaded Mexico at about the time, in 1519, as the Aztec priests and tradition had predicted the return of the white gods.[5] The Aztecs even offered the Spanish conquistadores the vestments of Quetzalcoatl and other gods and considered performing human sacrifice to them in case they were fatigued after such a long journey. Throughout the Inca Empire, the Spaniards were greeted as *Viracocha*, the Inca name of the great White God they had been waiting for. It is only when the Asiomericans were completely horrified and disillusioned by the brutalities and merciless killings, that they recognized their mistake. The realization that the Spaniards were not gods but *popolocas* (barbarians), however, came too late.

The European conquerors of South and Central America not only destroyed practically all the records and literature of Asiomerica, but created an utterly distorted image of the American past by taking some of its ugly features out of context and magnifying them out of proportion. For instance, the human sacrifice practiced by the Aztecs was repeatedly stressed without explaining its extenuating features, and without pointing out that human sacrifice had not been unknown to other peoples, such as in Egypt and Rome. Taking their technique a step farther they contrasted this picture with that of their own deeds in Asiomerica in which European misdemeanour, caprice, and criminality were soft-pedalled and civilized and humane behaviour emphasized. No wonder the Asiomerican past did not attract much attention and even today remains popularly unknown and historically uncertain. Most people believe that Asiomericans were uncivilized hordes with an occasional freak of knowledge, who had contributed nothing of permanent value to civilization by 1492. Despite a good deal of information to the contrary, there is resistance to accepting a change in this image. Misconceptions multiply fast but die slowly.

In the second half of the eighteenth century explorers and historians began to take an interest in America's ancient history. Alexander Von Humboldt was the first man to recognize the Inca and Aztec civilizations in their own right, and the first to give a serious account of their religious traditions. He also saw the manifestations of artistic achievement in Aztec monuments.

As interest grew, many explorers and writers gave their lifetimes and even their fortunes to reconstructing America's past. Lord Edward Kingborough, who attempted unsuccessfully to prove that Asiomericans were one of the ten lost tribes of Israel, painstakingly collected enormously valuable data and published nine volumes of his *Antiquities of Mexico* between 1831 and 1848, but ended in a debtors' prison. Yet, without his work the ancient American history would be much poorer.

Good luck played a part in John Lloyd Stephens' discovery of the first major complex of pyramids, temples, and terraces covering twelve acres—the Copan ruins in Honduras—in November 1839. He bought the site from the local owner for fifty dollars, and although Stephens was not a professional archaeologist but an American lawyer and antiquarian, his find opened the way to Asiomerican archaeology. Edward Herbert Thompson discovered the Chichen Itza in 1855, with its brilliant temples, pyramids, and sculpture. Soon, others pursued similar work with as much devotion as skill and competence.[6] Amongst the pioneer scholars, the works of William Prescott, who wrote during the second quarter of the nineteenth century, are commonly accepted as standard writings.[7] They are still of incalculable value, and in some respects remain unsurpassed, certainly in the English language.

However, such was the nature of the discoveries and research that it was inevitable that this subject should have lent itself to divergent interpretations and conflicting opinions. In this battle, not only historians, anthropologists, archaeologists, and, of necessity, scientists, especially botanists, actively participate, but also institutions and Church organizations, such as the Rosicrucians, the Theosophists, and the Church of Jesus Christ of Latter-day Saints (the Mormons), maintain strong positions. It is indeed ironic that the world should have so little information about the origins and early civilization of a people who first cultivated the food its inhabitants eat in various regions; after all, civilization began as a result of cultivation. Potatoes, maize, beans, yams, squash, mangoes, peanuts, cashews, pineapples, cacao, avocados, tomatoes, peppers, papaya, strawberries, and blackberries, are all Asiomerican contributions to civilization.

Much of the discussion revolves around the origin of man in America, and consequently early civilizations of ancient America. It is generally conceded that man is not indigenous to America, for no anthropoid apes, the ancestors of man, either extant or fossil, have been found in America. The absence of such remains, however, is not definite proof of their non-existence, yet, until such evidence turns up, the theory of indigenous Americans would remain untenable. Even the theory of Continental Drift, propounded by Wegener in 1912, which has recently been considerably reinforced by studies in rock-magnetism, and which claimed that the world was once a solid land mass that broke up into continents and islands, may explain certain facts of geology, geography, and prehuman biology, such as South American monkeys, but cannot account for man's presence on the American continent. For the continents would have drifted away from each other before any form of man existed in terms other than those of his simian ancestors. Even if man had existed originally in America, this cannot exclude the possibility of early human migration, of which there is undoubted evidence. But the great debate that has already lasted for centuries continues and seldom has so much bitterness, so much militancy, not principally overlaid by nationalistic passion, been noted in academic disputes as in this one.

Some of the theories which have been advanced to account for the presence of the Asiomericans on the continents are hardly more than extravagant assumptions. Of those that have enjoyed popularity at one time or another, the following are regarded as major hypotheses. Some religious zealots have suggested that Asiomericans are the descendants of the Lost Tribes of Israel who had wandered to America. This theory was something of a fad with the earliest explorers. On the other hand, the eighteenth- and early nineteenth-century classicists liked to find Carthaginian-Phoenician traits in Asiomerican culture. Later, the

Egyptian origin theory became the favourite, and even now enjoys occasional currency.

Of the numerous Egyptian enthusiasts, the most devoted was Augustus Le Plongeon, whose intellectual arrogance and egotism initiated a militancy, acrimony, and bickering in this academic debate which has filled proceedings of numerous congresses of Americanists and pages of historical writings. But he died a disappointed and discarded scholar. After him, the greatest champion of Egyptian origins was Elliot Smith, who wrote *Elephants and Ethnologists,* and who was ably supported by William Perry. They amassed a staggering body of evidence in their support, but before they could gain general acceptance of their theory, they were confronted by one of the most meticulous of scholars, Ronald B. Dixon, who minutely scrutinized their evidence. His verdict was categorically against this theory which was seriously discredited, despite the bitter counterattack against Dixon. Yet, this Egyptian theory, in complete disregard of professional and scholarly opinion, stubbornly persists, presumably because Egyptian archaeology is so well known to European scholars, and because they are so used to tracing their own early culture to Egypt. It is one of those academic irrationalities which has gradually built up immunity to its own antidotes.

Similarly, two other schools, the Lost Tribes of Israel and the Lost Continent of Atlantis, have substantial supporters who refuse to respond to the weight of evidence to the contrary. Both these beliefs use Egyptian parallels with ancient America but claim that Egypt acted only as an intermediary. The Lost Tribes of Israel theory is held by, amongst others, the Mormons, and members of other religious organizations. The theory of the Lost Continent of Atlantis is almost as old as the Columbian discovery of America itself. It was championed by Gonzalo Fernandez de Oviedo y Valdes in 1535, and later held by many eminent European scholars. As late as 1924 and 1925 it was effectively advocated by H. Lewis Spence in his works, *Atlantis in America* and *The Problem of Atlantis.* This theory of Lost Atlantis continues to be a favourite and is revived now and then by new editions of the Spence and Ignatius Donnelly best sellers. There is a Pacific counterpart of Atlantis, popularly called Mu, or the lost continent of Lemuria. Its best known exponent was James Churchward, who published his last book on the subject in 1931. The idea of the lost continent of Atlantis providing a partial land bridge from Europe or Africa to America, or that of a transatlantic sea-migration which would conveniently explain the vague affinity between the Aztec and Mayan calendar systems and those of the Nile Valley, or that of a Pacific Ocean lost continent, Mu, linking

45

Asia with America, are all far too speculative to merit serious attention.

A post-war theory of Thor Heyerdahl, widely known as *Kon-Tiki*, bravely supported by a daring voyage on a balsa raft, advances the view that Asiomericans sailed westwards across the Pacific and populated Polynesia. Heyerdahl does not deny, however, the Indonesian or Melanesian origin of the present Polynesian race and culture, but suggests that Indonesian culture reached Polynesia through a circuitous northern route via Japan, America, and thence to Polynesia. Before Heyerdahl, a Spanish missionary, J. de Zuniga, in 1803, and a British missionary, William Ellis, in the 1830's had similarly suggested that the eastern group of Polynesian islands was peopled from America.

An Atlantic Kon-tiki was proposed by De Bourbourg, who argued that the Egyptian civilization was derived from the Atlantean colonists from America. Recently a view has been put forward that the Mayan script came from Crete and the entire civilization revolves round the emergence of a White God in ancient America, who may have come from the Western world.

Some scholars, such as A. Hyatt Verrill, believe that men came to America in a variety of ways, some from Europe via Greenland, others across the Atlantic, some from Lost Atlantis or southern Europe, some via the Bering Straits, and many more across the Pacific. He suspected that professional archaeologists suppressed information contrary to their theories.

An eminent amateur anthropologist, Harold S. Gladwin, who also distrusted the common sense of the professionals, wrote in his book, *Men Out of Asia,* of a series of waves of migrants going out from the various parts of Asia to settle in ancient America. He also suggested that after the death of Alexander in 323 B.C., some survivors of the wrecked fleet under Nearchus sailed eastwards, picked up artisans from India and Southeast Asia, crossed the Pacific and reached America, where they and their descendants founded the ancient civilizations. Whilst the feasibility of such a voyage cannot be conclusively refuted, it is not generally accepted.

Without diverting attention from subtle distinctions, it may be said that all these divergent opinions fall into two broad groups— the transatlanticites, who believe in western migration across the Atlantic, and the transpacificites who support Asian settlers having gone across the Pacific either through a northern route, a middle route or both. Of these, the former view has been considerably challenged by later researches, but lingers on.

Divergent views prevail amongst the enthusiasts of the Asian origins of Asiomericans. Baron Von Humboldt, whilst visiting Mexico, found similarities between Asian and Mexican astrology.[8] He founded the systematic study of ancient American cultures and was convinced of the Asian origin of the American-Indian high civilization. He said, "if languages supply but feeble evidence of ancient communication between the two worlds, their communication is fully proved by the cosmogonies, the monuments, the hieroglyphical characters and the institutions of the people of America and Asia."[9] In 1761 a French scholar, De Guignes, published his opinion that some Buddhists were sent from China to Mexico, which was identified as Fu-Sang in early Chinese annals, in the fifth century. He appears to have based his hypothesis on the tradition of a Chinese legend which spoke of a Buddhist priest, Hwui Shan, who was said to have come from ancient America. Later, H. J. Von Klaproth endeavoured to disprove this theory on the grounds that the monk in question had come from southeastern Japan, and not from America. Many scholars since, however, especially from France and some from Germany, have rallied round the theory of Buddhist influence. M. de Paravey renewed the theory of Buddhist influence in 1844. A year later, a German orientalist, Friedrich de Neuman, supported the view. Rivero and Tschudi urged that Quetzalcoatl in Mexico and Mango-Capac in Peru were Indian missionaries. Channing Arnold and F. J. T. Frost even traced the chronological passage of Buddhism from India to Central America. They argued that as Buddhism had spread all over eastern Asia by the eighth century, it was rightly poised to launch itself farther eastward across the sea.

Considering that at this time Buddhism was flourishing in Southeast Asia, as well as in China and Japan, and was backed actively by powerful Asian kingdoms, such as that of the Khmers, it would not appear surprising that some Buddhist monks had voyaged across the Pacific. Meanwhile, John Ranking, in his *Historical Researches on the Conquest of Peru, Mexico etc.*, suggested in 1827 that the Inca Empire was founded by the crews of a few ships of Kublai Khan wrecked and driven across the Pacific. In 1834, John Dunmore Lang, a minister of the Scots Church at Sydney, declared that Polynesians had crossed the Pacific Ocean from Easter Island to America under a violent gale of westerly wind, landing somewhere near Copiapo in Chile. It was the descendants of these Polynesians, he claimed, who progressively populated and civilized the whole continent of America from Cape Horn to Labrador.[10] In 1836, J. Mackintosh favoured the view that Koreans were the first to visit ancient America. In 1866, the French architect,

Viollet-le-Duc, also noted striking resemblances between ancient Mexican structures and those of South India.

All these scholars were also greatly impressed by the similarity between the Hindu Trinity—Brahma-Visnu-Siva—and the Mexican Trinity—Ho-Huizilopochtli-Tlaloc—as well as the likeness between Indian temples and American pyramids. Later, two English scholars, Channing Arnold and Frederick J. Tabor Frost, in their *The American Egypt*, made a detailed examination of the transpacific contacts, reinforcing the view of Buddhist influences on Central America. In 1947, Harold S. Gladwin suggested successive waves of Asian migrants belonging to specific archaeological cultures and linguistic groups, including Alexander's sailors. The most recent and by far the most systematic, well-reasoned, and effective case has been advanced by the eminent archaeologists, R. Heine-Geldern and Gordon Ekholm, who favour Indian and Southeast Asian cultural influences on ancient America through migrations across the Pacific.

It is likely that man first came to America from Asia towards the end of the last glacial period, probably between twenty thousand and ten thousand years ago, across the Bering Straits. He may have gone by sea or, more likely, crossed on ice. The water distance is only about sixty miles, interrupted by the Diomede Island almost in the middle of the gap, and ice may have paved the whole way at the time. The Aleutian Islands have also been suggested as a route of migration, but the chain of islands is long, and the gap at the western end of about a hundred miles would have required skilful negotiation. Whether there was a land bridge so far south of the Bering Straits is questionable because of the ocean depths of ten to twenty thousand feet. Long before, in geological antiquity, there was a land bridge from Siberia to Alaska which horses, camels, cattle, elephants, deer, and other species had crossed. This, however, does not explain human migration, for man's entry belongs to a much later period when the two continents had probably separated.

There are just as many conflicting opinions about the Bering Straits theory as any other. Arguments in favour of the theory are: many Asiomericans share physical characteristics with North Asians; even today there is some migration between northeastern Asia and the extreme tip of northwestern Alaska; and, distinctively Asian dialects are spoken by many Alaskan and northwestern American tribes. Examples of arguments against this theory are: the physical characteristics of a race are likely to be altered by environment, or admixture of blood with other races if encountered during the course of migration; not all Indians of North, Central, and South America possess Mongoloid or North Asian features; the Asian dialects disappear completely as soon as one goes far from the northwestern coast tribes.

Widely distributed over the vast continent, Asiomericans show considerable ethnic diversity. Generally speaking, Asiomericans are yellowish or reddish brown in skin-colour, and usually have coarse black hair, broad faces with prominent cheek-bones, and often a well-developed chin. They are described broadly as Mongoloids, but they are a composite race. Whilst they have some characteristic Mongoloid features, they lack others. For example, the pigmentation of their skin, usually darker than that of the Asians and sometimes more reddish than yellow, their hair-form, and their facial size are Mongoloid, but the Mongoloid eye-fold appears only occasionally. Their eyes do not slant. Their brow-ridges are often well-developed, whilst the Mongoloid forehead is typically smooth. The nose of any American Indian is very rarely as flat as that of a typical Mongoloid; it may be hooked, straight, or sometimes concave. The hawk-nose of so many of the Asiomericans is, in fact, recognized as inherently Aryan, associated with the races of the Iranian plateau. Asiomerican types have also been identified with the Dravidians of the Indus Valley. There is concrete evidence to support the belief that many of the early American peoples were of Indo-European stock. For instance, the Toltecs, apart from various references to bearded white gods, were, as Edward Tylor has pointed out, large of stature and fair in complexion. In contrast, the Aztecs of later times were small and dark.

Again, the Sirionos of Bolivia, an isolated, primitive tribe with slightly wavy, fine hair and great bushy beards, who bear no resemblances at all to any other known Asiomerican tribe, resemble Polynesians. Also amongst nearly all the tribes of western South America are found words—not one or two but scores—which are strikingly like and, in many cases identical with, words of the same meanings in Oceanian dialects. In some of their arts, habits, and religious beliefs there is a great similarity between the Polynesians and the Asiomericans of western South America. The evidence of blood grouping would indicate kinship between the Asiomericans of North America and Polynesians. They share a relatively high incidence of M, and they also share some of the highest known frequencies of the rhesus gene cDE. This similarity may imply transpacific contact.

In the 1930's, Baron Erland Nordenskiold noted numerous cultural traits—forty-nine to be exact—common to both South America and the Pacific islands. This could have been due either to accidental or

49

deliberate migrations from Polynesia to America, or simply to parallel and independent growth. It is significant, however, that four-fifths of these common traits were found in Colombia and Panama, the precise areas where Polynesian sailors would land if they were drifting with the Equatorial Counter-current.

This evidence would seem to support the view that during the course of the uncounted thousands of years, successive waves of immigrants spread over the two continents of America. The migrants had clearly been filtering across Asia and had added to their respective characteristics—Eurafrican or Dravidian or Iranian—traits which they shared with the Mongols. Gladwin, pointing out that the Americas are populated by many different kinds of men, recounts no less than five successive migratory waves of Pygmies, Australoid Negroid, Mongoloid, and Melanesian-Polynesian peoples to America.

At the time of the discovery of America, there were perhaps thirty million Asiomericans distributed over the two Americas, comprising more than six hundred distinct societies. Hence, it would require far more time than is usually allowed for a few nomadic people to multiply, develop an ethnic admixture, spread from the Arctic Circle to Cape Horn, and to give rise to the diversity of tribes, dialects, customs, and beliefs found amongst the original inhabitants of America.

As the inquiry into the cultural past of ancient America has to rely heavily on anthropological data, its students have come to reflect the controversies that divide anthropologists. Broadly speaking, cultural historians of Asiomerica are divided into two camps, "diffusionists" and "evolutionists." The former believe in an early diffusion of Asian and Pacific culture through America, whilst the latter assert the independent and local development of the American-Indian culture. Inevitably both sides have their relentless and uncompromising champions many of whom, by reversing the process of historical scrutiny, mould evidence to fit their conclusions, rather than draw conclusions from actual material. There are some extremely plausible arguments on both sides, but it appears that more and more material is coming to light reinforcing the diffusionist theory.

According to the evolutionist, man, being a creative animal, can invent in one place as easily as he can in another. And under similar circumstances and needs, and at similar cultural levels, widely distributed men can produce similar inventions. Hence, identity in achievements is no evidence of cultural borrowing. The diffusionists accept the fundamental basis of this assertion, but go a good deal further in interpretation. They argue that whilst coincidences are possible, identical complex inventions in details of common cultural trends cannot be purely coincidental. In any case, for every instance of parallelism, many more of diffusion—almost in the ratio of one to a hundred—can be traced in history.

In the second half of the nineteenth century ideas based on Adolf Bastian's concept of the *Elementargedanke,* psychic unity of mankind, captured the imagination of anthropologists. Whilst Bastian recognized the importance of geographical conditions on the development of culture, he did not ascribe any creative power to them; they could only modify a culture, not create one. Hence, he explained the sameness of thought in widely separated lands as due to the similarity of the psychic structure of man the world over. However, the evolutionists appear to have disregarded Bastian's stress on the similarity in elementary ideas and on his admission that at a higher stage contact with other cultures might constitute a superior external stimulus. As they interpreted this theory, the psychic unity, together with the similarity of circumstances in which culture tends to develop, was bound to lead to parallel and independent developments which produced similar or even identical results. Even the most highly complex beliefs and myths were regarded as natural products of the human mind. The underlying thought of these conceptions was that the manifestation of ethnic life represents a time series, which progresses from simple beginnings to complex modern civilization.

The publication of *The Origin of Species* in 1859 and the popularity of Charles Darwin's concept of evolution also had repercussions on the writing of cultural history. Cultural historians borrowed the concept of evolution from ethnologists, who in turn had borrowed it from biology and applied it, somewhat indiscriminately, to cultural phenomena. In their zeal to make use of new-found knowledge, nineteenth-century anthoropologists failed to reflect sufficiently on the capacity of man, as of all living beings, as Darwin himself had pointed out, to respond to changing environmental conditions and to improve his position. Only now has anthropological inquiry begun to note the concepts of function and adaptation. Broadly speaking, evolutionist historians applied the theory of evolution to culture in the same way as it is applied to biological organisms; one form grows out of another. Elaborate arts, complex institutions, and abstruse knowledge were held to be the results of gradual development from an earlier and simpler form.

The earliest pioneers of cultural evolutionism, Herbert Spencer,

51

Edward Tylor, and Morgan, however, were somewhat anterior to Darwin, although their ideas gathered force after Darwin had published his thesis. In 1852, Spencer had published a paper, *Development Hypothesis*, a brilliant defence of the theory of organic evolution which laid the beginnings of cultural evolutionism. Edward Tylor pioneered cultural evolutionism in Britain and introduced the term culture into anthropological literature as a specific technical term. He was, however, always willing to concede transmission of cultural traits if he were satisfied with the evidence. Franz Boas (1858–1942), whilst accepting the validity of the concept of evolution in biology, was opposed to its application to cultural history. He could not accept the contention that cultural similarities were the outcome of identical processes, because it was based on the assumption that the human mind behaves identically everywhere. He had wide support amongst fellow anthropologists.

England was the main home of evolutionist theories and, despite its far-flung empire, it remained partial to its island mentality and isolationist theories long after the weight of opinion had moved away from evolutionism elsewhere. Whilst on the Continent evolutionist concepts had been considerably discredited by the last quarter of the last century, it was not until 1911 that W. H. Rivers, a leading British exponent of evolutionism, announced his conversion to diffusionism. Since then evolutionist concepts, which were found very convenient by writers seeking to fan nationalist-purism, have lost much of their impact, although the discussion has by no means ended either amongst ethnologists or historians. With some exceptions, mainly in Britain, most historians today seem to agree with V. Gordon Childe in making a clear distinction between cultural evolution and biological evolution and oppose notions of total parallelism in cultural growth.[11]

The opposition to the isolationist theory gained credence in 1949, when two eminent scholars, Robert Heine-Geldern and Gordon F. Ekholm, presented overwhelming evidence of innumerable Asian-Pacific-American similarities before the Congress of Americanists at New York. The theory of identically independent cultural development in distant lands can be, as it has often been, taken too far. Like any other people, Asiomericans, no doubt, have made original contributions to civilization, such as rubber and numerous foods, including the development of tapioca from a poisonous root called manioc, but it is a very different matter to independently duplicate those inventions previously made in other parts of the world. It seems almost unbelievable that the evolutionists are prepared to concede to Asiomericans what is not conceded to the inhabitants of the British Isles nor to Europeans in general. No serious and non-partisan scholar today credits prehistoric

Europe with having independently invented the wheel, bronze-casting, writing, pottery, weaving, and similarly important innovations. Europe borrowed them from Asia. Thus, whilst Europe invented with the assistance of Asian experience and heritage, ancient America is not supposed to have borrowed from or been influenced by anyone else. What is still more baffling is the premise that a series of complex techniques, such as casting by the lost wax method, the extraction of tin from cassiterite, the alloying of copper and tin, the colouring of gold by chemical processes, weaving, tie-dying, and batik could have been invented twice, independently of each other, in two different areas of the world.

Whilst the diffusionist theory has been gaining popular support, there is no conclusive evidence to dissuade the isolationist or evolutionist. Whatever evidence there is, is fragmentary, insufficient, and mainly in the form of parallels between the cultures of Asia and ancient America. But these parallels are so many and so close in detail, that the theory of contact and exchange is quite logical. Many of these similarities, identified as emanating from a single source, belong to much later periods, cutting well into historical times, and suggest that periodic migrations from Asia to America continued to take place until the first century, and possibly later. Many of the Asian parallels with America are of Indian origin. As direct migration from India has not been suggested, it is claimed that diffusion of Indian ideas and cultural traits took place through the media of China and especially Southeast Asia.

The first Asians to travel to America during prehistoric times were perhaps East Asians. The archaeological work done since 1961 on the Pacific Coast at Valdivia in Ecuador, by scholars such as Emilio Estrada, Betty J. Meggers, and Clifford Evans, has added considerably to the documentation of similarities between South America and eastern Asia, and suggests that the Japanese crossed the Pacific in prehistoric times. Pottery made by shellfish-gathering people of Ecuador and that of Japan (Honshu island)—both belonging to the same period of prehistory, between 3000 and 2000 B.C.—are very similar. Whilst Valdivian pottery is different from other early Asiomerican artifacts and archaeological finds, it is very close to the pottery from the Jomon period of Japan which would suggest Japanese landings in Ecuador. Other items, belonging to a much later period, the last two centuries B.C., include pottery, house models with certain alien architectural features, neck rests, seated figurines, symmetrically graduated Pan pipes, net weights, ear ornaments, coolie yokes, and sea-going rafts with centreboards.

The first Asians to travel to America during historical times were possibly the Chinese, as is suggested by some of the sculptures of the Chavin culture, the oldest of the higher civilizations of Peru. This most ancient site of all the American civilizations discovered so far, was not found until 1941. It was discovered by Julio C. Tello, the Asiomerican archaeologist, and derived its name from Chavin de Huantar in the north Peruvian highlands. Chavin sculptures show motifs which closely correspond to those found only in China of the ninth and eighth century B.C. (848 B.C. ± 167 years), which corresponds exactly with the date of the Chavin culture as determined by the Carbon-14 method.

There was no prior local tradition, no bridge or direct transition from an earlier beginning to explain satisfactorily the evolution of this era of Chavin culture. It appeared suddenly, embracing the whole of Peru and producing works of art that were inspired by profound religious feeling. Maize (radio carbon dating 714 B.C. ± 200 years) and decorated ceramics for ceremonial use also appeared in Peru during this period. Traces of metal (gold only) and weaving appeared for the first time in South America during this period. The art of the goldsmith required metallurgical techniques, such as hammering, embossing, annealing, welding, soldering, strap joining, incising, champleve, and cut-out designs. From where did these techniques suddenly emerge? Whilst scholars such as Heine-Geldern suspect a Chinese link, Vale and Clifford Evans suggest Central America, and Julio C. Tello favours its local evolution. Archaeological investigations on this site have to be carried further before puzzling questions can be, if at all, resolved.

The art of the following period, the Salinar culture at El Salinar in Chicama Valley, again contains motifs that correspond with those of seventh and sixth centuries B.C. China. Chinese influences probably came from the ancient eastern states of Wu, in the lower part of the Yangtze Valley, and Yueh, in modern Chekiang. After some interruption, presumably caused by the unsettled conditions in China, it appears that Asians resumed migratory voyages from the coasts of Vietnam, and traces of Dong-son culture are far more numerous in South America than those of Chinese influence. These migrations, possibly, came to an end with the conquest of Tonkin and north Annam by China during the first century.

It appears that the vacuum created by the disappearance of Vietnamese and Chinese transpacific voyages to South America was filled by the Indianized peoples of Southeast Asia. This view has gained strength from the recent researches of Heine-Geldern and Ekholm. They have unearthed astonishing parallels in architecture and art, religious symbols, cosmological theories, government institutions and royal courts, insignia of kings and dignitaries, and even games. The contacts between Cambodia and the Maya and Olmec areas seem to have been particularly close from the seventh to the tenth century and it is likely that they more or less continued until the fall of the Kambuja Empire before the Thai incursions.

Indeed, the parallels between the arts and culture of India and those of ancient America are too numerous and close to be attributed to independent growth. A variety of art forms are common to Mexico, India, Java, and Indo-China, the most striking of which are the *Teocallis,* the pyramids, with receding stages, faced with cut stone, and with stairways leading to a stone sanctuary on top. Many share surprisingly common features such as serpent columns and banisters, vaulted galleries and corbeled arches, attached columns, stone cut-out lattices, and Atlantean figures; these are typical of the Puuc style of Yucatan. Heine-Geldern and Ekholm point out that temple pyramids in Cambodia did not become important until the ninth and tenth centuries, a time coinciding with the beginning of the Puuc period. The use of half columns flanking the doors and of groups of small columns set in panels is characteristic of both the Cambodian and Mayan civilizations. Atlantean figures, which appeared in India in the second century B.C., are found at Tula in Central Mexico and Chichen Itza in the tropical forest of Yucatan.

The oldest Mayan city to be excavated was Uaxactun, where the first Mayan observatory was found, and also the oldest Mayan fresco. Quite near Uaxactun was the city Tikal, where archaeologists have found colossal mounds of rubble and immense buildings, including five of the steepest pyramids that have ever been seen; the tallest rose to a height of two hundred and thirty feet with the temple standing at the very top. Similar towering, narrow pyramids are found in the ancient Cambodian city, Angkor Thom.

Mayan art reached its highest point in the cities of Yaxchilan, Palenque, and Piedras Negras. Numerous pyramids and sculptures have been excavated there. One of the best pieces of Mayan sculpture in the pyramid temple of Piedras Negras, Guatemala, appears to be a Buddhist scene. The subject matter of the scene is not clear but the theme is somewhat alien to Mexican art tradition. It bears remarkable likeness to a Jataka bas-relief of the Borobudur stupa in Central Java, and the technique of placing the figures at several levels in the composition is also very similar to the one used in Borobudur.

The buildings of Chichen Itza show certain influences from Southeast Asia; for example, the lotus motif occurs in the Mercado (covered market) at Chichen Itza. As a vaulted gallery, closed by a wall on one side and with pillars along the other, the Mercado is strikingly reminiscent of the galleries so typical of the Cambodian architecture that eventually blossomed into the galleries of Angkor Vat, dated about the middle of the twelfth century—the precise time that the Mercado and similar buildings at Chichen Itza were built. What is more significant is that the gradual development of these galleries follows very much the same pattern in both Cambodia and the northern Mayan region.

The lotus motif, interspersed with seated human figures, which has a deep symbolic meaning in Hindu and Buddhist mythologies and as such is an integral part of early Indian art, especially of Amaravati, is found at Chichen Itza as a border in the reliefs of the lower room of the Temple of Tigers. The lotus plant in Indian art, as reproduced on architraves and in border designs, shows not only the flowers and leaves, but the whole plant, including the rhizome, a kind of root-like stalk which grows horizontally under water or deeply buried in the mud. Whilst the flowers and leaves generally resemble their natural forms, the rhizome is represented by a decorative undulating creeper. This occurs in the art at Chichen Itza. If these two representations are not connected in some way, it must be an extraordinary coincidence that in India as well as in ancient America the generally invisible rhizome should have been not only made the basic element of a whole motif but also stylized in a similarly unrealistic manner.

Again, as in the early Indian art, the lotus motif at Chichen Itza is used as a border around an imaginary landscape and as a frame for other motifs such as the human figures. Even the figures' postures and movements are similar to those in India. Whilst the figures naturally differ in racial type and in costume, the motif is essentially the same. The similarity between the art of Amaravati and that of Chichen Itza is particularly noticeable in reclining figures holding on to the rhizome of the lotus.

In Indian art the lotus rhizome frequently protrudes from the mouths of makaras, sea monsters with fish-like bodies and elephant-like trunks. At Chichen Itza, stylized figures of fish are found at both ends of the lotus plant, in the same position as the makaras in India. "Such a combination of highly specific details cannot be accidental. It suggests the existence of some kind of relationship between Maya art and not only Buddhist art in general, but the school of Amaravati of the second century A.D. in particular."[12]

If the gap of almost a thousand years between the Amaravati period and Chichen Itza appears long, it is because evidence of the connecting links has not survived. In any case, it is not uncommon for decorative or symbolic motifs to survive even longer. Furthermore, the lotus occurs in Mayan art in the middle of the Classic period, several hundred years earlier than the date of the Chichen Itza reliefs. It is also a reasonable assumption that wooden sculptures and buildings, which have not survived, existed in Central America and carried on the tradition of this motif. There is evidence of wood carving amongst the Aztecs and there is little reason to believe it was not equally important in earlier times.

Eventually the lotus motif in both India and Southeast Asia assumed new forms: totally unrealistic, purely decorative designs of foliage-like scrolls. It then merged with another motif, *kirttimukha*, combining features of the lion, the death's head (*kala*) and the serpent or dragon, which appears in the Gupta art of India. The new form, found for the first time in the Pallava art of the seventh century, became a favourite in Southeast Asia, particularly Cambodia and Bali. In Cambodia, the creepers with ornamental foliage which had replaced the lotus are frequently seen on door lintels of the period between the ninth and the eleventh centuries, surging from both sides of the mouth of a demonic face without lower jaw, a mythical sea monster with a fish's body and an elephant's trunk. Lotus rhizomes extending from both sides of the mouth of a demonic face without lower jaw occur also at Chichen Itza. This similar use of the lotus motif not only indicates cultural intercourse between South Asia and America, but also suggests that it lasted well after the seventh century.

The makara motif, a makara head with upturned snout and with a human face in its mouth, from India, Java, Bali, and Sumatra, is comparable to the Mexican Xiuhcoatl, the so-called fire-serpent found at Palenque. Whilst this fire-serpent of Mayan art and its Aztec counterpart differ from the numerous more realistic representations of reptiles of the same areas, they correspond in many details, such as fish-like bodies, elephant-like trunks and forms of the teeth, to the makara. In Indian and Mayan art variants with paws occur, which resemble a crocodile rather than a fish, and in both regions a human figure often emerges from the mouth of the monster.

The makara and kirttimukha are the most frequent motifs on ancient and mediaeval temples in and outside India, and seem to have gained widespread popularity abroad in both the East and the West. Ananda K. Coomaraswamy pointed out in a study of Indian iconography in 1931 that the makara occurred frequently in mediaeval European art. Long before him, in 1875, E. Viollet-le-Duc suggested that the kirttimukha

Makara from Amaravati (a) and makara from Chichen Itza (b); the lotus-motif from Amaravati (c) and the lotus-motif from Chichen Itza (d). *After R. Heine-Geldern and G. F. Ekholm.*

God on the lion throne from India (e), and Mayan jaguar throne (f). *After R. Heine-Geldern and G. F. Ekholm.*

The Tree of Heaven in shadow play figures from Java (a), and the so-called "Cross" from Palenque, Mexico (b).
After R. Heine-Geldern and G. F. Ekholm.

occurred at Poitiers, a twelfth-century Romanesque cathedral, but few scholars took notice of this assertion. Recently, a director of the Seattle Art Museum has pointed out further examples: "There can be little doubt that Coomaraswamy was correct, while Viollet-le-Duc's observation that the kirttimukha occurred at Poitiers was an understatement. While makara and kirttimukha forms appear on the majority of French and Spanish Churches built in the 12th century, earlier Romanesque Churches were not decorated with such designs."[13] This makara motif seems to have been incorporated into the Chinese dragon concept. Islamic structures, such as the old Talisman gate at Baghdad, have also preserved variations of the kirttimukha. This motif was probably taken to England from France by the Plantagenets, and a motif known as the "Green Man" which appears on the Romanesque churches of some twenty-three English counties is thus ultimately of Indian origin.

The reputed "Cross" of Palenque, a stylized tree with a demonic face in its branches, appears to be a copy of the *Kalpa-Vrksa*, depicted in Indian sculpture as growing on the cosmic Mount Sumeru. The Javanese version of this tree, as seen in the *Wayang kulit*, with a demon's face between the beams of a cross, resembles the Mexican Cross. The motif also appears in a highly conventionalized form amongst the reliefs of the Angkor Vat in Cambodia. Porches with figures of monsters, lotus walls, and a "cross-shaped-holy-arch" have been discovered in the temples of Palenque, as in the temples of Cambodia, where the holy-arch was particularly common from the eighth to the tenth centuries.

Ancient American sites have revealed a galaxy of teocallis, despite the fact that many were demolished by European invaders. These pyramids are of various sizes and belong to different periods. Many of them escaped the onslaught of the intruders because they had been swallowed up by the jungles, thus remaining disguised until discovered by archaeologists. The ruins of Teotihuacan remained more or less unnoticed until the beginning of this century, even though they were not hidden by the jungle. Teotihuacan, meaning "the place where gods were made," was supposedly the most glorious and ancient city of Mexico. The two world-famous teocallis of the Sun (Tonatiuh) and the Moon (Meztli) have been excavated on this site. These pyramids are surrounded by numerous smaller pyramids. A number of scholars have suggested that the inspiration for these teocallis came from Egypt, but American pyramids are very unlike those of Egypt; it may even be a misnomer to describe them as pyramids. The teocallis of ancient America are really step-pyramids, in which several rectangular terraces, each of diminishing size, are built on top of one another, with an outside stairway leading up to the platform. The Sun Pyramid at Teotihuacan has four such terraces; the temple at Tulahas has five. At the top is a temple for which the rest of the pyramid merely serves as a base, or a plinth. The Egyptian pyramids had neither platforms nor temples at the top and there was no stairway outside. Certainly, until later times their side walls were plain. The interior chamber, in which the bones of the Pharaoh were entombed, was reached by a low passage through the stone, which was sealed with earth after the entombment of the king. But the American pyramid is similar to the temple-pyramids of Cambodia, and is reminiscent of a prevalent concept in the Hindu-Buddhist world. It expresses the idea of erecting an artificial mountain, like the Indian Mount Sumeru, the Mountain ascending to Heaven.

There are, however, certain difficulties about the chronology of the pyramids of Southeast Asia and Mexico. The earliest American pyramids are older than the earliest similar pyramids known in Southeast Asia. For instance, the temple-pyramids of Cambodia date from the eighth century, and the Sun Pyramids of Teotihuacan, despite the difficulty of obtaining reliable radio carbon dates and taking into account the additions and alterations made from time to time, possibly had its earliest foundations laid in the second century B.C. Whilst there may be certain difficulties in satisfactorily setting out the similarities between the temple-pyramids of Cambodia and those of Mexican-Mayan areas, there are none in respect to other parallels. Nor are there any chronological discrepancies in the case of the Southeast Asian parallels in the Mercado at Chichen Itza.

Ancient Indian chronology is still subject to dispute, and any theories about Indian influences travelling across the Pacific to America must remain somewhat tentative. However, it seems that this cultural intercourse between Southeast Asia and America took place intermittently during the first six centuries of the Christian era. Whilst evidence from the Southeast Asian side would suggest the most likely period to be from the third to the fifth centuries, American evidence suggests that contact must have taken place not later than the middle of the classic period of Central America, since some Hindu-Buddhist traits appear in the Maya area at that time. This does not, however, preclude an earlier date. The lotus designs of Chichen Itza would bear testimony to cultural exchange during the first half of the first millennium. Atlantean figures and the motif of gods standing on crouching human figures may belong to the same time.

The makara motif may have been introduced more than once over a prolonged period. Indeed, a more detailed comparison of the various forms in which it appears in different regions may yield valuable chronological clues. At any rate, the combined motifs of the makara and the lotus would seem to indicate contacts in the period from the ninth to the twelfth century. And the similarities between the buildings of the Puuc style and Cambodian temples, particularly those of Isvarapura, would reinforce the evidence of contact around the tenth century. Finally, the Mercado at Chichen Itza reflects characteristics of Cambodian galleries of the eleventh and twelfth centuries.

There are indications that Java and possibly Sumatra and Champa may have participated in transpacific contacts with America, but Asiomerican parallels with Cambodia are much closer. The ports from which the traffic was carried on must have been located on the coast of what now is Vietnam, a region Cambodia lost to her neighbours in the eighteenth century. Long before that, however, after a period of unprecedented political power and cultural achievements around 1200, the collapse of the Cambodian Empire must have caused the cessation of transpacific voyages.[14]

There is little material available to enable historians to visualize even the broad lines of ancient American thought. Their astronomical calculations give some indication of their concept of the universe, but they reveal little of their gods and their religious system. However, similarities between the gods and temples of Central America and those of India are far too striking not to compel consideration, even if adequate allowance is made for the fact that some kind of polytheism had existed in all primitive societies, and gods were conceived of in all shapes and sizes by primitive men. Ancient America was as rich in gods and temples as was India. The Asiomerican term for god, "teo," is close to the Sanskrit "deva." E. G. Squire noted similarities in both major and minor features of Buddhist temples of South India and Southeast Asia and those of ancient America. Both in ancient India and Mexico they were round and different colours were used on each of the four quarters. In 1866, Viollet-le-Duc pointed out some striking similarities between ancient Mexican structures and those of southern India.

The similarity extends also to their gods. The parallels between the Hindu Brahma-Visnu-Siva Trinity and the Mexican Ho-Huitzilopochtli-Tlaloc Trinity, and the resemblances between the attributes of certain Hindu deities and those of the Mayan pantheon are impressive. Discussing the diffusion of Indian religions to Mexico, a recent scholar, Paul Kirchhoff, has even suggested that it is not simply a question of miscellaneous influences wandering from one country to the other, but that China, India, Java, and Mexico actually share a common system.[15] Kirchhoff has sought "to demonstrate that a calendaric classification of 28 Hindu gods and their animals into twelve groups, subdivided into four blocks, within each of which we find a sequence of gods and animals representing Creation, Destruction, and Renovation, and which can be shown to have existed both in India and Java, must have been carried from the Old World to the New, since in Mexico we find calendaric lists of gods and animals (or their substitutes) that follow each other without interruption in the same order and with attributes and functions or meanings strikingly similar to those of the 12 Indian and Javanese groups of gods, showing the same four subdivisions."[16]

There is some similarity between the iconography of American gods and Hindu and Buddhist art motifs. The disc of the sun as a quoit, the mussel shell with a plant, and the figures of Visnu, who despite his Mexican features, is so recognized from the mace (*Gada*) and *Cakra* that he holds in his two hands, appear on both sides of the Pacific. Moreover, the Mayas used the umbrella as a mark of dignity and a symbol of rank, and the umbrella comes from Southeast Asia, where it was known in the third millennium B.C. The friezes of Chacmultun in Yucatan exhibit two types of umbrellas like those still used in India and Southeast Asia. The Mayan goddess, Ix Tub Tun, who spits out precious stones, possesses attributes of an Indian *nagini* of Kubera, the Indian god of treasure.[17]

E. B. Tylor showed in a lecture in 1894 the four Mexican pictures, known as The Vatican Codex, that corresponded so closely to the pictures of Buddhist hells or purgatories painted on Japanese temple scrolls, as to "preclude any explanation except direct transmission from one religion to another."[18] He also found the counterparts of the tortoise myth of India in ancient America.

The Toltecs achieved greatness mainly because of the inspiration they derived from their white-bearded legendary god-man, Quetzalcoatl, who was exceptional in moral virtues, loved the sciences, was the source of all agricultural prosperity, and the inventor of all arts. His two institutions, priesthood and princedom, were the foundations of all Aztec social and religious life, creating a new religious concept of a higher spirituality. The historical reality of Quetzalcoatl is somewhat obscure.[19] The myth of Quetzalcoatl has been described as having its basis in a belief in a rain-and-wind god who brought fructifying showers to the dry earth of Mexico. Later, a number of stories and legends grew about him and he was credited with powers of wisdom and the attributes of a hero. Yet his humility, his burning need for self-purification, and emphasis on achieving mystic union with divinity through a life of contemplation, chastity, and penitence, could not have sprung from a society which, like that of the Aztecs, was given to armed conquests and bloodshed. Quetzalcoatl is said to have lived a rigorous life of abstinence in his palace, oriented towards the four points of the Universe, practicing several types of penance. Above all, he devoted himself to meditation, *mo-teotia,* to conceive the supreme God and all that exists. It has, therefore, been suggested that behind Quetzalcoatl was Buddhist inspiration. Considering that the tradition of the Toltec beliefs is posterior to the Buddhist expansion in Southeast and East Asia, and to the fresh waves of migrants from Asia, particularly from Indo-China, it is quite likely that some Hindu-Buddhist thought had crept into Toltec beliefs.[20]

In fact, it was about the beginning of the Christian era, referred to as the classical period, that evidence appears of new ways of thinking in ancient America as well as fresh migrations from Asia. It would be extremely unlikely if these two were not connected. The new migrants are described as a people with a high degree of culture, possessing books of pictures, music and song, and worshipping a Supreme God who was Master of the Everywhere (Tloque-Nahuaque) and "was held to be the dual god (Ometiol), Master and Mistress of our flesh, who in a mysterious cosmic coupling and conception, has given origin to all that exists."[21] The Supreme God caused the birth of his four god-sons, who made up the primordial forces which were to generate the history of the world. It is from these myths and beliefs that several of their principal rites were derived. "The belief in a supreme dual principle, mother and father of the gods and of man, as well as a concept of the world with the four corners of the universe, their characteristic colours, the four elements, the heavenly tiers and the nether world of the dead, are undoubtedly analogous to some concepts in the civilizations of India, China, and Tibet. Are these simply parallelisms, or did there exist in ancient times some kind of cultural dissemination?"[22] According to Leon-Portilla, a definitive answer cannot be formulated as yet. But he reminds those who are inclined towards the idea of cultural dissemination of the inexplicable absence of such cultural elements as the practical use of the wheel, the concept of weight and the development of balance scales, amongst other things, in the pre-Columbian world. Besides, it cannot be ignored that the innate capacities of all human beings make them apply relatively similar solutions to similar problems.[23]

Mackenzie and some other scholars, however, are of the definite opinion that the ancient Mexicans and Peruvians were familar with Indian mythology and cite in support close parallels in details. For instance, the history of the Mayan elephant symbol cannot be traced in the local tradition, whereas it was a prominent religious symbol in India. It is not a motif imported from Egypt, for there are divergences between the African elephant and the American representation of it. The African elephant has larger ears, a less-elevated head and a bulging forehead without the indentation at the root of the trunk, which is characteristic of the Indian elephant. It is the profile of the Indian elephant, its tusk and lower lip, the form of its ear, as well as its turbaned rider with his *ankus,* which is found in Meso-American models. Whilst the African elephant was of little religious significance, it had been tamed in India and associated with religious practice since the early days. The elephant was associated with the Nagas, snake deities, who were rain-gods "wholly dependent on the presence of water and much afraid of fire, just like the dragons in many Chinese and Japanese legends."[24] The Nagas were regarded as the guardians of treasures, especially of pearls, and there is a good deal of additional evidence that the cults of Nagas and elephants in India had overlapped frequently. The religious significance of the elephant is typically Indian and there appears to be little doubt that the Mayan representation is similarly religious.[25] Mayan elephants are represented with the conventional ornamentation of the elephant-like figures on the bas-reliefs in Cambodia. Even Bancroft, who did not subscribe to the theory of contact between Indian and American mythologies, thought the elephant motif deserved attention.

A kind of caste system prevailed amongst the Incas of Peru. Peruvians worshipped an omnipotent and invisible Supreme Being, Viracocha, creator and preserver of the world. Imprints of the *Ramayana* and the *Mahabharata* have been noticed on the poetry of Peru. The American story of Yappan resembles the story of Indra of the *Mahabharata* so closely that Mackenzie comments that with this piece of evidence alone a good circumstantial case can be made for the diffusion of Hindu thought, myths, and practices to ancient America.

The Mexican doctrine of the World's Ages—the universe was destroyed four consecutive times—is reminiscent of the Indian *Yugas.* Even the reputed colours of these mythical four ages, white, yellow, red, and black, are identical with and in the same order as one of the two versions of the Indian Yugas. In both myths the duration of the First Age is exactly the same, 4,800 divine years. The Mexican Trinity is associated with this doctrine as is the Hindu Trinity with the Yugas in India.[26]

Only four chemical elements were known to the peoples of ancient Greece and India. They were earth, water, fire, and air. The Hindus, in the *Bhagavad Gita,* describe the four ages of the world as corresponding to the four points of the compass, and they were the ages of earth, water, fire, and air. The Mayas divided each of their four ages into five periods, with each period ruled by a god. These are the twenty gods of the Mayan myths and they provide names for the twenty days of the Mayan months. In this way the Mayan calendar is somewhat akin to the Hindu Yugas. The Mayas distinguished between thirteen heavens, each ruled by a god; the lowest was earth. Below earth were nine underworlds with nine head gods; the lowest of these underworlds was ruled by the god of Death, Ahpuk.

Scholars who insist that pre-Columbian American religion and civilization were of independent origin are obliged to explain why the myths, beliefs, and practices of ancient America assumed such complex features at the very beginning, whilst in Asia they resulted from the fusions and movements of numerous peoples after a period of time much greater than that covered by American civilizations from beginning to end. The isolationists must also explain why the American race should have been the last to emerge from an uncivilized state and why, once they emerged, their progress should have been so phenomenally rapid.

Considering the missionary zeal and religious enterprise of Indian monks and priests, it would seem unlikely that they would have missed an opportunity to spread their respective religions. The traces of Hindu-Buddhist influence in Mexico and amongst the Maya correspond in kind precisely to those cultural elements which were introduced by Buddhist monks and Hindu priests in Southeast Asia. If Indian religions were not found in Central America at the time of the Spanish conquest, this cannot by itself be held as evidence that they had not existed at an earlier date. The history, especially of Southeast Asia, shows how easily religions may disappear or be submerged in local cults. Amongst the Cham of Annam, Hinduism and Buddhism had been firmly established for almost a millennium and a half, from the second to the fifteenth century. Yet, Buddhism disappeared completely after the fall of the Cham kingdom in 1471 and Hinduism declined so rapidly that its influence at present is hardly recognizable. Amongst the non-Muslim Badui and Tenggerese of Java, traces of Hinduism and Buddhism are exceedingly slight, although these must have been the

66

predominant religions as late as the sixteenth century. The Batak of Sumatra were under Buddhist and Hindu influences from probably the third to the fourteenth century, but in the nineteenth century they were pagans. "We have little doubt that a sober but unbiased comparative analysis of the Mexican and Mayan religions will reveal many traces of the former influences of either Hinduism or Buddhism or of both. To mention but one instance, the conceptions of hell and of the punishments inflicted there resemble those of Buddhist and Hindu belief to such an extent, both in a general way and in specific details, that the assumption of historic relationship is almost inevitable."[27] It is, however, interesting that whilst in Mexico and amongst the Mayas, traits of apparent Hindu-Buddhist origin abound in the fields of art, religious architecture, government, cosmology, mythology, and iconography, there is hardly any Indian influence in the technical fields. Whatever little there is appears to have been the by-product of artistic and religious beliefs.

Parallels between the Pan-pipes of the Solomon Islands and those of South America are indeed startling. The Pan-pipe is a primitive wind instrument mythologically associated with the goat-footed Greek god Pan. But here are pipes which are pre-Columbian, and have tone and pitch identical with their Polynesian counterparts. The odd pipes differ, each from the next, by the interval of a fourth. The even pipes have notes half-way in pitch between the odd ones, and thus form another "circle of fourths." What is more significant is that the absolute pitch of the instruments examined from both areas is the same. Consequently, the vibration rates in successive pipes are 557 and 560.5; 651 and 651; 759 and 749; 880 and 879: too close to be within the bounds of accidental convergence.

Elliot Smith, who had lived in Egypt for years working as a professor of anatomy, and who was a British diffusionist, points out that Asiomericans and East Asians practiced the same method of mumification. Some scholars have noted other parallels between the symbols, postures, dress, and etiquette of Indian and Southeast Asian royalty and those of Mexico and Peru. It is pointed out that the four queens of the last Ayar ruler performed *sati* after the latter had been killed by the Spaniards. The Mexican Lion-throne and Lotus-throne remind one of Indian *Simhasana* and *Padmasana*. The parasol, a mark of royalty amongst the Mayas, the Aztecs, and the Incas, may be an adaptation of the royal *Chatra* in use in India and Indianized Asia from the earliest times. Both types of parasols shown in the frescoes of Chak Multun in Yucatan correspond to types still in use in Southeast Asia. The use of the throne, of the litter, and of fans mounted like standards on long poles as insignia of rank and royalty, closely resemble similar paraphernalia of royalty and aristocracy in Southeast Asia. Not only Aztec court ceremony, but even their form of government, was similar to that of Southeast Asia; for instance, the institution of four chief officials in Mexico corresponds to the four ministers of state and governors of the four quarters of the empires of Southeast Asia. What is of particular significance is that, in both cases, this institution is based on Indian cosmological principles.

William MacLeod pointed out that the Mexican *Volador* ritual is similar to an Indian rite of hook-swinging, the *Charak Puja* of Bengal and South India. In Mexico the participants normally hang by their feet, and in India by their shoulders. However, an old description and illustration of hook-swinging in India in which the participants hang by their feet has been unearthed by Heine-Geldern and Ekholm. A relief at the Bayon at Angkor Thom in Cambodia represents a rite similar to the Volador of Mexico.

Similar routines of everyday life of Indians and Asiomericans have also been noted. For instance, betel-chewing with lime and coca-chewing and tobacco, as well as the gourd-container for the lime are common to both peoples. The Peruvian substitute for tobacco, which was used for medicinal purposes, was a shrub, called cuca (coca). The leaves are first dried in the sun and then mixed with a little lime to constitute "a preparation for chewing, much like the betel-leaf of the East."[28] Vegetarianism has been popular both in India and Mexico, and Indian food is similar to Mexican. The Indian *roti* or *chapati* and the Mexican *tortilla,* similar in size and shape, are made in the same way. Both peoples have an unusual respect for corn, and share the custom of offering bits of food, before eating, to God in expression of their gratitude for the meal provided.

Mirrors of pyrite; shell money; birchbark shelters, canoes, and containers with identical curvilinear design from Siberia and North America; string crosses for prayers from Tibet, India, Assam, Mexico, and Peru; the custom of fishing with poison; shell fishhooks; the use of agricultural terraces in Southeast Asia, Peru and Bolivia; and the cultivation of cotton, were common from early days in both Asia and America.

Some linguistic kinship between India and ancient America has also been suggested. Miles Poindexter, a former ambassador of the United States to Mexico, proposed that primitive Aryan words and people came to America by the island chains of Polynesia. The Mexican name for boat is a South Indian Tamil word, *Catamaran,* and Poindexter gives a long list of words of the Quichua languages and their analogous forms in Sanskrit.[29] Similarities between the hymns of the Inca rulers of Peru and Vedic hymns have been pointed out.[30] Kroeber has also found striking similarities between the structure of Indo-European and the Penutian language of some of the tribes along the northwestern coast of California.

Tylor, writing in 1881, pointed out that the ancient Mexican game, *patolli,* a favourite of the Aztecs, was very similar to *pachisi,* played in India. The two games were connected in a series of independent features, such as divining by lot, a sportive wager, realization of the law of chance, transfer of the result to a counting board, and rules of moving and capturing.

Ethnobotany, a relatively recent discipline not hitherto fully utilized, provides conclusive evidence of both cultural contacts between Southeast Asia and ancient America, and of transpacific crossings. The publication of *The Evolution of Gossypium* in 1947 by Hutchinson, Silow, and Stephens brought home to many historians the value of the study of ethnobotany in tracing the processes of cultural diffusion and the migrations of people through plants.

A study of cultural intercourse would reveal that the transfer of knowledge is a slow and uncertain process. Intermittent contacts lasting even over centuries may not result in any influence. Settlement, on the other hand, may result in the rapid introduction of numerous culture traits. As far as plants are concerned, their transplantation is a very complicated procedure. It requires the adoption of a whole complex of knowledge about the plant's ecological requirements, and often also about its human uses. Hence, the presence of even one transferred plant would mean that a quite effective and probably relatively durable contact had been made between two peoples. The presence of a number of plants would indicate a major cultural contact.

Cotton, which plays such an important part in world economy and is grown at present in Asia, Africa, the Americas, and to some extent in Europe, is one of the tantalizing mysteries of history and science. In Egypt, the first definite proof of its use dates from the fourth century B.C. But long before this, about 3000 B.C., cotton was cultivated in the Indus Valley. During the excavations at Mohenjo-daro a small fragment of cotton fabric and a small piece of cotton string in the neck of a silver vessel were recovered. These fragments were made from raw material indistinguishable from the indigenous coarse *bengalese* cottons found in the region today. The quality of both the fabric and the string leaves no doubt that a mature textile craft had existed in the Indus Valley civilization. It is from this cotton that the perennial forms of East Asia, Africa, and the West have developed.

Although it is certain that cotton was first used in the Indus Valley, no evidence of its wild ancestors has been found in India. There are various interpretations of the cytogenetic evidence but it is suggested that the progenitors of the early cottons of India may have been introduced from southern Arabia or northeastern Africa. This is puzzling enough, but when South American cotton is studied scholars and scientists are thoroughly baffled. Evidence of the Asian ancestry of American cottons is irrefutable, but substantial proof of the migration of Gossypium is inconclusive.

On the north Peruvian coast known as the Huaca Prieta woven fabrics of unexpectedly elaborate pattern, dated about 2400 B.C. and made from a highly cultivated species of cotton, have been discovered. Archaeological evidence concerning cotton is incomplete because both cotton plant material and cotton fabrics have survived only in the driest areas. It is, therefore, principally the botanical evidence, together with whatever archaeological finds there are, which is relied upon in fixing the origins of the cotton plant of America.

American cottons are tetraploid in chromosome constitution, and their chromosome complement is made up of one set homologous with the complement of the diploid Asian cottons and one set homologous with the complement of the diploid species of America.[31] After a series of painstaking experiments, experts have agreed that one parent of the American cotton undoubtedly came from Asia: in other words, from the Indus Valley area.

The vast diversity of cultivated cottons falls into four species, distinguished from each other by their respective number of chromosomes. The species, Gossypium herbaceum and Gossypium arboreum, are diploid (with thirteen chromosomes each) and the other two, Gossypium hirsutum and Gossypium barbadense, are a more sophisticated species, the tetraploid, with twenty-six chromosomes each. The first two are of Asian origin, with Gossypium arboreum coming from the Indus Valley region, the other from Africa and Arabia. The two tetraploids are of American origin and are hybrid, with half Asian ancestry. The linted diploid species which were the Asian ancestral species of the Peruvian tetraploid cotton was Gossypium arboreum, which is typically an Indus diploid widely distributed over Southeast Asia.

But how did the two come together? Did the Indus ancestor travel through Africa across the Atlantic to Peru? This view has been rejected—not so much because of the inability to explain the feasibility of its transatlantic journey, which is in itself a difficult problem—because of the difficulty in understanding how the two parents came in contact, once the Asian species had reached South America. Not only is the closest known American wild ancestor of the Peruvian cotton confined to the Peruvian coast, but the whole group of the American wild species of Gossypium are found on the Pacific side of the continent. Since the American diploids are all static or relic species with limited distribution, it would appear that the two met because the Asian diploids are aggressive and spread rapidly. And as the centres of variability of these major allopolyploids are within the area at present occupied by the American diploid on the Pacific side, it would also support the theory that the Indus diploid entered Peru from the Pacific. If this is true the Asian diploid must have been the Gossypium arboreum or a species ancestral to it, for no other linted diploid species could have been carried across the Pacific to western South America. "There is no evidence that Gossypium herbaceum ever reached the Pacific and the present eastern limit of the distribution of Gossypium aboreum coincides apparently with the limit of the area in which it has recently been used."[32]

S. C. Harland, whose researches led to the modern studies of the origins and evolutionary history of cultivated cottons, suggested that they met on a land bridge across the Pacific Ocean. But objections to this theory are insuperable. Neither birds nor winds could carry cotton seeds for a distance of at least three thousand miles and, in fact, the Pacific Ocean from New Guinea to Peru is about ten thousand miles wide. In any case, birds do not eat Gossypium seeds, and sea-water would have destroyed their germinal power. Recently, Skovsted, carrying Harland's researches further, has demonstrated that the American cottons are amphidiploids of the constitution 2 (AD), which makes it essential that an A genom diploid cotton must have reached Central America through man's efforts, where it hybridized with an ancestral D.

Again, from the longitude of Guam to that of the Revillo Gigedo islands there is no record of the occurrence of a diploid cotton north of Australia. This fact, together with the scientific evidence suggesting that the growth of A-genom bearing linted allopolyploids has taken place only since the origin of human civilization, would lead to one conclusion; cotton seeds must have been carried by man who took them with other seeds of his crop plant and with the tools of his civilization.[33]

Also, the contact between the Asian and the American species could not have come about by migration around the Pacific, either by a northern route, by way of China and Alaska, or by a southern route, by way of the Antarctic. For, as Hutchinson points out, "Gossypium is a genus of Xerophystic perennial shrubs adapted to the arid tropics. No member of the genus would grow in an ecological situation where temperate woodlands existed and until the modern development of short-term annual cottons under domestication, no member of the genus would survive in a climate with winter frosts."[34]

Scientific evidence is supported by archaeological remains. In the pre-Inca Peruvian graves not only have woven fabrics been found, but also instruments for weaving and spinning. This would amply support the theory that cotton was introduced by civilized men, for the development of fibres into threads and thence into weaving is an important advance in the skills of man, and a landmark in the history of civilization. It is also significant that the spindles in Peru used the same device as did the fine spinner of the Dacca muslins in India. Their two-barred type of cotton loom has been used in Asia, Europe, America, and everywhere else. But, as Crawford points out, the fact that this two-barred type of loom originated in India and spread to Europe, and that it is found with its technical subtleties of fabric construction in the cotton areas of South America, would be difficult to explain except in terms of direct or indirect cultural contact between India and ancient America.

Contact between Asia and America probably was two-way. If Asians went with the intention of permanently settling in America, this cannot exclude the possibility that some may have returned, possibly accompanied by some descendants of the early settlers. It is not unlikely that early American cultures were founded by the impact of Asian immigration, but they then developed mainly under their own stimulus. Later the Americanized Asian cultures might have diffused back across the Pacific giving a new impetus to their original homelands. Cotton is such an example. It was the Indus cultivated cotton that crossed over to America, and, having been hybridized with American cotton, returned to Asia in a new and more advanced form.

Another plant which appears to have been imported to America from Southeast Asia is the coconut, *cocos nucifera,* which is regarded as a characteristic plant of the Pacific. It is a pan-Pacific species which probably originated along the shores of the Indian Ocean. Because of the uniformity of its nomenclature throughout the area stretching from Madagascar to Tahiti, it is concluded that its distribution must have taken place through the agency of man. However, as "coco" is a

Portuguese word, it is likely that it was the Portuguese who carried it to South America. Ridley's suggestion, made in 1930, that the original home of the coconut must have been Costa Rica and Panama was probably based on the Spanish traveller Oviedo's accounts of the early sixteenth century. It is refuted by the references made by Marco Polo to coconut in Sumatra, the Nicobar and Andaman islands, and South India in the last quarter of the thirteenth century. Indian sources from about the first century refer to coconuts. Again, coconut palms are represented in the carvings of both Angkor Vat in Cambodia, and the Borobudur in Indonesia. The coconut plant was already widespread in Polynesia on the eve of the first European contact. The suggestion that the coconut could have drifted from America to Polynesia during the pre-Columbian period is invalidated by the absence of any evidence that coconuts have floated to and established themselves on remote islands. The embryo within the fruit can survive only for a limited period, and the waves could at best carry it to near-by islands, although there is no evidence that this occurred. It must have been planted throughout Polynesia by man before the arrival of Europeans in the Pacific.

Maize, *Zea Mays*, is widely grown in Asia and Africa. At one time it was believed to have originated in Asia, but evidence of extensive cultivation in pre-Columbian America made an American origin seem most likely. Early this century, Laufer and Merril concluded that the Spaniards took maize to Asia, by way of the Philippines, from America during the early modern period. Since then further research has renewed claims that maize was in use in Asia before Columbus discovered America. There is no doubt that maize was of enormous importance in pre-Columbian America. It was, as it is now, the basic staple of life in Mexico. Consequently, there are various versions, including mythical and speculative, about its origin. The Aztecs believed that their hero-god, Quetzalcoatl, who created the human race with his own blood, assumed the shape of an ant to steal away a single grain of maize from the mountains where the ants had hidden it. This grain he gave to man to cultivate. Whilst evidence supporting the claims of maize originating in Asia is at present inconclusive, it is more misleading and unwarranted to assert, for instance, as Van Hagen has recently done, that maize was cultivated at Huaca Prieta in Peru as early as 3000 B.C. In fact, the Huaca Prieta site is noted for its lack of maize pods, although the evidence of the most ancient maize has been found in other regions of Peru. The earliest remains of an extremely primitive form of cultivated corn came from a once-inhabited rock shelter at the Bat Cave in New Mexico. Excavated by Herbert Dick between 1948 and 1950, these remains have

73

been dated by radio-carbon analysis as belonging to the mid-third millennium B.C., but there is no evidence for maize agriculture in the Valley of Mexico until more than a thousand years later.

The maize plant has never been found in a wild state and its immediate progenitor, despite several speculative theories, is unknown. One theory is that maize developed from a wild ancestor that was at once a popcorn and a podcorn; another is that it descended from teosinte or tripsacum. Two scientists, C. R. Stonor and Edgar Anderson, working independently, concluded that certain distinctive varieties of maize widely cultivated by the Nagas in Assam in India, had been in cultivation there from the pre-Columbian period. Whilst, on the whole, these varieties were similar to those of maize grown in early Peru and Chile; the popcorns, green corns used as a fresh vegetable, and brewing corns did not fit into the picture at all. The Asian popcorns are not at all like the popcorns of Central America. After a period of collaboration and further experimentation these two scientists found the conclusion inescapable, that "there are at least two races of maize in Asia and that one of these must have crossed the Pacific in pre-Columbian times. The direction (or directions) in which it travelled, however, is still uncertain."[35] It seems somewhat surprising that the post-Columbian maize should reach such remote areas as the Naga hills and the interior of New Guinea, and be cultivated by the hill tribes of Upper Burma and Siam, the Lolo of Central Asia, and the Aborigines of Hainan, without reaching the surrounding highly civilized Asian countries. Yet it is a significant crop of Asian countries. Why should India, China, and other Asian countries have taken maize from the hill tribes, and not from the Europeans before it passed through their territories on its way to these hinterlands? It may be possible that maize, like cotton, crossed the Pacific from Asia to America in prehistoric times, and was later repatriated.

Whatever its exact origin, the maize plant certainly went through a long process of skilful cultivation in the hands of Asiomericans. Thin pancake-like bread made of maize flour, called *tlaxcatti* by the Aztecs and *tortillas* by the Mexicans today, accompanied by beans and peppers, and washed down with drinks made from maguey or cacao were the standard diet of the Aztecs and other Asiomericans.

Evidence of the origin of the sweet potato, *Ipomoea batatas*, mainly cultivated in Southeast Asia and Central America, is inconclusive despite numerous studies. Various hypotheses on its original home have been proposed by scientists supporting Southern Asia, Central and South America, or Africa. Of these, the theory of its American origin is generally accepted, for it is datable in Peru at least to the beginning of the Christian era. However, recent cytological research has thrown considerable doubt on this theory. In spite of its wide distribution, it is a single species, as is suggested by the continuous ranges in individual morphological characters, and the consistent chromosome numbers. Although the sweet potato came to be widely distributed throughout Europe and Asia during the post-Columbian period, it existed in Polynesia well before that. It is known that the sweet potato was in Hawaii by about the middle of the thirteenth century, and no more than a century later it was in New Zealand. The American prehistorian, Ronald B. Dixon, was convinced that the sweet potato had reached Polynesia before Columbus reached America. Whether the original species travelled from Southern Asia or the Pacific areas to America or vice versa, the fact of its common origin and diffusion would lend further support to the theory of transpacific contact. What makes this plant more important for the historian is that if the transpacific voyages were long and arduous, the sweet potato tubers would have either been eaten or spoiled. But this did not happen. The migration of the sweet potato alone shows that voyages were made relatively easily across the Pacific.[36] At any rate, the sweet potato was certainly transplanted via the Pacific irrespective of the direction of the journey. This is further substantiated by the fact that the name for the sweet potato, *kumara* or *kumala,* is found in the entire Pacific area, and that cognates were prevalent amongst the Aztecs and the peoples of Panama and the Caribbean.

Another typical feature of American culture, the *quipu,* the device of the ancient Peruvians for recording events, sending messages, etc., consisting of cords or threads of various colours knotted in various ways, has a replica in Hawaii. Something like quipu was used in early China and is referred to in the Tao-toh-chiang.

Whilst the importance of cultural similarities must not be over-emphasized, it would be equally untenable to regard them as incidental results of sporadic or accidental transpacific crossings from Southeast Asia. To justify the volume of the cultural parallels, there must have been repeated and consciously undertaken voyages between the two continents. But the evidence of ethnobotany must clinch the argument in favour of the transpacific voyages during historic times. Indeed, acceptance of the theory of Asian migration to Central America across the Pacific would resolve a problem in tracing the origins and interrelationships of world cottons. Scientists have provided definite proof of cultural diffusion; historians must now provide the evidence of migrations.

75

The only plausible argument against cultural diffusion from southern Asia to the Pacific is the distance involved. It is asserted that it would have been unlikely for a large number of people to have crossed the vast expanses of the Pacific without well-equipped boats and skilful voyagers. The argument, however, falls upon closer scrutiny. It would not be at all difficult for a large canoe or catamaran to cross from Polynesia to South America even at the present time, and the ancient Asians were skilled and enterprising seafaring men. Also, in prehistoric times the Pacific was divided into relatively small areas of navigability studded with small islands. Within these areas, off-shore voyages of two hundred miles or so were practical.

However, the migrations with which the present argument is most concerned are the ones which took place later in historic times, when cultural traits were sufficiently developed to be transmitted. Asian ability to cross the seas during that period is undoubted. The art of shipping and navigation in India and China at the time was sufficiently advanced for oceanic crossings. Indian ships operating between Indian and Southeast Asian ports were large and well equipped to sail across the Bay of Bengal. When the Chinese Buddhist scholar, Fa-hsien, returned from India, his ship carried a crew of more than two hundred persons and did not sail along the coasts but directly across the ocean. Such ships were larger than those Columbus used to negotiate the Atlantic a thousand years later. According to a work of mediaeval times, *Yukti Kalpataru*, which gives a fund of information about shipbuilding, India built large vessels from 200 B.C. to the close of the sixteenth century. A Chinese chronicler mentions ships of Southern Asia that could carry as many as one thousand persons, and were manned mainly by Malayan crews. They used western winds and currents in the North Pacific to reach California, sailed south along the coast, and then returned to Asia with the help of the trade winds, taking a more southerly route, without, however, touching the Polynesian islands.[37]

In ancient times the Indians excelled in shipbuilding and even the English, who were attentive to everything which related to naval architecture, found early Indian models worth copying. The Indian vessels united elegance and utility, and were models of fine workmanship. Sir John Malcolm wrote: Indian vessels "are so admirably adapted to the purpose for which they are required that, nothwithstanding their superior science, Europeans were unable, during an intercourse with India for two centuries, to suggest or at least to bring into successful practice one improvement."[38] It is also known that in the third century a transport of horses, which would have required large ships, reached Malaya and Indochina.

Emilio Estrada, Clifford Evans, and Betty J. Meggers, who have pointed out many striking similarities between Ecuadorian archaeological remains of the early Bahia and early Jama-Coaque cultures (the last two centuries B.C.) with relics of approximately the same period of Japan, India, and Southeast Asia, also support the feasibility of trans-pacific voyages. The Equatorial Counter-current, running eastward just north of the equator, leads directly towards the northern coast of Ecuador, and farther to the north the Japanese current flows eastwards to join the Mexican current moving down along the Pacific coast to Ecuador. Asian vessels were already carrying a flourishing trade and traffic from East Asia to the western world via Southeast Asia. By the third century, their ships were capable of carrying six hundred men and one thousand metric tons of cargo. The nineteenth-century geographer and Confederate naval Commander, Matthew Fontaine Maury, believed that Chinese mariners would have had no serious difficulty in discovering America. "One could go from China via Japan, the Kuriles, the Kamchatka coast, and the Aleutians to Alaska without losing sight of land for more than a few hours."[39]

The New Zealand prehistorian, S. Percy Smith, tries to show in his *Hawaiki—the Original Home of the Maori* that the ancient Polynesian wanderers left India as far back as the fourth century B.C. and were daring mariners who made, more often than not, adventurous voyages with the definite object of new settlements.[40] A people who reached as far east as Easter Island could not have missed the great continent ahead of them.[41]

In contrast to the Pacific, the Atlantic is comparatively small and its winds and currents head directly toward Central America. Hence, one may ask why the Asian, rather than the Mediterranean, migration to Central America be found more feasible? The answer lies in the art and technique of shipping. The Pacific people first developed advanced watercraft. Their oceangoing canoes were equipped with masts, sails, paddles, bailers and stone anchors; some boats even had three masts. For a long time the Mediterranean-Atlantic propulsion technique was rowing, which did not give way exclusively to sail propulsion until the end of the Middle Ages. Indopacific people had made this shift much earlier due to their two pieces of sophisticated sailing equipment—the fore-and-aft-rigged sail made of plaited pandanus mats sewn together in a triangular form with wooden yards and booms to strengthen the long sides of the triangle, and the centreboard, both of which employ the same aerodynamic principle of lift as does the airplane wing. Consequently, they could paddle forward much more freely and efficiently. Whilst the Vikings were sweeping across the northern seas in their long ships, the Polynesians in their long canoes, mounted with reinforced triangular sail, were negotiating thousands of miles of sea, often at seven knots an hour if favoured by a powerful wind.

What was the motive that urged Asians to undertake long journeys to America? It was probably gold, which initially attracted Indian adventurers and merchants to Southeast Asia. The remains of Dong-Son culture are mainly found in gold-producing areas. It is also possible that the daring ancient mariners were looking merely for new areas for food and settlement. But it seems more likely they were prospecting for precious metals, stones, and pearls to cope with the demand in the centres of ancient civilization. This view is substantially reinforced by W. J. Perry who was the first scholar to point out the distribution of the pearling beds of the world, and why, wherever pearls are found, similar complex religious myths, beliefs, and practices are also found. It is therefore significant that the mythology of the pre-Columbian American civilizations "was deeply impregnated by the religious beliefs and practices and habits of life that obtained amongst the treasure-seekers of the Old World."[42] Equally significant is the fact that the Mayas preferred to settle in that part of Central America which was unhealthy but rich in precious stones and gold. Somewhat like the Indians, the Asiomericans accumulated stones and gold and made symbolic ornaments from them. Mexican temples and idols, as in India, were lavishly decorated with gold and precious stones.

Whatever the motive, transpacific traffic would seem to have gone on regularly for about two thousand years, from about the eighth century B.C. to the twelfth century. The number of Asian migrants was perhaps not very substantial and they were absorbed in the local populations of early Asian settlers, but their cultural influence was profound. The foreign civilization implanted upon more primitive indigenous cultures by small groups of immigrants was soon absorbed by the local population and, in consequence, new civilizations were born which, despite their original character, nevertheless also reveal the features of both foreign and indigenous sources.

In view of so many parallels in fundamental conceptions and detail, in mythology, ritual, iconography, architecture, religious beliefs, crowns, thrones, plants, together with the evidence of migration, it appears incredible that isolationists should continue to insist on the independent evolution of Asiomerican civilization. Each correspondence in itself, with the exception of a few very unusual ones, may not amount to much, but in aggregate the evidence of cultural diffusion is formidable. Heine-Geldern and Ekholm declare unequivocally:

The large number of highly specific correspondences in so many fields precludes any possibility of mere accidental coincidence. Nor would it help us to take refuge in any kind of explanation based on some alleged psychological laws. There is no psychological law which could have caused the peoples on both sides of the Pacific to stylize the lotus plant in the same manner and to make it surge from the mouth of a jawless demon's head, to invent the parasol and use it as a sign of rank and to invent the same complicated game. There is no explanation other than the assumption of cultural relationship. We must bow to the evidence of facts, even though this may mean a completely new start in our appraisal of the origin and development of the American Indian higher civilization.[43]

Chapter III

SUVARNABHUMI: ASIANIZATION
OF INDIAN CULTURE

ONLY SINCE World War II has the term Southeast Asia been used to describe the area to the east of India and to the south of China, which includes the Indochinese Peninsula, the Malay Archipelago and the Philippines, roughly forming a circle from Burma through Indonesia to Vietnam. Before the term Southeast Asia became common usage, the region was often described as Further or Greater India, and it was common to describe the Indonesian region or Malay Archipelago as the East Indies.[1] The reason may be found in the fact that, prior to Western dominance, Southeast Asia was closely allied to India culturally and commercially.

This region was broadly referred to by ancient Indians as *Suvarnabhumi* (the Land of Gold) or *Suvarnadvipa* (the Island of Gold), although scholars dispute its exact definition. Sometimes the term is interpreted to mean only Indonesia or Sumatra. It has been suggested that the term was mainly applied to Burma, but this interpretation is not convincing. Arab writers such as Al Biruni testify that Indians called the whole Southeast region *Suwarndib (Suvarnadvipa)*. Hellenistic geographers knew the area as the Golden Chersonese. The Chinese called it *Kin-Lin; kin* means gold. Although the exact region meant by the term is not clear, it is not unlikely that the name was applied to the whole Indochinese Peninsula and the Malay Archipelago.

Southeast Asia is a complex of races and languages. In its mountains and jungles live a wide variety of peoples with varying degrees of advancement and divergent historical experiences. During the last two thousand years, this region has come under the influence of practically all the major civilizations of the world: Indian, Chinese, Islamic, and Western. Of these, Indian culture appears to have blended best with the indigenous culture.

It is not known precisely when contact began between India and Southeast Asia, for Indian writers seldom recorded historical or topographical details with any degree of accuracy. The modern historian has to reconstruct the picture from fragmentary references in literary sources, archaeological remains, and non-Indian writings. The archaeological sources remain insufficiently tapped. Nor are the excavations always conducted by experts, for easy accessibility to the sites and the chance of generous rewards often attract pseudo-scientists.

Contemporary indigenous historical narratives are conspicuously inadequate, and the information in Greek literature is casual and defective. The references made by the Arab travellers of the ninth century onwards and by Marco Polo, although of great importance, are impressionistic and insufficient. Chinese sources reveal considerable information about the areas geographically and historically close to her, but distant countries such as Malaya and Indonesia are inadequately treated.

Modern historical research on Southeast Asia is in its formative stages and the attention accorded its ancient past has been much less than that given to later periods. Western scholars were mainly stimulated by their colonial involvement in the area and generally concentrated attention on their own activities. An idea of the extent of knowledge about Southeast Asia may be gained from an European scholar who wrote in 1861, that, except for Burma, "the Indian countries situated beyond the Ganges hardly deserve the attention of History."[2] Burma was presumably excepted because the British by that time had fought two successful wars against her and had annexed Lower Burma to their Indian Empire, and a few British administrators, such as John Crawford, Henry Yule, and Arthur Phayre, had written accounts of their missions and the country. Stamford Raffles in 1817 produced *A History of Java* from materials collected by a staff of collaborators, but it does not seem to have stimulated much interest amongst British writers who remained, almost until the end of World War II, excessively preoccupied with the British in India. Neither the realization of the close and ancient Indian cultural contact with Southeast Asia nor the fact that Burma, Malaya, and their other territorial possessions in eastern Asia were tied to Indian administration, evoked British interest in the study of early Southeast Asia. Even today, with the exception of a few notable orientalists and scholars of cultural history such as Richard Winstedt, G. H. Luce, H. G. Quaritch Wales, Reginald Le May, and Roland Braddet, British historians have made little serious inquiry into the cultural past of these Asian countries. A people with no long cultural history of their own perhaps could not be expected to be attracted by the ancient cultural past of the people they dominated. What is surprising, however, is that British intellectual interest in Asian culture remained much less and much more inhibited than even that of France and Holland whose own cultural pasts were only, if at all, slightly better, but whose political and economic interests in Asia were less than those of the British.

Equally strange is the attitude of Indian historians towards the cultural past of Southeast Asia. With their appetite for knowledge Indian scholars could be expected to make an impressive study of Asian culture. But on the whole they have remained generally indifferent, not even attempting to integrate their own ancient history with that of their neighbours. Presumably this is because they have generally followed a prescribed course of study and inherited a set system of academic training, which is only gradually adapting itself to new consciousness and need. Indeed, in their newly found zeal of independence and Asianism, they tend to lean too much on the nationalist side, although there are notable exceptions, such as K. A. Nilakanta Sastri, R. C. Majumdar, B. R. Chatterjee, B. Ch. Chhabra, H. B. Sarkar, and Manmohan Ghosh. Indian interest, however, has been growing in this field and various publications have emerged in recent years.

Although the interest of the French and Dutch scholars in early Southeast Asian history was also limited, it was, in fact, their work which paved the way for its advancement. Studies concerning the ancient past of Indochina were stimulated by the discovery of the temples at Angkor in 1862 and of the account of the exploratory voyage of Doudart de Lagree and Francis Garnier. Later, works by E. Aymonier, Victor Goloubew, George Coedès, H. Parmentier, M. G. Maspero, René Grousset, G. de Coral-Remusat, Philippe Stern, S. Lévi, B. P. Groslier, and others, appeared.

The Dutch set up a society to study the culture of the Indonesian people in 1778 in Java and this inspired numerous studies in early Indonesian history and culture. Hendrik Kern, Brandes, Cohen Stuart, and Holle published important studies on Indonesian epigraphy. Later, N. J. Krom, W. F. Stutterheim, R. Goris, P. V. Van Stein Callenfels, F. D. K. Bosch, C. C. Berg, J. C. Van Leur, H. J. de Graaf, J. G. de Casparis, and many other Dutch writers made notable contributions on Indonesia's early history. Amongst the better known Indonesian scholars in this field are R. Ng. Poerbatjaraka, Sanusi Pane, Mohammad Yamin, Prijono, and Hussein Djajadiningrat.

But the eastward expansion of Hindu civilization has not yet been fully traced. Whilst historians have begun to understand its results, its origin, and its progress in the various individual countries, there still lies a long road ahead before a substantial assessment of the entire regional phenomenon can be made. There is, of course, less expectation of reaching agreement on detailed interpretations. There is a tendency amongst some Indian scholars to overemphasize Indian influence on Southeast Asian civilization, and some of them insist on analyzing the process in terms of cultural domination or colonization. On the other hand, some non-Indian scholars, especially modern writers of secondary works, tend to play down India's importance in the evolution of Southeast Asian civilization. For a balanced and dispassionate interpretation the degree of Indian influence should not be overemphasized nor the local genius overestimated. Dispute amongst historians, however, is not always along nationalistic lines; often there are genuine differences of well-considered opinion. For example, whilst F. D. K. Bosch, Parmentier and E. B. Havell suggest limited local contribution, others, such as Coedès, Quaritch Wales, and Stutterheim see more surviving influences of the local cultures.

Sociologists who have entered the field in recent years tend to disregard the evidence of literary sources, philology, archaeology, and epigraphy, and overrate somewhat uncertain and overstretched ethnological formulations, and the surviving features of pre-Indian civilization. Briefly discussing the limitations of this approach, and emphasizing the need for the greater study of inscriptions in local languages, Georges Coedès says, "I am convinced that such research will reveal numerous facts which will indicate a much deeper Indianization of the mass of the population than the sociologists will at present admit."[3]

The advent of Indians in Southeast Asia has hardly a parallel in history. It cannot be equated with the arrival of Europeans in America, because the Indians did not go to Southeast Asia as strangers. There appears to have always been some form of contact. But at a certain point which is at present indefinite, and due to circumstances which are not yet determined, an influx of merchants and immigrants into Southeast Asia resulted in the foundation of indigenous kingdoms, which practiced the arts, customs, and religions of India, and used Sanskrit as the sacred language. If the Indianization of Southeast Asia appears to be a new phenomenon around the beginning of the Christian era, it is because Indians arrived at this time in noticeable numbers, accompanied possibly for the first time by educated persons who were able to spread India's religions and culture with the Sanskrit language. In fact, the most ancient Sanskrit inscriptions of Southeast Asia are not very posterior to the first Sanskrit inscriptions of India proper. However, the earliest archaeological finds in these areas are not necessarily evidence of the earliest Indian influence. The priests who consecrated the first Hindu or Buddhist temples, and the scholars who composed the first Sanskrit inscriptions, must have been preceded by navigators, merchants, or immigrants, who founded the first Indian establishments. These establishments, Oc-eo in Indochina and Kuala Selinsing in Perak, for instance, were not always completely new creations, but were founded on neolithic sites, which Indian navigators may have frequented from time immemorial.

In view of the ethnic affinities between the prehistoric Austro-Asiatic races of India and those of Suvarnabhumi, contact between the two regions may well go back to the remotest antiquity. Opinion on this question, however, is by no means united. Mainly basing their evidence on linguistic affinities between Malaya and certain tribes of India, which they believe belong to the Austro-Asiatic family, Schmidt and Kuh, for example, favour the view that the Malay race emigrated to the Malay Archipelago in prehistoric times. Some scholars dispute this theory and deny even the existence of the Austro-Asiatic family. There are other theories, one of which suggests that first the Malays went to India and then the process was reversed.

Whatever be the ethnic and cultural relationship between India and Southeast Asia during the prehistoric period, the transplantation of Indian culture into Southeast Asia began in historic times with trade contacts. The Buddhist Jatakas tell many stories of enterprising merchants and princes, sailing to Suvarnabhumi for trade. For instance, in the *Mahajanaka Jataka*, Mahajanaka, the son of a banished King of Videha, undertook trade in order to make money to finance his campaign against the usurper of his father's throne. Having collected goods, including pearls, jewels, and diamonds, he embarked on a ship with some merchants bound for Suvarnabhumi. There were seven caravans on board with their beasts (or three hundred and fifty men, depending upon the interpretation of the original text), and in seven days the ship travelled seven hundred leagues. The story is told for religious instruction; mention of trade and sea journeying is incidental. Hence, the geographical and chronological data are very inadequate.

Reference to Suvarnabhumi is also found in the accounts of the third Buddhist Sangiti (council) held at Pataliputra in 247 B.C. during the reign of Asoka. The tradition as contained in the *Mahavamsa* refers to two missionaries, Sona and Uttara, who were said to have been sent to Suvarnabhumi, possibly to Burma, with the message of Buddhism.

Nothing, however, has been found in the countries of Southeast Asia to corroborate the tradition, and no reference to this incident has been found in the inscriptions of Asoka.

Accounts of sea voyages, some of which ended in disaster, are also recounted in other ancient texts, such as the various recensions of the lost Paisachi text *Brihatkatha* of Gunadhya, *Kathakosa,* and the Jain *Jnatadharmakatha.* The *Kathakosa* tells the story of Nagadatta who went to Suvarnadvipa with five hundred ships to conduct a profitable trade. Whilst this story, like similar stories of romance, adventure, and instruction, must have a touch of the imagination of the tale-teller, and the size of the merchant fleet may be somewhat magnified, it suggests that the trade between the two regions was considerable. The *Jnatad-harmakatha* mentions that a party of merchants, having braved a storm, reached an island called Kaliyadvipa and found mines of gold, silver, diamonds, and other jewels. There are numerous references in the *Arthasastra* to those lands and places in eastern and Southeast Asia, which were worthy of note from the economic, commercial, or political viewpoint. For instance, it refers to a kind of sandalwood, called *taila-parnika,* which was produced in Suvarnabhumi. The *Ramayana* reveals some knowledge of the eastern regions beyond seas; for instance Sugriva dispatched his men to Yavadvipa, the island of Java or Sumatra, in search of Sita. It speaks of Burma as the land of silver mines.

Tamil literature contains references to tall roomy ships laden with goods returning from eastern ports. Puranic cosmology and geographical divisions into *varshas* and *dvipas* point to Indian knowledge of this area, although the knowledge of the Puranic compilers was somewhat vague and inexact.

The *Milindapanha* and the *Mahaniddesa,* both Buddhist texts ascribed to the first centuries of the Christian era at the latest, refer to trading voyages to eastern ports. The *Niddesa* enumerates a series of Sanskrit or Sanskritized toponyms whose identification with localities in Southeast Asia has been proposed by Sylvain Lévi. At the present neither archaeological and epigraphic evidence nor the non-Indian literary sources allow historians to go further back than the *Niddesa* with any degree of certainty. However, if the *Niddesa* contains older tradition, the date of Indian voyages could be put back to a few centuries before the Christian era.

India's contact by sea with China would also imply Indian contact with Southeast Asia. On the authority of the *Annals of the Former Han Dynasty,* which gives the itinerary of a sea journey starting from the coast of Tonkin (Te-nan) and ending on the Indian coast, belonging to the period of Emperor Wu (140–80 B.C.), and which also contains a reverse itinerary relating to the reign of Wang Mang (A.D. 1–6), Bagchi suggests that regular sailing from the Gangetic Valley to Tonkin was taking place in the second and first centuries B.C.[4] S. Lévi, who was the first scholar to analyze the evidence of such itineraries and who held the view that the detailed knowledge of the sea route as contained in these accounts could not have been acquired before the second century, did not make use of the Chinese evidence, upon which Bagchi based his opinion.

Beyer, the first to conduct systematic archaeological investigations in the Philippines, finds formidable evidence to strengthen the view that there was pre-Christian contact between India and Southeast Asia. He concluded that all the artifacts found during the excavations at the Novaliches site in the late 1920's, including pottery, iron implements and weapons, beads and bangles, were brought to the Philippines from India over a long period of trade between the two countries. Both the iron and glass objects found are similar to, and in some cases identical with, the prehistoric glass and iron finds in South India. In 1948, having re-examined the theory and its criticism, Beyer substantially reaffirmed his earlier view. If Indian contacts reached as far as the Philippines in the centuries before Christ, it would be reasonable to conclude that the countries en route were also in touch, perhaps more intimately, with India. If this evidence is accepted, there must have been Indian settlements in coastal Southeast Asia well before the commencement of the Christian era.

Evidence, however, of Indian migration in the first century is definite. This evidence is archaeological rather than historical, and suggests that Indians sailed as far as the Sunda Islands. Indian works of art have been found all along the route from India and, more significantly, all the cultures that emerged in the area about the same time carry unmistakable marks of Indian influence. Just why that should have happened remains obscure, for nothing in written sources explains it.[5]

Information about trade routes between India and Southeast Asia is found in Chinese and Greek sources. The Greek and Roman writers did not know of the world east of the Ganges, including China (*Sinai* or *Thinai*), until the first century but they do corroborate the Chinese evidence of the trade routes. About the middle of the first century, Pomponius Mela mentions Chryse and Argyre, the islands of gold and silver beyond the Ganges. Substantial evidence for the existence of a sea route to China via Southeast Asia comes from the anonymous author of the *Periplus of the Erythraean Sea,* who had undertaken a journey to India.[6] But the first extant description of Southeast Asia as a whole is found in Ptolemy's *Geography,* written in the middle of the second century.

Land routes between India and Southeast Asia lay through eastern Bengal, Assam, and Manipur. Proceeding to Upper Burma through the passes in the Manipur hills, travellers reached Lower Burma through Arakan. Part of this route was common with the Indian route to Szechwan and Yunnan in southwestern China, and although difficult, it was often used.

The two extreme points in India for sailing to Southeast Asia were Bharukachha (Broach) on the western coast and Tamralipti (modern Tamluk in the Midnapore district of Bengal) on the eastern coast. Between them there were many good ports on both coasts. From Tamralipti, ships sailed regularly along the coasts of Bengal and Burma to Malaya, Indonesia, and Indochina. Some ships sailing from India for the ports in Malaya and beyond first made the journey along the coast as far as Palura in the Ganjam district, and then travelled across the high seas, to the Malay Peninsula. Further voyages to the islands of the East Indies and to the coast of the Indochinese Peninsula were routed through the Malacca Strait. However, archaeological evidence suggests that many voyagers disembarked and negotiated the short land journey across the Isthmus of Kra to the east coast of southern Thailand. From there the sea journey recommenced across the Gulf of Siam to Indochina. There were probably also direct sailings from South India through the channel between the Andaman and Nicobar Islands to Takua Pa in Siam or Kedah in Malaya. Voyages also commenced from the Andhra coast, and proceeded either along the coast or directly to Tavoy in Lower Burma. From there, the travellers headed for the Menam Delta negotiating the mountains through the Three Pagoda Pass. A route not generally used was to skirt Singapore and reach either what is now Bangkok, through the Gulf of Siam, or Funan and Champa across the China Sea. At all these points of embarkation and disembarkation, and all along the inland routes, the harvest of archaeological finds has been rich and has enabled historians to piece together a coherent account of journeys between India and Suvarnabhumi.

The popularity of these routes varied from time to time. The earliest settlers, it appears, embarked at Amaravati or at Guduru and landed at Martaban in Burma. Some of them moved up to the Pegu region and settled there, whilst others pushed southward through the Three Pagoda Pass as far as the fertile rice plains of Thailand. Later, during the reign of the Guptas, the port of Tamralipti was more frequently used, possibly because of its proximity to the Gupta capital at Pataliputra. It was from here that Fa-hsien started his sea journey back to China. In Pallava times, Kanchipuram—though not a port, being about forty miles inland—was more popular for journeys to Burma, Malaya, Java, or Sumatra.

The journey from India to Burma by land was so exacting that travellers generally preferred to take an alternate route. The Indochinese Peninsula was covered with mountain ranges, wild and thick jungles, treacherous rivers, and other perils. Inland communications were few and difficult. The major means of inland communication were the rivers—the Red River, the Mekong, and the Menam; the overland routes were, and still are, few. The only regular land route between Burma and Siam was through the Three Pagoda Pass, although at times some Burmese armies and migrants did cross over to Siam in the north. There was no regular road link between Laos, Tonkin, and Annam, and there is still none. The hostility of nature is such that more than four-fifths of Indochina is almost barren and uninhabitable.

That Indian traders and settlers repeatedly undertook journeys to Southeast Asia, despite the hazards and perils involved, speaks well for their physical prowess, courage, and determination, even if allowance for the pull of profit is made. But they were more than enterprising and courageous. This is illustrated by the fact that they were able to radically transform whole civilizations by spontaneous individual effort, without state aid, planned organizational backing, or political domination. It was the Indian merchants who opened up the region for Indian religions and settlements, and who sustained Indian cultural intercourse with Southeast Asia. In marked contrast with what happened in Central Asia and China, where once the process had been initiated the principal burden of cultural diffusion fell on scholars, pilgrims, and monks, the cultural role of Indian settlers and traders continued undiminished in Southeast Asia. There were numerous coastal merchant settlements both in India and Southeast Asia, constantly in touch with each other. To deny them the qualities of mind and body which they no doubt possessed, would be extraordinarily prejudicial. Suggestions have been made in the past, and recently repeated, that the Indian traders were poor and untutored and could not effectively transmit ideas.[7] In view of the ample archaeological evidence and of the opinions of specialist scholars in the field, such as Coedès, Winstedt, and Groslier, it is surprising that this suggestion, without any substantial arguments to back it, should ever have been put forward.

Indians were not the only people trading in Southeast Asia at the time, but it was the Indians who proved most skilful in winning the confidence and friendship of the local peoples and in transmitting their cultural influences. In ancient Indian society, the trading community was wealthy and, after the ruling houses, the chief patron of priests and learning. Even today the distinction between the trader and the labourer is clear enough to a discerning observer. In the ancient period those who came to Southeast Asia and set up establishments there, whether temporary or permanent, were wealthy merchants or their agents in charge of foreign depots: men of skill, enterprise, and culture. Reflecting upon the extraordinary difficulties involved in these journeys and remembering that often they were feats of ingenuity, stamina, and perseverance, one cannot but regard the early Indian traders as remarkably well-equipped to spread ideas. They were good traders and good sailors and loved to acquire wealth through risk and honest bargain. Not only were the Indian traders vehicles of culture in this part of the world, but everywhere trade has been a major factor in the dissemination of culture. The Indian commercial relations with the Western countries is one example of it. The Arabs, as traders, have been the most outstanding transmitters of culture. Arthur Waley, writing on a similar subject, categorically declares that merchants were undoubtedly the main carriers of information about the outside world, and disputes the assertion which is derived from false analogy between the East and West that merchants are not likely to have been interested in philosophy. Indian or Chinese merchants, in contrast to European traders, were "reputedly capable of discussing metaphysical questions" and there is ample testimony in Buddhist legend of such merchants.[8]

No doubt cultural contact was stimulated by the inherent spirit of human adventure and the desire to give and take; the main reason for Indian expansion and the eventual radiation of Indian culture was profit, not missionary endeavour. Indian trade was already brisk by the beginning of the Christian era, and later it became far more extensive. The discovery of monsoons made sea journeys between India and the Western world safe and punctual, and the Roman demand for the luxury goods of the East had reached fantastic proportions—far beyond what India alone could supply. Consequently, the Indians went in increasing numbers to Southeast Asia looking for those things that could be sold to the Romans at such good prices that Pliny the Elder was to bewail this loss of blood inflicted on the Roman economy. Spices, sandalwood, camphor, and benzoin, were amongst the products of the countries beyond the Ganges: Takkola, "cardamom market"; Karpuradvipa, "the camphor island"; Narikeladvipa, "the coconut palm island," and many more Sanskrit toponyms reveal the type of interest which attracted Indians toward these regions. The growing demands of maritime trade stimulated the development and expansion of Indian shipping. The consequent economic revolution was so vigorous that it has been compared to the epoch-making change brought about by the discovery of the direct sea route to India from Europe fourteen centuries later, which altered the entire commercial map of the world.

The attraction of lucrative trade was no doubt further strengthened by the reputation of Southeast Asia for rich gold resources. Perhaps by modern standards Southeast Asia would not seem to have been so rich as to justify this reputation, but gold was far more scarce in ancient days, and the prospects of finding gold were accompanied by a certain expectation of profitable trade. In the beginning of the Christian era, India lost Siberia as her most important source of gold, because political upheavals and large-scale movements of the peoples of Central Asia in the last two centuries B.C. cut off the trade route.

That Indonesians adopted various Indian numbers would further endorse the view that Indian trade with Southeast Asia, particularly with the East Indies, was unusually active. Numerals, terms for family relations, and terms for parts of the body, generally remain unchanged in a language affected by foreign influences.

Since profit, not religious zeal, was the driving force behind Indian cultural expansion, it is somewhat superfluous to argue whether Hinduism or Buddhism came first to Southeast Asia. At any rate no definite answer can be given, for in thought and culture both religions are inextricably interlinked and the differences are at best sectarian. Hinduism probably arrived first but certainly existed simultaneously. Whilst Hinduism must have been due to the presence of Hindus from India and those local peoples who had imperceptibly absorbed elements of Hindu culture, Buddhism, an organized missionary religion, must have been introduced by monks. That Hinduism was not a proselytizing religion, and yet had a powerful hold for centuries in Southeast Asia, would suggest the existence of large communities of Hindus or gradually converted peoples.

Although the Buddha is recorded to have instructed his disciples "let not any two of you go in the same direction," early Buddhism was not a proselytizing religion; in fact, it did not begin as a religion at all. However, it soon developed into one with an unprecedented zeal for proselytization. During the reign of Asoka, zealous missionaries carried Buddhism to foreign lands as well as the distant regions of the vast Mauryan Empire. Innumerable stupas sprang up all over the country, the finest of which, the stupa of Sanchi, still stands.[9] As communication improved between northern and southern India, Buddhism migrated to South India. After the fall of the Mauryan Empire, the Satavahanas founded the first historical empire in the west and the south. It was then that the ancient trunk route of northern India, which was the main artery of traffic linking Ujjayini, the western capital of the Imperial government, with the capital of the Mauryan Empire, Pataliputra in the east, was extended to the capital of the Satavahanas at Pratisthana. From Pratisthana the route proceeded southward, bifurcating in both eastern and western directions. Thus, centres of political power, missionary religion, and maritime commerce were linked by road transport in an unprecedentedly intimate contact, bringing Buddhism to the Indian coastal areas of brisk international trade. From there it was but a short step for a dynamic religion, as Buddhism no doubt was, to the countries of Southeast Asia.

The Hindu Satavahanas, at first, only tolerated Buddhism. Later it was actively patronized, and consequently flourished throughout the Satavahana period. It was, however, during the first two centuries A.D., after the Satavahanas had recovered from a short political set-back (ca. 35–90), that Buddhism had its greatest success in South India. This was also the period when Indian trade, mainly from South India, with the West had reached its height, and was expanding in the East. The Satavahanas, and the Kshaharatas, their rivals in the west, competed in building Buddhist monasteries, patronizing the monks, and granting lands and gifts of money to Buddhist temples. In the eastern sector of the Empire, particularly along the southeastern coast of India, Buddhist stupas and other structures were built mainly through private effort, which would suggest that Buddhism was even more popular in these areas. The remains of Amaravati and Nagarjunakonda lend considerable support to this view. Both cities were situated on the river Krishna; the distance between the two by land was about sixty miles, and by river a little more than one hundred. Amaravati was contemporaneous with the Satavahanas, whereas Nagarjunakonda was developed after their fall, and is associated with the Buddhist teacher, Nagarjuna. It was from this area and during this time that Indians sailed mostly to Southeast Asian ports, which makes it likely that they were either Buddhist or at least familiar with Buddhist teachings.

Whilst Hinduism may have been more popular with the settlers, courts, and aristocracy, Buddhism with its simplicity and doctrine of human equality may have gained more attention from the common people as it did in China. Both in their respective ways, however, helped cultural intercourse until the whole of Southeast Asia professed Buddhism, Hinduism, a mixture of both, or an admixture of these and their own indigenous beliefs. Practically all sects and schools of Hinduism and Buddhism, from vedic worship to Tantric beliefs, entered these countries. Siva, generally speaking, was a more popular Hindu god than Vishnu. Many Cambodian and Indonesian kings had their images installed in the likeness of the deity they worshipped, superimposing on their own personality the attributes of their favorite god. In some countries, such as Indonesia, Hinduism was so intermingled with Buddhism that Siva and the Buddha were described as brothers. Indeed, in Balinese temples where the religion is Balinese Hinduism, Saiva and Buddhist priests sit side by side, although dressed differently, as they bless the laity. Theravada Buddhism found a far greater following in Southeast Asia than the Mahayana School. In countries such as Indonesia and Malaya, which became Muslim in the fourteenth and fifteenth centuries, the earlier beliefs still survive. Most have been given an Islamic veneer, but in some cases they are still in their original form. In comparatively inaccessible mountainous regions of interior Indonesia, indigenous beliefs are combined with Hindu and Buddhist practices, and in many cities, such as Jogjakarta and Surabaya, Muslims, theoretically not supposed to worship icons, can be seen kneeling in prayer before beautifully sculptured Hindu-Buddhist images of the ninth century and later.

It seems that the Indian immigrants made no conscious attempt to convert local peoples to their faith or culture; they certainly did not impose it by force. Proselytism was precluded by the very nature of the Hindu faith, which perhaps would explain the general unconcern of Indians with the Indianization of Southeast Asia, as well as the absence of references in Indian literature relating to the processes of change. However, there were Buddhist missionaries who worked for the spread of their faith, and some centres and monasteries earned a widespread reputation for their learning.

Whether they were monks or merchants, the culture of these Indians deeply affected the countries they visited or settled. Groslier gives a graphic description of Indian traders who came to Spice Island with the southwestern monsoon looking for goods for export to the Mediterranean world. They had to temporarily settle in the deserted land waiting for the favourable wind to return, and gradually the demands of increasing trade compelled them to establish permanent depots in these lands.

Intermarriage must have played an important role in this cultural synthesis. Soon complete fusion of population and culture was achieved. This fact should dispel any arguments of Indian caste rigidity at the time. The argument, first advanced by Coedès long ago and almost mechanically repeated by certain other scholars, that since the caste system, which was an integral part of the Hindu social organization, did not exist in Southeast Asia, Indian cultural influence must have been partial, ignores the fact that the Indian culture which radiated abroad was a blending of Hinduism and Buddhism, and that the caste system was not so rigid at that time. Also, many settlers and sailors were Buddhists and opposed to the caste system.

Whilst there was a continuous influx of merchants, priests, monks, and settlers into Southeast Asia, and whereas Indian scholars and traders constantly went to other lands to preach or to make profit, unlike the Portuguese and other Europeans, there is no account of any Indian adventurer or merchant seeking employment at the local courts purely for reasons of amassing wealth. However, once Indians had become a part of Southeast Asian life, they were often employed by the local rulers. Later, Indianized kingdoms emerged either as a result of an Indian imposing himself on the local population or else through a local chief adopting the foreign civilization. With time it was inevitable that there should emerge able men of enterprise and ambition who sought power and authority. Those who succeeded in setting themselves up as rulers brought to their court and household, at least in the beginning, the required staff of priests, scribes, goldsmiths, weavers, bards, sculptors, scholars, bodyguards, and so on, as well as Indian texts on law and jurisprudence, the arts, and the like. All aspects of the culture of the rulers penetrated the society of their adoption. In time, local people were employed in various positions and local influences were assimilated by the Indian rulers and settlers.

Despite the large-scale influx of Indians of various economic classes and intellectual levels over a long period, there is no evidence of any local resistance to their arrival. The friendly reception accorded Indian settlers is in marked contrast to the strong distrust and opposition encountered by European settlers and traders practically everywhere, not only from highly civilized and sophisticated communities but also from primitive and aboriginal peoples. There is no evidence that the Indians regarded these new lands as outlets for their excessive population or an exclusive market for their growing trade, or that they insisted on the superiority of their culture. Wherever Indians settled they gave what they had and took what they could. Thus was evolved, by mutual consent, a new culture whose dominant note was Indian.

Southeast Asian traders or Buddhist pilgrims who visited India brought back Indian traditions. Consequently, an Indian political system, centring around the king, with a Hindu-Buddhist cosmological basis of kingship; Indian epic and sacred texts; Indian mathematics and astronomy; and Indian skills in husbandry and handicrafts, became increasingly entrenched in the new lands. Sanskrit became the official language, and along with Pali, was used for religious texts. The various schools of Hinduism and Buddhism found a following in these countries, and even Indian Islam entered Southeast Asia. The impact of Indian civilization was such that it did not remain confined to settlements or coastal areas, as one would expect in an age of slow transport, but penetrated to the centre and distant corners of mainland and inland Southeast Asia.

According to Quaritch Wales, Indianization, although a continuing process, proceeded in successive peaks, which he calls the Four Main Waves of Indian Cultural Expansion.[10] These waves, which correspond to the peak periods of Hindu-Buddhist civilization, are the Amaravati in the second and third centuries, the Gupta from the fourth to the sixth centuries, the Pallava from about 550 to 750, and the Pala from about 750 to 900. He adds a fifth wave, supplementary to the fourth, the late Pala influence in the twelfth and thirteenth centuries, after the disruption of Nalanda University. Perhaps a sixth wave of Islam could also be added, for it was principally Indian Islam that travelled to Southeast Asia. This is a simplified classification of a complex process which does not lend itself to neat categorization, but it does reflect the fact that the Indian cultural encounter with Southeast Asia assumed different forms in different periods, and that it was closely connected with the changing patterns of Indian society. The Indian impact was a kind of chain reaction, in which each successive wave of Indian immigrants worked out a cultural synthesis with the local people, including localized Indians, with varying degrees of concentration and assimilation.

Besides commercial profit and cultural propaganda, there were other reasons that prompted this vigorous, sustained, and extraordinary maritime expansion by a people who today are not particularly noted for their adventurous spirit or material pursuits. One conclusion is obvious: the ancient Indians were very different from their modern descendants in their spirit of commercial enterprise as well as missionary zeal. They were not reluctant to go out seeking people with whom they could exchange goods and ideas. However, various other explanations have been suggested. For example, a remote cause is to be found in the third century B.C. in the conquest of Kalinga by Asoka, and in the resultant exodus of population. Others believe that the pressure felt by the mass of the Indian population because of the Kushana invasions in the first century led to Indian emigration; this would be chronologically more plausible. It is also suggested that a wholesale migration of coastal people might have been caused by Samudragupta's conquest of South India; this would explain the simultaneous rise of the Hindu states in Southeast Asia. However, none of these explanations would appear to be correct, because the available data clearly indicate that Indian expansion in the first centuries was of a commercial nature, and not a haphazard movement of groups of people seeking asylum from unrest. No evidence has been advanced to show a systematic displacement of large Indian populations. If invasions or internal chaos were normally to cause an exodus of Indians to foreign lands, then there would have been many more migratory waves, especially during the period beginning with the disastrous incursions of Mahmud of Ghazni.

That the introduction of Indian culture was a gradual process presupposes that the indigenous cultures were sufficiently well developed to exchange knowledge. The local cultures adopted only those Indian features of which they approved. It is possible that the local element was subordinated to Indian influence but it was never eclipsed, and the local people never completely lost their freedom of initiative. A people who could feel the stimulus of an alien culture and respond to it in accordance with their need cannot but have attained a certain degree of civilization. The facility with which the Indians were able to expand their culture in Southeast Asia may lend some weight to the view that in their beliefs and attitudes the indigenous peoples could see a reflection of their own traditions.

What sort of civilization existed in Southeast Asia before the advent of Indian cultural diffusion? Because of the earliest racial and cultural movements, it seems that by the last phase of the Neolithic Age, the entire region was inhabited by ethnically intermixed peoples. The most characteristic feature known of this period is the different forms of adzes with quadrangular sections. These adzes are found in North India, Burma, Malaya, China, and Japan. Probably this quadrangular adze-culture came to the Malay Peninsula and Indonesia through China and central Indochina (Laos and Siam) sometime between 2000 and 1500 B.C. It brought to Indonesia what are called the Austronesian languages (which later developed into Indonesian languages), and introduced the outrigger canoe, rice cultivation, domesticated cattle or buffaloes, head-hunting, and the custom of erecting megalithic monuments.[11] This culture was the most widespread and important of the Stone Age cultures of the region, because of its artistic development, especially in pottery and weaving.

Whilst Heine-Geldern considers that originally Indonesians migrated from Yunnan and southwestern China, Hendrik Kern, who wrote in 1889 and relied on linguistic evidence, suggested it to be Indochina and the neighbouring areas, in which sugar cane, bananas, cocoanut, bamboo, and possibly rattan were grown. Rice was the staple food of this seafaring people. The Neolithic wave of migration, however, does not seem to have gone beyond the Moluccas and did not reach New Guinea.

The next stage in the development of these countries, known as the Dong-son culture, which has been defined as the culture of the Indonesian peoples of the coastal belt of Annam, took place between the fifth and second centuries B.C. It was characterized by extensive use of bronze and considerable knowledge of iron. The bronze work was quite advanced and bronze kettledrums are a special feature of this period. Of superb workmanship, they were widely used for ritual purposes. They have very thin walls and the bronze is an alloy of copper and lead as in the mints of China in the Han times. Later, in the Indian period, the usual copper-tin alloy came back into use. In addition to the drums, swords, daggers and helmets, household utensils and small statuettes, all of bronze, and ornaments of shell and semi-precious stones have been found. The first find of drums was made near Thanh-hoa in Annam. However, they have subsequently been discovered all over the island area.

The Dong-son people were skilled agriculturists, fishermen, shipbuilders, and sailors. Their navigation was more developed than that of their predecessors and they had some knowledge of astronomy. They were well-travelled merchants and, significantly, some of their names for weights and measures, such as *kati* and *tahil*, are still used in Malaya and Indonesia.

It has been suggested recently that the Dong-son culture can be traced back to the Yueh people who inhabited the coastal regions of China about 2000 B.C., and whose typical traits, according to Eberhard, were: "A developed navigation; the practice of holding boat races, with its outgrowth, the dragon boat festival; the use of bronze drums decorated in a way showing connection with that rite; and the concept of the dragon as the river god. Elements of this culture were the worship of serpents, of sacred mountains—the latter developed into important temple festivals—and of certain trees."[12] However, as Eberhard himself points out, the subject of the affiliations of these early cultures of the Pacific lands can be tackled only in a tentative manner.[13]

96

There are various other theories, all disputed and unresolved, concerning the relationship between Austro-Asiatic or Austric culture—the culture which spread across the Indo-Chinese peninsula to the extremities of northeastern India—and pre-Aryan India. If some are valid, Indian contact with Southeast Asia began many cenuturies before the Christian era and continued vigorously until about 1500. Even if the possibility of cultural contacts during the prehistoric times, of which there is only fragmentary and indefinite archaeological evidence and legendary accounts, is discounted, direct Indian contact with the countries of Southeast Asia lasted for about fifteen hundred years. Whilst Hinduism stagnated and Buddhism almost disappeared in India during the mediaeval period, they both flourished in Southeast Asia. Burma, Thailand, Ceylon, Laos, Cambodia, and Vietnam are even today predominantly Buddhist nations, and Malaya and Indonesia—with the exception of Bali which still professes Balinese Hinduism—remained Hindu-Buddhist until the rise of Islam in the fifteenth century. However, Islam did not dislodge Indian culture; it became another tributary in the river of Malay culture. South India by far exerted the greatest influence on Southeast Asia, although Gujarat, Bengal, and Malwa made significant contributions.

The line of demarcation between Chinese and Indian cultural influence in Southeast Asia may be drawn from eastern central Tibet southward through the Indochinese Peninsula, then in a southeasterly direction into Indonesia; but there was much interpenetration. Formosa, Tonkin, and the Philippines remained on the Chinese side, whilst Laos, Cambodia, Siam, Burma, Malaysia, and Indonesia came within the Indian sphere. Chinese influence, however, does not seem to have been very great. Formosa is really a part of the Chinese nation, and in the Philippines, both India and China made contributions, as well as other regions, including the West. Even Tonkin, which is physically, ethnologically, and often politically allied to China, retained Buddhism and a good deal of Indian culture.

The nature and depth of Indian and Chinese influences differed considerably, as did the processes of their advance. Whilst the Chinese migrants had little inclination to mix with local populations, even though there was an ethnic affinity between them, the Indian settlers intermarried freely with indigenous people. Even within the Indian sphere of influence, the Chinese, who established themselves at selected trading points, remained colonies of foreigners with little inclination to mix with the local population. Chinese cultural expansion was the secondary outcome of political domination, for China seldom exported culture for its own sake but gave it as if to soften the blow of conquest.

Except for some political interference in Ceylon and for the naval expedition sent by Rajendra Cola against the Sri Vijaya Empire in 1025, no Indian state ever made any serious effort to dictate political terms, much less culture, to the peoples of Southeast Asia. Chinese culture remained confined to the people of Chinese descent in these regions, and nowhere, with the possible exception of Tonkin, is there any trace of the total assimilation of Chinese culture.

Indian and Chinese cultures have met in other areas, but in Indochina the meeting was on a large scale, and their interaction with the existing culture has been a unique phenomenon in history. Although India was farther away from Indochina, it does not appear that this was much of a handicap. Tonkin, over which China ruled for long periods, was the only area in the whole Southeast Asian region where the local people absorbed more Chinese than Indian culture. Even then it accepted Buddhism and, in turn, transmitted it to southern China. Describing the contrast between the methods and effects of these two influences, Groslier observes: "China quite simply conquered and annexed Tonkin, making a clean slate of the past to impose her civilization, and finally turn the country into one of her provinces; a province scarcely recognizable as distinct from others in her vast empire. Whereas India only touched on the southern coasts of Indo-China, and vanished again from the scene, when her seafaring activity practically came to an end in about the fifth century A.D. But in that short space of time the peoples thus drawn out of their isolation, on their own initiative took over her culture, and very soon in turn created new civilizations of profound originality. China dominated, whilst India scattered seed, and between them they were to shape the double aspect of Indo-China."[14]

Indeed, as Coedès has pointed out, Southeast Asia was able to make progress mainly during those periods of history when it was left alone by a China weakened by her own internal political upheavals. China never liked the establishment of powerful empires in her neighbourhood, and the states of Southeast Asia found a favourable climate for political and cultural progress at a time when China was politically unstable. The ascendancy of Funan during the fourth and fifth centuries coincides with the chaotic period of the Three Kingdoms in China; the consolidation of Champa's power in the seventh century, the peak of pre-Angkor Cambodia, the blossoming of Angkor Cambodia in the tenth century and the growth of the Khmer, Cham, and Burmese kingdoms at the end of the eleventh century coincide with periods of weakness in Chinese history. In contrast, the strength of cultural movements in India is reflected in similar movements in the countries of Southeast Asia.[15]

Even the remarkable Hellenization of the Mediterranean world does not compare with the Indianization of Southeast Asia. India was far from Southeast Asia and had never dominated any of the local kingdoms; nor did any purely Indian dynasty, unlike the Greeks in Egypt or Syria, ever rule the area. Hellenic civilization directly expanded in those areas that were in the Greek neighbourhood and had been dominated by Hellenic dynasts. There were far fewer Indians in Southeast Asia than Greeks in the Hellenistic world, and those Indians had to contend with an equally powerful Chinese civilization in an area mainly frequented by Chinese, and in which most of the local peoples were racially closer to China than to India. On the other hand, Greek civilization did not confront such a contrast of cultural and ethnic types. In fact, the Greeks were not successful in influencing Persians, West Asians, or Indians. On the contrary, they were considerably influenced by them. Even in effect, Indian culture in Southeast Asia left behind more than was left by Hellenism in the Mediterranean world. There is nothing in the Hellenistic world to compare with the Angkor Wat or Borobudur. Whilst Hellenism merged into Hellenisticism and absorbed many traits of other civilizations, Indian culture has continued to grow quite distinctly. Again, India contributed not only philosophy and thought, but also a religion that still survives in most areas of Southeast Asia. Greek religion is a thing of the past.

Whatever be the precise nature of the process of Indian cultural alliance and influence, its extent was deep and extensive, and its effects were felt in all aspects of culture from religious thought to the technical skills in agriculture and handicrafts. First the Indian alphabetic system, which is still used in Burma, Siam, Cambodia, and Laos, was introduced, followed by the introduction of Sanskrit and Sanskrit literature, "playing just the same part as Latin in Mediaeval Europe. India also taught her political system centred on the king, and her main religious beliefs. Her sacred texts, and her great epics, were so well learnt throughout this India beyond the seas that they became naturalised in each of these lands. Finally, India unfolded the secrets of her mathematics and astronomy, making possible calendar calculations of much greater accuracy than in the past, and all her technical skill in husbandry and handicrafts."[16]

Ceylon

Sri Lanka, Sinhala, or Ceylon, which is India's closest neighbour to the south, was possibly the first country in southern Asia to feel the impact of Indian immigration. Ceylon's cultural relations with India, often reinforced by close political ties, have been almost continuous to the present day. Strictly speaking, Ceylon is not counted as part of Southeast Asia but it did act both as an intermediary and a base for the eastward migration of Indian culture and religions. In the history of Buddhism and Hinduism, as well as in the contemporary Indian world, Lanka occupies an eminent position. The Hindu epic, *Ramayana*, narrates the story in which Rama's conflict with Ravana, the king of Lanka, is the central theme. Although the history of ancient Ceylon, when it was known as Lanka in India, is largely a complex of myths, legends, and plausible conjectures, and the beginnings of the earliest migrations are indefinite, it is undoubted that the early settlers of Ceylon came from India.[17]

The Vaddas were possibly the earliest peoples of Ceylon, but it is the following Aryan migration which has been authenticated. The language of the Aryans gave rise to Sinhalese, now the national language of modern Ceylon. The Aryan migrants, members of the *Sinhalaa, Sinhalas,* or the Lion Tribe, named their new home Sinhaladvipa, from which have derived its later variations: the Portuguese *Ceilao* or *Zeylan,* and the English Ceylon.

The coming of Aryans is represented in the *Mahavamsa* by the story of Prince Vijayasimha who came from northern India in the sixth century B.C. In spite of the legends that surround him, his historical existence is generally acknowledged. It was, however, at the time of the introduction of Buddhism during the reign of Asoka that close contact between India and Ceylon began. This contact became so constant that it is not always possible to separate the history of South India from that of Ceylon. Indeed, the period before the arrival of the Portuguese in 1505 is sometimes referred to as the Indian period of Ceylonese history.

By the time Buddhism arrived, the Aryans, who were not altogether cut off from their kinsmen in India, had opened up the country, established settlements in the dry zone, introduced the use of iron, organized a system of government, and spread Hindu doctrines. The existence of Hinduism is undoubted, but the extent of its popularity is not precisely known; other faiths, such as Jain and Ajivika, were also practiced. Certain elements of Hinduism, such as the caste system, are known to have existed in pre-Buddhist Ceylon. It is also possible that the fame of Buddhism had reached Ceylon before the third century B.C. when Asoka sent in the mission headed by his son (or brother), Mahinda (or Mahendra), the first foreign missionary and the real founder of Buddhism in Ceylon. According to the *Mahavamsa,* the King of Ceylon,

Devanampiya Tissa (247–207 B.C.), received Asoka's mission with great respect and, deeply impressed by the new faith, he and his people soon embraced Buddhism. Mahinda delivered a number of sermons during his initial stay of twenty-six days at Anuradhapura, the capital, and when he left there were already sixty-two monks. Whatever be the accuracy of the story of his spectacular success, there is no doubt that the visit of this young man, who worked for the next forty-eight years of his life in Ceylon, marks the beginning of Sinhalese culture as we know it, and the phenomenal rise of Buddhism throughout the country.

Because no monk was allowed to ordain nuns, Asoka later sent Sanghamitra, Mahendra's sister, to Ceylon to ordain Queen Anula and other women who expressed the desire to enter the Sangha. It is said that she brought with her a sprig of the Bodhi Tree, under which Gautama Buddha had attained enlightenment. The branch was planted at the capital in an impressive ceremony, and the sacred tree which resulted still exists.[18] The idea for this transplantation of a branch of the Bodhi Tree is attributed to Asoka. The Tree served as an inspiration to the people who had recently embraced the Buddhist religion, became symbolic of Buddhist supremacy in Ceylon, and strengthened the cultural links with India. Later, other sacred relics were imported to Ceylon from India. A returning Ceylonese mission from Pataliputra brought the alms bowl of the Buddha, which was housed in the Thuparama Dagoba, and one of the Buddha's teeth was enshrined in a specially built temple, Dhammachakka. These events in the early history of Ceylonese Buddhism left a deep impression on the Sinhalese people and still evoke pious enthusiasm amongst millions of its votaries.

There are various legends about the tooth, but it is known to have been in Ceylon when Fa-hsien visited the country in the fifth century. The tooth has a chequered history, for powerful monarchs, both within Ceylon and outside, longed to possess it. Some hostile powers sought to destroy it; the Portuguese claimed to have captured and burned it in the marketplace of Goa during their suzerainty over Ceylon from 1517 to 1600. It has, however, survived all such attempts and is now preserved in the Temple of the Sacred Tooth at Kandy where a colourful festival is held each year.

The reign of Vattagamani (ca. 29–17 B.C.) is an important landmark in the history of Buddhism in Ceylon, for it was then that the sacred scriptures, which had been committed to memory, were written down through the efforts of hundreds of reciters and scribes. The sacred Pali canon, the Tripitaka, which survives today and the original of which has long since vanished from India, was the result of this mass effort.

INDIA AND WORLD CIVILIZATION

Buddhism became so powerful in Ceylon that kings went out of their way to identify themselves more closely with it and to extend it special patronage. Monks began to pour into Ceylon from India and monasteries were erected all over the country with generous endowments made for their maintenance. Hundred of thousands of men and women embraced the new faith and thousands entered the Sangha.

Ceylon's particularly enthusiastic response to Buddhism was presumably because Buddhism was seeking support amongst a people who were already ethnologically and culturally closely associated with India. By the time it came to Ceylon, Buddhism had assumed a popular form. It did not stress its abstruse doctrines but sought to emphasize the personality of the Buddha as an inspiring teacher and as a saviour of supernatural power. It was this image which was most appealing and comprehensible to the common man. Buddhist literature was rich and comprehensive enough to satisfy both monks and laymen. It was therefore easy for Buddhist preachers to communicate with the masses in Ceylon.

The adoption of Buddhism as the national religion was followed by major changes in the social and religious life of the people, as well as in the royal household and court. The court was additionally influenced by India because the Ceylonese royalty established matrimonial links with South Indian royal houses, and continued to maintain them. During certain later periods, parts of Ceylon and South India were joined under one ruling dynasty, and trade contacts between India and Ceylon were further strengthened. Pali—also much Sanskrit—became the literary language of Ceylon, and Ceylonese literature has close affinities with its Indian counterpart. The art of writing possibly came to Ceylon with the Aryans before the introduction of Buddhism; the earliest known specimens of writing, however, are associated with Buddhism.[19] Whether the Ceylonese alphabet was introduced during the period of Asoka or before, it is undoubtedly Indian in origin.

The rise of Buddhism also witnessed a blossoming of Ceylonese art and architecture. King Devanampiya Tissa was the first to promote the building of sacred monuments, the earliest of which is the Thuparama Dagoba at Anuradhapura, built during the days of Asoka. A successor of his, Dutthagamani (101–77 B.C.), built the Lohapasada, the brazen palace, and began the Ruvanvelisaya Dagoba, which was completed after his death. King Mahasena (334–362), who is famous for his large irrigation tanks, also built the largest *dagoba* (or stupa), commonly called the Jetavanarama, at Anuradhapura. The 251 feet high Jetavanarama Dagoba stands on a platform which covers nearly eight acres of a fourteen acre walled enclosure. The Abhayagiri Dagoba, almost equally massive, is reputed to have been built in the first century B.C.

The main architectural remains are found at Anuradhapura and Polonnaruva, the two most famous capitals of ancient and mediaeval Ceylon. The former was the royal capital for more than a thousand years, until it was superseded about the eighth century by the latter which remained the capital until the thirteenth century. Ceylonese antiquities, therefore, belong to two widely separated periods. Anuradhapura architecture goes back to the third century B.C. although most of it dates from the early centuries A.D., whereas the important structures of Polonnaruva belong to the second half of the twelfth century. The most conspicuous structures at Anuradhapura are the Buddhist dagobas, far exceeding in dimensions anything extant in India. But the magnificent stupas and the ornamental and decorative architecture, the sculptures of dwarfs and of Naga deities, the moonstones, and the stone railings of Anuradhapura recall those of Sanchi and Amaravati. The latter phase of this period is characterized by influences typical of Andhra art, as seen in the Buddhist sculptures of Amaravati.

During the Polonnaruva period, Ceylonese architecture was mainly influenced by the South India Pallava art of the seventh century. Examples in Ceylon of the sacred shrines of the Pallava period are the Koneswara temple at Trincomallee, and the ancient temple of Tiruketiswaram. The Tivaka Vihara at Polonnaruva, built by Parakrama Bahu (1153–1186), has a high pyramidal roof in Dravidian style; indeed, the buildings at Polonnaruva in general have a distinctly Dravidian character.

In Buddhist shrines, Hindu deities occupy honoured places; Vishnu is particularly popular in Sinhalese Buddhist temples, for he is not considered a rival of the Buddha but the protector of Ceylon, and is worshipped as subordinate to the Buddha. Hindu temples were also built: for example, the Siva temple at Polonnaruva dating probably from the eleventh or twelfth century resembles the South Indian Chola buildings. Ceylonese sacred monuments and monasteries, however, are distinguished from those in India by certain features common with Buddhist structures in Indochina.

Painting and sculpture in Ceylon, although modified by indigenous influence, generally followed Indian models. But often the mark of Ceylon is so deep on certain works of art that its Indian origins are not very evident. The Ceylonese "moonstone," a semi-circular slab placed at the foot of a staircase and carved elaborately in low relief, although developed from the plain Amaravati type moonstone, is especially characteristic of Ceylonese art. Its design is invariably based on the open lotus flower.

Indian influence on Buddhist iconography is unmistakable. Large statues of the Buddha, seated, standing, or reclining, are abundant in the country, and some of them go back to the beginning of the Christian era. The earlier type of Buddha image known in Ceylon is that of the Andhra School, and the folded drapery style of the early Buddha images closely resembles that of Amaravati.[20] The stone Buddha statue, from the Toluvila ruins at Anuradhapura, with a local devotee seated beside it, is comparable to the best Gupta sculpture, and Pallava influence can be seen in the sculpture of Polonnaruva. Some Ceylonese sculpture may have even been cast in India. The human panel-figures generally resemble those at Sanchi, although they are more advanced in style.

Early Sinhalese pictorial art is said to have been inspired by Amaravati, and the frescoes at Sigiriya bear striking similarities to those of Ajanta. Situated on an isolated hill, Sigiriya was constructed as an impregnable refuge by King Kasyapa I, who reigned during the last quarter of the fifth century, and the paintings, comprising twenty-one female portraits, are placed in two irregular rock chambers, usually called pockets. Some recent observers have noticed the reflection of the Amaravati style and technique in the art of Sigiriya. Whatever be the foreign influence, the Sigiriya frescoes are remarkable productions of their age. There is nothing to suggest who the artists were, where they came from, or how they learned their art.

Apart from the ancient Pali Chronicle, *Mahavamsa*, the main sources of the history of dance and music in Ceylon are art and literature. Details of sculptured dancing figures, and wood and ivory carvings undoubtedly reveal the relationship of the Ceylonese dancers' art with that of Indian, particularly Bharata Natyam, which spread to Ceylon from South India. The *Mahavamsa* mentions musical instruments such as *mridanga, kahala, maddala,* and *vina,* which are still in common use in India. Most of the musical instruments listed in the *Thupavamsa* and *Dalada Sirita,* belonging roughly to a period between the thirteenth and fourteenth centuries, are of Indian origin. Some of the drums are identical with those of South India. A number of technical terms current in Indian music are referred to in the Sinhalese poem, *Kavislumina.*[21] In Sinhalese folksongs, for example harvest songs, is seen the reflection of the folksongs of Malabar which accompany the transplantation of paddy seedlings in the fields.

In turn, Ceylon has contributed a good deal to India and the world by carefully preserving the original Buddhist doctrine and practice. It was from Ceylon that the world learned the most authentic account of the rise of Buddhism. The Pali canon has had great influence upon Burma, Cambodia, Thailand, and Laos: the countries where Theravada Buddhism flourishes today.

Burma

Burma is the largest country in the Southeast Asian mainland with an area of a quarter of a million square miles. Although there was a land route between India and Burma from very ancient times, trade and contact between the two countries developed by sea rather than by land because Burma lay across the highly inaccessible Assam and Manipur hills, and the Arakan hill ranges. In contrast, the sea route to lower Burma was relatively easy. It was an important stage in the route from India to China, although today Burma lies off the main road of world commerce, which goes by sea through the Strait of Malacca.

It was mainly through Buddhism that Indian thought and culture made an impression on Burmese life and civilization. The Ceylonese chronicles speak of two of Asoka's missionaries, Sona and Uttara, who were dispatched by the Third Buddhist Council to Burma to revive Buddhism. This would suggest that Buddhism had been in existence in Burma for some time. Whilst the accuracy of this account has been questioned, its possibility cannot be denied outright, and there is hardly any other legend so widespread in the Buddhist tradition of Burma, and held with such deep conviction. There is a Burmese tradition that Buddhism came to the country through the good offices of two Mon merchants, Tapussa and Bhallika, who were graced by the Buddha with some hair from his head and who enshrined the hair on the top of the Singuttara Hill, at the place where the famous pagoda, Shwe Dagon, now stands. Amongst other traditional accounts emphasizing the antiquity of Buddhism in Burma, a prominent story is connected with the commentator of the Pali canon in the fifth century, Buddhaghosa, who is said to have been born in Burma, went west to Ceylon, and finally returned home with a complete set of the Pali Tripitaka. Whilst the historicity of the episode is obscure, the Burmese chronicles strongly insist on its reality.

Outside the Buddhist tradition, the earliest reference to Buddhism in Burma is found in the Chinese chronicles of the third century, which mention a Buddhist kingdom of over one hundred thousand families and several thousand monks in Lin-Yang in central Burma. Chinese interest in Burma was awakened because, during the Han dynasty, parts of the land had fallen under Chinese overlordship, and occasional military expeditions were sent from China. After the collapse of the Han rule, China relaxed her hold on Burma.

Despite Chinese domination of large parts of Burma for centuries, the foundations of Burmese civilizations as we now know it were not laid until the arrival of Indian cultural influences, and there is no evidence of Chinese influence on Burmese civilization whatsoever. Except for its Buddhist content, Chinese culture remained alien to Burma. The Burmese claim that the beginnings of their culture and civilization came with the Sakyan migration from India. According to the Burmese legend, Taganng, their first capital, was founded in Upper Burma by Sakyan princes from Kapilavastu. The Chinese texts also observe that the Indians' arrival laid the beginnings of Burmese civilization, and that whilst Buddhism was strong in central Burma, Hinduism had made some progress in southern Burma.

Indians settled along the coast in Burma and inward on the river. The *Periplus* refers to Sino-Indian trade through the wild Sesatai people, who possibly lived in the north of Burma, between China and Assam. Some of the Sanskrit place names mentioned by Ptolemy in the second century have been identified with places in Burma. Although his descriptions, especially of the interior, suffer from mistakes, he gives place names in abundance, sometimes as if he is enumerating numbers like a mathematician. The ports of Takkola and Vesunga appear to be Ptolemy's Takola and Besynga. Ptolemy speaks of the Irrawaddy Delta as it was at the beginning of the second century. He refers to Kirrhadia, beyond the mouth of the Ganges, in which the finest cinnamon was to be found, and above which lived the Tiladai people (variously spelled). These people are identified as the Kiratas or the Cilatas mentioned in an inscription discovered at Nagarjunakonda. They inhabited the regions now known as Arakan and Lower Burma and were converted to Buddhism about 250 by monks from Tambapanna.

Although Indian culture must have travelled to Burma well before, possibly in, the pre-Christian era, the evidence of Indo–Burmese cultural contact from about the fifth century onwards is definite. Its greatest impact came in the beginning before the Burmese national genius had attained maturity. "The basis of her script, her literature, her art, her thought, her religion, Burma owes to India, and a fair number of her economic products."[22]

The people of Burma are broadly divided into three racial groups, the Mons, the Burmese, and the Shans. Today the Burmese are by far the largest group, but the Mons, who are related to the Khmers and who once occupied wide tracts in Lower Burma and the Malay Peninsula, are the earliest known people in Burmese history. Originally they held most of Thailand and, in Burma, the eastern plains from Kyauksu to the sea, and thence to the Isthmus of Kra. Pegu remained their main centre of power and activity until 1757. The Burmese belong to the same racial stock as the Tibetans, Nepalese, and other peoples of the Himalayan region. The exact date of their immigration to Burma is not known but by the ninth century they had become the dominant power in Upper Burma. When they arrived, the Buddhist kingdom of Pyu with its capital at Sri Ksetra, was flourishing, and after the overthrow of the Pyu in 832, they settled at Kyauksu, where they adopted the language, religion and culture of the Mon. Later, they founded the kingdom of Arakan, but their main centre was Pagan (Arimaddana).

The Shans, related to the Thais, came after the Burmese and acquired principalities in Upper Burma. They share the Buddhist culture of the Burmese. The Mons were often persecuted by the Burmese during the mediaeval and early modern periods, and were forced to flee to Thailand in large numbers. Today they are relatively small in numbers, mainly concentrated near Moulmein, and have more or less assimilated with the Burmese.

The Mons were, however, an accomplished people; it was they who gave Burma its writing and its religion. They were possibly the first to come into contact with Indian culture in the first century through the seafaring Telinganas of the Andhra–Pallava country of South India. The earliest Mon inscription found on a pillar at Lopburi in Thailand is in the Pallava script of the fifth century.

So far only the Pyu capital site, about five miles from Prome, has been worked with any thoroughness. Archaeological finds, ranging from about the beginning of the sixth to the end of the tenth century, comprise numerous Buddhist monuments, stone and bronze statues, terracotta tablets with inscriptions, and reliquaries. The earliest relics are fragments of the Pali scriptures discovered at Moza and Maungun, on the Pyu site. Dated approximately 500, these are written in a script resembling the Kadamba script of South India of the same period. They were first discovered in 1897 and then supplemented by further finds at Hmawza, including a manuscript of twenty gold leaves and stone statues of the Buddha, bearing imprints of Gupta style. Some of these statues carry inscriptions in Pyu and Sanskrit. These remains indicate that by this time Buddhism was widespread and well established in Burma, that Pali was known and understood—certainly in the capital city—and that Buddhism was fed and nourished from the Andhra–Pallava region of

South India from centres such as Amaravati, Nagarjunakonda, Kanchi-puram, and Kaveripattinam. It is significant that all these places were intimately associated with the Buddhaghosa tradition.

Epigraphic documents point to the prevalence of the Theravada School of Buddhism, stressing the doctrinal and metaphysical aspects more than anything else. Although Buddhism in Burma at this time was predominantly Theravada and was greatly influenced by the emergence of the Theravada Buddhist centre at Kanchipuram under the commentator Dhammapala, evidence is also found that Mahayanism, which probably came from eastern India, also existed there.

Kings of the Pyu dynasty and others bore the Indian titles of Varman and Vikrama: for instance, Surya Vikrama (died in 688), Hari Vikrama (654–695), and Jayacandra Varman. Their capital, Sri Ksetra, was built according to Indian cosmological beliefs, like an image of Indra's city Sudarsana—also called Amaravati—on the summit of Mount Meru, with thirty-two main gates and a golden palace in its centre. The division of the Pyu kingdom into thirty-two provinces with the king presiding over them would even suggest that the entire layout of the empire was organized as a replica of the heavenly realm of Indra. The Pyu country was mentioned by the Chinese scholars, Hsüan-tsang and I-tsing, in the seventh century as a Buddhist kingdom. The Chinese chronicles of the T'ang period provide further evidence of the flourishing state of Buddhism in the Pyu kingdom.

In addition to various Buddhist objects, images of Vishnu, Siva, Ganesa, Brahma, and other Hindu gods have been found at Hmawza, Mergui, and over a wide area of Burma. In Prome, ruined stupas and other objects going back to the sixth century have been discovered. One of the stupas is a majestic structure rising from five superimposed terraces. The stone figure sculptures attached to these temples and the terracotta votive tablets recovered from the debris of their relic chambers reveal influences not only of the contemporary Pallava art of South India, but also of the Gupta style of the north.

The principal southern Indianized neighbours of the Pyu were the two Mon kingdoms of Pegu (Hamsavati) and Thaton (Suddhammavati), where Hinduism and Buddhism flourished side by side. Sometime before the eleventh century Thaton became a very important centre of Buddhism. There is also some evidence of a Hindu dynasty, Sri Dharmara-janujavamsa, ruling Arakan from 600 to 1000.[23]

Earlier, to the north of Prome, a debased form of Tantric Buddhism seems to have prevailed: the Ari cult amongst the Mrammas, a Tibeto-Dravidian tribe who were a somewhat uncouth people and had set up a kingdom with its capital at Pagan. In 1044, Anawarhta (Aniruddha) ascended the throne of Pagan, and thus began a new and distinguished era in Burmese history. Our knowledge of the Burmese and their culture from the eleventh century onwards is more reliable and unbroken.[24] Anawarhta openly endeavoured to destroy the Ari cult, and himself embraced Theravada Buddhism from a Mon monk, Shin Arhan (Dharmadarsi). A patron of art and culture, he built numerous temples and monasteries with the zeal of a new convert. He began work on the Shwe Dagon (or Shwe Zigon) Pagoda which was completed during the reign of his son, Kyanzittha (1084–1113), and he imported complete copies of the Tripitaka from Ceylon. In 1057 he even declared war on the Thaton Mon king, Manuha, who had refused to give him canonical texts. Manuha was defeated, and Anawarhta returned with thirty-two white elephants laden with sacred texts, Buddhist relics, and monks.

The results of the sack of Thaton were of great importance for religion and art in Burma. From now onwards Theravada Buddhism became the principal religion of the state, with Pali as the language of the scriptures. Burmese law came to be based on the *Manusmriti* as interpreted and modified by Buddhist teachers. The Burmese adopted the Mon alphabet, and the great influx of craftsmen from Thaton to Pagan ushered in an era of religious and educational reform which lasted for over two centuries.

There were many features of Hinduism in the prevalent form of Buddhism at Thaton, including the place of prominence given to Hindu deities in temples. This led G. E. Harvey to call it a form of Buddhism which was largely Hindu in spirit. The artists from Thaton influenced the building of temples in the Pagan kingdom. In the Bidgat Tail Library built in the twelfth century to house scriptures from Thaton, ten Hindu avataras are reproduced with the Buddha as the ninth, and the building is dedicated to Vishnu.

During the twenty-eight years of his reign, Kyanzittha carried on the work of his father. He built numerous temples and stupas, including the great Ananda Temple, and restored the famous Mahabodhi Temple at Bodhgaya in Bihar, where the Buddha had attained enlightenment. Since Buddhism was declining in India at the time, this restoration was most opportune. By the end of the eleventh century, the Pala dynasty of eastern India, under whose rule of three hundred and fifty years both Buddhist and Hindu art had flourished, and the Nalanda University had risen to great fame, was drawing to an end.

The Ananda Temple at Pagan with its glittering gilt spire is one of the most beautiful sights in Burma. On the outside there are fifteen hundred plaques illustrating the Jataka tales, each with an inscription in Pali or Mon, and inside the aisles there are eighty niches with sculptures of the early life of the Buddha. These were made by Indian artists or by artists following Indian styles and models, and with Indian inspiration. Kyanzittha, whose mother was Indian, patronized Hinduism as well and had many Brahmans amongst his advisers. Kyanzittha's reign is regarded as the most creative age in the history of Burma. After Kyanzittha's death, his son, Alaungsithu, came to the throne. He, too, was a great temple builder—and built the temple of Thatbyinnyu at Pagan, which, according to Harvey, dominates all others in majesty of line, and which was built after the model of contemporary temples in North India.

In the last quarter of the twelfth century, a significant episode occurred in the history of Buddhism in Burma when it was split by the establishment of a Ceylonese order of monks by Capata. From then on, Ceylonese Buddhism was the chief influence on the religion of Burma. Ceylon at that time had witnessed a revival of Theravada Buddhism under Parakrama Bahu I, and for the next four centuries was looked upon with the utmost veneration by other Theravada Buddhist countries such as Thailand, Burma, and Cambodia. During these centuries Indian trade with Burma had been as brisk as ever. An inscription at Pagan alludes to a Vishnu temple built by Nanadesi merchants and to a gift made to the temple in the thirteenth century by some Malabari merchants.

Whilst Buddhism was declining in India, many Buddhist monks crossed over to Burma, taking Pala art and Tantric Buddhism with them. But this Burmese link with India was weakened when the Turki–Afghan rulers took over northern India. Burma herself was not in a very stable condition. In 1287 Pagan fell to Mongol invaders, and Burma lapsed into a state of political disintegration, prolonged anarchy, and confusion. Buddhism suffered in the general decline. The Sangha split up into sects, and although pagodas were built, none of them could rival even the lesser temples of Pagan. This condition lasted until the second half of the fifteenth century when Dhaddacedi ascended the throne; a more stable kingdom was set up, and religious reforms were introduced, restoring the Sangha to its former prestige and power. From now onwards, Buddhism was firmly entrenched in Burmese society and although there were schisms on trivial matters, its ascendancy has never been questioned.

The rulers of the later dynasties, such as the Toungoo (1531–1752) and the Alaungpaya (1753–1886), were devout Buddhists, and Buddhism and its culture continued to grow in Burma, making notable contributions to world Buddhism. During the reign of Mindon, a remarkable statesman who ruled his country most wisely at a critical period when British pressure on Upper Burma was continually mounting, Buddhism made further progress in Burma. Under Mindon's patronage, religious studies were pursued with increasing vigour and zeal, and some of the best works of Burmese Buddhism were produced. Emulating the tradition of Asoka, Mindon summoned the Fifth Buddhist Council to make a redaction of the Tripitaka. The Council met at Mandalay from 1868 to 1871 under the direction of the King himself, and the text adopted was incised on 729 stone slabs, which are still carefully preserved. This text formed the basis of the revision of the Tripitaka carried out under the auspices of the Sixth Buddhist Council held in Rangoon during 1954–1956.

Buddhism not only dominated the cultural life of the people but played a significant role, at times decisive, in the political history of Burma. It helped to unify the peoples of Burma by bringing the Mons, the Burmese, and the Shans together into one national religion, culture, and consciousness. It encouraged the growth of art, education, literature, and social and cultural life. Although Burmese culture absorbed other influences, Buddhism represents the crystallization of Burmese national tradition. It inaugurated a society in Burma based on equality of social standards; few societies enjoy such democratic social life as does Burma.

Thailand

The story of Siam, or Thailand as it is now called, is unique in that although the country has a long history, the Thais, who dominate it today, have a common history of only about seven centuries. The Thais came to Siam in the thirteenth century, having been driven out of their former home in southwestern China by the military campaigns of Kublai Khan. They had founded in Yunnan around the seventh century a powerful kingdom, Nanchao, which played an important role in the history of Southeast Asia until their expulsion.[25]

Nanchao was in close proximity to the Indianized Pyu kingdom, and lay on a route between India and China at a time when intercourse between these two countries was active. Hence, it had been exposed to Indian culture for centuries.[26] Buddhism was popular in Nanchao. Two bells with Buddhist inscriptions in Chinese and Sanskrit that have been dated about the eleventh century have been found there. Brahman advisers to the government are referred to in their folklore.

There were Indian settlements in Nanchao. The most important Thai kingdom in Yunnan was Gandhara; one portion of it was also called Videharajya.[27] Their capital was known as Mithila, and the king, entitled "Maharaja," was reputedly descended from Asoka. The people of Nanchao used an alphabet of Indian origin, and, according to a local legend, Avalokitesvara came from India and converted the people to Buddhism. Names of places and symbols in Yunnan were associated with Buddhism: for example, the sacred hill Gridhra-kuta, the Bodhi Tree, and the Pippala Cave. According to a tenth-century Chinese traveller, there was even a local tradition asserting that the Buddha attained enlightenment in Yunnan. Writing in the thirteenth century, Rashiduddin not only calls the country Gandhara, but asserts that its people came from India and China.[28] The Pali chronicles and the Chinese annals also endorse the view that the Thais, although ethnologically related to the Chinese, had acquired more Indian culture than Chinese before they were forced out of their homeland. In northern Siam, where they settled first and which was close to southern China, there is no trace of Chinese influence either in customs, dress, literature, art, or religion.

Even before the Mongol incursions, some of the Thais had begun to move out of their state and slowly penetrate the adjoining areas to the south and west, such as the Pyu kingdom, the Shan states, and the Sip-Song Panna, a no-man's land to the northeast of Siam. According to the standard Siamese history of North Siam, the *Pongsawadan Yonaka,* the first Thai settlement of any importance was made in 860 when a Thai prince named Brahma crossed the Mekong and founded a principality at Chai Praka in the district of Cheingrai, in far northern Siam.[29] In 1215 the Thais founded the principality of Mogaung to the north of Bhamo, and eight years later, that of Mone (or Muong Nai). It was, however, after the conquest of their kingdom by the Mongols in 1253, that their mass migration from Nanchao commenced.

By the time these Indianized Thai people reached Siam, the country had been in close cultural contact with India for more than a thousand years. Whilst there is archaeological evidence indicating Indian influence on early Siamese culture, specific references to Siam in the ancient literature of India are rare. Frequent references to Suvarnabhumi, however, do suggest that the ancient Indians were familiar with the Menam Valley. The Siamese scholar, Prince Damrong, whose researches were based on Siamese annals and inscriptions as well as on Chinese chronicles, has even suggested that Suvarnabhumi was actually in southern Siam, near the mouth of the Menam Chao Phya. Coedès is also of the opinion that this region with its many toponyms like Supan,

Kanburi, U Thong, all meaning gold or the land of gold, perhaps had a better claim than Burma to represent Suvarnabhumi.

Thailand comprises four geographically distinct areas—the northern region embracing the circle of Bayab, the central region formed by the valley of the Menam River, the northeastern plateau region, and the southern peninsular region. The earliest inhabitants of Siam were the Lavas—some of whom still survive in the northern hill ranges— and the Mon-khmer, who stretched from present-day Cambodia through the Menam Valley and the Malay country as far as Pegu. All these regions were deeply influenced by Indian culture. The north felt the impact for the first time when it was conquered by the Mons of central Siam in the eighth century and it seems likely that central Siam may have come into direct contact with Amaravati even before the Mons arrived from Lower Burma, as is suggested by the archaeological finds at Pong Tuk and Phra Pathom (or Nagarama Pathama). The Buddhist symbol, the *dharmacakra,* has been found amongst the relics at Phra Pathom which suggests that Buddhism possibly had reached Siam even before the Christian era, because the dharmacakra belongs to a very early period of Indian art, when the Buddha was not represented in human form but only by symbols. The specimen found at Phra Pathom may not be so old, but it is not later than the first or second century.

The northeastern area had come under the influence of the Hindu kingdom of Funan at a very early period. Later, when northeastern Siam fell to the Khmers, its Indian character was further strengthened. The southern part of Siam, however, was most directly and continuously in contact with India. Large numbers of Indian merchants, settlers, and teachers came to southern Siam in successive waves either directly from India or through Burma. Southern Siam is full of remains of Indian culture, most prominent of which is the city of Nakhon Srithammarat.

The traffic along the trade routes between India and Siam varied from time to time. It seems that the earliest Indian immigrants to Siam came by sea from the Amaravati region. Having landed at Martaban, they proceeded towards the south through the Three Pagoda Pass into southern central Siam. Later, during the Gupta period, when the capital was at Pataliputra, the routes from the ports in Bengal, such as Tamralipti, were busier. Southeast Asian travellers proceeded either to Martaban or to the Burmese ports of Akyab and Arakan, and thence overland to Siam via Thaton. During the period of Pallava ascendancy in South India, the route from Kanchi either straight to Mergui and Tenasserim, or to Takuapa in the Siamese part of the Malay Peninsula, was commonly used. In addition, there was the sea route around the island of Singapore up to the Gulf of Siam where Bangkok stands today; although long, this route was often used.

Numerous excavations have yielded extensive evidence of Indianization and some remarkable pieces of art. Because Siam increasingly assimilated Indian art and culture into a local pattern, relics of pure Indian descent are more ancient than those reflecting local influence.

The most ancient objects of culture excavated in Siam in 1927 at Pong Tuk and Phra Pathom are all relics of Indian culture. Pong Tuk, situated less than thirty miles west of Bangkok on the Mekong River very close to Kanburi, was on the route to the Three Pagoda Pass leading to Martaban, and was thus in direct contact with Amaravati. Indian settlements flourished on this site for several centuries. Excavations have revealed a variety of objects, including the remains of a temple sanctuary and other buildings, a small statue of the standing Buddha and, curiously, a Graeco-Roman lamp of Pompeian style. The discovery of this lamp in Siam has been regarded as indicative of collaboration between Indian and Greek navigators east of India. Coedès considers the lamp to be of Mediterranean origin, not a copy made in Asia, and places it in the second century.[30] This date is also confirmed by the small bronze statue of the Buddha in the Amaravati style of the second century. In addition, other objects, such as votive tablets of the Bodhgaya style and bronze Buddha images, show Gupta influence and could not be later than the sixth century. Since no Khmer or Thai images or objects have been found on this site, and all the relics are Buddhist, it is suggested that a centre of Buddhist worship existed at Pong Tuk from early in the Christian era up to the sixth or seventh century. Buddhism may well have come even earlier if the representation of the Buddha by the dharmacakra found at Phra Pathom is taken into consideration. The very early inhabitants of western Siam must have principally remained Buddhist for a long time, for there are no early Hindu relics found in the area. However, Indian cultural influence continued to grow throughout; first through its contact with Amaravati in South India, and later with neighbouring Dvaravati in the Menam Valley, an Indianized kingdom of Siam of which Pong Tuk may well have been a part. Hsüan-tsang mentions that Tu-ho-lo-po-ti (Dvaravati) was a flourishing kingdom between Sri Ksetra (Pyu) in Burma and Isanapura (Khmer-lang) in Cambodia.

Situated in central Siam, Dvaravati was founded by the Mons or Talaings from Lower Burma in the second or third century. It became prominent after the decline of Funan. By the seventh century Dvaravati had become important enough to dispatch embassies to China and extend her frontiers from the borders of Cambodia to the Bay of Bengal. This kingdom flourished until the rulers of Kambuja extended their supremacy over the Lower Menam Valley in the tenth century. The bronze Buddhas of Amaravati style, Gupta images from the Ganges Valley, ruins of stupas and monasteries, and tablets bearing Buddhist beliefs written in Pallava script have been found there. The art of Dvaravati shows clear Gupta affiliations. The Hindu and Buddhist images of Vishnu, Siva, and the Buddha appear to reflect the art of Sarnath, Mathura, and Ajanta. Even after the Thais had broken the Mon power and set up their ascendancy, Dvaravati retained something of its Hindu character. Under the Thais the city came to be known as Ayuthia, which remained the Thai capital until it was captured and destroyed by the Burmese in 1757.

The archaeological and sculptural remains belonging to the succeeding period are somewhat scanty; they nevertheless point out that during the eighth and ninth centuries the people of central Siam practiced Theravada Buddhism, and that their art was influenced by Gupta art. As they were politically a part of Kambuja (Cambodia) during this period, it seems they were further influenced by Hinduism, of which many traces are found.

One of the oldest sites in central Siam, eighty miles north of Bangkok, is Lopburi (Lavo), a minor city at present but for centuries a centre of Mon-Indian culture which later became the capital of the central Siamese province of the Kambuja Kingdom in 1002. Here are ancient monuments, including the temple of Maha-tat, and standing images of the Buddha, one of which bears a Sanskrit inscription.

One of the most remarkable sites in the centre of Siam, is Srideb (Crip-tep), where statues of Hindu deities bearing Sanskrit inscriptions of the fifth or sixth century have been discovered. The art of Srideb is of excellent quality and provides a link between Indian art and the art of Indochina. Quaritch Wales considered Srideb the oldest known Hindu temple in Indochina. Le May, however, has some misgivings, not because of its architectural conception, which is definitely Hindu, but because of its laterite base.

In peninsular Siam, as well as in Malaya, evidence of the existence of hitherto unsuspected Hindu states and settlements has recently come to light, and some Buddhist and Hindu images have been excavated. Present knowledge is based on archaeological finds and Chinese notices, which do not easily lend themselves to interpretation. Of the several states in this region mentioned by Chinese annals, one was Tambralingo with its capital at Ligor, modern Nakhon Srithammarat. A Sanskrit inscription of not later than the sixth century has been found here. As the Pali *Niddesa* refers to this kingdom, it must have been flourishing in the second century. Although it was a strong Buddhist centre many Hindu relics have been unearthed here. Three sanctuaries—the Bot Prahm with numerous Sivalingas, the San Pra Isuon containing bronze statues of Siva, Parvati, and Ganesh, and the Na Pra Narai with its renowned statues of Vishnu—are amongst the excavations made at this site. The political history of this state is obscure, but the ambitions of one of its princes initiated an era of Indian culture which has been designated the Cambodian period of Siam.

According to the *Liang Shu*, there possibly existed in the region in the first or second century a Hindu state, Lang-ya-hsiu, which sent several embassies to China. This may have been the Lankasuka of the Malay and Javanese chronicles, located on the east coast of the Malay Peninsula, south of Ligor.[31]

The Isthmus of Kra, in addition to Nakhon Srithammarat, has produced a rich harvest of archaeological finds. The Vat Phra That at Chaiya of the Sri Vijaya period is constructed according to the classical Indian architectural principles of *silpa-sastra*. An exquisite black bust of Lokesvara, inspired by Pala art, has been found in this vicinity.

Towards the end of the tenth century, Lopburi was seized from the reigning Mon king by a prince from Nakhon Srithammarat, thus bringing the whole of central and southern Siam under one authority. In 1002, his son, Suryavarman I, captured the throne of Kambuja at Angkor during a civil war. Although he came from southern Siam, his dynasty claimed kinship with the Khmers, and Suryavarman claimed the Khmer kingdom as his right. Thus central and southern Siam were united with Kambuja under the Khmer Kingdom of which northeastern Siam was already a part.

The Khmers or Cambodians had begun to penetrate the northeastern part of Siam from the seventh century, but it was not until Khmer ascendancy had been established that Siam felt the full impact of Khmer culture. Both regions belonged to the same Indianized culture. The Khmers patronized both Buddhism and Hinduism, leaning a little more to one or the other at different times. Whilst their temples at Panom Rung and Muang Tam are clearly Hindu in character, one of the scenes portrayed on a large square stele is of a Buddhist character which resembles reliefs from Bharhut and Sanchi.

Whilst the Khmers were ruling northeastern and central Siam, the Thais began to penetrate the land. They settled first in the north as a dependent state of the court at Angkor. Their migrations, unimportant at first, became formidable by the middle of the thirteenth century. One of their attacks led to the foundation of the Shan states in Upper Burma, and in 1229 the kingdom of Sukhotai was founded. The rise of Thai power is associated with Rama Kamheng (or Gamhen), who succeeded to the throne about 1276. During his reign the Thai kingdom was extended to include both Pegu and Nakhon Srithammarat, and political relations with China were opened up. A patron of Buddhism, Rama Kamheng was well versed in both the Tripitaka and Hindu ritual and astrology. He built a school for Hindu and Buddhist priests, and dispatched a mission to Ceylon to fetch Buddhist relics and texts. Buddhism prospered in Sukhotai, and it received impetus from Ceylon when the Thai king persuaded the Ceylonese monk, Mahasami Sangharaj, to come to Siam. Rama Kamheng was an admirer of Parakrama Bahu, the king of Ceylon, and sought to emulate him. Under Kamheng's influence, Buddhism and Pali literature were firmly established in Sukhotai and even the neighbouring Hindu kingdoms came more and more into the Buddhist orbit. Hinduism then declined, leaving its mark only on ceremonies and customs. The Sukhotai School of Buddhism is often characterized as the blending of the Chiengsen School, which may have come from China, and the Theravada School of Ceylon. In Sukhotai's many temples and remarkable bronze standing Buddha images can be seen the beginnings of Thai art, which is a fusion of the art of the Khmers and the legacy which the Thais brought with them from the north.

By the middle of the fourteenth century, Sukhotai declined and the centre of power moved to Ayuthia. A Thai prince crowned himself king in 1350 under the title of Ramadhipati, and he is traditionally regarded as the first king of Thailand. Religious contact with Ceylon continued and during the Ayuthia period, particularly the fifteenth century, Buddhist activity greatly increased under the influence of Sinhalese Buddhism. Politically, it was a period of wars with Burma on one side and Cambodia on the other. The Khmer kingdom was destroyed by the Thais in the fifteenth century, reducing it to Siamese vassalage; the Siamese captured Angkor three times, and finally annexed it in 1460. The Siamese victory over Angkor in 1431 led to an influx of Cambodian scholars and priests. The Siamese king, taking advantage of Cambodian scholars and statesmen, reorganized the state administration and remodelled the court ceremonials on Cambodian lines, a reform that survives even today.

The Thais were ethnologically Chinese and the chronicles of the

Sui dynasty give details of the court life at Nanchao, which resembled that of the Chinese. Many words are common to both Thai and Chinese; for instance, most of the Siamese numerals are of Chinese origin. The only obvious Chinese influence on Siam today lies in architecture, particularly the tiers of roofs of Siamese temples. Very little else of Thai culture can be traced to China. In fact, it appears that even when they arrived in Siam, the Thais had not absorbed much Chinese culture. For in northern Siam, where they settled first and which was close to southern China, there is no trace of Chinese influence in customs, art, literature, or thought. Chinese culture, without the medium of Buddhism, has not generally attracted non-Chinese peoples, even in China's immediate neighbourhood. The Thais do not appear to have been very culturally advanced at the time they came to Siam. When they found themselves face to face with the highly advanced kingdom of Cambodia, they were simply awe-stricken and fascinated.

It is scarcely surprising that the Thais took to the prevalent form of Mon-Khmer culture enthusiastically and in time made notable contributions of their own to it. Today Thailand is replete with temples. The present-day capital, Bangkok, alone has many famous temples, some of which are amongst the most impressive monuments in the whole of Asia; for example the Wat Phra Keo, the temple of the Emerald Buddha, next door to the royal palace. The main object of worship in this temple is a single-stone jasper image of the Buddha which is dated to a very ancient period, and around which numerous legends have grown. The image was first discovered in 1436 at Chiengrai in northern Siam. Wall paintings, bas-reliefs, and other pieces of sculptural art enhance the artistic beauty of the temple.

Although Thailand is predominantly Buddhist, there are traces of Hindu influence, visible mostly in the court ceremonials. The kings of Sukhotai recruited their court Brahmans from Cambodia and adopted much of the Cambodian Hindu court ritual. Later, during the Ayuthia period when Hinduism in Cambodia had fallen into decline, Brahmans were obtained from southern Siam. Until recently, the court Brahmans cast horoscopes, consulted omens, and performed worship of both Hindu and Buddhist deities. Ceremonies of coronation, tonsure, cremation, and lesser rites connected with agriculture were developed by the Brahmans. The Siamese call their coronation by its ancient Sanskrit designation, the *rajabhiseka*. The entire complex of coronation ceremonies, such as *homa* (sacrifices to Fire), purificatory rites, ablutions, anointment, and the actual coronation, are closely modelled on Hindu rituals, and are presided over by the *Brah Maha Raja Guru*. The Buddha, as well as the chief Hindu deities, are represented in these ceremonies. The tonsure ceremony in Siam is a rite of initiation of youths, corresponding to the Hindu *Cudakarma Mangala,* which is a very important Hindu *Samskara.* Cremation, an old vedic rite, is the only means of disposal of the remains of deceased royalty in Siam, and the chief method of disposing of all their dead. The people of Thailand take these ancient ceremonies very seriously, which partly explains why state ceremonies are still conducted by Brahmans.

There are some eight families of court Brahmans in Thailand who claim that their ancestors came originally from the sacred Indian city of Varanasi. As no Brahman women appear to have come with them, they intermarried with local people. Today they speak only Siamese, and have a very limited and corrupt knowledge of Sanskrit. Amongst their texts, which are mostly mantras, they have a Tamil hymn written in an Indian character.

Some of the domestic ceremonies performed in Siam are of Hindu origin. The royal title is Rama, a Hindu *avatara,* and the royal temple at Bangkok contains illustrations from the *Ramayana.* Hindu festivals, such as Dashahara, commemorating the victory of Rama over the demon king Ravana, are still observed in Thailand. In Chi Mai *Sankranti* (called *Songhurant*) is still observed as the New Year's Day. The Thais, like the Hindus, still believe in Vishnu or Narayana (Phra Narain), and Mahadeva or Siva, and dislike the asuras (*asuns*) as the enemies of the devas.

The Siamese lent their own ideas to Buddhist sculpture. This led to the development of the typical Siamese image of Buddha, in the form of a slender figure with flame-crowned oval face wearing a strange all-pervasive smile, and to the distinctive pagoda style which is a unique combination of Indian inspiration and Chinese architecture.

It is not always possible to separate the Indian influence in Thai language and literature from the Siamese genius. The Siamese alphabet, consisting of forty-four consonants and thirty-two vowels, is derived directly from the Kambuja alphabet which, in turn, owes its origin to the alphabet of the inscriptions of southern India during the sixth and eighth centuries. Numerous Thai words are taken directly from Sanskrit: for instance, *akas, rath, maha, racha* (raja), *cakra, sathani* (sthan). The pronunciation of the language is, of course, very different.

Siamese fiction and mythological literature have drawn freely upon Indian stories. Their religious literature is almost wholly Buddhist. Famous Indian works, such as the *Ramayana,* the *Mahabharata,* and the *Sakuntala* have formed the basis of some of the outstanding Siamese literature. The *Ramayana*, known in Siam as the *Ramakien* (or *Ramakirti*), is regarded as a Siamese classic. Knowledge of this work is as essential for a cultured Siamese as Homer used to be for an European. The characters of Rama and Sita are known everywhere by all classes of people. The epic and Puranic literature of India constituted the principal source of inspiration not only for Siam but for the whole of Southeast Asia. It provided the themes for classical theatre, shadow theatre, and marionette shows.

Indian influence is clearly seen on Siamese dance, drama, and music. Many of the themes of Siam's various dance-dramas (*lakhon-ram*) are drawn from Indian mythology: for example, the story of Savitri and Satyavan. Many Thai musical instruments closely resemble those of India. Unlike India, dancing is an integral part of the social life of Thailand, and the ancient plays and tales from Indian epics, which are almost dissociated from the artistic world of India, are continually staged in Thailand. The Siamese dance is generally performed in a very slow and steady motion, as it was done in ancient days in the presence of royalty.

The Siamese legal system is directly descended from the *Manusmriti*. The Hindu *Dharmasastras* provided the framework for Siamese justice. The earliest available legal corpus dates from 1805, but many of the earlier collections of manuscripts were destroyed when Ayuthia, the capital of Siam at the time, was sacked by the Burmese. The first volume of this work is justifiably entitled the *Phra Dharmasastra*.

Indochina

Indochina is divided into several interlinked regions with distinctive characteristics, and her states throughout the course of history have been subjected to periodic boundary changes and foreign interference and domination. These factors have rendered her culture complex, rich, and varied, giving her the quality of diversity in uniformity.

In the north is the delta of Tonkin (northern Vietnam) which had direct sea contact with India and played a significant role in transmitting Buddhism to China. South of Tonkin, divided by an almost impenetrable chain of mountains, is Annam (southern Vietnam), where the Dong-son culture developed, followed by one of the earliest and most brilliant Southeast Asian civilizations, Champa. West of Tonkin lies Laos, south of which is Cambodia. Both these countries have been important areas of contact between Indian and Chinese culture.

Because of the almost insurmountable geographical barriers, Indochina has been isolated from the mass of the Asian continent. The only overland route to India lay through Burma over the difficult mountains of Assam. The journey over the Bhamo Pass to China was also tedious. Travelling up the rivers meant reaching the inhospitable wilderness of Yunnan and Szechwan. However, the sea routes with both India and China were open and carried most of the traffic.[32]

Our knowledge of the history of Indochina, before the arrival first of the Chinese and then of the Indians around the beginning of the Christian era, is very fragmentary. The Dong-son culture flourished mainly along the coastal belt of Annam, developing remarkably between the fifth and second centuries B.C. This was the period when China was vigorously expanding her frontiers, and had come to dominate Tonkin. Consequently, China influenced the art and culture of Dong-son, especially on the eve of the Christian era. It was, however, not until Indian culture entered the scene, that Indochinese civilization got a real start and gathered momentum.

Indian and Chinese cultures have met in other areas but not on such a large scale as in Indochina, where they interacted with a vigorous local culture. Whilst China ruled over Tonkin for long periods, India only touched on the southern coasts of Indochina and vanished from the scene in about the fifth century when her seafaring activity practically came to an end. But in that short space of time the peoples of Indochina were so inspired by Indian culture that they voluntarily accepted it and in turn created new civilizations of profound originality: "China dominated, while India scattered the seed, and between them they were to shape the double aspect of Indo-China."[33]

The oldest and most important of the Indianized states was Funan occupying the lower valley of the Mekong, roughly corresponding to modern Cambodia and South Vietnam.[34] Funan was possibly the result of a confederation of tribes. Finot suggests that Funan is a Chinese variation of the old Khmer word *bnam* (meaning mountain), *phnom* in modern Khmer. The Chinese texts on Funan were first collected and properly interpreted by Pelliot, and Coedès, as in many other sections of Indochinese archaeology, initiated the serious interpretation of the archaeological evidence. Precise information concerning the people of Funan and their civilization is still lacking. The discovery of Indian objects together with objects of advanced Dong-son style suggests very early Indian contact. However, it is generally agreed that civilization began with the arrival of Indian traders. Funan was rich in all that Indian merchants were looking for and, in addition, was an ideal halfway house on the sea journey to China.

A Chinese writer, Kang Tai, who visited Funan in the middle of the third century—the period of the oldest of four Sanskrit inscriptions found in that country—reports that an Indian Brahman, Huen-Chen of Ho-fu, led by a dream, landed in Funan, married a local princess, Lien-Ye, and founded the kingdom in the first century. A variation of this story is found in the Cambodian annals. This literary tradition is confirmed by a seventh-century inscription from Champa[35] wherein the Indian is identified as Kaundinya of the Somavamsa. Under Kaundinya's successors, Funan's domination spread over most of the neighbouring lands by the third century, and diplomatic contacts were established with India and China; one of Funan's missions visited India in the third century. It is said that the direct descendants of Kaundinya were overthrown about 200 by the commander of the troops, Fan-cheman, who founded the political greatness of Funan.

Until the fifth century the history of Funan is fragmentary, but enough is known to suggest its increasing Indianization. About 357, for instance, it is known that an Indian was ruling Funan. Local Sanskrit inscriptions, supported by the *History of the Liang Dynasty* which provides precise dates and facts, tell of the arrival of another Indian Brahman, Kaundinya-Jayavarman, who ruled over Funan between 478 and 514.[36] With the assistance of an Indian monk, Nagasena, who carried statues of the Buddha and other gifts to the Chinese emperor, he cultivated good relations with China, seeking Chinese help to defeat the neighbouring Chenla. Although the kings of Funan professed Saiva Hinduism, Nagasena reported to the Chinese emperor that both Hinduism and Buddhism were flourishing in Funan. The Funanese monks were well versed in Sanskrit and some of them went to China and translated Buddhist texts into Chinese.

Rudravarman, the son of Jayavarman, ascended the throne in 514 and ruled for the next twenty-five years. During his reign he sent at least six embassies to China. He was an ardent devotee of Vishnu, and the last great king of Funan. He was responsible for the first great work of sculpture preserved in Indochina. After a prolonged struggle, Funan was conquered by the neighbouring Indianized state of Chenla.

The country was wealthy, and its trade, stretching from Rome to China, was brisk. Even the Chinese were full of praise for Funan's material prosperity. According to them the country was overflowing with gold, silver, pearls, and spices. Considering that the Indians had already developed techniques of irrigation and land reclamation, it is possible that they were responsible for the agricultural prosperity of the land.

Not much of the art of Funan has survived. The Funanese archaeological site, Oc-eo, has produced various important objects, including a gold medallion, dated 152, bearing the effigy of Antoninus Pius. The Roman medallion was found with various Hindu objects, notably intaglios and seals with Sanskrit inscriptions of the same and following periods. The medallion is striking evidence of the close Indo-Roman trade relations, which were one cause of Indian exploration of Southeast Asia.

Influence of Gupta or post-Gupta architecture is found in many Funanese buildings, and numerous statues of the Buddha and Hindu gods, such as Vishnu and Siva, gold ornaments, tin amulets with symbols of Vishnu and Siva, and merchant's seals with inscriptions in Sanskrit, have been excavated from sites in Funan. Some of these pieces were directly imported from India and others were copied locally from Indian models. A Buddha head discovered at Ba-the, clearly of Gandhara inspiration, is perhaps the oldest Indian object. The images of Harihara and Ardhanarisvara, found in southern Funan and now preserved in the museum at Phnom Penh, are brilliant examples of sculptural art, both in conception and execution.

Funan inscriptions are in pure, flawless Sanskrit. Their content shows that Indian religion, philosophy, and mythology were widely understood, and that the secular knowledge of India, such as phonetics (sabda), logic (nyaya), and political theory (arthasastra), were studied in Funan.

Champa, on the coast of Annam, was another Indianized state, about which more information is available. It constantly clashed with the nearby Chinese colonies established in Tonkin during the Han period, and hence Chinese historians frequently refer to Champa. The kingdom (called Lin-yi) is first mentioned in 190–193. The name Champa is clearly Indian whether it was named after the capital of the Anga country in the lower Ganges Valley, or as Sastri suggests, after the Cola capital of the same name.[37] The Chams were probably of the same Indonesian stock as the founders of the Dong-son culture further to the north.

Situated on the main sea routes from India and Java to China, and at the foot of spice-bearing mountains, Champa soon attracted the attention of Indian traders, and played a significant role in spreading Indian culture in eastern Asia. Sri Mara was the first Hindu king of Champa, and established his dynasty about 200 over an extensive area, including Tonkin and part of northern Annam. Champa maintained close relations with Funan, a fact which must have been largely responsible for the penetration of Indian influence there. Since the early history of Champa is reconstructed from Chinese sources, we have the Chinese derivation of the names of Champa kings. They all begin with *Fan,* such as Fan-hiong and Fan-wen, which is possibly a corruption of the common Indian royal suffix, *Varman.* Fan-wen, who had expanded the frontiers of his empire by a vigorous, aggressive policy, died in 349. His grandson, Fan-hu-ta, was probably the king referred to in the Sanskrit inscriptions as Bhadravarman. He was a noted commander and scholar. He dedicated a temple to Siva at Mison which was called Bhadresvarasvami and became the centre of royal worship in later centuries. It is said that Bhadravarman abdicated his throne to spend his last days on the banks of the Ganges.

Champa passed through various dynasties, and war with China continued intermittently, particularly during the third and fourth centuries. This was a period of political unrest in China, which probably gave Champa the opportunity to expand into Chinese territory. However, once China was unified under the Sui dynasty towards the end of the sixth century, Champa was attacked and its power broken by the Chinese emperor. The Chinese took back with them the golden tablets of eighteen kings of Champa and 1350 Buddhist works. Champa continued as a tributary state of China, but it never recovered its old power.

Recent excavations in Tra-Kieu, the most ancient capital of Champa, have revealed ample evidence of Indian influence in the form of Sivaite and Vaisnavite shrines and bas-reliefs. The earliest inscription found in the region and possibly the whole of Southeast Asia, is the Vo-canh inscription written in a South Indian script and dating from the second or third century. The most ancient bronze statue found in Champa is that of the Buddha of Dongduong (Quang-nam) which is one of the most beautiful specimens of Amaravati art; even a principality in that area was called Amaravati. Inscriptions of Bhadravarman, both in Sanskrit and Cham, have been found; they belong to about 350 and are the earliest inscriptions found in Champa proper. This bronze Buddha image of the Amaravati School indicates that Buddhism had obtained a footing in the country by the third century, and in 605 the Chinese captured more than thirteen hundred Buddhist monks. I-tsing also alludes to the prevalence of Buddhism in Champa. Mahayana Buddhism was possibly most generally practiced, as it was occasionally patronized by the Kings.

During this period, remarkable sculptures and original brick temples were created which are notable for their decoration and ornamentation. The doorways and pillars are adorned with an incredibly intricate stone foliation of leaves, buds and flowers, inset with medallions of anchorites and celestial dancers. Three groups of temples, Mi-song, Po-nagar, and Dongduong, are very famous. In the days of their splendour the Chams were Sivaites, and Siva, his Sakti, and his two sons, Ganesa and Skanda, were prominent amongst the gods worshipped. Champa statues followed Gupta models, not only in subject matter but also in technique, which was simple, dignified, and majestic. Sanskrit inscriptions, one of which carries a date of the Saka era, have also been found.

The beginnings of Chenla, the Indianized kingdom that demolished Funan and later blossomed into the Khmer Empire, are obscure. Chenla is the name of the Kingdom as found in the Chinese texts, but the derivation of the name is not known. Chenla was certainly in existence by the end of the sixth century, and was beginning to emerge in the northeastern parts of Cambodia along the middle reaches of the Mekong whilst Funan was flourishing. It is possible that until the end of the fifth century Chenla was confined to the tableland watered by the Semun, whilst the Bassac region was dominated by the Chams. It was a vassal state of Funan and had its capital at Sreshthapura, near Vat Phu.

Chenla is claimed to have been the original home of the Kambuja people. The Kambuja royalty, however, traced its descent from rishi Kambu Svayambhuva, the king of Aryadesa (India) and the *apsara* Mera, which is another version of the recurrent motif of foundation myths of royal families in South India. The two earliest known kings are Srutavarman and his son Sreshthavarman, who secured Chenla's freedom from Funan. About the middle of the sixth century, when the last king of Funan, Rudravarman, died, the king of Chenla, Bhavavarman—possibly a grandson of Rudravarman of Funan—undertook to conquer Funan with the help of his brother Chitrasena. Their partial conquest of Funan made Bhavavarman the undisputed master of the Mekong Valley; his successors completed the conquest of Funan. It seems that the Khmer people of Chenla, unlike the people of Funan, did not cultivate the deltas, but preferred to depend on rain in the high lands. Hence, they were possibly attracted by the rich plains of southern Funan.

A good deal is known of Bhavavarman from inscriptions, one of which, written in Sanskrit verse, announces the consecration by the King, of a Sivalinga named Tryambaka. Another describes him as King of Kings, strong as Mount Meru. When he died in 598 the unification of the two kingdoms was well advanced, and he has been described, therefore, as the founder of the glory of Kambujadesa. After his death, his brother Chitrasena ascended the throne as Mahendravar-man. He built numerous Siva temples throughout his domains. All the known inscriptions of Mahendravarman resemble Pallava inscriptions of the early seventh century.[38] In marked contrast to Funan and other Southeast Asian states which frequently sent embassies to China, Chenla dispatched its first embassy to China in 616–617, during Chitrasena's reign.

After Chitrasena's death, his son Isanavarman ruled over the whole of Cambodia, Cochin China, and the valley of the Mun River to the north of the Dangrek Mountains. On the site of the modern Sambor Prei Kuk (Kampong Thom) on the Mekong River, he founded a new capital city, called after his name, Isanapura. It was in this city, which served as the capital of the Kambuja kingdom until the ninth century, that the art of Chenla, known as the Sambor style, and the early phase of Khmer art developed. One of his inscriptions commemorates the consecration of a statue of Harihara and of an *asrama* for the *Bhaga-vata* or *Pancaratra* priests. These inscriptions attest to the power of the king and the prosperity of his reign, but say little of his conquests.

The Kambuja or the Khmer kingdom gradually emerged from the fusion of Chenla and Funan, and became the most powerful state in Indochina. It survived for almost seven centuries and attained an unparalleled height of political prestige and cultural advancement until destroyed by the Thais in the fifteenth century. At about the same time this empire emerged, the Pyu kingdom of Sri Ksetra in Burma, the Mon kingdom of Dvaravati in Siam, and the Empire of Sri Vijaya in Indonesia were flourishing. The seventh century was a formative one in Southeast Asia.

Until the end of this century, the Khmer kings concentrated on consolidating their hold over the lower Mekong region and around Tonle Sap. Both Hinduism and Buddhism were practiced, with the former predominating; Saivism appears to have been the court religion. The worship of Harihara, in which Siva and Vishnu are united in a single body, was the main feature of this period. Most inscriptions are in Sanskrit and the literary culture was based upon the *Ramayana,* the *Mahabharata,* and the *Puranas*.

The eighth century is a complete blank in Khmer history; possibly it was a period of unrest and confusion all over Southeast Asia. But at the beginning of the ninth century the whole country came under the authority of Jayavarman II, whose long rule of fifty-two years (802–854) marks the beginning of the Angkor period and of classical Khmer art. At this time, inscriptions indicate the Khmer Empire was confined to the eastern and southern portions of Cambodia and Cochin China.

Until the rise of Jayavarman II the capital of the Kambuja was in the south at Isanapura where the earliest types of Khmer temples are found, all dedicated to the Hindu religion. Indian models, especially of the post-Gupta style, were generally imitated, but the wood originals in India have perished. Indian influence in early Khmer or Sambor art is so marked that some scholars have suggested the artists came from India. The statues are extremely beautiful, but only a few have survived. The most exquisite of these are the statues of Harihara, Uma, and Lakshmi in the Phnom Penh museum. This Sambor phase was one of the most beautiful in Khmer art, and a worthy forerunner of the brilliant later period.

There is some mystery about the exact origins of Jayavarman II. He is said to have been a descendant of an ancient dynasty of Cambodia who had lived at the court of the Sailendras in central Java, and returned to his country steeped in Javanese culture. According to one inscription he came from Java to reign in Indrapura but another records that he simply appeared like a fresh lotus. B. R. Chatterji holds the view that Jayavarman II did not come from Java in Indonesia but from a place named Java in Laos,[39] but Groslier accepts the theory that he did come from Java. Indeed the impact of the Indianized culture of Indonesia ignited the renaissance of Cambodia.[40]

Jayavarman introduced into Cambodia with the help of a Brahman guru, Hiranyadama, the cult of the Deva Raja (the king-God) which was somewhat similar to that of the Sailendra King of the Mountain cult. This cult claimed universal supremacy for the king, and inspired the period of temple-building in Cambodia. According to scholars, such as Coedès, the Sailendras had resuscitated the title of King of the Mountain which had previously been an attribute of the kings of Funan. If so, then Jayavarman was only repatriating something which the Sailendras had borrowed from his predecessors. Significantly, the proclamation styling him as the Deva Raja specified that Cambodia was no longer dependent on Java, and this may imply, as Groslier suggests, that the Sailendras had occupied parts of Cambodia during the eighth century. Jayavarman based his power on religion. He organized the state, founding several capitals—Hariharalaya, modern Roluos, Amarendrapura, probably a city built around Akyum, and finally Mahendra-parvata on the Phnom Kulen—which provide impressive evidence of his progress. There are many remains from Jayavarman's reign at Sambor Prei Kuk, at Banteay Prei Nokor, at Roluos, and on the Phnom

Kulen, the last being the most important. Excavations on the summit of Phnom Kulen have revealed a number of temples that were completely hidden by thick forests and were mainly discovered by Phillippe Stern and Henri Mouhot. In style, they provide a link between pre-Angkor and classical Angkor art.

The Khmers were accomplished builders; Jayavarman's successors built temples enthusiastically. The cult of the King of the Mountain inspired each king to erect a magnificent shrine to perpetuate his memory. Thus arose the complex of Angkor Thom. Yasovarman I (889–901) was one of the outstanding rulers of the dynasty, and the founder of the first city of Angkor. This covered a much larger area than Angkor Thom, which was founded later by Jayavarman VII at the end of the twelfth century. These two cities partly overlap, but the former lies outside the southern wall of Angkor Thom. Yasovarman issued a large number of Sanskrit inscriptions written in Kavya style and built the Saiva temple of Phnom Bakheng. Six of his successors ruled during the tenth century when building activity dominated political events. The last king of this dynasty was Jayavarman V (968–1001), in whose reign Mahayana Buddhism prevailed and numerous Buddhist texts were imported from abroad. He was followed by Suryavarman (1002–1050) from Siam, who initiated a new dynasty of great kings. Primarily a Buddhist, he is said to have erected temples of Siva and Vishnu. Cambodia reached its peak during the reign of Suryavarman II (1113–1152), the builder of the matchless Angkor Wat, an epic in stone. With the death of Jayavarman VII (1181–1220) the kingdom began to decline, falling finally before the advancing Thais.

After the fall of the Khmers in the fifteenth century, the temples gradually fell into disuse. Their ruins were discovered only in 1860, and are perhaps the most awe-inspiring to be found anywhere. Scattered throughout the mountains and jungles of Cambodia in an area of about ten thousand acres, more than six hundred Khmer monument ruins can still be counted. Of these, twenty are of major importance. They range from temples and palaces to reservoirs and bridges, and cover the reigns of more than twenty kings. The great monuments are near the capital Angkor Thom, which alone covers an area of two thousand acres; Angkor is a derivative of the Sanskrit *nagara,* meaning city, and *thom* a Khmer word meaning great.

The ruins of Angkor Thom are the remains of the latest city built by Jayavarman VII. He planned the whole city to give it a cosmic meaning. According to Hindu belief the world consists of a circular, central continent (Jambudvipa, the ancient name of India) surrounded by seven annular continents. Beyond the oceans an enormous mountain range encloses the world. In the centre of Jambudvipa is Mount Meru, surrounded by the moon, sun and other stars. On the summit of Meru is the city of the gods, encircled by the abodes of eight *Lokapalas*, the guardian gods of the world. Buddhist conception is fundamentally the same, with differences in detail. Both hold Mount Meru as the centre of a circular universe with concentric zones around it. Thus, a miniature image of this cosmological arrangement carries a symbolic meaning for both Hindus and Buddhists.

In Angkor Thom the central mountain is the Bayon, the temple of the Bodhisattva Lokesvara, the Lord of the Universe, and the city is surrounded by a wall and moat forming a square almost two miles on each side. The balustrades of the causeways leading over the moat to the city gates are formed by rows of giant statues, on one side of gods, devas, and on the other of demons, asuras, holding an enormous serpent. Thus, the whole city is a representation of the Puranic story of the churning of the primeval milk ocean (kshirasagara) by the gods and the demons, using the primeval snake, Vasuki, as a rope and Mount Meru as a churning stick.

Outside Angkor Thom is the Angkor Wat, covering an area of five hundred acres. This is the largest and the most impressive temple in the world. According to Henri Mouhot, who discovered it for the modern world: "This architectural work perhaps has not, and perhaps never has had, its equal on the face of the globe."[41] Since his day, countless people, both admirers and sceptics, have stood spellbound before this majestic temple of Vishnu. The genius who conceived this temple, like all other Khmer artists, is unknown to us.

A raised causeway of flagstones, lined by a naga-balustrade, leads from the main road over a moat to the main gate of the temple. This gate house, which is a spacious building forming the front part of the wall that goes around the enclosure, is in itself a remarkable creation. A paved road 400 yards long leads to the temple. At the base, the temple is 223 by 242 yards, and its main tower is about 80 yards high. Structurally it is a three-stepped pyramid. Each storey is punctuated by towers at the corners and pavilions in the centre. The main tower is on the third storey. The temple rises steeply in the form of three concentric rectangular galleries, each double the height of the preceding one, and connected by stairs and intervening open terraces. The innermost gallery is dominated by five tall domes, the central one of which dominates the plain below. The entire building is constructed in sandstone, and if any wood was used, it has long since perished.

129

The building has been chiselled with endless bas-reliefs and beautiful designs and patterns. Flowers, birds, and dancing maidens decorate the walls. Hundreds of Khmer artists must have spent their entire lives on the work, yet it is impossible to detect a single flaw in these acres of carved panels. The sculptors of Angkor who executed many scenes from the *Ramayana*, the *Mahabharata*, and the *Harivamsa*, must have had an intimate knowledge of Indian epic literature. Vishnu predominates but other gods also adorn the temple with their various incarnations and emanations. Kings are also introduced and the Khmer language can be seen engraved in some places. Evildoers are shown being condemned and the virtuous rewarded by Yama with Chitragupta as the keeper of the records. The outer gallery, running around the whole building, itself contains a half-mile of bas-reliefs on the back wall, and there are about 1750 life-size *apsaras*, practically every one in a different, magnificent head-dress.

Although the Khmers are so admirably remembered for their superb achievements in art, they patronized all branches of Indian learning. All the princes received training in Indian philosophy and literature. A number of persons of apparent Indian origin were present in the Kambuja kingdom and Brahmans were held in high esteem. For instance, Hiranyadama came from a *janapada* in India to teach Tantric texts to the royal priest, Sivakaivalya. According to a Chinese tradition, there were a thousand Brahmans in Tuan Siuan, an area in Funan, alone. The presence of so many Hindus presumably influenced the social structure of Kambujadesa on caste lines, creating divisions and relationships. Kambuja records mention four *varnas*, and the emergence of a new class, *Brahmaksatra*, resulting from intermarriage between Brahmans and Ksatriyas. Other classes were created during the period of Jayavarman V, such as Khmuk and Karmantara. The Brahmans seem to have enjoyed a position of privilege, and their social life, as well as marriage customs and funerary rites, was much influenced by Indian practices. Although Hinduism remained the dominant religion, Buddhism also flourished. In the ninth century, King Yasovarman erected a Saugatasrama for Buddhist monks. Suryavarman I, who came from Siam, possibly adopted Buddhism; his inscription contains an invocation to the Buddha as well as to Siva, and he was posthumously named Nirvanapada.

Jayavarman VII was an ardent Buddhist and the public utility works undertaken by him were remarkably extensive. His Ta Prohm inscription containing 145 Sanskrit verses expresses his feeling of charity and compassion towards the whole universe. The magnitude of his resources and the depth of his religious sentiments can be gauged by the scale of his donations and charities. About sixty-seven thousand people were employed in the temples and the revenues from approximately three and a half thousand villages were given to defray their expenses. More than fourteen hundred professors and scholars were engaged in study in these temples, and their daily necessities were supplied. According to the evidence of his inscriptions, there were about eight hundred temples and more than a hundred hospitals in the kingdom, that were given over thirty million pounds of rice every year. Whilst these figures must be exaggerated, they do give an idea of his devotion to Buddhism. Despite this devotion, he was "the most arrogant and the most lustful for glory of all the Khmer kings, attributes in which they all excelled themselves."[42] He built so many temples that it is said he shifted greater quantities of stone than all his predecessors put together, and put statues of himself in the chief temples of his kingdoms.

When Buddhism became the paramount religion of Cambodia is uncertain. It had long been flourishing and occasionally enjoyed royal patronage, but it was never the state religion and never held a dominant position. It seems likely that Siam, which was first influenced by Cambodia, later aided Cambodia's conversion to Buddhism. The change was almost complete; today Hinduism is practically extinct in Cambodia, except in a vestigial form in certain ceremonies and festivities. For instance court Brahmans, called *Bakus,* perform domestic rituals in the royal household. These Brahmans, although a survival of Hinduism, are Buddhists as are other Cambodians; their performance of the royal ceremonies appears to be rather a matter of profession than of faith. Hindu deities have been absorbed by Buddhism and relegated to subordinate positions, and even the Hindu gods in the great temples, such as Angkor Wat, have long been replaced by the images of the Buddha. Numerous Buddhist images have been found in the temple and it appears that by 1550 it had become a Buddhist pilgrimage place.

Unlike some other countries, Cambodia does not minimize Indian influence on the local culture. On the contrary, the people of the country generously acknowledge it. For instance, inaugurating the Maha Vithei Jawaharlal Nehru Boulevard on 10 May 1965, Prince Norodom Sihanouk recalled the close cultural ties that have existed for two thousand years between India and Cambodia. He said: "When we refer to 2000 year old ties which unite us with India, it is not at all a hyperbole. In fact, it was about 2000 years ago that the first navigators, Indian merchants and Brahmans brought to our ancestors their gods, their techniques, their organisation. Briefly India was for us what Greece was for the Latin Occident."

Malaya

Malaya has historically been a meeting ground of diverse races and cultures. Certainly, the Malay Peninsula, which includes modern Malaya and southern Thailand, has played a central role in Indian sea trade with the countries of East Asia, as well as in the transmission of Indian culture throughout Southeast Asia. Takkola, modern Takua Pa in southern Thailand, was the first landfall of traders and settlers coming from India. From here the travellers went on in different directions. Some crossed over the mountain range to the fertile plain on the eastern coast and then proceeded either by land or sea to Siam, Cambodia, and other regions of Indochina, and further east. Others went to Burma or travelled by land southward toward Malaya or by sea through the Strait of Malacca to destinations in the Archipelago or East Asia. But all who wished to travel further east had to negotiate Malaya either overland or by a circuitous coastal voyage. It is therefore not surprising that this region was much Indianized, and ruins of shrines, images, Sanskrit inscriptions, and other remains of Indian culture have been found throughout the Peninsula.

Land communications within Malaya were adequate, including rivers and elephant tracks through thick jungles. Kedah was connected with Ligor in the northeast, and with the east coast region encircled by the Patani Sai, Belum, and Pergau Rivers. The goldfields of Pahang could be reached both by land and by sailing down the Kelantan and its tributaries. The northern part of Malaya, including part of what is today southern Thailand, was more advanced than the southern part of the country, as most of the important places and harbours, such as Tambralinga, Kataha, and Takkola, were located in the north, close to the trade routes. Southern Malaya also remained in a state of neglect because of the power and prosperity of Sumatra.

Malaya's fortunes have often been subjected to external pressures. Malaya has been rich enough to attract attention but not powerful enough to repel unwanted guests. Prior to Western domination, her northern neighbours, first Funan and later the Thai kingdom, held sway over her; from the south the Sri Vijaya and Majapahit Empires dominated Malaya for long periods. All these political contacts affected her cultural life.

Of the written records tracing the antiquity of the Indo-Malay contact, one has to rely again on Chinese chronicles, which refer to Indianized principalities in the Peninsula, although many of the place names are not positively identifiable. Ancient Indian literature contains very few references to Malaya.

In the first or second century, the kingdom of Langkasuka (Lang-Kia-su, Lang-Ya-hsiu, or Tun Sun), mentioned several times in Chinese chronicles, was founded on the east coast in the neighbourhood of Patani. There is some controversy as to whether Langkasuka was on the west or the east coast of Malaya, but latest opinion appears to favour the latter view.[43] More than four hundred years later, in 515, King Bhagadatta (Po-chi-ieh-ta-to) of Langkasuka sent an envoy, Aditya, to China. During the sixth century at least three other embassies were sent to China. References are also found to other states, such as Pan Pan, which was conterminous with Langkasuka and was frequented by the Brahmans from India. It was from this state that the second Kaundinya went to Funan. Southeast of Pan Pan was Kolo (Ko-lo-fu-sha-lo), placed by Coedès in the area of Kedah or Kra; this was prominent enough in the sixth and seventh centuries to attract envoys from China. Chinese records speak of embassies coming from Malaya to China in the sixth century and of Indian kings reigning there and using the Sanskrit language.

Indian literature also mentions kingdoms, Kalasapura and Kamalanka (Karmaranga), which were probably in the Malay Peninsula, Kala (Kedah), and Pahang. In the *Puranas*, mention is often made of Katahadvipa (Kataha), which was included amongst the nine divisions of the world across the seas, and to which regular voyages were undertaken from Tamralipti. Various other references to Katahadvipa are found in Sanskrit dramas and stories. The Tamil epic, *Silappadikaram*, of the second century contains a description of tall, roomy ships entering a city in South India laden with a variety of goods and spices from a Malayan port called Tondi.

Both Indian and Chinese literature contain references to Kedah, situated on the west coast, and the most important Indianized principality in Malaya proper. From the third to the fifteenth century, Kedah was an important port. A well-known Tamil poem, *Pattinappalai*, of the second or third century, mentions regular trade between Kalagam, possibly Kedah, and Puhar (Kavirippattinam). Later, the Chola inscriptions of the eleventh century refer to Kedah in various forms, such as Kidaram, Kadaram, and Kataha.

Although the Chinese had become aware of Langkasuka earlier, Kedah was neither noticed nor recorded until the T'ang period, presumably because it was not in contact with China. I-tsing was the first Chinese scholar to refer to Kedah (Chieh-cha), which he visited in 671. Later, the Arab writers also mention it as Kalah placing it on the way from India to China, and some mention it as a dependency of Zabaj, Sri Vijaya.

The remains excavated in the Malay Peninsula generally confirm the deductions made from literary sources, although much work still needs to be done. Excavations so far have not yielded any substantial evidence from the time of the kingdoms of Langkasuka. The Sanskrit inscriptions that have been discovered do not date back further than the fourth century, although the literary references fix the date of the Indianized states in the Malay Peninsula much earlier. Lately, however, some evidence has been building up to strengthen the conclusions reached from literary sources. It was probably an Indian ship that brought an Attic vase of the fifth century B.C. to Perlis. The Roman beads found at Kota Tinggi in Johore were probably brought by Indian traders at the beginning of the Christian era.[44] The remains of a Siva temple excavated by Quaritch Wales on a low spur of Kedah Peak have been interpreted as an important link in the transition from the sepulchral shrines of South India to the *Chandis* or tomb shrines of Java. Thus it seems that Indian culture was centuries old in Kedah in the seventh century, and flourishing enough to become the centre of cultural diffusion to Java. Malacca also must have been an early Indian centre. A *makara* fragment built into the wall of a Portuguese church must have come from an ancient temple destroyed by the Christian conquerors.[45]

Kedah, however, is by far the most important of Malayan sites. Following the explorations of James Low and later of Evans, made in 1925, Quaritch Wales carried out extensive investigations in Kedah on about thirty sites. Further archaeological work has been done recently on these sites by members of the Malayan universities. Of the thirty sites excavated by Quaritch Wales, eight appear to be Buddhist, as many as twelve are possibly Saiva and Hindu, and three are the remains of secular buildings.

The Pallavas founded settlements in Kedah, on the Bujang River, whose temple ruins have yielded an image of Ganesa and other objects of Saiva faith. Kedah was an important centre of Indian culture in the fifth or sixth century; Indians, both Hindu and Buddhist, came continuously for several centuries to settle, and gradually Kedah became a repository of Indian art styles and cultural traits which in due course were further diffused. They came mainly from South India, but many Indians arrived from other parts of the country. A stone inscription found at Guak Kepah in Kedah mentions a *mahanavika*, literally a great sailor, Buddhagupta. He is described as an inhabitant of Raktamrittika. which is identified with Rangamati, twelve miles south of Murshidabad in Bengal.

Some of the inscriptions testify to the presence of both Hinayana and Mahayana Buddhists in Kedah in the fourth century. A bronze statue of Buddha in the style of Amaravati found in Kedah and two Buddhist images of Gupta style from the Kinta Valley in Perak, belong to the fifth century. An inscribed clay tablet found near Kedah, which is assigned to the sixth century, contains three Sanskrit verses embodying some Mahayana philosophical doctrines. Two of these three verses have been found in Chinese translations of Madhyamika texts and all three are found in a Chinese translation of the *Sagaramatipariprccha*. In the eighth century the Palas of eastern India reinforced Mahayanism in Malaya.

Bruas in Perak is supposed to contain the relics of the ancient Gangga Nagara mentioned in the Blagden recension of the Malay annals. Higher up the west coast, Kuala Selinsing in Perak has been identified by Evans as the site of an ancient Indian settlement on the strength of a Sanskrit inscription "Sri Vishnuvarmmasya," found on a cornelian seal.[46] Spelled incorrectly, the inscription is written in boxheaded characters of a South Indian variety of about the sixth century or earlier; hence, it is generally regarded as a Pallava seal. This site has yielded many other significant finds pointing to the existence of a continuous settlement there for several centuries. These include a remarkable number and variety of beads, some of which, such as the complicated stone beads, appear to be imitations of those of India or cultures farther west.

Some important Buddhist relics have also been excavated from Perak, which has been a rich mining area from ancient times. A fine bronze Buddha statue from Pangkalan, and another bronze image of the Buddha mined from a depth of sixty feet in a tin mine at Tanjong Rambutan, reflect the Gupta style of the fifth century.

In the southwest corner of Kedah, in Province Wellesley, a group of seven Sanskrit inscriptions probably belonging to the fourth century, were discovered by James Low at Cherok Tokun in the central part and four more in the north. From Bidor comes a fine bronze image of Avalokitesvara with Tantric emblems in Pala style of the eighth and ninth centuries. Two more bronze statues of the same Bodhisattva, one of which is a standing four-armed image, have been found in open

135

cast tin mines at Sungei Siput. A bronze statue representing a Brahman ascetic found recently at a site in Tinkus Valley, Sungei Siput in Perak, resembles the effigies of the vedic sage, Agastya, of whom numerous specimens have been discovered in South India, Ceylon, and Java. Whilst the Agastya cult was common in Indonesia, this is the first evidence of its presence in Malaya. Of the six hundred or so beads found at Kota Tinggi in Johore about eighty are of early Indian origin, more than a hundred are Roman (probably brought by Indian merchants), one Hittite, and two Phoenician.

The present political border between Malaya and Thailand is not a meaningful division in respect to their cultural past. The monuments in southern Siam, at places such as Chaiya, Takua Pa, Nakhon Srithammarata (Ligor), and Yala (near Patani), are impressive examples of the local Indianized art, resembling Pallava or Gupta architecture. Of all the Indianized states in the Peninsula the most important was Ligor, now Nakhon Srithammarata, in southern Thailand. It was essentially a Buddhist settlement. Some of the fifty temples that encircled the stupa belong to a very early period, yet there are also Brahmans of Indian descent at Patalung, who trace the arrival of their ancestors by an overland route from India across the Malay Peninsula. In addition, numerous relics of Hindu origin have been excavated from this area.

The history of the Malay region from the eighth century onward is a little better known, for it came under the domination of the Indonesian Empire of Sri Vijaya and the Sailendras, and the ruins of this period, which lasted almost until the end of the thirteenth century, are found throughout the Peninsula. In the fourteenth century, when the Indianized Majapahit Empire displaced Sri Vijaya, Kedah, Patani, and Kelantan were greatly influenced by Majapahit culture; for example, linguistic traces in Kedah and the shadow play in Kelantan still contain Javanese Hindu characteristics.

Although Malaya was in close contact with India for over a thousand years and Hindu and Buddhist influences were strong, the remains unearthed are surprisingly few, and Malaya proper has not yielded a single temple or stupa approximating the splendour of even a minor structure of Thailand or Indonesia. Perhaps the adverse climate and corrosive soil took their toll of early structures which may have been of wood. Moreover, the empires of which Malaya formed a part had their seats of government outside the Peninsula, particularly in Indonesia. Another possible explanation of this, as Winstedt points out, is Muslim iconoclasm: *"The Kedah Annals record how on conversion to Islam the Malays destroyed all the idols they were accustomed to wor-*

ship, together with the idols handed down from their ancestors."[47] Islam is indeed uncompromisingly iconoclastic and has a long history of image and temple destruction in other countries, including Indonesia —and India itself—where most of the many statues surviving from the pre-Muslim past are headless.

Indian contacts with Malaya during this period can be better studied as a part of the whole phenomenon of developing cultures in the Archipelago. Soon after, Islam and Europeans came to Malaya effecting deep changes in her life and culture, yet the cultural background of Islamic Malaya is distinctly Indianized. Malays still perform many ceremonies which bear the marks of Hinduism; some Sanskrit words are still used in rituals. The Malay ceremony, *Melenggang perut,* performed in the seventh month of pregnancy to achieve the birth of a son, is reminiscent of a Hindu practice. Various other rituals connected with childbirth are the relics of an Hindu past. Elaborate ceremonies pertaining to the student life, laws and customs regulating family life, inheritance and social behaviour, wedding ceremonies, and temperamental similarities all suggest the harmonious blending of the two cultures.

Concepts of state and kingship in Malaya, royal titles such as *Seri Paduka,* ceremonies connected with coronation, and royal prerogatives are clearly of Indian inspiration. Malaya's literature and folklore are deeply influenced by the Hindu epics, the *Ramayana* and the *Mahabharata.* Her language has many Sanskrit loan words, and until the introduction of Arabic and, later, Roman script, Indian scripts were used in Malaya and the Archipelago.

Indonesia

Sea trade between India and East Asia had begun to flourish in the first century, and Indian settlements had been established in Southeast Asia; Palembang in Sumatra was a port of call en route from India to China.

The oldest report on Indonesia is found in the Han annals of the Emperor Wang Mang who ruled China in the first quarter of the first century. Specimens of Chinese ceramics of the Han period found in Sumatra endorse the existence of regular contact between China and Indonesia at that time. A Chinese source mentions an embassy sent to China in 132 by King Pien (Tiao-pien) of Ye-tiao; the name is a Chinese transcription of King Devavarman of Yavadvipa (Java Island).

The fact that there was an Indianized kingdom in Java powerful enough to dispatch an envoy to China in the early second century would suggest the prior existence of Indian influence. Believing that Java was already Indianized by 132 and assuming that this Indianization had only been effected slowly in the course of many years, G. Ferrand believes that the beginnings of Hinduism in Indochina and in Indonesia must be anterior to the Christian era. Fa-hsien, who visited Java about 414 for five months, described the country as a stronghold of Hinduism. From Java, Fa-hsien sailed for Canton in a merchant vessel which had two hundred Hindu traders on board. Less than twenty-five years later, the Buddhist monk, Gunavarman, stopped in Java on his way to China and laid the foundation of Buddhism there. References to Indianized Java of later periods are numerous and specific in the Chinese chronicles.

Ptolemy's reference in the second century to *Iabadiou* certainly represents the Prakrit form of the Sanskrit Yavadvipa. He also mentions several places in the Archipelago and the Peninsula under their Sanskritic names. The evidence indicates that Indian civilization had found a firm foothold in Java by his time.[48]

The chief sources of early Javanese history are elaborate local narrative verses and poems. People in Java believed that Rishi Agastya came from India and settled there. Usually called Bhatara Guru, Agastya is an extremely popular legendary figure in Indonesia, and he was widely worshipped and venerated; numerous reproductions of his image in art and sculpture are found in the country. According to Javanese chronicles, twenty thousand Indian families came to Java from Kalinga in the second century. A century later their prince, Kano, emerged. Various other Javanese traditions and legends associate the original settlers and their leader, Aji Saka, with the heroes of the *Mahabharata*. The Javanese era commences from Aji Saka in the year 78, the epoch of the Saka era in India. Another tradition in Java mentions the foundation of a Hindu state in 56.[49]

The archaeological remains excavated so far are somewhat posterior to the literary references relating to Indian culture in Indonesia. Amongst the earliest finds are the images of the Buddha, in the Amaravati style, discovered at Sampaga in the Celebes; in the south of the Jember province in eastern Java; and on Mount Seguntang at Palembang in Sumatra. Sanskrit inscriptions of a King Mulavarman from Kutei in Borneo, dating from the fourth or the beginning of the fifth century, have also been found. These inscriptions are not dated, but their script closely resembles that of the early Pallava inscriptions of South India and the early inscriptions of Champa and Kambuja. The next series of inscriptions comes from West Java and refers to a King

Purnavarman; these scripts suggest that they were engraved in the middle of the fifth century. Because of its closer proximity to India, Sumatra was probably the first island visited by Indians in this area, but it has yet to be properly investigated by archaeologists.

However, in the various parts of Indochina and Malaya numerous stone inscriptions belonging to the third century, at the latest, have been found. These inscriptions, covering a period of centuries, bear recognizable family likeness, and are usually composed in Sanskrit and written in a South Indian script. The earliest of these inscriptions is the rock inscription from Vo-Canh in Champa, written in Sanskrit, dating from the third or even possibly the second century. It is therefore plausible to assume that before Indian culture spread as far as Champa, it may have found a foothold in lands nearer to India, such as the Malay Peninsula, Sumatra, and Java.

The earliest chief Indianized kingdom in Indonesia was Sri Vijaya with its capital at Palembang, in Sumatra. The Chinese called it Shih-li-fo-shih (San-fo-tsi, Kan-te-li or, briefly, Fuche). It is generally believed that this kingdom was founded in the seventh century, but Majumdar believes, as does Ferrand, that it was founded in or before the fourth century, reaching greatness at the end of the seventh.[50] In any case, it is in the last quarter of the seventh century that the first clear allusions to this kingdom are found in epigraphy and literature. Qua-ritch Wales, whilst admitting the existence of Sri Vijaya in the seventh century, suggests that it was supplanted by a powerful kingdom called Javaka, under a Mahayanist dynasty of the Sailendras newly arrived from India. Whether Sri Vijaya and Javaka were one or two states, the cultural pattern of Indianization remained the same.

Sri Vijaya ruled over an extensive area stretching from Java to the Malay Peninsula and southern Siam from at least the seventh to the twelfth, possibly the thirteenth, century. A group of inscriptions found at Palembang, some of them dated 683–686, refer to the conquest of Jambi (Malayu) and the island of Bangka. An inscription dated 775 from Nakhon Srithammarat refers to the might of the king of Sri Vijaya and to several Buddhist temples built there under the king's command. Thus, it seems that by the eighth century Sri Vijaya dominated the whole of Sumatra, West Java, and the greater part of the Malay Peninsula. Control of the northern part of Malaya and the two straits added to the increasing prosperity of Sri Vijaya. Indian traders who chose the sea route had to go through one of the two straits, and those who took the overland route to Indochina and China had to cut across the north-ern part of the Malay Peninsula. According to Coedès, Sri Vijaya succeeded to the commercial hegemony of Funan and control of the southern area.

Material progress accelerated the growth of learning and art. I-tsing stayed in Palembang for six months in 671 learning Sanskrit grammar, and again fourteen years later, on his return from India, spent four years, copying and translating several Sanskrit texts into Chinese. He was so impressed by the Buddhist studies in Palembang that he advised Chinese monks to go through a course of preliminary learning there before proceeding to India. He himself came back to Palembang for the third time with four of his colleagues from Canton and wrote his two *Memoirs* there. At the time, Buddhist monks in Sri Vijaya numbered more than a thousand. From the seventh to the eleventh century Buddhism remained most powerful in Indonesia, attracting famous scholars from India, such as Dharmapala, a scholar from Nalanda University, who visited Indonesia in the seventh century. Atisa Dipan-kara (eleventh century), the monk who became the head of Vikramasila University and inaugurated the second period of Buddhism in Tibet, went there in his early life to study Buddhism.

Whilst Sri Vijaya was at the peak of its power, another kingdom was emerging in central Java, the Sailendras, with whom Sri Vijaya had friendly relations at first. Before the rise of the Sailendra kingdom in the eighth century, there were several Indianized states in Java. Two of these, called by the Chinese Cho-po and Ho-lo-tan, sent embassies to China in the fifth century. Amongst the earliest archaeological remains of West Java are four Sanskrit stone inscriptions of a king Purnavarman of Taruma who reigned in the fifth century. As these inscriptions refer to his grandfather as a *rajarshi,* and another ancestor as a *rajadhiraja,* it would seem that an Indianized society flourished in Java during the fourth and fifth centuries.

Chinese historical works mention various kingdoms in Java and other islands, although not all of these are easy to identify. The most important kingdom in Java during the T'ang period was Ho-ling, a Chinese variation of the Indonesian Kaling or Kalinga, which was also the name of a region on India's east coast. About this time a number of Indians from Kalinga are said to have emigrated, and it is possible that they settled in a part of Java; they certainly were numerous enough to name the state after their home area.

Attempts have been made to connect the Indian Kalinga with the origins of the Sailendras in Java. It is argued that the two ruling dynasties of Kalinga, the Gangas and the Sailodbhavas, were defeated by the Calukya dynasty of the south in the seventh century. The defeated rulers thereupon set out for the renowned islands of the east and founded the Sailendra Kingdom. Nilakanta Sastri, however, finds this theory open to objection and suggests that the Sailendras may be an offshoot of the South Indian Pandyas. Various other theories of their precise origins have been advanced but none is clearly established. It seems that in Java there were numerous centres of power, usually referred to as *kratons,* which meant king and his court. The more powerful kratons struggled for political supremacy, and out of this conflict emerged the Sailendra dynasty in central Java, in the eighth century, which was to attain not only great political power but also a degree of cultural advancement seldom surpassed in history.

The accounts of Arab writers, such as Ibn Khurdadhbih, Abu Zayd Hasan, Al Masudi and Al Biruni, testify to the political, commercial, and cultural accomplishments of the Sailendras. The Sailendra Empire is referred to by the Arab writers as *Zabag (Zabaj),* from the empire of Maharaja; some scholars believe that the term refers to the Maharaja of the Sri Vijaya Empire. The most detailed account of Zabag is by Abu Zayd Hasan, who wrote about 916, basing his account on one originally written by Sulayman in 851. Sulayman recounts various islands forming part of the kingdom and speaks of the great fertility of its soil and of its dense population. The king is described as so rich that every day he threw a solid brick of gold into water saying "there is my treasure." His daily revenue amounted to two hundred *mans* of gold, fifty of which came from cock-fights. The Maharaja was the overlord of a number of islands and, according to Al Masudi, his Empire was so large that even the fastest vessels could not complete a round trip of it in two years.

The data to reconstruct the history of this Empire are inadequate, and the details of its relationship with Sri Vijaya are not clear. We do not know whether the Sailendras were a branch of Sri Vijaya, whether they had taken the latter under their protection, or whether they shared a peaceful coexistence. It is, however, generally accepted that a Sailendra prince, either having been driven out of his home or by virtue of kinship, became the ruler of Sri Vijaya at Palembang in the ninth century and his dynasty lasted there until the thirteenth century.

The Sailendras brought the greatest part of the Malay Archipelago under one central authority. Their Empire extended as far as Champa and Kambuja; the Sailendra fleet raided the distant coast more than once in the eighth century. This was a troubled period in the history of Southeast Asia, especially Indochina, and our knowledge of it is more obscure than that of others. Why these naval raids were carried out is

141

not clear. Why did the Sailendras temporarily bring Cambodia under their domination? It is known that Jayavarman had declared the independence of Kambuja from Java in 802, and although it is not certain, there are reasons to believe that the successive Sailendra expeditions and incursions caused the collapse of the royal dynasty of Champa.

The Sailendras were evidently a great naval power, and their relations with the fellow-Buddhist Pala Kingdom of Bengal were quite close; as early as 782, Kumaraghosha of the Pala Empire was the royal preceptor, guru, of the Sailendra kings. A copper plate inscription, found at Nalanda and dated about 860, records the erection there of a monastery by King Balaputradeva of Suvarnadvipa. Visitors and scholars from Indonesia to Nalanda became so numerous that a separate monastery had to be built to lodge them. A Chola inscription from South India records that two Sailendra kings, Chudamanivarman and his son, Sri Maravijayottungavarman, constructed a Buddhist monastery at Nagapattana (modern Negapatam). In both cases the respective Indian kings granted lands and villages to these monasteries.

The Sailendras maintained good relations with the Chola rulers of South India. The Cholas were also a great naval power, and by the beginning of the eleventh century under Rajaraja the Great (985–1014) and his still more powerful son, Rajendra Chola (1014–1044), they became the paramount power in southern India. The friendly relations between these two powers deteriorated in the eleventh century, and two Chola inscriptions of 1024 and 1030 speak of Rajendra's military expeditions and conquests of several countries in Southeast Asia, including Sri Vijaya and the Sailendra Kingdom. Another Chola king, Virarajendra (1063–1070), is also said to have led a successful military incursion to Sailendra. The conflict between the Cholas and the Sailendras, which persisted throughout the eleventh century, considerably crippled the power of both.

The Sailendra period is one of the most important eras in the history of Southeast Asia. Buddhist art, inspired by the Mahayanism and Tantrism of the Palas, reached a new peak. Indonesian civilization during the Sailendra period became a model for other Southeast Asian countries. The Sailendras introduced a new kind of script, Devanagari, from northern India, built world famous monuments, such as Lara Jonggrang and Borobudur, and gave Malaysia a new name, Kalinga. Whilst Mahayana Buddhism had its votaries at the court and amongst the governing classes, Sivaism was prevalent amongst the common people; whilst Borobudur represents the peak of Buddhist art in Indonesia, the temple of Lara Jonggrang at Prambanan is Saiva.

In the tenth century the scene of power and civilization moved to eastern Java. Just before the Sailendras emerged in central Java as a supreme power, a powerful dynasty was ruling there with its capital at Mataram, and, under its ruler Sanjaya, had led successful expeditions to Sumatra and Cambodia. Sanjaya is said to have been a great conqueror and he was deified as Divine Sanjaya. An inscription found at Changal in the district of Kedu mentions that Sanjaya had erected there a monument for a Sivalinga in 732. After his death, central Java was conquered by the Sailendras and his successors were pushed eastward. In the ninth century, however, it appears that Mataram had shaken off the political supremacy of the Sailendras in eastern Java, which became a prominent region where Indian culture found a strong repository for the next five hundred years.

Mpu Sindok, who ascended the throne in 929, was the first known king of the house of Mataram to settle in eastern Java, under the regal title of *Sri Isana Vikrama Dharmottungadeva*. By this time, the culture and civilization in central Java had visibly declined. Sindok is an eminent name in Javanese history, and the later kings eagerly sought to trace their descent from him, but the exact accomplishments which gave him this prestige are lost to history.

Princess Mahendradatta, the great granddaughter of Sindok, married a prince of Bali, Udayana. Their son, Airlingga, who ruled over the Mataram Kingdom from 1010 to 1049 was one of the greatest kings of Java. He brought the whole of Java under his authority and established commercial and political relations with other countries. According to an inscription, he built a dam to stop the Brantas River from flooding. He was regarded as an incarnation of Vishnu, and at Balahan, where he was cremated, there is a fine statue of Vishnu on his mount, Garuda. He was a patron of literature, and Kanva's poem, *Arjunavivaha*, the first book of its kind, was written under his patronage.

Before he died, he divided his kingdom between two of his sons. The two resulting states, Kadiri and Djanggala, survived in eastern Java until the beginning of the thirteenth century, when a new dynasty, Singhasari, emerged. Kadiri was the center of intellectual activity during this period.

Singhasari was founded by Ken Angrok, who styled himself as an incarnation of Bhatara Guru; he has been the subject of many popular legends. But the dynasty attained its highest power and prestige under the rule of Kritanagara (1268–1292), who is portrayed in literature in striking contrasts. A Javanese chronicle, *Pararaton*, describes him adversely, whilst a well-known historical poem, *Nagara-Kritagama*, hails

143

him as an expert in Buddhist scriptures and polity. He was certainly a devout Buddhist and practiced Yoga and Samadhi. Marco Polo, who visited Java during this period, described Singhasari as a prosperous kingdom ruled by a great king. Kritanagara initiated an aggressive imperial policy. He subdued Sumatra, Bali, parts of Borneo, and the Malay Peninsula. Emboldened by his successes, he even picked a quarrel with Kublai Khan, but before the Chinese punitive expedition could reach Java he was dethroned by an internal rebellion led by the governor of Kadiri.[51]

From the chaos and unrest that followed the rebellion in Singhasari, in which the Chinese expedition played an active part, there emerged the kingdom of Majapahit in central Java under Vijaya, a son-in-law of Kritanagara. Vijaya, having subdued other contenders for the throne, proclaimed himself the king of the whole of Java in 1294, assuming the regal name of Kritarajasa Jayavardhana. The most eminent name of this dynasty, however, is not that of a king, but of a commander, Gajah Mada, who became the prime minister and the effective ruler from 1331 to 1364. He extended the authority of Majapahit over Sumatra where he completely demolished the weakened Sri Vijaya kingdom as well as dominating Bali and other islands. He is believed to have initiated the "Javanization" of Bali.

The Empire attained the peak of its power under Rajasanagara (1350–1389), commonly known by his personal name, Hayam Wuruk. He ruled over all the principal islands in the Archipelago and the large part of the Malay Peninsula. He established cultural and trade relations with neighbouring countries, such as Kambuja, Champa, China, Siam, and India, which sent a large number of Brahmans and Sramanas to his capital. After his death the kingdom disintegrated and supremacy over the various islands, including Sumatra and some states of Malaya, gradually passed to Ming China, which became the suzerain of the Archipelago.

The Majapahit Kingdom, however, continued until 1520. About the middle of the fifteenth century Islam had begun to penetrate Java; the new religion gradually became powerful enough to bring about the downfall of the last great Indianized kingdoms in Java, as of others in Indonesia. Only a small Hindu state of Balambangan retained its independence, and continued to do so for two and a half centuries. Today only Bali still professes a kind of Hinduism, called Hindu-Balinese.

Soon the arrival of European merchants, soldiers, and missionaries changed the pattern of Indonesian society. In fact, Western culture came to Indonesia at about the same time as Islamic culture, but whilst the former scarcely affected the indigenous culture of Indonesia at first, the latter quickly began to take root in Indonesian soil. The explanation of this contrast may be that whilst Western culture was completely alien and had come to Indonesia in association with political domination, Islamic culture was familiar and completely unattended by foreign military force.

Indian Muslim traders and teachers, chiefly from South India, embarking at Gujarat and Malabar, carried Islam to the Malay Archipelago. They were mainly interested in profit, and were not religious zealots. They were not willing to sacrifice life or property for the holy cause, nor were they the instruments of an Islamic Church. Even teachers who arrived later from Egypt, Mecca, and Arabia came in search of gain through rich patrons. Their language was Indian—Hindustani, Gujarati, Malayalam, Tamil, or some other—and the books they brought were Indian versions of Arabic or Persian originals. From these Indian versions, translations into Malay were made.

Islam made easy conversions, mainly because of the simplicity of its beliefs, in marked contrast to the complex doctrines and traditions of Hinduism and Buddhism, in which very sophisticated and varied philosophies had admitted a variety of ugly traditions and superstitions over a period of centuries; Sufism also found a ready reception in Indianized Indonesia. Whilst Islam made religious converts, it could not impose a new culture, for Indonesian culture was far too developed and distinctive itself at the time. Change of religion was bound to affect the existing religious cultural character, but even in this sphere Islam accepted many features of Indonesian culture. For instance, Islamic fasts in Indonesia are still called *puwasi upavasa,* a term of Sanskrit origin; a Muslim teacher is called guru; and Muslim sultans bear titles such as *Maharaja, Srinara,* and *Mandulika.*

Today, Indonesia is the largest Muslim country in the world, yet Indonesian culture is perhaps the only one which Islam has not penetrated beyond the surface. In Malaya, too, the culture has few Islamic features but the Malays at least have Muslim names, whilst most Indonesians have retained their original names. Islam is not a culture in the true sense of the term, but it has certain recognizable features, acquired from the Arab and Persian cultures, which it has always sought to impose on its adherents. The French traveller, Jules Leclercq, having seen *hajis* (Muslims returned from Mecca) joining in the worship of ancient Hindu images, remarked that the advent of the Muslim faith has not alienated the Javanese from their old beliefs.[52]

Indonesian language, art, social customs, legal and political systems, literature, folklore, and philosophy, were affected by Indian cultural currents. "To gain a correct idea of the extent of the influence of Hindu culture in the islands that came under it," says Sastri, "one must contrast Sumatra, Java and Bali with the islands farther east which were not touched by this influence. It will then become clear that all the elements of higher culture, the form of organized state-life, trade and industry, art and literature were practically gifts of the Hindus to these islands, and that the archipelago falls easily into two divisions—one which accepted the new culture and advanced with it into civilization, and the other which lagged behind."[53]

The Kawi language, Indonesian in essence, is full of Sanskrit loan words. The oldest extant script in the Malay Archipelago is the so-called Pallava script—the language being Sanskrit—named after the Pallava dynasty. By the eighth century Java had evolved its Kawi or Old Javanese script from the Pallava, which was given the Sanskrit appellation of Akshara Buddha, meaning Buddhist letters. Another Indian script used in the Archipelago was an early form of Devanagari, possibly introduced in the eighth century as a result of the close intercourse between the Palas and the Sailendras. Madurese, Sundanese, and Balinese scripts also derive from the Pallava. Batak writing in central Sumatra has undergone much simplification perhaps owing to the writing materials used—bark or sapwood—but it is also derived from the same source. Peoples in the south of Sumatra, the Rajang and the Lampong, use writing closely resembling the Kawi. The ancient alphabets of the Bugis and Macassars of the Celebes were derived from an Old Malay or Sumatran script of the Pallava family. The alphabets used by the Tagalogs and others in the Philippines, when the Spanish first met them in the sixteenth century, were likewise closely allied to the Sumatran script, although the number of characters had dwindled considerably. Thus at one time Indian scripts were in use in the whole of the Malay Archipelago. With the introduction of Islam they were partially superseded by the Arabic script, and with the coming of the Europeans by Roman characters.

Numerals generally remain unchanged in a language affected by foreign influences, but Indonesians adopted various Indian numerals. Before the arrival of the Indians, Indonesians had their terms for 1-10, 100, and 1000. Numbers higher than that, however, were represented by words meaning "innumerable," "obscure," or by borrowed terms. The Sanskrit *laksha*, which means 100,000, is used throughout the Archipelago to denote 10,000, so when the problem of appropriate terminology for 100,000 arose, the Archipelago adopted the Sanskrit word *koti* representing 10,000,000.

Whilst the Sanskrit laksha and koti are given a lower value than the original, Sanskrit *ayuta*, 10,000 assumes the higher value of 1,-000,000 *(yuta)* in Malay and Javanese, and 100,000 *(samyuta)* in Tagalog. It is possible, however, that yuta is derived from the Sanskrit *niyuta,* meaning a very high number. In Balinese, *ha-laksa* stands for 10,000, *ha-koti* for 100,000, *ha-yuta* for 1,000,000, and *ha-bara* (in Sanskrit *bhara* means weight, a large quantity) for 10,000,000. The lower Indian numerals that have been adopted in the Archipelago are mostly used in compounds: thus *pancanana* (five-faced), or *dasaguna* (tenfold).

The formation of ordinals from the cardinals is interesting. In India, *prathama* (foremost or first) was excluded from the list of ordinals because the functions of the first are different from those of other ordinal numbers. The Malay differentiates between its first and the following ordinals by using *pertama* (prathama) with *yang* preceding it for first, but for all others it merely uses the prefix *ke* before the original cardinals; thus *ke-dua* is second, *ke-tiga* is third, and so on.

Tagalog expresses fractions by the use of the term *bahagi* (part) from the Sanskrit *bhaga* (share). In Malay bahagi means to share or to apportion. As for the numeral co-efficient *biji,* which also means seed in Malay and some other languages of the Archipelago, the origin may be sought in the Sanskrit *bija* (seed). The Javanese *siji* (one) is short for *sa-wiji* meaning one or a certain. *Wiji* alone stands for piece in counting, or for seed, and in a literary sense for offspring. Likewise in Malay it means not only seed or pip but also testicle. The Javanese wiji may share the same origin with the informal Dayak *ije* (one), which may represent a word etymologically cognate with the Sanskrit bija. As for the connection between bija and biji, it is common to find the Sanskrit "a" being changed into "i" in the languages of the Malay Archipelago.

Language is merely a vehicle of ideas. Whilst its introduction was dictated by utilitarian reasons like the need to communicate, it soon assumed the additional role of transmitting ideas and cultural traits. Some Sanskrit inscriptions suggest that Indian philosophical and literary texts were carried to Java from very early times, although there is no record of it. The most ancient texts composed in Indonesia appear to belong to the fifth century; they deal mainly with grants of land, etc. Later, under the patronage of the great empires, Indonesian literature flourished, and Indian epics, such as the *Mahabharata* and the

Ramayana, were translated and adapted in the Javanese language.

Several recensions of the *Ramayana* exist in both verse and prose in Indonesia. Episodes from it are used as themes in the popular Indonesian *wayang-kulit* (shadow play). The Indonesians have made alterations in Valmiki's version, combining it with material from other Indian versions of the *Ramayana* and with their own imaginative embellishments. Some scholars, such as Stutterheim, believe that some of the traditions preserved in the Indonesian version may even be anterior to Valmiki's *Ramayana.* The Rama tradition, however, principally in its Indian form, is still a living force in Indonesia. The Indonesian concept of chivalry is closely modelled on this epic and on Rama's ideals. In the education of Indonesian girls frequent references are made to the lofty examples of Sita. The main river of central Java, Sarayu, is named after the Indian river on the bank of which was situated Rama's capital, Ayodhya.

The other Indian epic, the *Mahabharata,* is even more popular. First translated into Old Javanese in the tenth or eleventh century, it has been repeatedly translated and adapted. The *Mahabharata* is like an encyclopaedia of Hinduism containing a wide variety of tales of heroic deeds and exploits. It appears to have captured the imagination of Indonesian peoples, who consider themselves to be the descendants of the heroes of the *Mahabharata,* and believe that all the drama took place on their soil. They endeavour to model their own lives and deeds in accordance with the ideals and examples of its heroes. The major hero of the epic, Arjuna, is the national hero of Indonesia. The name of the leader of the Indonesian Revolution, Sukarno, is taken from Su-Karna, a hero of the *Mahabharata.*

The style of early Javanese literature closely follows Sanskrit. Courtly poetry began in Indonesia with adaptations of Indian epics and other works. The Old Javanese work, *Amaramala,* is modelled on the Sanskrit *Amarakosa* and other Indian lexicons. Such adaptations as a category are known as *Parva.* Parvas were followed by *Kakawins,* which were the adaptations of Indian poetical works. These are called *Nitisas-tra-Kawin* in Java, and in Bali just *Nitisastra.* The first important literary work of Indonesia, *Arjuna Vivaha,* was written during the reign of Airlangga (Erlanga, or Rake Halu Sri Lokesvara Charmavamsa Erlanganantavikramottungodeva, the only Balinese prince to rule over both Bali and Java), and deals with an episode from the *Mahabharata.* The theme and style of this work made the Indian epic extremely popular in Indonesia and are reflected in other literary works and folk tales. During the Kadiri period two poetical works of outstanding quality, *Krishnayana,* describing Krishna's fight with Jarasandha, and *Suman-*

148

asantaka, based on Kalidasa's *Raghuvamsa,* were written. Another masterpiece, the *Bharatayuddha,* portrays the conflict between the Pandavas and the Kauravas. It was written in the second half of the twelfth century by Mpu Sedah and possibly completed by Mpu Panuluh. Many other Javanese works, such as *Harivamsa, Bhamokavya, Smaradahana,* and *Nagara Kritagama,* drew freely from Indian literature. The *Hitopadesa* and the *Pancatantra,* which so deeply influenced the fables and fairy tales of the Western world, were well known in Indonesia and other parts of East Asia. Their stories form the basis of Indonesian fables and folklore known as *Tantri.*

The Indian tradition of puppet shows, *Kathaputali,* is not only well preserved, but nowhere in the world are these shows as much an integral part of the social life of the people as they are in Indonesia. All over Java and Bali, and now also elsewhere in Indonesia and Malaya, wayang shows are frequently performed before large audiences. It is an exquisite art developed over centuries. The beautifully cut leather puppets are operated by the *dalang* (performer) with incredible ingenuity and skill. The performance is accompanied by the Javanese *gamelan* (orchestra), and the puppets represent the heroes and heroines of the Indian epics, with the size, appearance, colour, and ornaments of each character fixed by convention. The influence of the wayang on the life of the people is enormous, and even the dominance of Islam has not lessened its popularity. For the Javanese, says Wagner, "the wayang-kulit is not just a show; but represents an abstract world in which ideas take human shape and imagination becomes reality."[54] Stamford Raffles, at the beginning of the nineteenth century, found eager multitudes of people listening for whole nights with rapturous delight and profound attention to wayang-kulit. The nationalists adopted wayang for patriotic shows during their struggle for power, and without it they might not have succeeded in gaining mass support for their movement.

The orgin of wayang is a subject of dispute, but there is no doubt that the culture introduced from India greatly influenced it. Indian myths, tales, and sagas were increasingly adopted; Indian gods, heroes, and demons also soon found their way into wayang. As might be expected, Indian tales and heroes over a period of centuries were hopelessly interwoven. Indian characters and situations drawn from a variety of long forgotten tales may be woven into a new context with a local character. Indian traditions also mingled with indigenous myths and tales. Indian influence, however, is noticed not only in the subject matter of the *lakons* (stage version of stories) but also in the technique of the whole art.

149

Indian imprints on Javanese music, village organization, rural economy, and customary laws of property can also be seen. Hindu influence in Indonesian music was perhaps felt somewhat later than it was in Indochinese music. The reliefs on the Hindu and Buddhist shrines of the Sailendra period illustrate the musical instruments of that time. These, especially the ones depicted at Borobudur in the eighth century, contain most of the local and Indian instruments that make up the modern orchestra, which is composed almost entirely of percussion instruments. There is no doubt that the instruments found in the household of the ruling and upper classes in Indonesia mainly bore Hindu characteristics; later, in the tenth century, small ensembles such as drum, conch horn, and crooked trumpet came into use.

Of the two principal scale systems of Indonesian music, *pelog* and *slendro* (*salendro*), the former is indigenous but the latter is of Indian origin and was named after the Sailendras. The deity *Batara Endra* is said to have invented this system at the command of Siva, but it seems that it was really given currency by Buddhists in Sumatra. It is a five note scale with three different modes, which divides the octave into more nearly equal parts than the pelog, namely into intervals of about six-fifths of a tone. It is said that Indonesia treats slendro as masculine, exalted, and severe, and pelog as feminine, friendly, and sad. The most important influence in developing Indonesian music was the Sanskrit dance-drama which promoted the development of the wayang-kulit, providing scope for dancing and narrative song.

In Indonesia singing and poetry go together, and many ancient Indian metres are found in Javanese songs. The art of dancing matured in the kratons of central Java, and bears recognizable marks of Indian style. The symbolic gesture of the hand, *mudra,* and the meditative seated posture, with legs crossed under the body, for example, are obviously Indian. It is, however, in Bali that Indonesian dancing has found its highest expression, associated with religious worship and the traditional Hindu-Balinese ceremonials. Whilst Javanese music absorbed certain new traits under the impact of Islam, Bali retained its older traditions. In fact, it was the Balinese who fled from the advance of Islam, settled in Bali, and created the first musical notation of Southeast Asia, based on the vowels in the names of the five notes of the scale—*ding, dong, deng, dung, dang.* Islamic influence on Javanese music was not significant, and its chief legacy is a two stringed spike-fiddle called *rebab,* which reached Indonesia through Muslim India.

Both Hinduism, mostly Saivism in contrast to Vaisnavism in Cambodia, and Buddhism flourished in Indonesia and both have left an indelible mark on the life and culture of her people. At about the beginning of the eighth century, the Puranic form of Hinduism, involving the worship of the Hindu Trinity, Brahma, Vishnu, and Siva, was popular in Java; in Indonesia Siva occupied the supreme position. Buddhism had very little hold on the people of Java at the beginning of the fifth century, but soon after, due to the missionary zeal of an Indian monk, Gunavarman, it gained considerable support. By the time I-tsing visited Sumatra, the kingdom of Sri Vijaya had become an important centre of Buddhist learning in southern Asia.

The influence of religion and philosophy was naturally to be felt in art and architecture. The religious structures in Java are commonly called *chandis*, a term which originally meant a commemorative building. With rare exceptions, all the relics of Indo-Javanese art are temples, sanctuaries, and sacred statues. These are found throughout the islands but chiefly in Java, where most of the Indonesian population appears to have been concentrated. In Sumatra also, many remains have been found. Bronze statues and a large stone image of the Buddha in the Amaravati style have been discovered in the district of Palembang. Considering that attention was not paid to some of these monuments until the twentieth century, it is not unlikely that most of them may have been lost forever. But there are enough left to reveal the high standard of Indonesian art. Whilst it was Indian in conception, it became increasingly local in character, evolving a well-integrated and distinctive regional style. For instance, the plan of the temple was Indian but the motifs were modified and the Indonesians excelled in the creation of decorative elements.

The numerous temples situated on the Dieng Plateau probably belong to the eighth century, and are the oldest in Java. At least some of them were erected during the dynasty that preceded the Sailendras. They are not large monuments but are fairly compact with sparse ornamentation. Images of Siva, Ganesa, Durga, Vishnu, and other Hindu deities indicate South Indian influence. Pallava or Calukya art was the main source of inspiration of these buildings, but Pala art also might have influenced the Javanese art of this period.

Chandi Kalasan is perhaps the oldest shrine to which an approximate date (778) may be given. The inscription commemorating this shrine is also the first Javanese record of the Sailendra kings. Erected by the first of the kings, it is dedicated to the Buddhist goddess Tara and appears to have been designed as a sepulchre for the king's consort. It is situated south of the Volcano Merapi in central Java. Above the entrance is found the kalamakara motif, which was originally a Pallava innovation.

The most important Indonesian monument is the stupa of Borobudur, which immediately followed Kalasan. The building is so enormous that it must have taken a decade or so to complete and is in marked contrast to the much smaller Hindu temples of the Dieng Plateau. In the Kedu Plain of central Java, Borobudur is a structure of overpowering majesty and splendour and commands an extensive view of the green rice fields and the distant towering volcanoes. It is rich and bold in conception, with grand decorations executed in an extraordinarily refined technique. Coomaraswamy describes it as a ripe fruit matured in breathless air—the fullness of its forms is an expression of static wealth that denotes the outward radiation of power rather than the volume.

Its exact origins are shrouded in mystery. Although there is nothing in India to compare with it, Havell regards it a descendant of Sanchi and Bharhut. Zimmer is more specific: "The Sailendra style is completely free of Polynesian elements. It is intrinsically Indian, even though, in the new, very gifted environment, it was guided by a new inspiration. The impulses of the Gupta style, and such subsequent mainland developments as are represented in the Pallava and Pala, have become infused in it with a new life. Specifically, its basic conceptions and formulae, as well as the refined, well-controlled execution, point to the Pallava area more directly than to the North."[55]

Unlike any other monument of the period, Borobudur is a whole mountain top carved into nine stone terraces, each of rising height and diminishing size, crowned by a simple stupa surmounted by an octagonal pinnacle. The result is a truncated, terraced pyramid supporting a relatively small central stupa, surrounded by seventy-two much smaller perforated stupas arranged in three concentric circles. The terraces have balustrades and there are galleries running around the four lower terraces. The outer side of the balustrades contains niches with 432 images of meditating Buddhas. Buddhas also appear on the other terraces. The most significant feature is the series of 1500 sculptured panels in the four ascending galleries of the lower terraces. The carvings, with extraordinary naturalness, depict the lives of the Buddha in his various incarnations, his travels throughout India, and other stories warning the wicked and inspiring the virtuous. The sculpture resembles certain Indian styles although typically Javanese scenes are depicted.

The unique beauty of Borobudur is inspired by the spirit of Buddhist devotion. Every detail is executed with care and refined realism. This freshness and originality was achieved not only by revolutionary changes in forms and techniques, but also by a novel application of the classical Buddhist vocabulary already perfected in its original Indian environment. All Buddhist monuments are associated with religious symbolism.

Borobudur represents the Mahayana Buddhist cosmic system and is one of the finest examples of iconological symbolism.

Not far from Borobudur there is an extensive group of Hindu temples, commonly referred to as the Prambanan group, which commands the veneration of the population. There are six buildings in two lines of three; the largest and the most beautiful, Lara Djonggrang, built by King Daksha of Mataram about 860, is dedicated to Siva, and the two smaller ones to Vishnu and Brahma. The largest temple derives its name from a statue of Durga Mahisasuramardini, which it contains. Opposite are the chandis of the mounts of the three gods of the Trimurti. Forty-two bas-reliefs representing the story of Rama are carved on the inner wall of the gallery. These reliefs are, if anything, superior to those of Borobudur, and certainly more dramatically conceived. The gate arches and entrances abound in ornamentation, with the head of Maha-kala, an incarnation of Siva, in the centre. Both the architecture and sculpture are inspired by Indian models.

The largest and most important group of monuments in eastern Java are the temples of Panataran. Although work on this site appears to have begun during the Singhasari period, the most important was done in the time of Majapahit.

Indonesian art is a syncretism of Hindu-Buddhist techniques and of indigenous traditions. The art of the Sailendra period is probably the most Indian, but later, Indonesian features became increasingly prominent. As Indonesian culture grew and gathered momentum, the Indian element weakened for want of immigrant reinforcements. By the time of Majapahit the synthesis between the Indian and Indonesian arts was complete, and from then onward the art of Indonesia was truly Javanese.

Although information about Borneo is at present scanty, seven inscriptions found at Maera Kaman in Kutei (East Borneo), inscribed on stone pillars in the Sanskrit script of the fourth century, point to a direct relationship between India and Borneo. These inscriptions speak of King Mulavarman and his ancestors and of a sanctuary called Vapra-kesvara, probably dedicated to Siva or Agastya. A beautiful bronze Buddha image of Gupta style has also been found in Kutei at Kota Bangum, and several statues of Hindu-Buddhist deities have been excavated at Mount Kombeng and in the estuary of the River Rata. Indeed, the earliest Hindu inscriptions in the whole of the Malay Archipelago have been found in Borneo. Although the Kutei inscriptions are simple, they reveal a fairly good knowledge of Sanskrit. There are other sites which have yet to be properly excavated. Two other objects, a gold Vishnu statuette and a gold tortoise, were found at

Kutei and were worn by the Sultan of Maera Kaman in his necklace on state occasions. Images of Siva have been found in various parts of the island, and other remains include a Ganesa image from Sarawak and a Pallava inscription from near Sangbetrang on the east coast. The name Borneo is said to have been derived from *Porunei*, and is identified with *Purnadvipa* mentioned in Kautilya's *Arthasastra*. According to the *History of the Sung*, Sri Maharaja, the King of Borneo *(Po-ni)*, sent a diplomatic embassy to China in 1082.

One of the most delightful spots in the world is the small island of Bali. In the whole of Indonesia, indeed in all Southeast Asia, it is only here that Hinduism has survived. The Hindu faith, however, has absorbed many local customs and traditions.

Little is known of the first Indian contact with Bali, and some scholars describe Balinese culture as an extension of Indo-Javanese civilization carried there by those who had escaped from the Islamization of Java. Others, such as Majumdar, hold the view that Bali had been in direct contact with India, for her inscriptions are in Old Balinese, which contains many Sanskrit loan words but is different from Old Javanese. The discovery of little clay tablets or circular seals bearing the confession of the Buddhist faith or Tantric Buddhist *mantras*, probably of the eighth century or before, suggests Indian influence for some time prior to that date. In addition to Sanskrit inscriptions and Buddhist formulae, images of Hindu gods and characters from the Hindu epics have been found. All these data indicate that Bali received Indian culture directly, but evidence of trade between India and Bali has not been discovered.

Bali has been justly called the island of thousands of temples. Despite the loss of about 2500 temples in an earthquake, it still contains more than 4500 large and important temples. The number of the temples and shrines may well be over 20,000. The most important is Pura Besakih, at the foot of the mountain Gunung Agung, and associated with the Hindu Trinity. This temple is said to have been founded by Wira Dalem Kesari (Warmadeva Keshari), probably in the beginning of the tenth century. It may have originally been a Buddhist sanctuary as well as the state temple of the Warmadeva dynasty. Even today the tradition is observed that only a Buddhist *pedanda* accompanying the ruler as his court priest may enter Pura Besakih. At important ceremonies, Buddhist and Hindu priests jointly conduct the rites and bless the devotees. Balinese literature and language, religion, worship and cremation services, and caste and social organization clearly reflect Indian influence.

Indonesia thus gives a remarkable example of a harmonious blending of local and foreign cultures. Few countries in the world have received so much from outside and yet have retained their own distinct personality. In the beginning Indian elements dominated, but they were all gradually acculturized. As an example, the Indonesian week comprised five days, called *pantjawarna of pasaran*. Indians, upon their arrival in 78, introduced the Saka calendar based on calculations made of the course of the sun, with a seven day week and a 365 day year. Its usage became common and at first all inscriptions were dated according to this system. But with the passage of time events were also recorded according to the Indonesian week of five days. Still later, the two systems were fused in a new one.[56]

The Philippines

Indian cultural waves went well beyond Bali and Borneo, reaching the Philippines and even Formosa. Both of these were for a time parts of the Sri Vijaya Empire, which has been described by a modern Filipino historian as "basically Malay in might, Hinduistic in culture, and Buddhistic in religion."[57] This contact of Indian culture with the Philippines also continued under the Sailendras. In the fourteenth century, the Hinduized Majapahit Empire emerged as a powerful state in Southeast Asia, extending its overlordship as far as Formosa and New Guinea. Whilst the control of Sri Vijaya and Majapahit over the Philippines was rather loose, their cultural impact was deep.

The influence of India over the Philippines was not as direct as that of China and later of Spain and the United States but, with the exception of modern European cultures, Indian influences have been the most profound. The manner in which Indian influence was brought and the date when it began are subjects of speculation; dates have been suggested ranging from the first millennium B.C. to the early fourth century.

The Philippines were near the sea route between India and East Asia, so they may have been visited by Indian sailors and traders. A series of remarkable excavations were carried out by Beyer in the late 1920's at Novaliches in the Philippines. His work was the first systematic archaeological investigation in the country, and his finds and conclusions were thoroughly examined by R. B. Dixon. Beyer concluded that all the artifacts found, including a large quantity of pottery, iron implements and weapons such as knives and axes, glass beads and bangles and beads of semi-precious stones such as carnelian, agate and amethyst, were brought to the Philippines from India over a long period of trade, well before the beginnings of the Christian era. Both iron and glass objects are similar to, and in some cases identical with, those of prehistoric South India. "There is no tribe in the Philippines," wrote the American anthropologist, Alfred L. Kroeber, "no matter how primitive and remote, in whose culture today elements of Indian origin cannot be traced."[58] Whatever its antiquity, it would be hard to deny the existence of trade between the two countries from the first centuries A.D. onwards. Pre-Spanish Philippine society with its nobility, code of laws, and political procedure, was largely of Indian cast. Some years ago when a new legislative building was put up in Manila, the capital, four figures were carved on its facade illustrating the sources of the Philippine culture, one of which is Manu, the ancient Indian lawgiver.[59]

A fleeting glimpse of Buddhism is noticeable in Philippine *Bathala* worship. The term *Bathala,* the supreme god of the ancient Tagalogs, originated from the Sanskrit *Bhattara.* The Hindu element in the ancient Philippine religious beliefs, and in the names of old Philippine gods, and of legendary heroes is quite apparent. Several religious objects which have been unearthed in the island of Mactan and in eastern Mindanao show the undoubted influence of India, but only two images of Hindu deities have so far been discovered. One image of solid gold shows "clear evidence in its tall pointed head-dress and other ornaments of the influence of Hindu-Javanese art of the tenth century."[60]

Spaniards of the sixteenth century found several related alphabets (one for each of the principal languages), all of which seemed to have derived from India some eight hundred years before. Malayan languages, including those of the Philippines, are unusually simple in their phonetic system, which caused them to discard much of the elaborate Sanskrit alphabet, but the salient characteristics of Indian writing were retained.

Whilst the most advanced Philippine peoples, such as the Tagalog and Bisaya, have long given up their old alphabets, remote descendants of ancient Indian scripts still linger on amongst the less advanced tribes in the interior of the country. Tavera and Paterno, two Filipino scholars, and Saleeby, an American, and others have concluded that about twenty-five per cent of the Philippine vocabularies is traceable to Indian influence. For instance: *bahagi* (part, portion) in Tagalog is *bhag* in Hindi; *bansa* (nation) is *bans* (family); *katha* (fiction, story) is *katha; diwata* (god or goddess) is *devata; dukha* (poor, destitute) is *duhkha; guro* (teacher) is *guru; mukha* (face) is *mukha; yaya* (nurse) is *aya:* and so on.

Philippine literature, mythology, and folklore are traceable to India. The Maranaw epic, *Darangan,* the longest in early Philippine literature, is basically Indian in plot and characterization. The tale of the *Ifugao Balituk* is reminiscent of the story of Arjunna getting water from a rock with his arrow for Bhishma who was dying of his wounds. A Philippine legend about the creation of different races from baked clay pots is quite popular in India with its local variations.

Indian influence through Sumatra brought the calendar, much of Buddhist folklore, and the syllabic alphabets; through Java came the more advanced arts of metal work, jewellery, and weaving. Modes of dress such as the *sarong* and *putong* (turban), personal ornamentation, especially by the people of Sulu and southern Mindanao, and old names for money, such as *salapi, siping, gatang, tanso, pilak,* and *bakal,* are said to be of Indian origin. The lotus design on the Philippine weapons was of Indian inspiration.

In 1762 during the Seven Years War in Europe, which was extended to the Philippines, eight hundred Indian soldiers formed a part of the British expeditionary force against Manila. A year and a half later, when the invading forces evacuated Manila, many of the Indian soldiers refused to go home, even at the risk of violating military regulations. They settled in the district of Morong in the community now known as Cainta, south of the town of Anitpolo, and married local girls. Their descendants today form an integral and useful part of the Philippine society. They have a reputation of being peaceful, law-abiding, and industrious citizens.

Except for this brief interlude, and some trade between India and Manila, nothing much was heard of India during the 333 years of the Spanish regime (1565–1898), largely because of the Spanish policy of sequestration, and also because of the similar though less severe restrictions of the British colonial government on Indians. During the American regime (1898–1946), freer intercourse with other countries was allowed, in consequence of which many British Indian subjects came to the Philippines as traders, businessmen, and a few as labourers. The contact between the two countries since independence in recent years has increased noticeably.[61]

Thus the history of Indian cultural penetration of Southeast Asia covers a period of more than fourteen hundred years up to the end of the fifteenth century. Hinduism was flourishing in Southeast Asia when it was in a state of decline in its homeland. Unbacked by political power or military conquest, the cultural development of Southeast Asia is indeed a remarkable tribute to the interaction of human ideas.

Chapter IV

IMPACT OF ISLAM ON
INDIAN SOCIETY

THE ADVENT of Islam was the most important event in the history of India since the coming of the Aryans, and it was the first major impact of an alien culture on Hindu society. So far, India had assimilated all immigrant peoples and cultures; on the other hand, Islam had usually assimilated the culture of the land to which it went. But in India, Islam neither lost its identity nor conquered the country culturally; both appropriated something of each other. The Muslims of the Indian subcontinent, who constitute the largest Muslim population found in any one country, are culturally distinct from their co-religionists in Arabia, Indonesia, or elsewhere. Although Islam assumed an Indian character, its adherents retained their distinctive religious and social organization. The political repercussions of this dichotomy have been far-reaching, resulting in the partition of India into two independent states.

The India to which Islam came was in a state of decline. Northern India especially had lost its old vigour, the reasons for which have often been debated but never conclusively explained. But for occasional sparks of brilliance in philosophy and science, cultural activity had given way to political adventurism. An era of intellectual stagnation and social degeneration had set in. Pride in past accomplishment superseded respect for change; progress meant not evolution but preservation of the ancestral heritage. Instead of investing their cultural legacy, Indians began to hoard it.

The spirit of enterprise was dislodged first by arrogance, later by timidity. Whilst Al Biruni, who accompanied Mahmud of Ghazni, considered Hindus to be excellent philosophers, accomplished mathematicians, and remarkable astrologers, he saw clear marks of stagnation and

158

decay and accused them of cultural arrogance rooted in past glory. According to him, the Hindus called foreigners *mleccha* (impure) and believed that there was no country but theirs, no religion but theirs, no science but theirs.[1] Having repelled the powerful Huns, who shook the roots of the Roman Empire and ravaged Europe, the complacent Hindus became consumingly conceited. The flourishing commercial and cultural intercourse which had thrived in the area from Rome to Japan, almost all of the known world, began to contract rapidly. Deprived of this stimulus, culture became static, Hinduism sectarian and ritualistic, and Buddhism gradually almost nonexistent, except in eastern India where it flourished until the thirteenth century. Common people were divided into innumerable castes and lived in narrow circles; caste discipline became corrupt and oppressive. The Brahmans tightened their monopoly of learning and took advantage of the common man's ignorance and credulity.

To the west of India the Roman world had collapsed and Europe had sunk into the Dark Ages. The Eastern Roman Empire at Constantinople, although it survived for some time, was in a state of decline. In contrast, China had emerged reunited under a powerful dynasty after a prolonged period of political unrest. In Southeast Asia and ancient America, new periods of progress began.[2]

The death of Harsha in 647 proved an irreparable loss. It marked the end of an era in Indian history. There were to be no more Asokas, Chandraguptas, or Harshas. For the next several centuries most of India, especially in the northern and central regions, was divided amongst independent kingdoms which, led by ambitious kings or pretenders, waged interminable wars against one another, often for petty ends. Although some of the rulers succeeded in establishing powerful kingdoms, they did not survive for long.

Most of the ruling dynasties of the North belonged to clans later known as Rajput. These suddenly emerged into prominence towards the end of the sixth century, and slowly gained political ascendancy in northern India which they held for the next five hundred years. They continued to play a major role throughout the mediaeval and modern periods, during which they did not dominate but were sought as allies by the paramount power in the country. After Indian independence in 1947, the numerous Rajput states, like all others, lost their identity and were merged into the Indian Union.

The origin of the Rajputs is the subject of historical controversy. The term Rajput is a derivative of the Sanskrit word, Rajaputra. According to legend, they are the descendants of either the sun, *surya-*

vamsi, moon, *chandravamsi,* or fire, *agnikula.* Some historians have suggested they were the descendants of the Scythians or Sakas who came to India, settled there, and eventually became unrecognizably mixed with the local warrior classes.[3] Others trace their origins to the Kshatriyas of the vedic period.

The Rajputs are renowned for their valour, chivalry, sense of honour, pride, patriotism, and lofty ideals of individual character. Indian legends and songs are full of praise for them. They were zealous patrons of Hinduism and it was, in a way, their courage and devotion which sustained Indian culture and traditions for nearly five centuries during the years of political unrest. However, their history is a wearisome chronicle of states continually rising, warring, and falling. They had no unity; they could not rise above parochialism and clan rivalries. Loyal to their personal ideals and prides, they perfected individual culture to the utter exclusion of national unity and social welfare.[4] It is, indeed, a tragedy of Indian history that such brave people, so earnestly devoted to their faith and heritage should have been inadvertently responsible for the failure to check cultural and social decline because of their constant dynastic feuds and internecine wars.

The history of South India during this period was less turbulent, although there were frequent wars. However, social organization and economic activity were relatively undisturbed, and cultural continuity was maintained in South India.

Art and literature, however, flourished under Rajput patronage; this period witnessed the perfection of temple architecture and the construction of some of the greatest buildings in India. But each Rajput dynasty was keen to retain its distinctive character in art, as in politics, and this led to the growth of several styles of architecture of which there are five main ones. Most important of the surviving buildings of the period are the remarkable temples of Khajuraho, built between 954 and 1002.[5] They are famous for their architecture and sculpture; some of their bas-reliefs are conspicuous for their eroticism. The Muktesvara Temple at Bhuvanesvara, the most beautiful of all Orissa temples, belongs to the Rajput period, having been built at the end of the ninth century. Some treasures at the famous Ellora and Elephanta Caves also belong to this period.

Despite the growing political unrest and internal decay, India remained practically free from foreign aggression from the early sixth century until the raids of Mahmud of Ghazni in the first quarter of the eleventh century, except for the brief incursion of Muhammad bin Qasim in Sind in 711–713. It is somewhat surprising that the Arabs,

160

who had emerged as great expansionist powers and brought the lands between Spain and China under Islamic domination during this period, should have left India alone. Possibly, the prevalent reputation of Indian glory and strength deterred aggression, but once Mahmud of Ghazni exposed the myth of Indian might, numerous attacks on India were made in quick succession by foreign armies. Another reason for the Arab indifference to the expansion of Islam into India may well have been the approval of Indian faiths by the Prophet himself, who is reported to have once said: "I get cool breezes from the side of Hind." In *Sahih Muslim*, Abu Horaira says that the Prophet mentioned certain rivers as belonging to heaven and one of them was a river of India. Two Indians, Sarmanak and Ratan, who collected the Prophet's sayings, *Al Rataniyab*, are reported to have visited Arabia during his time. Many Islamic traditions support the high standing of Indian culture with the Arabs: "Ibni Ali Hatim relates on Ali's authority that the Valley of Hind where Adam descended from Heaven, and the Valley of Mecca, which had the tradition of Abraham, were the best valleys in the world."[6] Certain words occurring in the Quran, such as *tooba, sundas,* and *ablai,* are of Sanskrit origin. A common legend suggests that after the Deluge some of Noah's sons settled in India. A son of Adam, Shees (Seth in the biblical form), was born in India and is now said to be buried in Ayodhya. The fourth Caliph is reported to have said: "The land where books were first written and from where wisdom and knowledge sprang is India."[7]

These and other traditions may be true, wholly, in part, or not at all, but they certainly indicate the affection and respect of early Muslims for India. Considering that the Arabs were convinced of their own superiority and had imposed their culture on the conquered, their high regard for India is a rare tribute. Even the highly developed civilizations of Iran and Egypt could not withstand the Arabs.

Muslim penetration into India was not a case of wholesale colonization, but of successive military attacks, migration of small groups of West and Central Asian Muslims to India, and large-scale conversion of local Indians over a long period of time. The first wave of Muslim conquerors originated with the Arabs, who gave Islam a foothold in India but did not press on with expansion. In 636–637, the Arab Governor of Bahrein and Uman, Usman Sakifi, dispatched an expedition to the coast of India, but India was still too strong to be successfully conquered. In any case, Caliph Umar was opposed to attacking India, even when he was told that "Indian rivers are pearls, her mountains rubies, her trees perfumes," for he regarded India as a country of complete freedom of thought and belief where Muslims and others were free to practice their faith.[8] Indeed, he rebuked Usman Sakifi for dispatching a military expedition, and threatened him with severe punishment if the experiment were repeated. About three-quarters of a century later, in 711–713 during the Umayyad Caliphate of Walid, Muhammad bin Qasim conquered Sind and Multan. This intervention, however, was occasioned not by any calculated designs of aggression; it was in the nature of a punitive expedition against the pirates of Kutch who rashly interfered with the trade and vessels of the Hajjaj, the Viceroy of the eastern provinces of the Umayyad Empire.

Politically, Islam remained confined to Sind and Multan for the next four hundred years, but a new era of intellectual collaboration between the Arab world and India began which was to have lasting effects. Although their conquest of Sind was politically insignificant, the Arabs acquired knowledge of vedantic philosophy, astronomy, mathematics, medicine, chemistry, and the art of administration. Elsewhere, the Arabs had tried to impose a composite culture on the local peoples which was based on their own language and script, and some elements of the indigenous civilizations. In contrast, the Arab rulers of Sind adopted local practices to a much greater extent than even the later, and not so accomplished, Turki-Afghan rulers of northern India. The Arab rulers dressed like Hindu rajas, and even followed a policy of religious accommodation. Despite their uncompromising iconoclasm, they did not apply to the Hindus the stringent provisions of Islamic law regarding idol-worshippers. On the contrary, they treated the Hindus as "people of the book."

Whilst the Arabs treated Indian culture with utmost consideration and hoped to profit from it, the Indians generally remained unresponsive to Arab culture, thus gaining very little in return. There are, however, a few examples on record which are suggestive of some Hindu interest in Islamic thought. In 886, a Hindu king commissioned an Arab linguist from Mansura, one of the two Muslim states in Sind, to prepare a version of the Quran in the local language. In the eighth century, Sind produced a scholar, Abu Maashar Sindi, an authority on the life of the Prophet and held in high esteem throughout the Caliphate; several other notable scholars from Sind made their mark in the Islamic world. Jurists from Sind were particularly noted for their mastery of the Hadith. Abul Ata and Abu Zila, two Sindi poets who wrote in both Arabic and Sindi, attained great fame.

The Arabs were as skilful traders as they were conquerors, and their merchants, under the stimulus of political supremacy, intensified their commercial activity, including maritime trade with India. With the traders came the new faith, but it was only a trickle compared with what was to come later, and it was confined to a few coastal areas. South India, with which the Arabs had trade relations long before the advent of Islam, at this time was involved in political upheaval as well as in religious rethinking. The Cheras were losing power, and new ideas were emerging in Hinduism. Indicative of the Arab influence in Malabar is the conversion to Islam in the ninth century of the last of the Cherman Perumal kings who, a few years after his change of faith, went to Arabia where he died. The memory of the event was kept alive in Malabar until recently. The Maharaja of Travancore, until the end of princedom in India, used to declare at the time of his coronation that he would keep the sword of power until the uncle, who had gone to Mecca, returned. Whilst the historicity of this conversion is mainly based on legends and its details are subject to doubt, that Islam had gained a firm foothold in Malabar at the time is not questioned. The Muslims in the area were designated as *Mappillas*, a title of honour, and various privileges were granted to them.[9] Under the patronage of the Zamorin who actively encouraged conversion, the influx of Arab merchants increased, the volume of Indo-Arab trade greatly expanded, and many Arabs settled permanently in India.

The real history of Islam in India begins with the Turki-Afghan invasions, although the invaders were mainly adventurers looking for plunder. Mahmud of Ghazni, ruler of a small Turki kingdom in Afghanistan, attacked India no less than seventeen times in the first quarter of the eleventh century, and carried back immense wealth, treasures which included the pillars of the Temple of Somnath and enormous quantities of jewels and gold. He was also responsible for the destruction of countless Hindu idols and temples. His invasions ended the rule of the Arabs in Sind in 1005. After Mahmud's death, his successors were unable to hold his kingdom together, and it was left to Muhammad Ghori, ruler of a small mountainous state in Afghanistan, to found the first Muslim state in India. In 1192 Muhammad Ghori gave a crushing blow to the Rajput power in northern India and appointed one of his Turkish slaves, Qutbuddin Aibak, as the Governor of his Indian territory. After Ghori's assassination in 1206 near Damiyak, probably by an Ismailite fanatic, Qutbuddin Aibak assumed sovereign power and founded the Slave Dynasty, which turned into an oligarchy of Turks, jealously guarding its doors against men of other races, whether Muslims or not.

It was only when the Turki-Afghan rulers had established their political authority in northern India that Islam began to make its impact on Indian society. It is, perhaps, a pity that Islam did not spread in India during its early period of Arab supremacy when it was young and vigorous. When Islam came to India, it had passed the peak of its power and glory. Worse still, it arrived through the medium of military adventurers and free booters whose own cultural attainments were almost nonexistent. The Turki-Afghans had raided and looted India for more than two hundred years before they began to organize an administration. In fact, the Turks almost devastated the Empire of Islam through misgovernment and interminable warfare. Whilst the Ottoman Turks at Constantinople were compelled to respect the dignity and traditions of Islamic culture, their kinsmen in India felt no such compulsion. The Ghaznavis, the Ghoris, the Khiljis, and the Tughluqs were much too concerned with the conquest of the country to devote much attention to religious or cultural matters. These conquerors were, in general, rough and crude people, ill-grounded in and uninspired by the Islamic faith. It was a great misfortune for both India and Islam that Islam fell into the hands of ruthless Turki-Afghan generals, whose sole aim was to establish themselves as sovereign powers and use the rich resources of India as funds for their almost ceaseless military campaigns.

When the Turki-Afghan conquests are compared with the early Arab invasions of India, the difference between the barbarity of the former and the culture of the latter stands out clearly. At first the Arab invasion was marked with cruelty, and Muhammad bin Qasim did commit rash deeds in his religious zeal or political nervousness in a foreign, reputedly mighty, country. Moreover, Muhammad bin Qasim was very young. Yet, as soon as the war ended, he compensated those whose property was wrongfully damaged, gave offices of responsibility to local representatives, permitted them to worship their own gods, practice their own customs, build their own temples, and gave protection to the people under his authority.[10] He even kept Hindu ministers and police officials in his service. Indeed, when he informed his Caliph that he had demolished temples, converted Hindus to Islam, and successfully waged war against them, he was reprimanded instead of receiving the commendation he had expected. His actions were held by the Caliph to be against the Islamic law, and he was ordered to compensate for the damage he had done.

Contests for political supremacy had been a feature of Islamic history from the very inception of the Caliphate. Whilst the first four Caliphs may have had religious motives for their political actions, the wars and conquests of later Muslim kings were never purely religious. India resisted the early Islamic invasions, as she would have any intruder, regardless of nationality or religion. Thus, the early armed conflicts between the aggressors and the nationals were not religious but simply political wars. Once Muslims states were founded in India, wars between Muslim kings were as common and natural as wars between Muslim and Hindu rulers. Most of the wars which the Muslim Emperors of Delhi had to fight were against Muslim sovereigns. All the Muslim invaders who came after Muhammad Ghori had to contend with a Muslim state. The invasions of Timur and Nadir Shah were not against Hindu kings but against Muslims. The cruelties of Timur were directed against Muslims and non-Muslims alike. It was Timur who built a human wall by piling up two thousand *shaikhs* of Islam one upon the other and plastering them alive. Babur had to defeat a Muslim king, Ibrahim Lodi, and he was opposed by the combined forces of Rajputs and Muslims. Humayun was dislodged by Shershah, and Akbar had to defeat other Muslim rulers to consolidate the Empire, and was actively aided by Rajputs. Aurangzeb spent the last years of his life in a long struggle to subdue the Muslim states of Deccan with the help of well-known Hindu generals. Even Mahmud of Ghazni made profuse use of Hindu generals and soldiers in his campaigns.

A Muslim king was first a king and then a Muslim. Alauddin Khilji abolished the supremacy of the Ulama and asserted the king's independent authority and responsibility for good government. Even the devout Aurangzeb did not undertake the holy pilgrimage to Mecca, Haj, for he was afraid of losing his throne in his absence. Neither the Sultanate of Delhi nor the Mughal Empire was an Islamic state in the real sense of the term. Although some rulers acknowledged but did not obey the authority of the Caliph, imposed *jizya* and many laws of the *Sharia* on Hindus, and patronized Muslim saints and nobles, all of them subordinated the demands of religion to the exigencies of politics. Few went to Haj, a major requirement of Islam. They extracted far more revenue from the cultivators than was allowed under the Islamic law, indulged in the lax and luxurious life forbidden by Islam, and, by claiming to be the "Shadow of God" on earth and assigning divine rights to themselves, usurped the sovereignty, which, according to Islam, belonged to none but God and which was exercised under rigidly prescribed conditions by the Caliph. Even the Caliphs did not govern according to the instructions of Islam. No Muslim rule, other than that of the first four Caliphs, was truly Islamic in character, and in a sense the Islamic state and Islamic culture lasted for only about half a century under the Prophet and the four righteous Caliphs.

The period of effective Muslim rule in India is generally divided into two parts—the Sultanate of Delhi (1206–1526) and the Mughal period (1526–1707).[11] Whilst the latter is a glorious period of Indian history, the former was very turbulent. The Delhi Sultanate did little to synthesize Hindu and Muslim cultures. With a few notable exceptions, the rulers were incompetent, cruel, and degenerate. Dynasties were short-lived, court intrigues and palace revolutions were rampant, and learning and the welfare of the people were completely neglected.

The five dynasties that ruled at Delhi before the rise of the Mughals were the Slave (1206–1290), the Khilji (1290–1320), the Tughluq (1320–1412), the Sayyid (1414–1451), and the Lodi (1451–1526). The Slaves jealously guarded their doors against non-Turks, but the distinctions between Turks and non-Turks vanished during the Khilji period. The Lodis were the first Afghan tribe to rule at Delhi but Babur wrested control from them in 1526. The early Turkish rulers of India had been Afghanized over the period of their stay in Afghanistan. Most of the later rulers were actually born in India, and many were of part Indian parentage; the proportion of these steadily increased with the passage of time.

Most of the Sultans were busied putting down rebellions of their own subordinates. No less than thirty-five Sultans belonging to the five dynasties sat on the throne of Delhi during a period of little more than three centuries, an average of about nine years for each Sultan. Of these thirty-five, nineteen were assassinated by Muslim rebels. As if this had not done enough damage to the prestige and power of Islam, Timur came in 1398 and left behind a trail of violence. He demolished a Muslim state, converted Delhi into shambles, and laid much of northern India to waste.[12]

Yet, the Sultanate of Delhi was the richest and most powerful Muslim state of the time, and attracted innumerable scholars, soldiers, and statesmen, who had been forced to leave Iraq and Iran after the fall of the Abbasid Caliphate. Whilst the frequent fluctuations in the political fortunes of the Sultans of Delhi did not allow them to either harness the accumulating talent for cultural progress or to impose their supremacy, usurping the Caliphate, over other Muslim states, the very fact that Muslim scholars poured into India stimulated Indian contacts with the outside world.

Whilst North India renewed its close contact with Western Asia and the Islamic world, South India continued some relations with Southeast Asia, and received visitors from the European world. Islam travelled to Southeast Asia from South India during this period. Marco Polo visited South India on his homeward journey from the Mongol Court of China towards the close of the thirteenth century. He commended Indian kings for good administration, and Indian merchants for their wealth, and declared that India was "the noblest and richest country in the world."

Of the visitors who came to India during this period the more prominent were: the Moroccan Ibn Batuta, who stayed in India for about twenty years in the middle of the fourteenth century; the Italian Nicolo de Conti in the early fifteenth century; the Persian Abdur Razzaq, who was an envoy to the Zamorin of Calicut in 1442–1443; and the Russian Athanasius Nikitin, who travelled through the Bahmani Kingdom in South India from 1470 to 1474, and was awed by the luxury of the nobles and the poverty of the peasants. In 1498, Vasco da Gama landed at Calicut, thus discovering the direct sea route between India and Europe which led to a regular influx of European visitors.

It was, in fact, after the commencement of European activities in the coastal areas of India that the Mughal dynasty was founded in 1526. During its rule, Indo-Islamic art and culture made rapid and memorable strides. All of the great Mughal Emperors were men of literary accomplishment and refinement and generously patronized art and learning. Akbar, although himself illiterate, far outstripped all the others in intellectual capacity, humanity, and cultural patronage. Babur wrote his memoirs, as did Jahangir, who was also interested in science and medicine. Shahjahan was well-read and knew Arabic, Turki, and Persian fairly well. His eldest son, Dara Shikoh, was a renowned scholar. Aurangzeb was proficient in several languages and a devoted student of the Quran. The last Mughal Emperor, Bahadur Shah II, who died tragically in exile in Burma after the revolt of 1857, was a sensitive and accomplished poet.

Islam expansion has been mainly attributed to coercion rather than persuasion. Whilst it is true that considerable official pressure, varying according to the zeal of the individual, and at times persecution and force were applied, much of the Hindu conversion to Islam was voluntary. Some Hindus, especially in Bengal, embraced Islam because of Hindu caste oppression, and others because they had had a genuine change of belief under the influence of Muslim missionaries. Others became Muslims in order to gain concrete benefits by embracing the religion of the rulers.

The development of Islam in India was a process of evolution rather than of imposition. Indifferent to culture, the Turki-Afghan rulers, in fact, sought neither to impose Islamic culture on India nor to enrich it by drawing upon the rich Indian heritage. But racial exclusiveness could not be maintained indefinitely. All the soldiers and officials could not be imported from Western or Central Asia. Even if there were enough men in these areas who were competent and prepared to undertake government positions in India, their recruitment would have been impossible on economic grounds alone. In addition, there were political and sectarian rivalries demanding the exclusion of alien Muslims. Muslim rule had to be Indianized to ensure success in India. This became inevitable as the Hindus who embraced Islam soon far outnumbered the few who had come from outside.[13] The Muslims in India were like the Buddhists in China, or the Christians in Europe. The Chinese Buddhists could not be called foreigners because they embraced a faith of alien origin, or the European Christians called Asians because Christianity was born in Asia. That the Muslims of India felt themselves to be Indians is well illustrated by Abul Fazl in his *Ain-i-Akbari*. He was so carried away by the beauties of Hindustan that he apologized for a digression which proceeded from "the love of my native country."

The Hindus gradually overcame their natural hostility against what had come from outside in the company of the sword. Slowly throughout India, the initial clash was followed by fusion and synthesis. In language and literature, scientific and philosophic thought, and art and architecture, a new character began to emerge which reached its peak during the Mughal period, especially under Akbar. He initiated measures to blend the two communities in a variety of ways. His *Din-i-Ilahi* (The Divine Faith), in which he sought to create a universal religion, was a noble effort. Dara Shikoh translated the Upanishads into Persian, and if he, instead of his younger brother and executioner, Aurangzeb, had come to the throne, the history of India might have been different. Both Akbar and Dara, in attempting to unite the two cultural groups, were following the main teaching of Islam, which is unity, human equality, and universal toleration. Islam rejuvenated Indian life, but it did not give rise to substantially new and enduring doctrines in Hindu culture. A possible explanation may be that Indian thought was highly intricate, whilst Islamic thought was simple and straightforward with a powerful appeal for the common man but a less strong one for the intellectual.

Islam was uncompromisingly monotheistic. The Quran lays great stress on the unity of God and on the belief that nothing can share a single attribute with God. This doctrine led to the mass destruction of Hindu temples and images, countless works of arts and learning, and created extreme bitterness in Hindu minds; but it also compelled Hindus to reflect on their own beliefs, many of which had become unrecognizable through tradition, superstition, and dogma. Consequently, Hindus began to modify their existing practice, mainly by returning to the original purity of their own scriptures. For instance, the vedantic philosophy of monism, the principal teaching of the Upanishads, was revived under the vigorous guidance of Sankaracharya (Sankara). Opinion is divided as to whether the new emphasis on the upanishadic thought was the consequence of the Islamic impact or a natural stage in the development of Hindu thought.

Whilst Islam preached the unity of God alone, accepting the universe as his creation, Sankara's vedantic philosophy stressed the unity of both the creator and the creation: the latter being *maya,* an illusion. "Brahman—the absolute existence, knowledge, and bliss—is real. The universe is not real. Brahman and Atman are one." Sankara is the unrivalled propounder of *Advaita Vedanta,* the non-dualistic aspect of the vedic teachings. His clarity, wisdom, and spirituality are deeply impressed upon the Vedanta—which is not only the primary Indian philosophy but is also widely popular abroad. However, the historical possibility that Sankara revived the upanishadic teaching because of Islamic thought cannot be altogether ruled out, for he was born about 686 in a village in Malabar, where Arab traders had introduced Islamic ideas.[14]

Islam opposed the caste system, and taught human equality and a personal pride in religion. The Sufi missionaries met with considerable success amongst the lower caste Hindus for whom conversion to Islam, as later conversion to Christianity, meant escape from a life of indignity and suffering. Islam's attack on caste and idolatory led to religious ferment which culminated in the Bhakti cult, single-minded, direct devotion to God and liberalism in religion.[15] There emerged a succession of remarkable teachers, such as Ramanuja, Madhava, Ramananda, Kabir, Vallabhacharya, Guru Nanak, Chaitanya, Dadu, and Mirabai, who advocated reconciliation of the two religious beliefs. Between them they covered a period of more than five hundred years, from the eleventh to the seventeenth centuries. Ramanuja and Madhava were amongst the early saint-reformers, and of the later ones, the most important were Kabir and Guru Nanak.

Ramanuja, of the eleventh century, ranks second only to Sankara amongst the great interpreters of vedantic thought. He argued that God and souls of men were not the same, although not separate from each other, and that the highest ideal was to love and worship God and to surrender completely to Him. Ramanuja's philosophy is known as *Visistadvaita* (qualified non-dualism), for he admitted the plurality of of both matter and souls.

Whilst Ramanuja was strict in culinary rules, his eminent follower, Ramananda, who probably lived during the end of the fourteenth and the first half of the fifteenth century, was not. Ramananda admitted disciples of all castes to his group, and they learned and dined together. His disciples included Dhanna the cultivator, Pipa the raj, Ravidas the leather worker, Sainu the barber, and Kabir the Muslim weaver. Chaitanya (1485–1533) of Bengal, in whose teaching is found the culmination and fulfilment of the religion of love, and who ushered in a new era in the spiritual life of Bengal, also had both Hindu and Muslim disciples. The cult of Krishna was particularly popular with Muslims.

Kabir (*ca.* 1440–1518), whose teaching is a synthesis of the finest Hindu and Muslim sentiment, condemned rituals and caste, opposed asceticism, and preached the religion of love.[16] He combined the zeal of a reformer with the humility of a devotee. He regarded the spiritual basis of Hinduism and Islam as one, and was revolted by the superstructures of dogma. Kabir was the embodiment of the process of Hindu-Muslim union in mediaeval India. He advocated a universal religion, to which no Hindu or Muslim could take objection. He denounced the Hindu worship of idols, ceremonial rituals and caste on the one hand, and on the other, the Muslim trust in one Prophet and his book, pilgrimage, and fasts. He repeatedly pointed out that Hindus and Muslims were one: they worshipped the same God and were children of the same ancestors.

> Make thy mind thy Kaaba,
>   Thy body its enclosing temple,
> Conscience its prime teacher.
> Then, O priest, call men to pray to that mosque
> Which hath five gates.
> The Hindus and Mussulmans have the same Lord.

Kabir had a large following amongst both Hindus and Muslims. Amongst his friends were several reformers who are remembered with respect even to this day, such as Taqui of the Sufi Suhrawardi sect, whose daughter Kamal married a Brahman, and Ravidas, who was a low caste, *chamar,* Hindu. Kabir is regarded as one of the great men of Indian history. He is an outstanding Hindi poet whose poetry is steeped in the love of God. Today there are more than half a million followers of Kabir, *Kabirpanthis,* in India. Other offshoots of his teaching are the Satnamis, Radhaswamis, and Dadupanthis.

Guru Nanak (1469–1539), a contemporary of Kabir and the Mughal ruler Babur, founded the Sikh faith.[17] Principally a social and religious thinker, Nanak lived in a period of Indian history filled with political upheavals, atrocities, and lawlessness. He condemned formalism and ritualism in religion and tried to blend the mystical ideas of the Hindu and Muslim faiths in Sikhism.[18] His first puplic proclamation was that there was no Hindu or Muslim, for all were the children of the same God. The ultimate goal of human beings was to enjoy divine beatitude. In many respects, he represents the high water mark of this Hindu-Muslim cultural synthesis and renaissance philosophy. He opposed all forms of idolatry and denounced caste and communalism. He preached devotion to one God, transcending religious divisions. His teachings were so liberal that they constitute a daily prayer not only for Sikhs, but also for many Hindus.[19]

All the reformers condemned caste, denounced polytheism and idolatry, advocated a puritanical way of life, preached communal harmony, goodwill and unity, exposed the futility of ceremonies, tended to emancipate the minds of men from the domination of priests and *mullas*, safeguarded fundamental religious beliefs, and encouraged local literature. They were nonsectarian, noncommunal, and nondogmatic. They realized the oneness of the God invoked by various religions under different names and believed in the *bhakti* as the principal means of salvation. Their chief contribution to Indian religious thought was a profoundly psychological analysis and comprehensive interpretation of bhakti.

Whether the Bhakti movement was inspired by Islam or was a logical extension of the developing Hindu thought during the mediaeval period is debatable. Certainly the excessive, if not exclusive, stress on devotion and love of God as preached by the leaders of the Bhakti movement was in contrast to the ancient Indian philosophical speculations which emphasized intellectual scepticism as the essence of religion. However, before the advent of Islam, Hindu mediaeval thought had departed from the questioning attitude, demanding logical explanations of conclusions, and had come to seek its validity in revealed truth. The earliest mention of bhakti is found in the *Svetasvatara Upanishad*. Later the *Bhagavad Gita*, composed before the Christian era began, emphasized the triple path of *bhakti, jnana,* and *karma* to obtain *moksha*, and by the middle ages bhakti had become a central doctrine of Hinduism.

The sacred language of Islam was Arabic, the mother tongue of the early invaders; later conquerors spoke Turkish and Persian, influenced and modified by Arabic. Whilst Arabic remained the language of

171

religion, Persian became the language of the court during the Muslim rule. Persian was, therefore, studied by both Hindus and Muslims if they sought administrative positions, but it did not become the language of the masses, not even of the Muslim masses.[20] The overwhelming majority of the Muslims in India were Indian converts, and the change of religion was easier than the change of tongue. Of necessity, Arabic and Persian had to intermingle with local languages. The result was Urdu, which is spoken in northern India and is a national language of Pakistan today. A combination of Persian and Hindi, Urdu is a fine example of Indo-Islamic synthesis. The evolution of a common language was indicative of growing intimacy between the two religious groups and an assurance of future understanding.

Originally a spoken language, Urdu came to be written in Arabic script. Its basic structure and grammar are Indian, as is most of its vocabulary. The emergence of a simplified and popular language helped the development of local languages too. A flood of literature appeared in the different languages of India. The Bhakti saints wrote and preached in the local languages, which gradually gained importance and respectability, and the snobbery attached to Sanskrit, which had discouraged the development of literatures in regional languages, was overthrown.

More important, however, was the growth of a common outlook which discounted religious ritualism and led to an extensive exchange of ideas at the common man's level and, consequently, to the development of common cultural patterns. As Urdu and Hindi were the expressions of the new common culture, Hindu and Muslim scholars wrote in both languages. Whilst Amir Khusrau, Rahim Khanikhana, and Malik Muhammad Jayasi wrote classical poetry in Hindi, many Hindus contributed to Urdu literature. Muslims contributed to the development of regional literatures also; for instance, Alaol (Alaul-Husan), the son of the Nawab of Jalapur, heralded a new age in Bengali literature. He translated not only Jayasi's famous Hindi epic, *Padmavat,* into Bengali, but also the Persian romance, *Saiju'l-Muluk wa Badi'ul-Jamal.*

Hindu and Muslim rulers in practically every region encouraged Indo-Islamic culture and literature. Muslim kings endowed Hindu temples and granted crown lands to learned Brahmans. During the reign of Qutbuddin Ahmad Shah (1451–1458), the first lyrical poem, *Vasanta Vilasa,* was composed in Gujarati. The Bengali translation of the *Mahabharata* was undertaken under the order of Nasir Shah of Gaur who ruled from 1285 to 1325, and to whom Vidyapati dedicated one of his poems. Similarly, Hussain Shah commanded Maladhar Vasu to render the *Bhagavad Gita* into Bengali. In South India, the Qutbshahi and

Adilshahi rulers, some of whom were poets in their own right, patronized the local languages even more than the Muslim kings of northern India.

The creative energy released by Indo-Islamic cultural intercourse achieved even better results in art. In many ways, Islamic art, which had assumed a synthetic character from a selective fusion of Arab, Syrian, Byzantine, Persian, and Central Asian traditions, was the antithesis of Hindu art. The divergence in natural background, religious beliefs, and political history of the two peoples was reflected in their respective art forms. Yet upon contact, instead of clashing they blended together, giving rise to a new form of art in India.

Because of religious taboos, Muslims were not initially interested in music and painting, but they soon acquired a deep affection for them. Before the rise of Islam, Mecca was not only noted for its shrines, but also for its dancing and singing girls. There is some evidence that even in the Quran a beautiful voice is indirectly praised. The Persians had always been fond of music. The oldest parts of the *Avesta,* named *gathas,* were recited in a musical voice. The Sassanian kings were famous for their patronage of music. With this background, Islam could not resist music for long. The serious study of this art began during the last phase of the Umayyad Caliphate and was well developed by the time the Abbasids ascended to their rule. The growth of Islamic music was a valuable contribution to world culture, as well as to that of India. Islamic music first came to Sind with the Arabs, and was soon blended with the prevalent Indian system.

The divine service in the mosque was performed without vocal or instrumental music, but when Muslim rulers saw that Hindu life was full of music, they adopted it into their social life, although they continued their *namaz* (prayer) without music. Muslim Sufi saints, who were as fond of music as the Hindu Bhaktas, even introduced it into their congregational meetings, where songs of divine love, *qawwalis,* were sung; qawwalis are extremely popular in India even today.

Some Muslim rulers became skilful musicians. A Muslim ruler of Jaunpur is credited with developing the imaginative *raga khayal* from the massive and solid *raga dhrupad.* Alauddin Khilji had a number of accomplished musicians amongst his courtiers. Singers and dancers—Hindu, Turkish, Persian, and others—resided permanently at Muslim *darbars,* often under the headship of a Persian officer. Devotional songs, such as *bhairavi, sarasrag, kalungra,* and *bhairon,* were sung at religious gatherings, and in the darbar, *malkos* and *darbari* were presented. Thus, by a fusion of Indo-Iranian music, North Indian music was formed.[20a] The Muslim poet, Amir Khusrau, was also a famous singer

173

who introduced new styles. From the fourteenth and fifteenth centuries onwards Persian modes were introduced into the music of northern India, thereby making it a little different from that of South India where the Iranian influence was not felt. The modern ragas and raginis developed under Muslim patronage. Many Indian instruments also owe their origin to Muslim artists; for instance, the *tabla, dilruba, sarod,* and *naqqara,* were introduced by the Arabs or Iranians. Amongst the tunes believed to be Iranian in origin are *zangola, zlif, zala,* and *khamaj.*

A synthesis of Hindu and Muslim musical elements had taken place even during the period of the Delhi Sultanate, and by the time of the Mughals, a musical art form existed which became highly developed under the enthusiasm and patronage of the Mughals. Music, as other aspects of Indo-Islamic culture, reached its zenith at the time of Akbar. During his reign about two hundred tunes were modified under Iranian influence. Darbari, or chamber music, was introduced in his time. The celebrated pupil of Swami Haridas, Tansen, lived at Akbar's court, and was one of his *navaratna* (nine jewels). Tansen's disciples gave rise to various schools of music. It is said that when the Mughals returned to the north after their conquest of Deccan, they took with them the most famous South Indian musicians along with other artists and sculptors.

Music in Muslim India was far more popular than it is sometimes made out to be. A major reason for this may well be that the vast majority of Muslims in India were of Hindu descent and disinclined to give up, like their tongue, their music. Even today some of the best known Indian musicians are Muslims, such as Ali Akbar Khan, Vilayat Khan, and Bismillah Khan.

The mediaeval period, in fact, appears to have been an age of accomplished musicians, both Hindu and Muslim. The great poet-singers, Tulsidas, Surdas, and Mirabai, belong to this period. Akbar's contemporary, Sultan Ibrahim Adil Shah of Bijapur, was also a composer, a teacher of both Hindu and Muslim musicians, and the author of a book, *Nau-Ras,* on music. In Kashmir, King Zainul Abidin patronized art and music and had a large number of Central Asian musicians at his court. Shahjahan, the prince of builders, who did not care much for painting, was a great lover of music. During Aurangzeb's reign, music, as well as other art forms, lost court favour but by that time North Indian music—often called Hindustani—had already assumed its new personality.

Today, Hindustani and Karnatak schools of music are prevalent in the north and south respectively. There may be minor differences of nomenclature and articulation but basically there is only one Indian music. The raga is the basis, and its development the goal of musical expression. Both systems have the same number of notes—seven *suddha* and five *vikrita*—in the octave. The classification of ragas under parental modes is also common to both.

Because of Islam's intense aversion to images, sculpture was not a well-developed art in the Islamic countries. Pre-Islamic Arabia had idols, and a few animal figures in stone, bronze or other metals are found in the palace of Alhambra in Spain and amongst the ruins of Egypt and Spain. Pre-Islamic Iran, under the Achaemenians and Sassanians, was rich in sculpture. Sculpture was also highly developed in India and remained almost unaffected by Islam.

At first Islam did not encourage painting, but later the Caliphs declared that the religious injunction against the representation of living creatures applied only to religious structures, not to residential buildings. Hence, the Umayyads and the Abbasids in Asia and the Caliphs of Spain had their palace walls decorated with floral designs and even human figures. The Mughal rulers loved and patronized painting. Babur brought with him some of the finest specimens from the ancestral collection of Timurid paintings. The Timurid school of painting, one of the two greatest Persian schools—the other being the Safavi—was begun by Timur's grandsons. The first patron of the school was Iskandar Sultan, son of Ulugh Beg, who ruled over Fars until 1414. Soon afterwards another Timurid ruler, Baysunghur (d. 1433), attracted artists to his library at Herat; it was there that Kamaluddin Bihzad flourished in the middle of the fifteenth century. Bihzad was the greatest artist of Persia—with the possible exception of Mani—and his interpretation of the Timurid style of painting greatly influenced Indian art. Both Babur and Humayun greatly admired Bihzad, and when Humayun returned to India after his exile in Persia, he took with him two of Bihzad's distinguished pupils, Mir Saiyid Ali and Khwaja Adbus Samad Shirazi.

In the course of time, three new schools of painting—the Rajput, the Jammu, and the Kangra—emerged in northern India, appearing first in the early sixteenth century in Rajasthan. Later, the Rajput style spread far beyond Rajasthan to the Himalaya states, Kashmir, and also to Mathura and Banaras. The new style was primitive but highly expressive and colourful. The eyes of the figures were almost hypnotic, with all expression conveyed through postures and poses of the body. However, Mughal art superseded this style by the middle of the seventeenth century.

Akbar was a great admirer of the realistic and forceful simplicity of the Hindu style and of the delicacy, linear grace, and decoration of the

Persian. He deliberately initiated a blending of the two styles under experts of both schools. Akbar rewarded good paintings generously, and both Hindu and Muslim artists were designated as officers of the state. His patronage, coupled with the use of paper as a medium, greatly advanced the development of the graphic arts. The importance of painting is stressed in the *Ain-i-Akbari*. Talented Iranian and Indian artists executed the miniatures of the illuminated manuscripts of *Hamzanama, Tutinama, Baburnama, Razmnama,* a Persian version of the *Mahabharata* which cost the Emperor about eighty thousand pounds, the *Akbarnama*, illustrated by Farrukh Beg, *Nala-Damayanti* of Faizi, the *Ramayana*, the *Harivamsa*, and others.[21] The *Akbarnama* paintings are noted for their unity of design, even though Mughal miniatures were usually painted by several artists. The miniatures of the Indian epics are not only fine art specimens, but also a valuable source of information about contemporary Hindu manners and customs.

At first the style was chiefly Persian in inspiration but later it was more influenced by Indian styles, and by the time of Jahangir's reign a new Mughal style of painting had been born. Jahangir, a talented painter himself, patronized painting almost exclusively; all the great painters of the school belonged to his court. He had a keen aesthetic sense and loved the beauties of nature. He was so attracted to Kashmir that he visited it thirteen times during the twenty-two years of his reign. He favoured naturalism in art, and the painting of landscapes, animals, and portraits reached its zenith during his reign. Mansur is the most renowned of the bird and animal painters of the period. From Jahangir's reign onward, the Rajput and the Mughal schools can be distinguished. Shahjahan carried on the tradition, but his chief patronage was given to architecture. His son, Dara Shikoh, patronized the arts, although he was more interested in philosophy. He left behind a valuable album of paintings, but before he could stamp his personality on Indian culture and society, he was executed by his younger brother, Aurangzeb.

Islam's richest contribution was in architecture and the whole of northern India is studded with beautiful buildings of the period. The Fatehpur Sikri complex, the Red Fort of Delhi, and the Taj Mahal are a few of the many outstanding buildings in which the blending of Indian and Islamic elements can be seen.

Muslim architecture, a fusion of Arab, Syrian, Persian, Turkish, Central Asian, and other traditions, is generally massive, with extensive buildings and mosques, mausoleums, domes, minarets, lofty portals, open courtyards, geometrical patterns, and calligraphic inscriptions. Its basic forms are the pillared hall, the dome resting on pillars, and the brick vault and cupola. The monotheistic puritanism of Islam delighted in the simplicity of the unbroken dome, the plain symbolism of the pointed arch, and the slenderness of the minaret. The inhospitable natural surroundings of Arabia had influenced the art of Islam, as they did its outlook on life, making it austere, vigorous, and purposeful. It is particularly conspicuous in mosques and sacred places by the absence of representations of living beings, whether in painting or sculpture. In contrast, Hindu architecture is renowned for its majesty, richness, and variety. Temples were carved with reliefs of all forms of the supernatural, and animal and plant life. Hindu art is decorative and at times voluptuous, whereas Muslim art is simple and puritanical.

By the time the Muslims came to India with a view to setting up an empire, they already had centuries of cultural tradition behind them which was influenced by the numerous peoples with whom they had come in contact in Europe, Asia, and Africa. Although Islamic architecture started in Arabia, it attained maturity through a period of sustained development in West and Central Asia, North Africa, and Spain, before reaching its zenith in India. Islamic architecture originated in the construction and design of the mosque and many of its finest buildings are mosques. Next in importance come tombs, followed by palaces, forts, and public buildings. In their early days in India, the Muslims were dazzled by the extraordinary richness and sumptuousness of Indian architecture. In the fourteenth century, they began to react against it, but this was a short-lived phase; soon syncretic tendencies reached their peak during the Mughal period.

The oldest extant Indian mosques are in the neighbourhood of Delhi where the Mughals built profusely. The most significant early Islamic building in India is the Qutb Minar at Delhi, which was completed about 1231 during the reign of Iltutmish. One of the most stupendous architectural achievements conceived by Muslims, the tower, comprising five stories and standing 238 feet high, forms part of the Qutb Mosque scheme. The Qutb Mosque was built by Qutbuddin Aibek in 1195 on the spacious substructure of a Hindu temple, and consisted entirely of spoils extracted from temples in the area. Such a second-hand building had little architectural beauty or order. However, four years later it was decided to project an expansive arched screen across the side of the structure facing Mecca; this screen is possibly the first surviving example of a structure in definite original Islamic style on Indian soil.

At about the time the Qutb Minar was being built in the eastern extremity of the Islamic world, Yusuf I of Spain, at the western extremity of Islam, was raising a tower even higher than the Qutb, the Giralda, at Seville. However, neither the Giralda nor any other tower in the Islamic world surpasses the Qutb in beauty. Another extremely fine example of the early Indo-Islamic style is to be seen in the adjacent Alai Darwaza, built in 1310. This and the ruined tomb of Alauddin Khilji, erected soon after, represent the early Sultanate style at the time of its greatest perfection.

Many palaces, mosques, mausoleums, baths, and educational institutions sprang up, especially during the reigns of Alauddin Khilji and Firuz Tughluq. After Alauddin's death there was a change in style, which had been foreshadowed for some time, and Tughluq architecture became marked by the absence of extravagant features. The Tughluq style, however, is vigorous and straightforward and readily adapted old structural features to its requirements. Its departure from Islamic traditions became clear; red sandstone and marble gave place to rubble and plaster.

The Lodi style was an elaboration of the Tughluq, enriched by new ornamental motifs from Iran and Turkistan. The most important feature of the tomb of Sikandar Lodi is the double dome, which subsequently played an important role in the evolution of Mughal style. This architectural invention, designed to preserve the symmetry and relative proportions of the body of the building, probably originated in Syria and came to India through Iraq and Iran.

The assimilation of forms and techniques in art naturally went on throughout the country. In Bengal, the prevalent brick construction was adopted by the Muslim conquerors who imitated Hindu motifs in their structural embellishments. The main features of Islamic architecture in eastern India are heavy stone pillars, pointed arches, and brick vaults. In Kashmir, the beautiful wooden architecture was readily appropriated, and Kashmiri tombs are quite different from similar structures elsewhere in India. In western India, Gujarati styles were similarly adapted. The rich ornamentation and delicate style of the Muslim architecture of Gujarat accord with the highly developed and rich Hindu architecture. In other regions of India, similarly, Islamic architecture absorbed prevalent local characteristics, emerging with a distinctive personality.

Unlike other Muslim rulers of India, the Bahmani rulers of the Deccan largely ignored the indigenous art with the result that the Deccan style was mainly influenced by the Imperial buildings at Delhi and the monuments of Iran. The Bahmani Kings, who were Shia Muslims, were patrons of the arts and sciences. They attracted eminent scholars and expert technicians from other countries, and it was probably because of this that their military architecture was much influenced by Europe and their civil architecture by Iran.

The Muslims acquired much from the Sassanian and Byzantine schools, and in all the countries they conquered they adapted the indigenous architecture to their own requirements. In India, mosques and temples required some ornamental decoration, and colonnades adorned the open courts of both but the contrasting styles were striking. The prayer chamber of the mosque was spacious, whereas the shrine of the temple was small; the mosque was light and open and the temple rather dark and closed in; Muslim construction was based on arches, vaults and domes, whereas Hindu construction was based on columns, architraves and pyramidal towers or slender spires. The Muslims readily adopted the Hindu trabeate, the system of using beams or long square stones as lintels and entablature instead of using the arch. They also made use of the bracket type of Hindu corbel—the stone or timber projection for support. In return, they gave to Indian architecture a sense of breadth and spaciousness and introduced new forms and colours. Like the Romans, they used concrete and mortar imaginatively. They spanned big spaces with arches, roofed large areas with magnificent domes, and introduced, amongst other architectural features, the minar. They introduced decorative arabesque or geometric devices, inscriptions in graceful lettering, gilding and painting in variegated colours, encaustic tile-mosaic and tesselate designs in coloured stones and marble.

With the establishment of the Mughal Empire in 1526, a new era of architecture dawned in India. By that time, even those Muslims whose families had come from outside had been largely Indianized, and the Indo-Islamic cultural synthesis had attained maturity. The Mughals gave it a new and vigorous impetus. In 1530, Babur, the founder of the Mughal Empire, was succeeded by his son, Humayun, who, after ten years of unsettled reign, was exiled for the next fifteen years. Because of the almost unending warfare throughout their brief reigns in India, Babur and Humayun were unable to contribute much of lasting value to Mughal architecture.

During Humayun's exile, his conqueror, Shershah Suri, famous for his revenue administration and public welfare works, ruled from Delhi, and architecture made considerable progress during the relatively brief rule of the Suri dynasty. At first Suri architecture was soberly elegant but toward the end it became highly decorative. It is the precursor of the Mughal styles, and an important stage in the development of Indian architecture. Shershah's finest building is the mosque constructed at

179

Delhi in 1541. The mausoleum of Shershah, in Sahasram in Bihar, built in a splendid Indo-Iranian style at about the same time, is an architectural masterpiece. It is indeed a suitable tribute to the genius of a ruler and to the skill and vision of its architect. Constructed of fine sandstone, the mausoleum is 250 feet wide and stands four square in the centre of a large artificial lake so extensive that each of its concrete sides measures 1400 feet in length. Whilst the style of Babur and Humayun was foreign, that of the Suris, although Muslim in external appearance, was influenced in details by Hindu architecture, especially in the construction of doorways.

The first outstanding monument of the early Mughal style is the mausoleum of Humayun (Humayun ka Makbara), built by his widow during Akbar's reign. She is said to have employed an Iranian architect, Mirak Mirza Ghiyas, who introduced certain Iranian features, such as a typically Iranian dome, an arched alcove as is found in the royal tombs of Iran, the interior arrangement of corridors, and the complex of rooms. Indigenous characteristics are to be found in the elegant kiosks with cupolas, and the excellent stone masonry. The style of this monument has been described as an Indian interpretation of an Iranian architectural conception. Both in spirit and in structure, Humayun's tomb is a captivating example of the synthesis of two great traditions of art.

All of the early Mughal buildings display the sober elegance of the Iranian style. At the beginning of the Mughal period, a fresh wave of Iranians came to India; this influx of noblemen and men of learning and culture more or less continued throughout the period. Iran thus played the same part in the development of Indo-Islamic art during the sixteenth century as Renaissance Italy did to the art of France. But early in Akbar's reign, Iranian influences were blended with Indian styles. This fusion is reflected in the mosque and palace buildings at Fatehpur Sikri, the capital city built by Akbar in 1570–1574 on a site near Agra. These buildings form a brilliant complex, with broad terraces and stately courtyards surrounded by numerous palaces and pavilions. The most imposing building is the Jama Masjid; its finest feature is the 176 feet tall southern gateway, the Buland Darwaza, which is made of marble and sandstone, and is architecturally the most perfect gateway in India, and the largest of its kind in the world. Indeed, the buildings at Fatehpur Sikri constitute one of the most spectacular structural achievements in the whole of India. The style of Fatehpur Sikri is mature in every respect, fully absorbing Iranian elegance into the exactness of Indian workmanship. A monument to Akbar's vision and

180

originality, it is, after the Taj Mahal, the most notable architectural achievement of the Mughals. This capital was built purely as a retreat from military strife. But Sikri's tenure as the capital was ironically short, lasting hardly more than a generation.

Akbar left scores of buildings at Agra, Allahabad, and elsewhere. The Agra fort, built in 1565–1573, is one of his outstanding structural achievements. It is important not only in providing an example of the military architecture of the early Mughals, but in testifying that the aesthetic taste and artistic feeling of its builders influenced even utilitarian structures. Unlike most Muslim rulers of India, Akbar encouraged indigenous construction systems and borrowed from other countries only when necessary. Most of his buildings are red sandstone, with white marble here and there for emphasis, and both arcuate and trabeate styles were used.

In the secular buildings of the time, of which the most important and complete is the palace of Akbar's Hindu queen, Jodh Bai, the carved decoration was unrestrained. Figures of elephants, lions, and peacocks, and other embellishments suggest that Hindu craftsmen predominated, under the supervision of accommodating Mughal overseers. Some of the civil buildings are more Hindu than others, and copy features of Hindu and Jain temples. Although this synthesis was a natural outcome of Indo-Islamic cultural exchange, Akbar's sympathies with Indian culture as a whole partly accounts for these unorthodox intrusions into Islamic art. In mosques and religious buildings, however, traditional Muslim construction was adhered to more closely.

By the time of Jahangir and Shahjahan, both of whom were sons of Hindu queens, the situation had changed. Islam had long been Indianized and so had Mughal rule. Muslim art had already assumed a predominantly Indian personality, in which Iranian influence can be detected only by experts. Although Jahangir inherited Akbar's artistic taste and built some magnificent structures, his reign was relatively unproductive in architecture. However, other arts developed, and a new school of miniature painting was established. Of the buildings erected by Jahangir, the tomb of Akbar, at Sikandra near Agra, is the most impressive. Built in 1613–1614, it was a departure from the conventional domed structure, and is a low, truncated, three-storied pyramid shape. Reflecting something of the nature-loving monarch whose remains it enshrines, a sense of space is given by the wide-terraced flower garden which surrounds it. The carvings and paintings, in both gold and colours, are exquisite. Its four minarets are in perfect harmony; nothing like these had been built in northern India since the Qutb Minar

181

centuries earlier. Whilst it does not compare with the mausoleum of Humayun at Delhi, it was a conception of such magnitude that it was not completed until eight years after Jahangir's accession, even though the Emperor took a personal interest in its construction.

Another interesting building of Jahangir's reign is the tomb of his father-in-law, Itmadud-daulah, at Agra, built by Empress Nurjahan. This small, elegant, and exquisitely finished mausoleum marks a transition between the styles of Akbar and Shahjahan, illustrating a fresh interpretation of the art of building. As an example of architecture in miniature, this building, with its garden and gateways, is one of the best of its kind. Built of white marble and decorated in stone of five colours, it is elaborately ornamental and embellished throughout with subtlety and delicacy. This mausoleum marks the beginning of the most sumptuous phase of Mughal building characterized by the profusion of gold, precious stones, and white marble, which replaced sandstone. The best known buildings of Shahjahan's period are the Jama Masjid; the Red Fort at Delhi, with its Diwan-i-Am, Diwan-i-Khas, and Moti Masjid; and the Taj Mahal. The Taj is the triumph of Indo-Islamic synthesis in art. Shahjahan built the mausoleum, which stands on the Jamuna River at Agra, to enshrine the remains of his queen, Mumtaz Mahal. Commencing work in 1631, twenty thousand Hindus and Muslims laboured for twenty-two years to finish it. Whilst the broad conception of this unique memorial is attributed to Shahjahan himself, there is some uncertainty about the identity of the architect who translated his ideals into stone. Some Western scholars have suggested that he was a Venetian jeweller and silversmith, Geronimo Veroneo. There is no evidence to support this suggestion except that the Italian was employed by the Mughal Court at the time and was invited, along with many others, to submit designs to a council of architects and craftsmen convened by the Emperor. But the design finally accepted was prepared by local master builders. That the Taj Mahal is wholly indigenous is obvious by the indisputably Indo-Islamic style of architecture. Contemporary manuscripts give full details of its construction, including the names of the architects and builders, amongst whom are found Hindus, Muslims, and West Asians, but no Italians.

Shahjahan's reign was followed by the long, austere, and autocratic rule of the intensely orthodox Muslim emperor, Aurangzeb, the last of the Great Mughals. Aurangzeb was not a patron of art, but was an accomplished calligrapher, and had made copies of the Quran to earn his living. After his death, the unity of India was broken and the country was plunged into political chaos and intrigue.

Just as the buildings constructed by Muslims blended Islamic designs with Indian details, the Hindu temples came under Indo-Islamic influence. The Govind Deo temple built in 1590 is the most notable of these and is a tribute to the versatility of Indian masons. It shows a sense of refinement and an appreciation of plain surfaces not often seen in temple designs. The secular architecture of Hindus, for example in Malwa and Rajasthan, was also influenced by Akbar and his successors. Royal residences and other state buildings, for instance at Bikaner, and palace fortresses, such as those at Jodhpur and Orchha, show the influence of the Mughal style.

Other arts and crafts which the Muslims transmitted from Iran to India, are enamelling, faience, the parcel gilt work of Kashmir, damascening, and papier mâché. Innovations were introduced in the manufacture of cotton and silk textiles, woollen shawls and carpets, and Nurjahan is credited with the discovery of the attar of roses.

Islamic political influence was considerable. In fact, the whole military organization was revolutionized and a new military oligarchy became the principal political institution of Muslim India. New weapons and techniques of warfare were also introduced.

The Muslims introduced into India the *Yunani* system of medicine. The large number of physicians, *hakims,* at the royal court held high *mansabs* and rendered inexpensive medical aid to the sick. The Yunani system is presumably so called because the Arabs had borrowed liberally from Greek medicine.

Islam made a greater impact on Indian urban life than on rural life. Influenced by the royal court, the urban population attained a high degree of sophistication in language and literature, arts and crafts, manners, dress, diet, luxuries and refinements. The centres of power, Delhi, Agra, and Lucknow, set fashions that were widely followed in all provincial courts, including even unfriendly states such as Rajasthan and the Deccan. This Mughal impress persisted in the parlours, the *zenana*, the wardrobe and the dining room, and continues to do so today amongst the upper classes of Indian society. Islamic court fashions, under Akbar and afterwards, exercised considerable influence on men's wear amongst the Hindu upper and middle classes, but not so much on women's clothing except in jewelry.[22]

Whilst the court played a significant part in determining styles, dress is principally governed by climatic conditions. Consequently, in large countries, the national dress has regional style. For instance, *pajamas* are worn in the Punjab by both Hindus and Muslims, as is the *dhoti* in the south; the variations in dress more often reflect class rather than

183

communal distinctions. Women's ornaments are common to both communities. Whilst the *shalwar* is worn by the women of the Punjab, the
sari is the most common dress of all Indian women. In India today
certain regional dresses, like dishes of food, have gained national
popularity. For instance, young girls in all parts of India prefer the
shalwar to the sari because of its suitability for active work and sport,
and the Afghan-type *karakuli* cap is a common sight in Delhi during
winter.

Even those Muslims who came to India from other countries largely
adopted costumes suitable to their new country. For instance, the Arab
amama, jubba, rida, tahmad, and *tasma,* as well as the Central Asian
kulah, nima, and *moza,* were replaced by the Indian *pugree, chira, kurta,
angarkha, patka, dupatta,* and *pajama.* The assimilation in dress was
primarily an upper class problem, and the large numbers of Hindu
converts felt no need to change their fashions.

In the rural Indian villages, where practically the entire Muslim
population was descended from Hindu converts, the traditional Hindu
outlook and social forms were retained. Even the caste prejudices, the
objection to widow remarriage, and the love of ritual and image worship
continued. Both Hindus and Muslims observed similar ceremonies of
birth, death, and marriage, and had much the same fairs and festivals.
The dress, the manner of cooking, the family system, and the style of
houses continued to be the same for both, and the common language
remained the regional tongue.

In social life, however, some effects of Islam on Indian society were
not too healthy, for example, the development of *purdah,* the seclusion
of women. Many Hindu nobles were required to offer their daughters
in marriage to Muslim sultans and noblemen, a demand which the
former found contrary to their religious beliefs. The caste-ridden Hindu
could not contract marriages for their children outside their own caste or
even subcaste, let alone their religious group. Consequently, they
responded to this pressure by adopting the Muslim practice of purdah,
which, in time, led to child-marriage and the general deterioration of
the woman's position in Indian society. Customs such as *jauhar* and
sati became more frequent. However, in the areas where Muslim influence
was weak, such as South India, the custom of purdah was not prevalent.

For all its emphasis on human equality, Islam, like Buddhism before
it, failed to demolish caste. From the Hindu point of view the Muslims
became another caste, and despite cultural similarity, they remained
a distinct social group. Because of the rigid Hindu caste system, intermarriage and inter-dining between orthodox Hindus and Muslims were

not possible. Also, no orthodox Muslim would allow his son or daughter to marry an unconverted Hindu. There was, however, no hostility based on group prejudice or religious consciousness. Cultural dissimilarities were regional, and power conflicts political.

A common Indian culture could not be evolved unless Islam in turn was influenced by Hindu culture and became Indian in character. Because of the Indian influence on their social life and customs, Indian Muslims today are a group distinct from Muslims elsewhere. Hindu caste affected Islam. Commonly, Muslims are regarded as belonging to two social groups—the *sharifzats* (high castes) and the *ajlafzats* (low castes). In fact, however, there are many more social castes and distinctions which divide Indian Muslims.[23] Whilst inter-caste marriages amongst Muslims were not prohibited, they generally did not take place. Social distinctions were preserved not by religious belief but by snobbery. The Muslim *bhangi* was as downtrodden as his Hindu counterpart, although the Islamic ideal of human equality was a major incentive for many caste-ridden and oppressed Hindus to embrace Islam. But in practice their social inequality remained. The foreign Muslims regarded themselves as somewhat superior to the local converts and, as a natural extension of this snobbery, the mixed Muslims, like the early Eurasians, tried to identify themselves with the ruling foreign class. Having been refused the superior status of the foreigner, they developed a class of their own. The terms *sayyid* and *shaikh,* implying Arab origin, carry highest prestige; the Mughal ranks next in importance. Outcastes and the converts from the lower Hindu castes were designated as *Nau* (New)-*Muslims,* somewhat in the same way as new migrants are called New Australians in Australia today.

Islam condemns priesthood, but it developed amongst Indian Muslims. They also showed a marked fondness for ritual and elaborate ceremony. Islam is monotheistic and iconoclastic, but Indian Muslims often venerate saints and their tombs. Numerous sacred shrines, such as Shaikh Chishti at Ajmer and Bhairava Nath at Mathura, are frequented by both Muslims and Hindus. A Muslim sect, *Panchpiriyas* (worshippers of five pirs), venerate saints to such a degree that an Indian census of 1911 described them as Hindus whose religion has a strong Mohammedan flavour. The Prophet rejected miracles, but Indian Muslims sanctify their heroes. Many Muslims even developed idolatrous practices. For example, the Chauriharas of Uttar Pradesh worship Kalka Sahja Mai and observe *sraddha;* the Meos of the Punjab worship many gods such as Siansi, Magti, and Lachi; the Mirasis take offerings to Durga-

Bhavani; the Turk-Nawas of eastern Bengal worship Lakshmi. Many Bengali Muslims worship Sitala, Kali, Dharmaraj, Baidyanatu, and other Hindu deities. The Avans of the Punjab use Brahmans as family priests, and the cow is revered by the Shins of the Indus Valley, who do not eat beef, as well as by the Momins of Kutch.[24] The Momins worship the Hindu Trinity—Brahma, Vishnu and Mahesh—and their salutation is "Ram Ram." Muslim ascetics are often tonsured and smear their bodies with ash; they also often act as guardians of shrines. The fire in some Muslim areas such as the Jhang district in West Punjab and Gorakhpur in Uttar Pradesh is looked upon as sacred. Many Muslims participate fully in Hindu festivities, such as Holi and Diwali.

Hindu women in Muslim harems formed a powerful influence in working out the Indo-Islamic synthesis. Hindu women who married Muslim men introduced their social customs and rites into the new homes. Muslims tended more toward monogamy under Hindu influence, the remarriage of widows became rarer. Many features of Muslim court life were borrowed from Hindus. The Hindu superstition of the evil eye, and Hindu habits of bathing and ceremonial purity were adopted by Muslims. Many Rajput converts retained their family names. The Malkana Rajputs, now Muslim, still perform Hindu rites and ceremonies. They prefer to be called Miyan Thakurs and admit to being a mixture of Hindu and Muslim. The Avans, although they are nearly all Muslims, retain their Hindu names and keep their genealogies in the Brahmanic fashion. Hindu titles, such as Chaudhari, Thakur, and Raja, are also found amongst Muslims. Some Muslim groups use the Hindu marriage ceremony, or perform the Hindu rites first and the Muslim ceremony afterwards. The Hindu joint family system and, in many cases, the Hindu property law were followed by Muslims.

Islamic thought was also affected by Hindu doctrines and philosophy. There were, no doubt, a number of people amongst both communities who bitterly resisted extraneous influences or innovations, but there were many more who regarded the spirit of religion as more important than its letter. Amongst them were mystics who interpreted religion for the common man. It was because of the endeavours of such people that the closeness of the two apparently irreconcilable doctrines came to be noticed: both stressed inner discipline, purification of mind, and unification with the divine.

The most mystical Muslim philosophy is *Tasawwuf*, known as Sufism, which is essentially the doctrine of the love of God, and which has exercised an incalculable influence on the intellectual and emotional life of Muslims, as well as on Islamic culture. Although Muslim orthodoxy often persecuted the Sufis, it was their interpretation which won the most converts to Islam in India, Africa, Indonesia, and elsewhere. It has been suggested that it is only because of Sufism that Islam became an international religion.

Sufism is not regarded by its followers as something which originated at a specific place or at a certain point in time. Jalaluddin Rumi said in his *Diwan* that the Sufis drank the wine of wisdom and knowledge before there were vines on this earth. Another Sufi scholar asserts that Sufism is too sublime to have had an origin. One theory derives Sufism from the esoteric doctrine of Muhammad himself, another from Neoplatonism, whilst yet another maintains it originated independently in the inherent mystical urge in all religious men. It has also been suggested that Sufism represents the reaction of the Aryan mind to a Semitic religion imposed by force.

The term *Sufi* comes from *suf* meaning wool; a Sufi is one who wears a woollen garment. The movement represented a reaction against the worldiness, luxury, and external piety of the period which followed the Muslim conquests. The early Sufis were simple, unsophisticated and pious people, who lived a life of self-discipline and poverty (*fakr*), devoting themselves to meditation and prayer in the quest of truth and righteousness. Their meditation was originally the continuous chanting of the name of Allah. Ascetics at first, they soon easily became mystics.

It was a woman, Rabia al-Adawiyya (717–801), who introduced a new dimension, the doctrines of divine love, into early Sufism by her concentration on serving God without being motivated either by the fear of divine punishment or expectation of reward: "O God if I worship Thee in fear of Hell, burn me in Hell; and if I worship Thee in hope of Paradise, exclude me from Paradise; but if I worship Thee for Thine own sake, withhold not Thine Everlasting Beauty." She thus marks the transition from the ascetic quietism of early Sufism to the advanced form it assumed with the introduction of the doctrine of *marifat*, gnosis, by the Egyptian Dhul-Nun al-Misri (d. 861), and that of *fana*, passing away into universal being, by the Persian Abu Yazid of Bistam (d. 875). Yazid was bold in his language and scandalized the orthodoxy. He was the first of the "intoxicated" Sufis who had drunk the "wine of knowledge" and who found God within his own soul through the mystic path. He was the first Sufi to give a detailed description of his *miraj*, mystical experience. From his time onward, the doctrine of fana became a central theme in Sufi theory. It was, however, Al Junaid of Baghdad (d. 910), the most original and penetrating intellectual of his time, who was responsible for developing this doctrine as an integral part of a well co-ordinated theosophy. Mansur al-Hajjaj (858–922) carried the philosophy still further. He did not merely see in the supreme mystical experience a reunion with God, but taught that man was God Incarnate, the doctrine of *anal-haqq* (I am the Truth).

By the end of the twelfth century Sufism so dominated the Muslim mind that every school of Islamic thought had become influenced by it. Imam al-Ghazali (1058–1111), who has been described as a "Renewer of Islam," was mainly responsible for this. His philosophy was the product of varied experience. After prolonged study, he attempted to reconcile orthodox Islamic teachings with mysticism and applied rational methods in interpreting its dogmas and doctrines. He became a wandering Sufi in 1095, asserted the futility of scholasticism, and declared that philosophy cannot unfold the mysteries of God and creation. He emphasized the value of direct experience as the vital element in religion, and taught that man's duty was to seek God and to love Him, whilst the role of the intellect was to realize its own limitations in this task. Ghazali took Abu Yazid, Al Hajjaj and Abu Said ibn Abil Khayr, who had reached the "reality of realities," as his models, and used their phrases, such as "anal-haqq," to express his belief in monism and "the annihilation of the soul and the sole vision of God." The greatest Muslim mystic thinker, Muhi al-Din ibn al-Arabi (d. 1240) was influenced by Al Ghazali. He built an imposing philosophical system and through his prolific writings Muslim mysticism attained its zenith. He was a complete monist: not only is there no other god but God, there is nothing but God and the world is His external manifestation. The evolutionary cycle of Sufism was completed in the fourteeth century with the rise of the school of Wahdat-al-Wujud, existentialist monism.

The early Sufis adhered to what was prescribed by Islam, but their ideal of life was renunciation, self-abnegation, and poverty. Later, Sufism gained greater spiritual intensity and breadth of outlook. Whilst retaining its mystical content, the Sufi vision embraces both heaven and earth and seeks to penetrate the innermost secrets of creation in order to comprehend the Divine mysteries that lie beyond ordinary human perception. The Sufis came to believe in the attainment of the vision of God and union with the Divine by adhering to the mystic path, *tariqa* or *suluk*. For them, spiritual life is a journey (*safar*) along this path; the journey has many stages and each state (*maqam*) has its corresponding achievement of certain virtues (*hal*). For Sufis, God or reality is the universal will, the true knowledge, the eternal light, and the supreme beauty, reflected in the mirror of the universe. As the nature of beauty is self-manifestation and desire to be loved, Sufis consider love to be the essence of all religions and the cause of creation and its continuation. The world is unreal, merely an illusion. Sufism thus teaches the doctrine of Wahdat-al-Wujud, unity of being, that being is one, that all apparent differences are modes, aspects, and manifestation of reality, and that the phenomenal world is the outward expression of the real, anal-haqq. "Know Thyself" is the core of Sufi philosophy, as it is in the Vedanta. It is through the path of self-knowledge that truth or reality is discovered in both Sufism and Hinduism, whether it is called *Jnana* in Sanskrit, or *Man araja Najsah Rabbahu* in Arabic.

Mysticism of the Sufi type has no place in orthodox Islamic teaching, for the strictly monotheistic religions, with the exception of Christianity, are not conducive to mysticism. Neither the Torah nor the Quran lend themselves to a mystical interpretation, as both assert most emphatically the complete otherness of God. Yet, the fact that mystic thought did develop in Islam is an illustration both of the powerful mystical strain in all religion, and of Indian influence on it. It is, therefore, not surprising that numerous scholars, both Muslim and non-Muslim, have been struck by the remarkable parallels between Sufi doctrines and those of Indian Vedanta and Buddhism.

One of the earliest examples of India's possible influence on Islam appears to have been the rise of opposition to legal Islam, known as *Zuhd* or asceticism. But in the further advanced philosophic concepts of Sufism, more definite Indian influence is suggested. R. A. Nicholson, strongly supported by Max Horton, insists that the Sufi idea of *jana* is of Indian origin, and strikingly close to the nirvana of Buddhism. Although recently A. J. Arberry has disputed this assertion as not proven, the weight of argument and opinion would seem to favour Nicholson and Horton rather than Arberry. The founder of this doctrine, Abu Yazid of Bistam, an uneducated man who disliked books, was a pupil of Abu Ali al-Sindi, who came from Sind in India (and not from a village called Sind in Khorasan, as Arberry asserts) and who was a convert to Islam from a foreign religion, evidently Hinduism. He instructed Abu Yazid, as Yazid himself admits, in the doctrines of divine unity (*tawhid*) and the ultimate truth (*haqa-iq*).[25] Even Abu Yazid's phraseology is reminiscent of Hindu philosophical expression. For instance, his usage of "That" for God is a typically Hindu way of referring to Brahman as the absolute, *Tat*. The phrase *Takunu anta dhaka* is indeed a literal translation of the upanishadic phrase, *tat tvam asi,* meaning "Thou art That" which is exclusive to the Vedanta. Considering that the vedantic teacher, Sankaracharya, had just revived and systematized the vedantic philosophy and made it a widespread and vigorous movement in India, it seems likely that Abu Yazid knew of it through his Indian teacher. Abu Yazid's extreme monism and his description of the world as illusion or deceit is remarkably close to Sankara's dismissal of the phenomenal world as maya, and his interpretation of vedantic monism.[26] A contemporary scholar, Zaehner, in fact, regards Sufism as "Vedanta in Muslim dress." It is indeed a remarkable illustration of cultural migration that through Sufism Indian monism should have found its way into Islamic philosophy which has been uncompromisingly opposed to any monistic or pantheistic doctrines.

Goldziher, who counsels that Sufism can be looked upon as an organized sect within Islam, points out that even the Sufi doctrine of Tawhid, or unity of God, is fundamentally different from the usual Islamic monotheistic concept, and is dependent upon Indian philosophy. "A Sufi goes so far to say it is *shirk* (giving associates to God) to assert that 'I know God': for in this sentence duality between perceiving subject and object to knowledge is involved; and this is also the current Indian view."[27]

The doctrine of anal-haqq is too reminiscent of the vedantic *aham Brahmasmi* to be attributed to parallel growth, especially since it is completely alien to Islamic thought. Its founder, Mansur al-Hajjaj, incurred the wrath of Islamic orthodoxy by his monist doctrine. He was condemned for blasphemy and was crucified in 922 for heresy. His theories were later incorporated into the system of Ibn-al-Arabi and Abdul Karim Jili. Jili's familiarity with Hinduism is testified to by his reference to ten major sects, including the Brahima (Brahman). Another exponent of Sufism, Jalaluddin Rumi (d. 1273), was also persecuted at first for opinions which were later accepted by the orthodoxy. Through his most important work *Mathnavi* containing reflections on Sufi thought, he introduced the practice of *sama,* a devotional dance akin to the Hindu *kirtan,* to Sufism. He taught that the heart is the mirror of divinity and that the "self is a copy made in the image of God," man's own true self belongs to the eternal self, which is God, to which it must return through fana, the annihilation of the self. All these doctrines closely resemble those of Hinduism.

Many of the mystical practices of the Sufis have Indian parallels. The *pasp-anfas* may have been derived from yogic breathing exercises; the Sufi *dhikr* is similar to the Hindu *japa,* and the *tasbih* (rosary) almost a replica of the Hindu *mala.* Both Indian thought and Sufism stress the approach to God not only through love but also submission to the *pir* or *guru,* who guides the way over the torturous path of self-knowledge to enlightenment.

It is probable that Sufism, although independent in origin, was assisted in its growth by contact with Indian thought. India and Iran, where Sufism developed, had long been exchanging scholars, merchants, artists, and envoys. Sufism first emerged as an eclectic philosophy in that part of Iran which is now Soviet Central Asia and Afghanistan, where Buddhist monks had been preaching for centuries, and which, until the rise of Islam, was a flourishing centre of Hinduism and Buddhism. The conversion of Ibrahim bin Adham (d. 777), prince of Balkh, to austerity became a favourite legend amongst the later Sufis. Admonished for his frivolity by an invisible voice during a hunting expedition, he is said to have pledged himself to an austere life. This story has often been compared with the story of the Buddha, and Al Junaid has called Adham the "Key to Sufism."

It is also clear that Sufism was more congenial to Iranians and Central Asians than to the Arabs. Buddhist monasteries flourished in eastern Iran and Transoxiana with a powerful centre at Balkh long before the Muslim conquest of India in the eleventh century. Wandering Indian monks were found as far as Baghdad during the Abbasid Caliphate, and are graphically described by Jabiz (*ca.* 866). A good deal of Buddhist literature had passed into Islam, often through a Manichaean medium.[28] By the eighth century, some Buddhist texts had been translated into Arabic along with many other Indian works. The Arabic version of the *Balauhar wa Budasaf* (Barlaam and Josaphat) had become a part of Arabic literature. The Buddhist story of the blind men describing an elephant according to their sense of touch recurs in the writings of Tawhidi, Al Ghazali, Sana-i, and Jalaluddin Rumi. The moral of the story is that, as each blind man felt only a part of the elephant and accepted it as the whole animal, so various religions know only partial truth, but in their spiritual blindness, claim it to be the entire truth. This denunciation of religious bigotry was an essential aspect of both Buddhist and Hindu teaching, and suited the Sufis admirably.

During the Arab period, many major Indian works were translated into Persian and Arabic. Al Kindi wrote a book on Indian religions; Sulaiman and Al Masudi collected and recorded information about India; during their travels, Al Nadim, Al Ashari, Al Biruni, and others discussed Indian religions and philosophic systems at length in their writings. Indian life and thought influenced the Islamic world in three areas: popular literature, science, and religious thought.

Indian mystic ideas were possibly transmitted to Jewish mysticism, known as *Kabbala,* through Sufism. Kabbala developed in Egypt and

Western Asia and was introduced into Europe about 900. Important modifications in the doctrine were made centuries later by Isaac Luria (1534–1572) who lived in Palestine. Many features of Kabbala, such as the marvellous powers assigned to letters, the use of charms and amulets, the emanations or phases of the deity, and the theory of the correspondence between macrocosm and microcosm, are amazingly like Indian Tantrism. Hindu influence is definitely discerned in the theories of metempsychosis and pantheism, so often found to have some connection with India when they exist in an extreme form. Although alien to the spirit of orthodox Judaism, the pre-existence and repeated embodiment of the soul is taught in the Zohar, and even more systematically by Luria whose school composed works called Gilgulim, or lists of transmigrations. The ultimate Godhead is called *En soph* or the infinite and is unknowable, not to be described by positive epithets and, therefore, in a sense nonexistent, since nothing which is predicated of existing beings can be truly predicated of *En soph*. These are crumbs from the table of Plotinus and the Upanishads.[29]

Many Sufis were attracted to India and settled there; eventually India became a centre of Sufism. Mansur al-Hallaj (858–922) was one of the earliest Sufis to visit India. Tradition also mentions a few other Sufis who settled in South India. However, Ali bin Uthman al-Julabi al-Hujwiri (d. 1072) was the first Sufi known to have made India his home, and in the middle of the eleventh century he wrote the first treatise in Persian on mysticism, called *Kashf-al Mahjub,* which has remained a standard text. He is revered by people of various faiths as a great teacher under the honorific title of Data Ganj Bakhsh.

Salar Masud Ghazi and Shaikh Ismail came to India in the eleventh century and made many converts to Sufism before Islam became a political force. Muinuddin Chishti came to India from Central Asia about 1192 and founded the Chishti order of Sufis, the largest Sufi order in India and Pakistan even today. His tomb at Ajmer is a popular pilgrimage place for both Muslims and Hindus. Later, Sufis came in large numbers with Muslim conquerors and began to preach Islam. They established monasteries, presided over by a pir, murshed or shaikh, who guided the disciples along the path of self-realization, *tariqa*. Their zeal, tolerance, and sympathy with Hindu thought brought success, but soon many of them gave up missionary work and devoted their attention to the study of Indian religions and thought.

Sufism in India aided the rapprochement between Hindu and Muslim beliefs and culture, for example in the Bhakti movement. Sufi thought to a limited extent inspired such eminent Indian thinkers as Kabir Guru

Nanak, Ram Mohan Roy, and Rabindranath Tagore. Sufis were influenced by Indian thought, particularly in the seventeenth century when they were repelled by Aurangzeb's intense adherence to the letter of Islam. Drawn towards the Vedanta, many Muslim mystics declared that nothing was real except God, and everything was illusion. They even adopted the doctrines of karma and the transmigration of the soul. They refrained from denouncing image-worship and preached *ahimsa*, nonviolence. Unlike the Sufis elsewhere, many Indian Sufis did not regard Muhammad as the perfect man, but as the equal of other prophets. He became a hero like Krishna in the *Mahabharata*. The Quran no longer remained the only holy book, but one of numerous holy scriptures, including those of other religions. The Sufis condemned religious bigotry and fanaticism, and preached the essential unity of all religions. In India the Sufis approximated the Hindu practices of meditation and asceticism.

As might be expected of any great religious movement with a long history and a succession of saint-philosophers, Sufism developed a number of sects. In India there were three chief ones—Dogmatics (*Kalam*), Philosophy (*Hikmat*), and Mysticism (*tasawwuf*). All these schools professed fundamentally similar philosophies but each was conditioned by a distinct intellectual tradition. The most original thinker of the Indian Dogmatics was Shah Wali Ullah of Delhi (d. 1762), who is compared with Al Ghazali. He endeavoured to reconcile theology and philosophy, and entered a powerful plea for moral reconstruction and social reform. The Dogmatics did not believe in conversion and considered all religious rituals and dogmas superfluous.

Dara Shikoh stands out amongst those who sought to harmonize Hindu and Muslim mystic philosophies, abandoned dogma, preached simple faith founded on the love of God, and stressed the fundamental unity of faiths. The eldest son of Shahjahan, he wrote a number of treatises on Muslim mysticism and expounded the identity of Hindu and Muslim mystic thought. In his *Majma al-Bahrain*, he sought to reconcile the Sufi theory with the Vedanta. He emphasized the yearning of the soul for unity with God (tawhid) and the conception of God as absolute. His assertion of the fundamental unity of being, and his teaching that the Upanishads and the Quran both sought the same truth provoked the wrath of Muslim orthodoxy. Dara translated several of the Upanishads into Persian under the title *Sirr-ul-Akbar*, and it was in this form that they first became known to European scholars. There was perhaps no other prince in the history of Muslim India who could match his scholarship and who was so passionately devoted to the spiritual life.

Chapter V

EUROPEAN DISCOVERY OF INDIA

INDIA was known to Europe in ancient times; indeed, parts of both Greece and India were under Iranian domination at the same time. Greek and Indian soldiers had fought together and against each other; diplomatic, commercial, and cultural relations existed for centuries between India and the Hellenic and the Hellenistic worlds; and countless adventurers, scholars, merchants, and missonaries had travelled to and fro. However, this close contact ceased after the emergence of Islamic power in the seventh century, and during the Middle Ages there was little or no direct intercourse between India and the West. European knowledge of India was remote during the Crusades, and was, at best, fragmentary during the mediaeval period. Something of India was known through travel accounts, such as those of Marco Polo, but here reality often gave way to romantic imagination. However, Indian influence can definitely be traced in some works of literature. For instance, in the *Alexander Song,* composed by Priest Lambrecht in the twelfth century, the flower girls, in their charming existence as half flowers—half humans, show a surprising similarity to the daughters of Mara who were supposed to seduce the Buddha. From the Alexander novel, the story, *Girl with the Poison,* entered the poetry of Frauenlob, Hugo von Trimberg, and others. This story belongs to Indian tradition in connection with the Maurya king, Chandragupta, and is found in Visakhadatta's play, *Mudraraksasa.* Again, the hero, Parzival, in Wolfram von Eschenbach's poetry becomes the embodiment of compassion and mercy as the positive result of the commandment not to kill. Remarkable, too, is the description of the "schastel marvel" and the "lit marveile" which is reminiscent of the Buddhist stupas. Moreover, the development of the legend of Priest John who spread Christianity in

India, and for whom the Portuguese went looking in vain, may well have a basis in some kind of cultural contact.

During the fifteenth century the Renaissance spirit drew Europe out of mediaevalism, and the new religious and commercial zeal inspired European explorers to find a direct sea link with India. It was the quest for India that led Columbus to stumble onto America in 1493. After persistent exploratory expeditions, the Portuguese, in their bid to reduce the power of the Muslims of North Africa and Western Asia, as well as in search of "Christians and spices," circumnavigated Africa, crossed the Arabian Sea with the assistance of an Indian sailor, and reached Calicut on the southwest coast of India, on 27 May 1498. This success eventually led to the almost complete elimination of Turkish supremacy on the Indian Ocean; the Arab trade monopoly between Asia and Europe was also destroyed by the incoming European powers. "It is to the discovery of the passage to India by the Cape of Good Hope, and to the vigour and success with which the Portuguese prosecuted their conquests and established their dominion there, that Europe has been indebted for its preservation from the most illiberal and humiliating servitude that ever oppressed polished nations."[1] This contact also slowly altered the whole character of Indian society. India became for the first time a political and economic appendage of another country, her weaknesses were exposed, and the processes of modernization were stirred into motion with increasing rapidity. The maritime activity of India, which had declined after the fall of the Roman Empire, was revived.

Although profitable trade was always one motive for their activities, the Portuguese, as the first European power to come to Asia, looked upon themselves as crusaders against Islam. Every injury inflicted on the Moors or Muslims was a gain for Christianity. Even the capture of the spice trade was described as a device to reduce the financial strength of the Muslims. It was both a religious duty and a patriotic pride to combat Islam everywhere. The centuries-old struggle for the Iberian Peninsula had made the Portuguese intensely hostile to Muslims. Alfonso de Albuquerque, the Portuguese Commander, reporting the capture of Goa, an important centre of international trade and commerce, gloated over the fact that he had put every Moor he could find to the sword, filled mosques with the bodies, and set them on fire. He calculated six thousand persons had been killed, some roasted alive.

These acts of terror and brutality, initially directed principally against Muslims, gradually became typical of Portuguese colonialism. They frequently attacked vessels carrying pilgrims to Mecca and set them on fire, sometimes with the passengers on board. The Portuguese were no less severe on Hinduism: "The fathers of the Church forbade the Hindus under terrible penalties the use of their own sacred books, and prevented them from all exercise of their religion. They destroyed their temples and mosques, and so harassed and interfered with the people that they abandoned the city in large numbers, refusing to remain any longer in a place where they had no liberty, and were liable to imprisonment, torture and death if they worshipped after their own fashion the gods of their fathers."[2] The Portuguese tried to build their empire in Asia on their bitter hatred of Islam and Hinduism. Their reign was devoid of scruples, honour, and morality, and was a major reason for the decline of Portuguese power.

As the Papal Bulls of Alexander III protected Portugal from other Catholic powers, especially Spain, the Portuguese were able to carry on their trade without rival or restriction for about a century. They established a highly organized and flourishing commercial empire, stretching from the coast of Malabar to the Philippines, which was incomparable to any empire in European history. The Portuguese supplied all of Europe with Asian goods, of which spices were the most considerable and precious commodity. Almost all the writers of the Middle Ages confirm the widespread demand for Indian spices in Europe. Most European dishes were highly seasoned with Indian spices; they were regarded as essential at every entertainment and were principal ingredients in almost all medical prescriptions. Despite the reduction in the cost of transport due to the discovery of the direct sea route, and the consequent cheaper price, the Portuguese conducted such a lucrative trade that the jealousy of other European nations eventually could no longer be contained. Consequently, by the beginning of the seventeenth century, when Mughal India was at the height of its glory, Dutch and British, and later French, trading companies emerged to capture the Asian trade.

The anti-Muslim aspect of European expansion in Asia was soon replaced by the rivalry between the Catholic and Protestant powers of Europe. Holland, inspired by the Reformation which began in Germany in 1517, revolted against Spanish tyranny and assumed independence in 1579. Soon England joined in, and the Protestant nations defied the Papal Bulls allocating the two halves of the world to Spain and Portugal. Their struggle for commercial supremacy in the East was one aspect of their religious defiance. During the reign of Elizabeth I, English world interests had broadened, and their triumph over the Spanish Armada gave the English confidence to expand their mercantile activity. Consequently, the East India Company was founded in 1600 to break the lucrative Portuguese monopoly of East Indian trade. The Portuguese were soon dislodged, and the European desire for profit and power made religious rivalry insignificant; indeed, by the middle of the eighteenth century religious rivalry had assumed the pronounced character of a political and economic struggle.

For over two hundred years, however, the Western powers remained confined to coastal commerce, and acquired only small territorial possessions in Asia because at this time the Mughals in India, the Mings and Manchus in China, and the Safavis in Persia ruled prosperous and powerful states. These Asian states were strong land powers with limited interest in maritime activities. This was especially true of the Mughals, who had come to India by land from the northwest and did not appreciate the danger to their security from the sea, or the importance of maritime power. When they did realize their mistake it was too late; they had become too weak even on land to reverse the process. The early Europeans came to India as traders, not as invaders, which possibly concealed the emerging trend in their activities for some time, but it seems incredible that the Mughals, who were so jealous of the integrity of their Empire, should have failed to detect it. The era of the great Mughals ended after the death of Aurangzeb in 1707, and throughout the eighteenth century local powers continued to decline. In due course, this led to the European domination of India and the industrial and technological advance of the West.

The Mughal period was in many respects a glorious period of Indian history, and the Mughals devoted much attention to art and culture, but they completely neglected practical and secular learning, especially the sciences. Throughout their long rule, no institution was established comparable to the modern university, although early India had world-famous centres of learning, such as Taxila, Nalanda, and Kanchi. There were flourishing universities in mediaeval Europe, as in other parts of the Islamic world, some of which had been in existence for some centuries. The University of Paris, which became the model not only for the universities of France but also for Oxford and Cambridge, had an organized pattern and legal status by the early thirteenth century. By the seventeenth century, a number of universities had come into existence in Europe. These universities nurtured intellectualism and laid the foundations of Western scientific culture through disciplined thinking, systematic investigation, and free discussion of knowledge. What is significant is that the European university had borrowed freely from the ancient Asian and Islamic models, which really were a part of the Mughal inheritance. Although their court was frequented by European visitors, the Mughals took no interest in European knowledge and technological accomplishments. Akbar received many European missionaries, and Ibadat Khana discussed religion and theology with them and protected them against the fanatic mullas. Christian missionaries at Akbar's Court came fully equipped, having learned Persian and read the Quran, and repeatedly had the edge in discussion over the Muslim mullas who argued with intense faith but with no knowledge of their opponents' holy book. Neither the nobles nor the mullas was stirred into learning Latin and investigating the Bible. Nor did Akbar show any curiosity in European science and philosophy, although both Hindus and Muslims had made notable scientific contributions in the past. Akbar was presented with printed books and a printing press, yet even the Indian classics were first printed by Europeans. It is, therefore, not surprising that during the period of European struggle for power, India was in a state of unparalleled decline, which not only made it possible for the Europeans to pursue their rivalries at will but also to do so with unique success.

The Mughals' power was gone, and a long trail of political upheavals followed. Intellectual inertia, already in evidence, became the prominent feature of Indian society, and the country lapsed into chaos, anarchy, and confusion. Eighteenth century India, in contrast to renaissant Europe, was so weak that it had little control over its affairs. It could not even tip the balance in favour of one of the European contenders struggling for power over Indian territory. It was the British who eventually triumphed in this contest, although it was the French who first conceived of European hegemony over Indian rulers.

In this struggle for power, technology, rather than diplomacy, played a decisive role. In purely military terms, the West won command of the East because of two things—ships and, more important, gunpowder.[3] To these could be added military organization and strategy. Superior armoury soon bred a military mentality and an aggressive policy. Immunity from retaliatory action led, at times, to unbridled tyranny. The West developed the bronze gun out of the bell-founding industry. Spain and Portugal, the first considerable ocean-goers of the times, borrowed northern European technology and met the cost of production from their overseas trade. England entered the arena later, successfully substituted cast iron for bronze, and, with the newer and cheaper technique, asserted her supremacy over others. By 1600 England was not only self-sufficient in artillery but also exported guns profitably. About the same time, France, and a little later Germany, entered the gun-making industry and eventually surpassed the English lead. Asians did not achieve any comparable results but fell farther and farther behind, and it was not until the middle of this century that they began to catch up with Europe in the race for arms.

Whilst the British were struggling for political supremacy in India, European scholars began an investigation into Indian literature and heritage. Some of these scholars were inspired by the spirit of inquiry, others by utilitarian ends, but they all began to explore India's past by working backwards from its current phase to its earliest one. They also began, understandably, by learning the languages spoken in the areas where they carried on their commercial and political activities. They soon became familiar with Persian, the court language of Mughal India, through which modern Europe first became acquainted with Indian literature and religion. It was only later that efforts were made to gain knowledge of the ancient classical language of India, Sanskrit, and finally of the vedic literature and the early civilization.

Discounting the mythical Sighelmus alleged to have been sent by Alfred on a pilgrimage to the shrine of St. Thomas at Mailapur, the first Englishman to visit India was a Jesuit priest, Thomas Stevens. He arrived in Goa in 1579 and was one of the first Europeans in modern times to study Indian languages seriously. He published a Konkani grammar, and in 1615 a remarkable poem entitled *Kristana Purana*, which was the story of the Bible intended for Indian converts to Christianity. He was a great admirer of the Marathi language, which he described as "a jewel among pebbles."

At about the same time, a Dutchman, Jan Huyghen Van Linschoten, published his *Itineratio* in 1595–1596 in which he referred to the imprisonments and tortures inflicted upon Indians by the Portuguese Inquisition. A Florentine merchant, Filippo Sassetti, who studied at the University of Pisa for six years (1568–1574) and lived at Goa for five years (1583–1588), collected a wide variety of data on India. Most of the letters in which his information was recorded deal with meteorological observations, but others deal with Indian folklore, science, and medicine. His interest in pharmaceutical texts awakened his interest in Sanskrit. He was, perhaps, the first person to declare that some relationship existed between Sanskrit and the principal languages of Europe.

Until the last quarter of the eighteenth century, several other isolated missionaries and travellers acquired certain, chiefly impressionistic, knowledge of Indian literature, language, and contemporary life but few made any serious attempt to understand Indian civilization. They accepted Indian culture at its face value without investigating its origins or studying it in its proper historical perspective.

Those Europeans who came to India at the time were a motley crowd of merchants and medicos, envoys and ecclesiastics, soldiers and sailors, adventurers and fortune seekers. They arrived from different countries by different routes with different motives; some eccentrics, such as Tom Coryat even walked all the way from Aleppo to Ajmer. Seeking pecuniary gain or excitement, these early Europeans were generally untutored and ill-equipped to either transmit or absorb ideas. The English were no exception. Trade, and only trade, was their object and they endeavoured to attain it, as merchants still do, not necessarily by sharing the beliefs of their customers or even by understanding their culture, but by making themselves agreeable to them. Consequently, they adopted Indian habits in food, often married Indian women, and respected Indian customs, beliefs, and authority. As traders they were concerned only with making money, regardless of scruples, morality, and learning. India was an "El Dorado" for enterprising young men in search of a fortune.

The travellers who carried information about India back to Europe were inadequately informed about the geography and society of the country as a whole, and their stay, in most cases, was too brief for accurate knowledge. Moreover, like most foreign visitors, they did not bring unprejudiced minds to the alien land, and whilst they fully understood and rationalized their own shortcomings and inconsistencies, they were much too willing to believe and record, if not magnify, anything which even vaguely had the ring of the extraordinary, unfamiliar, or exciting. And the complexities of Indian society and beliefs were far too paradoxical to lend themselves to easy comprehension. Furthermore, the impressions and the narratives of European travellers had unfortunately become stereotyped, and each visitor referred to practically the same things, as if he had come to India with preconceived ideas and was merely looking for reinforcement. Whilst some useful information reached Europe through these travellers, references to the exotic and romantic East became frequent and indiscriminate in European literature. At best, seventeenth-century India to the European was the India of the great Mughals, depicted with extravagant imagination. For instance Dryden's popular drama, *Aurengzebe* published in 1675, portrayed the Mughal Court quite fantastically. Unrealiable as these narratives were, they succeeded in projecting a picture of India in Europe which has never fully worn off.

It is significant that although the early European travellers were imbued with an anti-Islamic bias, they usually accepted the fanatic Muslim point of view about the Hindus, presumably because they shared the Judaic tradition with Muslims, knew a good deal about

Islam which was no longer so strange by that time, and also because they were taken by the splendour of the Mughal Court. They looked upon the Hindus as degraded and superstitious. This attitude was re-inforced by missionaries like Abbé Dubois, who focused their attention almost exclusively on the darker side of Hinduism, and sought to re-place it with their own faith. Alexander Pope's (1688–1744) couplet is typical of the British response to Indian ideas as they understood them:

> Lo, the poor Indian whose
> untutored mind,
> Sees God in clouds or hears
> him in the wind.

The French response to India was somewhat different from that of the British, possibly because many of the French travellers who came to India were known for their literary taste and gave interesting ac-counts of their travels. J. B. Tavernier, Thévenot, Francois Bernier, and Abbé Carré concentrated on the Mughal Court and Empire in their travel accounts. Tavernier, a jewel merchant, travelled to India as many as five times between 1641 and 1668. A competent business-man, he had no education or refinement, however, and wrote more to amuse than to inform. He probably saw more of India than any other traveller in the seventeenth century, although he said little that is worth remembering; his anecdotes are childish and often offensive. Bernier is better known, for he was an educated man, and was responsi-ble for bringing Indian ideas to some of the prominent French scholars of the day. He spent twelve years as a physician at the Mughal Court, and upon his return met the eminent French fabulist, La Fontaine, at Mme. de la Sablier's Salon, and shared his knowledge of India with him and Pascal, the philosopher and mathematician. Jean Racine (1630–1699) gave a flattering portrayal of Puru, Alexander's Indian adversary, in his *Alexandre*. A friend and disciple of Rousseau, Ber-nardin de Saint Pierre (1737–1814), who had lived in Mauritius for two years, wrote *Le Café de Surat* and other pieces with an Indian setting.

In 1778 a work was published dealing with Sanskrit literature, vedic legends, and doctrines, called *L'Ezour Vedam*, which created a sensa-tion in the West by attracting the attention of Voltaire. But it was later shown to be a work faked by a European missionary, Roberto de Nobili, for the purpose of converting Hindus in the seventeenth century.[4] Earlier, Voltaire had published a tragi-comic story relating the adventures of a Hindu and his wife, as well as his *Historical Fragments on India*. Whilst Voltaire's information on India came from unreliable sources, he believed that the West received its knowledge of astronomy, astrology, and metempsychosis from India, and he looked to India for truth with the eyes of a disillusioned European.

Several other well-known French writers of the Enlightenment were somewhat familiar with India. Diderot wrote several articles on Indian religion and philosophy in the *Encylopédie* of 1751. In 1770 Abbé Rayal, with the assistance of Diderot, d'Holback, and Naigon, produced the *Philosophical and Political History of the Europeans in the two Indias*.

Not long after the publication of Voltaire's works, Abbé Dubois fled France as a political refugee from the Revolution to live in India for thirty-one years. Typical of the class of people who regard themselves as charged with civilizing the heathens, and convinced of the superiority of his own civilization, he published his widely read *Hindu Manners, Customs and Ceremonies*, which, despite his laboriously collected data, is essentially a scathing criticism of Hindu belief and practices. Even if allowance is made for the Roman Catholic standards he applied to the Indian religions, many of his observations are grossly inaccurate and appear to be deliberate distortions. What is incredible, however, is that his work, despite the decisive exposition of its errors, has enjoyed almost continuous popularity in Europe, and was long accepted as a standard interpretation of Indian religions.

Jacquemont, who visited India during the reign of Ranjit Singh, wrote *Hindu Heroes and Heroines*. Lemierre's *Veuve du Malabar*, published in 1770, was epoch-making. M. de Jouy wrote the *Tipoo Sahib* and the opera, *Les Bayadères*, in 1810, which Napoleon himself attended.

Meanwhile a few missionaries had been taking a close interest in Sanskrit. In the beginning, having come first to South India, they learned Tamil or some other South Indian language. It was only after some time that they felt the need to learn Sanskrit. A German priest, Heinrich Roth (1610–1688) was the first European to produce a Sanskrit grammar, which was written in Latin and remained in manuscript form. In 1651, a Dutch preacher named Abraham Roger, who had lived at Pulicat near Madras as well as in Indonesia, published in Amsterdam *Open Door to Hidden Heathendom*. This book included about two hundred proverbs of the Sanskrit poet, Bhartrihari, from a Portuguese translation, and not only described the customs and religion of the Hindus but also mentioned the Vedas for the first time. Translated into German in 1663, it was drawn upon by Herder (1744–1813) for his *Stimmen der Volker in Liedern* (Voices of the Peoples in Songs). After the stories of the *Pancatantra,* this work was the first Indian literature to become known in Germany. A German Jesuit, Johann Ernst Hanxleden, who worked in Malabar from 1699 to 1732, compiled a Sanskrit grammar in Latin and one in Malayalam. His Sanskrit grammar also remained unpublished but was used by the Austrian missionary, Fra Paolino de St. Bartholomeo (whose real name was Johannes Philippus Wessdin), "undeniably the most important of the missionaries who worked at the earliest opening-up of Indian literature."[5] He lived on the Malabar coast from 1776 to 1789 and was well acquainted with Indian literature, languages, and religions. He wrote two Sanskrit grammars in Rome in 1790 and several learned treatises. Another missionary, Coeurdoux, suggested in 1767 that there was a kinship between Sanskrit and European languages. He reached this conclusion with the help of Maridas Pillai of Pondicherry. It appears that he was quite familiar with Sanskrit literature. He correctly describes its system of grammar and refers to the *Amarakosa* and other Sanskrit dictionaries as well as to the Indian system of poetics, called *alamkara*. He also describes the six systems of Indian philosophy, in addition to Buddhism and Jainism.

The English were most closely bound in political and cultural relations with India, and although they initiated a systematic investigation of Sanskrit literature, most of the work on the subject was done on the continent, particularly in France and Germany. Perhaps the Anglo-Indian political association, enforced and unequal as it was and often clouded by mutual distrust and fear, was not conducive to a deeper British appreciation of the Indian heritage. Morevoer, the remarkable practical qualities of the British in commerce, military organization, and administration, and their faculty for recognizing and making use of opportunities, inevitably, although not inordinately, subordinated their cultural and intellectual sensitivities. Hence, it was administrative needs which initially induced the British to study Sanskrit.

Despite the loss of countless texts, today there are scores of thousands of Sanskrit manuscripts in various libraries. When Alexander came, there existed in India an ancient literature far richer than that in Greece at the time. The first scholar to publish a real dissertation on Sanskrit learning was Alexander Dow, in a preface to his history of India, which appeared in Europe in three volumes in 1768. Whilst his history leaned heavily on Ferishta, his Preface carried a significant account of Hindu religion and customs. He pointed out the existence of innumerable ancient Sanskrit texts, observing that the authentic history of the Hindus went back farther than that of any other nation.

The turning point in the European discovery of India's past came during Warren Hastings' Governor-Generalship. By this time the British had gained control of Bengal and their commercial interests in India depended on their ability to eliminate rampant corruption in their own ranks and to rationalize the administration of their Indian possessions. The merchants of the East India Company were generally greedy and corrupt, filling their own pockets by cheating the Company and the Indians. Their contributions to India were political anarchy, economic exploitation, cruel taxation, extravagant wars, unjust intervention, and forged treaties. London was appalled at this tarnishing of the British name.

Born in 1732, Warren Hastings was the son of a clergyman from an old and once wealthy family. He went to India at the age of seventeen as a writer in the Company's service and, through his varied experiences in trade and administration, he acquired an exceptional knowledge of the Indian mind and temperament. Well-disposed towards Indian literature and culture, he stressed the need for the study of Sanskrit, albeit mainly for utilitarian reasons. Hastings also realized that British supremacy in India could rest only on a proper understanding of Indian religion and culture. Although he was impeached for acts of corruption and tyranny, he gave the beginnings of a sound administration to British India. For the codification of the laws of the land and for the efficient operation of the administration, it was essential to gain an accurate knowledge of the ancient Sanskrit legal texts. Hastings had the Indian law books compiled by the local learned pundits under the title of *Vivadarnavasetu* (meaning bridge over the ocean of dispute) but there was no one who could translate the resultant text into English. Hence, a Persian translation was made and an English translation of this was published in London in 1776. This was entitled *A Code of Gentoo Laws by* N. B. Halhead, a schoolmate of Sir William Jones.[6] This second-hand translation introduced the study of Sanskrit philology.

The first Englishman who, urged by Warren Hastings, acquired a knowledge of Sanskrit was Charles Wilkins (1749–1836). He was a founding member of the Asiatic Society of Bengal and had acquired considerable knowledge of Sanskrit at Varanasi (Banaras). He subsequently became the first librarian of the famous India Office Library at London, then known as the East India Company Library. He is described by his contemporaries as the first European who really understood Sanskrit, and he gave Europe its earliest acquaintance with actual Sanskrit writing. H. T. Colebrooke, a founder of Sanskrit scholarship in Europe, said that Wilkins had more information and knowledge respecting the Hindus than any other foreigner since the days of Pythagoras. In 1785 Wilkins published an English translation of the *Bhagavad Gita*—the first Sanskrit work rendered directly into a European language. Later, Wilkins published the *Hitopadesa* (1787) and the Sakuntala episode from the *Mahabharata* (1795). These Sanskrit works were translated principally to familarize European intellectuals with Indian ideas; their literary merit was a subordinate consideration, if at all. Thirteen years later, in 1808, Wilkins' Sanskrit grammar appeared, using Devanagari type (which he himself had carved and cast) for the first time in Europe. Wilkins also initiated the study of Indian inscriptions and translated some of them into English.

It was, however, the celebrated Orientalist, Sir William Jones (1746–1794), who pioneered Sanskrit studies. He came to India as a puisne judge of the Supreme Court at Calcutta in September 1783, having already gained competence in Asian learning, especially Persian and Arabic, and having formed a deep appreciation of Indian culture. He had ardently sought the Indian appointment, and had waited in uneasy uncertainty for five years, first, in order to make enough money to be able to retire early and conduct his researches without financial worries, and second, to "give the finishing stroke to his Oriental knowledge." He lived in India for about ten years, until his premature death, and was extremely happy there. He said that, although he was never unhappy in England, for it was not in his nature to be unhappy, he was never really content until he was settled in India.

His admiration for Indian thought and culture was almost limitless. "It gave me inexpressible pleasure to find myself in the midst of so noble an amphitheatre, almost encircled by the vast regions of Asia, which has even been esteemed the nurse of sciences, the scene of glorious actions, fertile in the productions of human genius, abounding in natural wonders, and infinitely in the forms of religion and government, in the laws, manners, customs, and languages, as well in the features and complexions, of men."[7] Even at a time when Hinduism was at a low ebb and it was quite fashionable to run it down, he held it in great esteem. Whilst Jones believed in Christ and Christianity, he was attracted to the Hindu concepts of the non-duality of God, as interpreted by Sankara, and the transmigration of the human soul. The latter theory

205

he found more rational than the Christian doctrine of punishment and eternity of pain. Writing to his erstwhile pupil and close friend, Earl Spencer, in 1787, after three years in India, he said: "I am no Hindu; but I hold the doctrine of the Hindus concerning a future state to be incomparably more rational, more pious, and more likely to deter men from vice, than the horrid opinions, inculcated on punishments without end."[8]

Although he had nourished political ambitions, which fortunately for Oriental learning did not materialize, and although he was a professional barrister, Jones was essentially a scholar. He was a brilliant Orientalist and linguist, for whom his eminent contemporaries, such as Burke, Gibbon, Sheridan, Garrick, and Johnson, had great respect. Literary London admired him so much that he was elected a member of the Club, Samuel Johnson's immortal coterie, a month before even Boswell was given that honour. He was made a Fellow of the Royal Society in April 1772 when he was learning Sanskrit during his initial years in India. His interest in botany was much more than mere pleasure; it was stimulated by his deep religious feelings, for in every flower, every leaf, and every berry he could see the attributes of God more eloquently illustrated than in the wisdom of man.

He learned Sanskrit with the assistance and encouragement of Charles Wilkins before the latter left India in 1786. In January 1784, a few months after his arrival in Calcutta, Jones founded the famous Asiatic Society of Bengal, of which he remained President until his death. The object of the Society was to inquire into the history, culture, literature, and science of Asia; it has done enormous work to advance the knowledge of Asian civilization both in India and abroad. It was in the journal of this Society, *Asiatick Researches,* that the initial attempts were made to unearth India's past. Within three years Jones became so proficient in Sanskrit that he could converse familiarly with Indian pundits. In 1789, five years after his arrival in India, he published in Calcutta his translation of the celebrated Sanskrit drama, *Abhijnana Sakuntala,* by Kalidasa.[9] This work became so popular that it went into five English editions in less than twenty years. In 1791 a German translation of the English version was made by George Förster, the world traveller and revolutionary. This inspired men like Herder and Goethe. Many other translations of the *Sakuntala* were made in the first half of the nineteenth century from Jones' English version, and later from the Sanskrit original.

In 1792 Jones brought out an English translation of Jayadeva's *Gita Govinda,* and published in Calcutta, Kalidasa's *Ritusamhara* in the original; this was the first Sanskrit text ever printed. Of greater importance, however, was his translation of the well-known legal text of ancient India, the *Manusmriti*, which was published posthumously in 1794 under the title *Institutes of Hindu Law or the Ordinances of Manu*. Three years later, in 1797, a German translation of the book appeared. Not only did Jones produce excellent translations but he also wrote original hymns to Indian deities, which are lasting monuments of Anglo-Indian literature. By the time of his death, his reputation as a Sanskrit scholar had eclipsed all his many other accomplishments.

Jones was the first British scholar to definitely assert the genealogical connection of Sanskrit with Greek and Latin, and possibly with Persian, German, and Celtic. In his third annual discourse of the Asiatic Socety on 2 February 1786, he declared that the Sanskrit language was of a wonderful structure, more perfect than the Greek, more copious than the Latin, and more exquisitely refined than either, yet bearing to both of them a stronger affinity, both in the roots of verbs and in the forms of grammar, than could possibly have been produced by accident. All three languages must have come from some common source.[10]

The greatest influence of Jones' work was, of course, on the study of Oriental learning itself. The interest in Indian literature awakened by Jones and Wilkins, led to scholars searching for Sanskrit manuscripts "with the avidity of explorers seeking Australian goldfields."[11] Of those scholars, the most outstanding was Henry Thomas Colebrooke (1765–1837), who put the study of Sanskrit on a scientific footing. "Had he lived in Germany," says Max Müller, "we should long ago have seen his statue in his native place, his name written in the letters of gold on the walls of acadamies; we should have heard of Colebrooke jubilees and Colebrooke scholarships. In England if any notice is taken of the discovery of Sanskrit—a discovery in many respects equally important, in some even more important, than the revival of Greek scholarship in the fifteenth century—we may possibly hear the popular name of Sir William Jones and his classical translation of Sakuntala; but of the infinitely more important achievements of Colebrooke, not one word."[12]

Colebrooke entered the service of the East India Company in 1782 and left India in 1815 at the age of fifty. During this period he had a distinguished career as an administrator and lawyer, but his claim to eminence is mainly based upon his being "the founder and the father of true Sanskrit scholarship in Europe."

He pursued his study of Sanskrit most energetically with the assistance of some excellent Indian instructors. A man of extraordinary industry and clear intellect, Colebrooke published many texts, translations, and essays dealing with practically all aspects of Sanskrit literature. His writings included works on Indian law, philosophy, religion, grammar, astronomy, and arithmetic. In 1797–1798, he published his first four-volume translation, *A Digest of Hindu Law on Contracts and Successions,* which immediately established his reputation as the best Sanskrit scholar of his day. His famous *Essay on the Vedas,* published in 1805, the same year as his *Sanskrit Grammar,* gave the first definite and reliable information on the sacred Hindu texts. In 1808 he published a critical edition of the *Amarakosa,* a Sanskrit lexicon. By this time Colebrooke had become President of the Court of Appeal, a high and lucrative position, but demanding; nevertheless, he continued his Sanskrit studies.

Unlike Jones, Colebrooke's interests lay chiefly in scientific literature. His love of mathematics and astronomy stirred his intellectual curiosity to investigate Indian work in these disciplines. Although some scholars such as Burrow and Strachey had preceded him, it was entirely through his work that scientists were able to form a clear idea of the Indian achievement in mathematics, especially indeterminate analysis. But it is chiefly for his philological researches and services to Indian jurisprudence that Colebrooke is remembered.

Apart from his writings, he collected a wide variety of Sanskrit manuscripts and presented them to the East India Company in 1818. This collection is one of the most valuable treasures of the India Office Library in London. In 1822 he founded the Royal Asiatic Society in London which has since done much to promote Oriental learning in Europe. He published many of his most valuable papers in this Society's *Transactions.*

An eminent English contemporary of Colebrooke, Horace Hayman Wilson came to India in the Medical Service of the East India Company and became deeply interested in Sanskrit studies. He pursued his interest with vigour and industry, and published his elegant translation of Kalidasa's *Meghaduta* in 1813; this made both an immediate and a lasting impact on European readers, and it has since been translated into many languages. In 1819, Wilson published his Sanskrit dictionary, and he translated the *Visnu Purana* into English. In 1832, he became the first occupant of the Boden Chair of Sanskrit at Oxford and this provided him a fuller opportunity to advance the study of Indology. By this time, however, Indian studies in England had lost their earlier vigour. The British, now masters of India and the supreme maritime power of the day, were less inclined to learn from aliens; they listened to Macaulay instead.

Two professors of Sanskrit, Wilson at Oxford and Lee at Cambridge, bemoaned the fact that not much attention was paid at their respective universities to Sanskrit, a language "capable of giving a soul to the objects of sense, and a body to the abstractions of metaphysics." The best philological works published in England were generally translations from the German.[13]

France began to take a closer interest in Indian learning and commenced a systematic investigation by the beginning of the eighteenth century. In 1718, Bignan, the librarian of the French king, asked travellers to purchase or make a copy of every book of note, as well as grammars and dictionaries, available in India or in regions where Indian culture prevailed. In response, many French officials, residents, missionaries, and visitors began to acquire Indian texts. The missionary, Calmette, obtained copies of the *Rig Veda,* the *Yajur Veda,* and the *Sama Veda,* although he failed to get a copy of the fourth Veda, the *Atharva Veda.* The *Rig Veda* was first sent to Paris in 1731, together with its *Aitareya Brahmana.* Other Sanskrit books, such as Gangesa's *Tattvacintamani,* which was very popular at the time in the southern and eastern regions of India, together with some Tamil books, a Tamil grammar, and a Tamil dictionary, were also sent to France about the same time by the Italian Jesuit, Beschi. A number of books were obtained from Bengal. Pere Pons, stationed in Chandernagore, succeeded in collecting main works in the different branches of classical Sanskrit literature. His catalogue containing one hundred and sixty-eight entries was astonishingly accurate for its time. Pons, who himself knew Sanskrit, had been assisted in the selection of his manuscripts by competent Indian scholars. His collection included a Sanskrit grammar which he had written in Latin, following the *Samkshiptasara,* and a Latin translation of the *Amarakosa.* Because of the labours of these men, the first printed catalogue of Sanskrit literature was published in Paris in 1739. The following year, Pons published in a letter, which has been repeatedly reproduced since, the first sound report on Sanskrit literature.

Whilst the difficulties of reading these manuscripts held up progress, French scholars learned something of Indian thought and history through Arabic, Persian, Chinese, Greek, and Latin works. The collection of Indian materials continued, however, and Joseph Deguignes accumulated as much material as was possible from non-Indian sources. Strictly speaking, Deguignes was not an Indologist; he was essentially a Sinologist who wrote a vast history of the Huns, but he gathered remarkably accurate knowledge about India. He was perhaps the first modern European to show, through his study of Chinese sources, the wide influence of Buddhism on Central Asian and Chinese peoples, and to give a tentative translation of a part of an ancient Chinese Buddhist text, the *Sutra in Forty-two Articles*. Still greater was his accomplishment in fixing the basis of Indian chronology. In this he had received invaluable help from an Indian scholar of Tamil, Maridas Pillai of Pondicherry, who knew Latin and French well. Both these contributions are extremely significant, and are worthy of much greater recognition than has hitherto been accorded to Deguignes. Possibly because of their background of English education, Indians have exhibited equal indifference to the contribution of Maridas Pillai. "All French scholars who visited Pondicherry during that period were indebted to him for most of the valuable information. He apparently played a part in the discovery of original links between Sanskrit on the one hand, and Latin and Greek on the other. The astronomer Le Gentil, one of the first who gave substantial account of Indian astronomy, wrote that he himself had been a grateful pupil of Maridas Pillai and of other Tamil scholars of Pondicherry in that matter."[14] Some of his translations and analyses of Indian texts were profitably used by French scholars. For instance, his translation of the *Bagavatam* was sent to Deguignes before its publication, and it was in this manuscript that the latter found the dynastic lists of the Suryavamsa and the Somavamsa kings who had reigned since Parikshit, including Chandragupta which Deguignes immediately recognized as the Sandrokottos of the Greeks. This synchronism was published in the *Mémoires de l'Academie des Inscriptions et Belles Lettres;* this same synchronism was rediscovered by Sir William Jones, who is generally given the credit for identifying it. Whilst Jones may not have been the real discoverer of Indian chronology, he indeed popularized it.

At about this time, Anquétil du Perron (1731–1805) visited India and later prepared the first European translation in Latin of the Upanishads from the literal Persian version made for the Mughal prince, Dara Shikoh, in 1636. As a young man of twenty-three, du Perron, whilst working in the Bibliothèque de Roi at Paris in 1754, saw a fragment of a mysterious manuscript which the Bodleian Library at Oxford had acquired in 1718 and which was reputed to be a book by Zoroaster. Du Perron was so moved by it that he at once decided to visit India and learn the language so that he could read it. He arrived at Pondicherry in 1754. This was the period when the English and the French were engaged in a bitter conflict for supremacy in India and du Perron was caught in it. He finally managed to learn Persian at Surat, and returned home via England in 1762. Whilst studying at Surat, he discovered the *Avesta,* and published his *Zend-Avesta* in three volumes in 1771. He also published an account of his travels, *Voyage aux Grandes Indes,* in 1781.

Du Perron acquired the Persian manuscript of the Upanishads in 1775 from M. Gentil, the French Resident at Fyzabad in North Bengal, and he translated them into French word for word, in the Persian word-order. Realizing his error, he set out to make a Latin translation of fifty Upanishads. He finished the work in 1796, but it was not printed until 1801–1802 in Paris. It is remarkable that this translation of the Upanishads, which had so profound an influence on European thought, was an incidental product of a venture undertaken for an altogether different purpose.

With Wilkins' version of the *Bhagavad Gita,* and du Perron's translation of the Upanishads, entitled *Oupenekhat,* the fundamental texts of Indian philosophy were available to Western thinkers. Du Perron did not know Sanskrit but, despite the imperfections of his translations, it made an important contribution to European knowledge. It caught the attention of the German philosopher, Schelling, and later of Schopenhauer, who in 1813 praised it as "a production of the highest human wisdom" and adopted an upanishadic motto, "whosoever knows God, himself becomes God."

For many decades, attention in France had been centered on China, about which much was heard from the sympathetic reports of Jesuit missionaries, mariners, and merchants; on Siam with whom France had come into diplomatic contact; and on Western and Central Asia, with which Europe had been closely linked historically and culturally. To Europe, China appeared culturally unique and politically powerful. Thus China came to influence European life in many respects, ranging from religious thought to opera. Hebrew had been taught regularly at the Collège Royal, later called Collège de France, since its inception in the sixteenth century. Syriac, Arabic, Persian, and Turkish were also actively cultivated. Consequently, when France awakened to Indian literature, there was already an existing tradition of learning into which Indology could easily fit. French possessions in India, and later domination over Indochina, provided further incentive for French interest.

A determined French scholar of Persian studies, Léonard de Chézy had become a passionate admirer of William Jones' translation of the *Sakuntala.* He was seized by the desire to read the masterpiece in its original. With the help of Pons' grammar of the *Amarakosa,* and later of Wilkins' translation of the *Hitopadesa,* he began learning Sanskrit. By sheer perseverance and remarkable ingenuity he was finally able to realize his dream—to read, and even publish, the text of the *Sakuntala.*

Léonard de Chézy, like many contemporary French thinkers, realized that Europe should be acquainted with the achievements of Asian nations. Consequently, there developed in France an influential body of opinion advocating the study of India as well as China. As a result, in 1814, a Chair of Sanskrit and a Chair of Chinese were created for Chézy and Abel-Rémusat respectively. These Chairs, a radical innovation in academic life, were set up between the disasters of 1814 and Waterloo, when the whole nation was undergoing political unrest and military conflicts. Only a nation like France, whose intellectual and cultural attitudes dominated most of Europe during the seventeenth and eighteenth centuries, could turn its attention to scholarship at such a time.

Although Abel-Rémusat was a Sinologist, he made important contributions to Indology by collecting Chinese data on India and translating the account of Fa-hsien's travels. Both de Chézy and Abel-Rémusat died of cholera in 1832, but their traditions did not die with them. Abel-Rémusat's successor was Stanislas Julien, who furthered research on Indian antiquity through Chinese documents. De Chézy was followed by several outstanding pupils. Amongst these were two Germans: Franz Bopp, the founder of the comparative philology of Indo-European languages, and August Schlegel. His French pupils included Loiseleur Deslongchamps, who published the *Manusmriti* and the *Amarakosa*, and Langlois, who was responsible for the first translations made directly from the manuscripts of the *Rig Veda* and the *Harivamsa*. But the most important of all was Eugène Burnouf, who in turn had many eminent students, including Max Müller.

Eugène Burnouf's father, Jean-Louis Burnouf, had been a student of de Chézy, and was an able classical scholar who was amongst the first to realize that much progress could be made in the morphology of European classical languages by a comparison with Sanskrit. Eugène Burnouf learned Sanskrit not so much to study philology as to investigate the depths of Indian culture, as well as comprehend hitherto unknown languages and the civilizations associated with them. With the help of Sanskrit, he was able to decipher Pali and discover the rules of Avestan and its relationship with Sanskrit. His *An Essay on Pali*, published in 1826 jointly with Christian Lassen, who was later to become a leading German Indologist, led to the recognition of a relationship between Pali and Sanskrit. Burnouf not only researched classical Sanskrit literature, but also the fundamental vedic literature, which had remained unused in the Royal Library for about a century. He translated the *Bhagavata Purana* into French in 1840, and devoted himself

212

to the study of Indian Buddhism. Making use of the work done by Deguignes and Abel-Rémusat on Chinese sources, he realized the importance of Buddhism in the expansion of Indian culture abroad. He made a comparative study of Buddhist texts in Pali and Sanskrit. He wrote his famous *Introduction à l'Histoire du Bouddhisme Indien* in 1844, and published *Lotus de la Bonne Loi,* an annotated translation of the *Saddharma-Pundarika,* the most important Mahayana text. His work thus led to a great advance in the study of Indian literature and culture in Europe. He succeeded de Chézy as Professor of Sanskrit from 1832 until his untimely death in 1853. According to him, the publications of the Asiatic Society of Bengal were widely sold and read in France, and people frequently bought copies of Indian classics that were available in various languages. He also refers to the exchange of learned publications between France and India.

Meanwhile, in 1822, the Société Asiatique, the first of its kind in Europe, had been founded in Paris. Many other French scholars had now come to take a deep interest in Indian thought. One of Burnouf's colleagues, the philosopher and translator of Aristotle, Barthélemy de Saint-Hilaire, who was later swept up to the Ministry of Foreign Affairs by the peculiar current of politics, published valuable studies on the Nyaya and Samkhya systems of Indian philosophy. Burnouf encouraged his pupil Ariel to study Tamil and its literature. Ariel collected many Tamil manuscripts and translated part of the *Tirukkural* and the poems of Auvaiyar. Burnouf helped Max Müller to publish the *Rig Veda,* and Rudolph Roth and Adolph Régnier to interpret it. The Piedmontese, Gaspere Gorresio, disciple of Barthélemy de Saint-Hilaire, published in Paris a monumental edition of the *Ramayana,* in five volumes, with financial assistance from the King of Sardinia. He also published two Italian translations of the work.

Fauche translated the *Ravanavadha Mahakavya* of Bhartrihari, the *Gitagovinda* of Jayadeva, all the works of Kalidasa, the *Dasakumara-carita* of Dandin, the *Sisupalavadha* of Magha, the *Mricchakatika* of Sudraka, the entire *Ramayana,* and the first nine parvas of the *Mahabharata* into French. Having read Fauche's translation of the *Ramayana* in 1863, the French historian Michelet said: "That year will always remain a dear and cherished memory; it was the first time I had the opportunity to read the great sacred poem of India, the divine *Ramayana.* If anyone has lost the freshness of emotion, let him drink a long draught of life, and youth from that deep chalice."

With the creation of the École des Hautes Études in 1868, a new centre for the study of Indology was opened up. Amongst many other Sanskritists who flourished in France were scholars such as Paul Régnaud, whose chief work was on Sanskrit rhetoric and on *Bharatiya Natyasastra,* Hauvette-Besnault, Auguste Barth, Abel Bergaigne, and Emile Senart. Barth devoted himself for more than forty years to the study of Indian religions in their historical perspective and to the criticism of works published in every field of Indology. Bergaigne wrote an epoch-making work, *The Vedic Religion according to the Hymns of the Rig-Veda.* This was followed by other works, of which the *Researches on the Samhita of the Rig-Veda* is most noteworthy. He brought about a revolution in the realm of religious history by his tireless work on the *Rig Veda.* The vedic hymns, which had been interpreted as songs of worship dedicated to the forces of nature, came to reveal through his interpretation an artificial pedantic religion surcharged with liturgy and rituals. Bergaigne founded the teaching of Sanskrit at the Sorbonne. Although at first purely a vedic and Sanskrit scholar, Bergaigne later turned to the study of Indian civilization and to the history of Indochina. Many inscriptions in impeccable Sanskrit, frequently elaborated in kavya style, were found in Cambodia and on the eastern coast of the Indochinese Peninsula. Bergaigne and Barth deciphered and translated many of these. With the help of such data, a part of the history of Champa was disclosed.

French scholars preferred to study Indian civilization in its broader perspective, including its phase of foreign expansion, through non-Indian sources. Foucaux, Professor of Sanskrit at the Collège de France, and Leon Féér worked on Buddhist subjects from Sanskrit and Tibetan works. The former published the *Lalitavistara* in Tibetan and French, and the latter translated many texts from Sanskrit, Pali, Tibetan, Mongolian, and Chinese.

With the increasing interest in the archaeological remains of Indochina, Indian art also attracted French attention. At the beginning of the nineteenth century, Langles compiled his comprehensive *The Monuments of Hindustan.* Later, Emile Guimet founded, first in Lyons and later in Paris, a special museum of history of religions, Musée Guimet, which became a world-renowned museum of Indian and East Asian art and archaeology.

Since every major Asian country had been in the closest possible contact with India in the past, an understanding of Indian culture was essential to appreciate other neighbouring civilizations. So in addition to their interest in Indian civilization or in Sanskrit, the French need to evaluate Indochinese society and culture led them back to India, and to

Central Asia. In Khotan, Dutreuil de Rhins bought a manuscript written on birch bark in Kharoshthi script. It was a Buddhist work, containing a middle Indian version of the *Dharmapada*. It was studied and published by Emile Senart. He published a new edition of Asoka's inscriptions, and of those found at Nasik and Karle. He edited the Pali grammar of Kaccayana and the *Mahavastu*, and wrote the *Essay on the Legend of Buddha,* in which he tried to show how the Buddhists introduced into the life story of the Buddha many elements taken from the saga of Vishnu-Mahapurusha.

The discovery of Dutreuil de Rhin's manuscript was the first in a series of finds. Since the end of the nineteenth century, a number of competent French scholars of Asian history and culture have undertaken historical explorations. Amongst the first of these were four friends of slightly different ages, Sylvain Lévi, Alfred Foucher, Edouard Chavannes, and Louis Finot. Edouard Chavannes was a Sinologist, but he contributed much to Indology through his studies on Chinese pilgrims, Chinese inscriptions of *Bodhgaya,* and the Chinese renderings of Buddhist stories and legends. However, his work cannot be separated from that of Sylvain Lévi.

In 1894 Sylvain Lévi, a former pupil of Bergaigne, succeeded Foucaux to the Chair of Sanskrit at the Collège de France, at the age of thirty-one. Earlier he had done field work in India, mainly in Nepal, looking for inscriptions and manuscripts. He was devoted to the study of Hindu-Buddhist literature and texts. He first published *The Indian Theatre* and then *Doctrine of the Sacrifice of the Brahmanas.* It was his findings in Nepal and his collaboration with Chavannes which finally led Lévi to Buddhist studies. Having learned both Tibetan and Chinese, he was able to correct the Sanskrit texts he rediscovered, such as *Mahayana-sutralankara* by Asanga, *Trimsika* and *Vimsatika* by Vasubandhu, and *Mahakarmavibhanga,* by checking them against their Tibetan and Chinese versions. With the help of the linguist, Antoine Meillet, Lévi also deciphered the Kuchean language. He found fragments of a Kuchean poem very similar to the *Karmavibhanga,* the sculptural illustrations of which he also later noticed in the famous Buddhist temple, Borobudur, in Java. Another French scholar, Paul Pelliot, in 1908 discovered many fragments of Indian texts in Central Asia.[15]

Albert Foucher came to India long before he succeeded Victor Henry at the Sorbonne. He was a devoted humanist who was greatly attracted to Sanskrit literature, its grammar, system of philosophy, and archaeology. It was he who connected the art of Buddhist India, widely known as the Gandhara School, with that of the Graeco-Roman world. He edited Maridas Pillai's French translation of the *Bhagavata Purana*, and in association with Finot, was responsible for the foundation of a research institute, the École Francaise d'Extreme-Orient, in Indochina, to study and preserve Indochinese culture. This institute helped to join Indology with Sinology. He also founded the French Archaeological Institute at Kabul, and the Franco-Japanese Mansion at Tokyo.

Many French Indologists, including Jean Przyluski and Jules Bloch, have worked in these institutions. Przyluski was attracted to Buddhist studies, linguistics, and ethnology, and wrote many books with the intention of tracing the remains of Munda, or popular, elements of non-Aryan origin in Indian documents. Jules Bloch, having first studied in Paris under Sylvain Lévi, Meillet, the famous linguist, and Vinson, the specialist in Tamil studies, came to India as a member of the École Francaise d'Extreme-Orient to learn modern Indian linguistics, where he worked with the Indian scholar, R. G. Bhandarkar. In addition to working on the grammatical structure of Dravidian languages and Asoka's edicts, he wrote a study of the Gypsies, *Les Tsiganes*. His work, *Formation de la langue Marathe*, contributed greatly to the study of modern dialects as well as to the rigorous science of linguistics.

The Belgian scholar, Louis de la Vallée Poussin (1869–1938), who studied with Emile Senart and Sylvain Lévi, contributed three volumes to the famous *Histoire du Monde* series between 1924 and 1935. His volumes form a complete political history of pre-Muslim India and are outstanding works of scholarship.

The French, even after withdrawing from their Indian territorial possessions, retained their interest in Indian studies. With the concurrence of India they have founded a centre at Pondicherry to continue research on Indian life and culture. Louis Renou, who died in 1966, was not only the leading French Indologist of his generation, but the most distinguished in the West. His output was phenomenal, but he was chiefly a scholar of the Vedas. Amongst his many books and articles were a Veda bibliography, a Veda index, a study of Indo-Iranian mythology, a Sanskrit-French dictionary, and a study of Panini, the grammarian. Jean Filliozat, who has made outstanding contributions to Indian studies, especially to the history of Indian science, worked for many years at the Pondicherry institute. Filliozat, a qualified medical practitioner and an accomplished linguist, has the rare competence to study ancient Indian medicine. His work, *The Classical Doctrine of Indian Medicine*, must remain a standard text.

Germany, unlike Britain or even France, was not at all politically connected with India, but undertook Sanskrit studies most enthusiastically. German Indologists produced work exceptional both in quality and quantity, and they soon became the leaders in the study of Sanskrit language and literature, as well as Indian thought and culture. Although the English scholars were the first to study Sanskrit, they did not maintain their lead for long, presumably because they were mainly motivated by considerations other than scholarship. Whilst a Chair of Sanskrit, which was first held by August Schlegel, was instituted at the University of Bonn in 1818, it was not until 1832 that the first Chair of Sanskrit was created in England, at Oxford, to recognize the work done by H. H. Wilson. Later, Chairs of Sanskrit were established at London, Cambridge, and Edinburgh Universities, and by the first quarter of the nineteenth century practically every intellectual capital of Europe had initiated a full fledged study of Sanskrit.

A contemporary of Jones and Colebrooke, Alexander Hamilton (1765–1824), who had learned Sanskrit in India, inadvertently introduced the language to Germany. Returning from India to England in 1802, he was detained in France when hostilities were suddenly renewed between England and France. By a remarkable coincidence, the German poet and philosopher, Friedrich von Schlegel (1772–1829), was also in Paris. By that time German interest in Indian literature had already been awakened by the work of the English scholars. Consequently, when Schlegel met Hamilton in 1803 he quickly took advantage of the opportunity and began learning Sanskrit.

In 1808 Schlegel published *Über die Sprache und Weisheit der Inder* (On the Language and Wisdom of the Indians), and thus became the founder of Indian philology in Germany. This work contained the first direct translation from Sanskrit into German. It gave an account of Indian mythology, and of the theories of incarnation and the transmigration of soul, all illustrated by translations from Sanskrit texts. Friedrich von Schlegel declared that a real history of world literature could be written only when Asian literature was included in it. However, his brother, August Wilhelm von Schlegel (1767–1845), whose translation of Shakespeare's plays is a German classic, became an even more active Sanskrit scholar. He had learned Sanskrit under Léonard de Chézy in France, and led the extensive development of Indology in Germany. He edited and translated a number of Sanskrit texts and wrote works on philology. He edited the original text of the *Bhagavad Gita,* together with a Latin translation, and paid tribute to its unknown authors: "I shall always adore the imprints of their feet." Schlegel insisted that the critical methods evolved in classical philology, of which he was an expert, should be applied to Sanskrit texts. He established a Sanskrit press at Bonn, at a time when the printing of Sanskrit was only beginning in India. With painstaking care he drew the Devanagari types, supervised their casting, and invented important technical improvements for their printing. He composed his first text, a critical edition of the *Bhagavad Gita* with his own hands. With the help of a subscription from Goethe, he then started a critical edition of the *Ramayana,* but only the first volume was published.

Franz Bopp (1791–1867), who had also studied Sanskrit in Paris, was, unlike the Schlegel brothers, more interested in language than in literature. Professor of Sanskrit at the University of Berlin, he published *On the Conjugational System of the Sanskrit language in comparison with that of the Greek, Latin, Persian, and Germanic languages* in 1816, thus laying the foundations for the new science of comparative philology. In addition, Bopp selected a number of episodes from the *Mahabharata,* especially that of Nala and Damayanti, translated them into German and Latin, and published them in 1819. His *Glossarium Sanscritum,* an important complement to this translation, appeared in 1830.

During the initial phase of Sanskrit studies, until about 1830, European attention was mainly focused on the classical period of Sanskrit. The vedic literature remained almost unknown except for Colebrooke's essay. Little was known of the extensive Buddhist literature. The Upanishads were better known through Anquétil du Perron's Latin translation from the Persian. The Indian linguistic genius, Ram Mohan Roy, edited the Sanskrit text of several Upanishads and published their English translation in 1816–1817.

Later, Paul Deussen (1845–1919) reinforced the study of the Upanishads with his translations and philosophical writings; he also made a selection of texts from the *Mahabharata* with philosophical commentary. Many Indologists reproduced consecutive depictions of the *Mahabharata.*[16] The pioneer in this field, however, was Hermann Jacobi, whose book, *Mahabharata-Inhaltsangabe, Index, Concordanz,* was published in 1903.

The real philological investigation of the Vedas began in 1838 with the publication of the first eight parts of the *Rig Veda* in London by a German scholar, Friedrich Rosen. Vedic literature contains many forms which became extinct in the later Sanskrit, but which existed in similar forms in Greek and other Indo-European languages. For instance, classical Sanskrit has no subjunctive mood unlike most of the older Indo-European languages, but it is common enough in vedic Sanskrit. Moreover, vedic Sanskrit has a tonic accent unlike the later Sanskrit, but similar to the Greek system. After his premature death, Rosen's work was continued by Eugène Burnouf.

One of Burnouf's students, Rudolph Roth (1821–1895), published his work on the history and literature of the Vedas in 1846. In association with another German scholar, Otto Bohtlingk (1815–1909), Roth produced the enormous Sanskrit-German dictionary, the *St. Petersburg Sanskrit Dictionary,* commonly known as the St. Petersburg Lexicon because it was published by the Russian Imperial Academy of Sciences between 1852 and 1875. Comprising almost ten thousand pages, this is the most outstanding of all the achievements of German Indology.

The most celebrated German Indologist, Friedrich Max Müller (1823–1900) continued vedic research by bringing out his splendid edition of the *Rig Veda* in six volumes between 1849 and 1874, and, from 1875 onwards, by editing the authoritative and annotated translation series, *Sacred Books of the East,* in fifty-one volumes, thirty-one of which are Indian texts. This work laid the beginnings of the study of comparative religion. It caused a tremendous sensation even in India, where a cultural renaissance and renewed national consciousness were taking place. Max Müller's translations of the Upanishads and the *Rig Veda* and other works, which have since been published in a variety of forms and editions, made Indian knowledge better known and appreciated everywhere. He guided considerable research in Indology, comparative religion, and mythology. The essays on mythology are amongst his most delightful writings.

Max Müller lived during the formative period of modern India. Armed resistance to the British rule in India had collapsed, having gained its momentum in 1857, but political opposition to British domination had become more organized and intensive. Whilst the Indian rebellion, especially the military revolt of 1857, enraged many British thinkers, such as Tennyson and Ruskin, to the point of writing unkindly of India, Max Müller remained a great friend and admirer, and his name is often Sanskritized as "Moksa-mula," meaning the root of salvation. Müller was the first European scholar to announce that India had a spiritual message for Europe, and he praised Indian thought and philosophy in almost lyrical terms: "If I were to look over the whole world to find out the country most richly endowed with all the wealth, power, and beauty that nature can bestow—in some parts a very paradise on earth—I should point to India. If I were asked under what sky the human mind has most fully developed some of the choicest gifts, has most deeply pondered on the greatest problems of life, and has found solutions of some of them which well deserve the attention even of those who have studied Plato and Kant—I should point to India. . . ."

Max Müller first came under the influence of German Orientalists, and later studied in Paris under Burnouf. He went to Oxford in 1848 to supervise the printing of his *Rig Veda,* and spent the rest of his long working life in England. An eminent classical scholar and a master of languages, including English, he was blocked from succeeding to the Chair of Sanskrit at Oxford in 1860 because he was of foreign birth and his liberal views on theological questions were unacceptable to the clergy in England. The Chair was given to Sir Monier-Williams, an important Sanskrit scholar who did a great deal to make Indian culture known in English-speaking countries. In 1868, however, Max Müller was appointed to a new Chair of Comparative Philosophy. Müller's influence on Indian studies has been extensive, deep, and lasting. For instance, when he pointed out that Alexander is not mentioned in the entire body of Sanskrit literature, historians felt compelled to revise their exaggerated assessment of his campaigns in India.[17]

By the middle of the nineteenth century, Indian texts began to appear in rapid succession, and knowledge about India was keenly sought. One of the most important works of this period was *Indische Alterthumskunde* by Christian Lassen (1800–1876), a pupil of August Wilhelm von Schlegel. The work was published in four large volumes between 1843 and 1862. Lassen, a Norwegian who regarded himself as a German, worked for many years as Professor of Sanskrit at the University of Bonn. His work, although somewhat obsolete today, is of outstanding merit.

The discovery of the vedic hymns also led to the emergence of a new science of comparative mythology. Theodor Benfey published in 1859 his edition of the Indian fable collection, the *Pancatantra,* which created a literary revolution. Benfey showed through meticulous research how the fables of India reached Europe, travelling step by step, through Pahlavi, Persian, Arabic, Hebrew, Latin, and the modern languages of Europe, till they supplied even La Fontaine with some of his most charming themes. Benfey's various Sanskrit grammars, founded as they were on the classical grammar of Panini, and his *History of Sanskrit Philology* are still important.

In 1852, A. Weber published his *History of Indian Literature* in German, the first connected historical account of Indian literature. The work was translated into English and has been printed several times. Weber brought out a second edition in 1876 which he updated by adding notes to the texts. He also opened up a new branch of Indian study through his work in 1883–1885 on the sacred writings of the Jains.

Towards the end of the nineteenth century, the literature on Indian studies had grown too vast and unwieldy for an individual scholar to master. Consequently, the need for an encyclopaedia surveying the work done in all branches of the subject was felt. *Grundriss der indo-arischen Philologie und Altertumskunde* (Compendium of Indo-Aryan Philology and Antiquities) began to appear in 1897 under the general editorship of the versatile Sanskrit scholar, Georg Bühler (1837–1898), who had studied under Benfey, and published many works of his own. This was an attempt by thirty leading scholars from throughout the world to give an encyclopaedic view of the work done in the various branches of Indology. The publication was continued under the editorship of other scholars and was one of the important developments in the field of Indian studies. Later, in 1900, A. A. Macdonell, a successor of Wilson at Oxford, published *A History of Sanskrit Literature* and in 1907 M. Winternitz, Professor of Indology at Prague, brought out *A History of Indian Literature* in German.

Today almost every library in Germany has a special collection of books on India and every university has a departmental library of Indology. Six universities—Bonn, Tübingen, Munich, Göttingen, Marburg, and Hamburg—have Chairs of Sanskrit, and practically every university provides for the teaching of Sanskrit within its department of comparative linguistics. Three German universities have their own magazines on Indology.

Holland's interest in India was direct, because of her commercial and political involvements in the East Indies, but Indology did not begin in that country until the nineteenth century. During the seventeenth and eighteenth centuries, a number of Dutchmen learned modern Indian languages, but only one, Herbert de Jager of the University of Leyden, is known to have been familiar with Sanskrit. The first professor to teach Sanskrit was Hamaker at the University of Leyden, who encouraged the study of comparative linguistics. But the real foundation of Sanskrit studies was laid by his eminent pupil, Hendrik Kern, whose work evoked much interest. A Chair of Sanskrit was consequently established at the University of Leyden in 1865, and was filled by Kern. Before Kern began his professional career, he had taught in England and India. By his publications and through his pupils, several of whom became eminent Indologists, Indian studies made considerable progress in Holland. Later, Holland produced such scholars as Speyer, Vogel, Gonda, Th. P. Gabestios, Bosch, and Faddegon. Today Chairs of Sanskrit exist at Leyden, Utrecht, Amsterdam, and Groningen.

In Italy, also, there developed a keen interest in and systematic study of Indology. Italian missionaries, merchants, and mariners continuously visited India. Those who left valuable accounts of their travels included Marco Polo; Florentine Filippo Sassetti, who made the first suggestion in his letters of a possible link between Italian and Sanskrit in the sixteenth century; Nicolo Manucci; Florentine Francesco Carletti; Pietro della Valle; Giovanni Francesco Gemelli Careri, who wrote *Giro del Mondo,* one volume of which is devoted to India; and Roberto De Nobili. Indian studies in Italy did not begin, on a scientific basis, until the middle of the nineteenth century. Italian interest in Indian thought was initially inspired by German romanticism. The father of Italian Indology was the Piedmontese, Gaspare Gorresio. As soon as Italy achieved political harmony and the kingdom of Italy was formed in 1870, the first Chairs of Oriental Studies were set up. Since then Italy has produced famous Indologists from Graziadio Ascoli to Giuseppe Tucci of the present day.

Even in those small nations of Europe which were not directly concerned with India, the knowledge of ancient India spread. In Czechoslovakia, which has a long tradition of learning, Indology was to occupy a place of prominence. Czech scholars were first attracted to Indian studies through the work of a Jesuit missionary, Karel Prikryl (1718–1795), who arrived in Goa in 1748 as director of the Archbishop's seminary. During his fourteen years in India, he studied Marathi, and is reputed to have written several books. Only one of these, *Principia Linguae Brahmanicae* (The Principles of the Brahmanic Tongue), has survived; this was probably the first grammar of Konkani dialect to have been written. Inspired by Prikryl's works, Josef Dobrovski, a philologist and historian, learned Sanskrit during the last part of the eighteenth century and pointed out the similarities between many Indian and Slav words and forms. In 1812 Joseph Jungmann wrote on Indian prosody and metre, and nine years later his brother, Antonin Jungmann, published the first Sanskrit grammar in Czech.

Of the numerous comparative philologists, Joseph Zubaty made notable contributions to Sanskrit philology and to the history of vedic literature and classical Indian epic and dramatic literature. He published his *Qualitative Changes in the Final Syllable in Vedic* in 1888, and, two years later, a study of Indian metrics entitled *The Construction of Tristubh and Jagati Verses in the Mahabharata.*

Alfred Ludwig (1837–1912), Zubaty's teacher, and Moriz Winternitz (1836–1937) were the first scholars who advanced Indian studies from comparative philology to Indology proper. Ludwig's philological studies were important but he is better known for his German translation of the *Rig Veda* in six volumes, published in Prague in 1876–1888, and for his studies of classical Indian literature. Ludwig was the first Czech scholar to study Dravidian languages.[18]

222

Winternitz succeeded Ludwig to the Chair of Indology at the University of Prague and held it for several decades. He wrote the three-volume *History of Indian Literature* in German, the first two volumes of which were translated into English and published in India in 1927–1933. In addition, he wrote many shorter studies on Indian literature, some of which were published in book form in Calcutta in 1925 under the title, *Some Problems of Indian Literature.*

After World War I, a new Chair of Indology was founded at the Charles University of Prague, the oldest university in Central Europe. Its first occupant, Wincerc Lesny (1882–1953) had travelled extensively in India, and was a scholar of Indian, as well as of Iranian, languages. He published a number of books on India, including a monograph on Rabindranath Tagore, and translated many of Tagore's works directly from Bengali. His work, *Buddhismus,* analyzing the Buddhism of the Pali canon and its development in India and abroad, is yet to be translated from Czech into other languages. Lesny also founded the periodical, *The New East and the Indian Society,* before World War II.

In Hungary, Indian studies did not reach such an advanced level as in some major countries of Europe, but Indian thought made a significant impact on Hungarian intellectual life, and Hungary has made some contributions to Indology. One of these is the work of Sir Aurel Stein (1862–1943), a British citizen of Hungarian origin whose archaeological surveys and work in Central Asia are classical contributions to the study of Indian culture abroad. Born in Budapest, he studied in Austria and Germany, and taught Sanskrit at the University of the Punjab, before he led Indian archaeological expeditions to the hitherto unexcavated ruins in Serindia. He bequeathed his valuable library to the Hungarian Academy of Sciences.

The first Hungarian Orientalist was Alexander Csoma de Körös (1784–1842) who visited India in 1830 at the invitation of the Asiatic Society of Bengal, and who died at Darjeeling in 1842 during his second visit. His work and that of Tivadar Duka (1825–1908) were the beginnings of Indian studies in Hungary. Some of the scholars whose contributions to Hungarian Indology are particularly notable are Karoly Fiolk (1857–1915), who translated several Sanskrit classical texts; Sandor Kegl (1862–1920) and Josef Schmidt (1868–1933) who made Indian philosophy accessible to Hungarians; Charles Louis Fabri, whose writings on Indian art and aesthetics are well known to Indian scholars; Ervin Baktay (1890–1963); and Ferenc Hopp, who founded the Museum of East Asiatic Art in Budapest, which is named after him.

Some Rumanian scholars and poets were also fascinated by Indian culture. G. Coshbuc (1866–1918), called "the singer of the Rumanian peasantry," translated the *Sakuntala* from a German version in 1897, and compiled a Sanskrit anthology. B. P. Hashdeu studied the problems of Sanskrit literature or linguistics. His disciple, Lazar Saineanu, went to Paris where he studied Sanskrit at the Sorbonne with Abel Bergaigne. Constantin Georgian (1850–1904), who had worked with A. Weber at Berlin, was the first Rumanian Orientalist to make persistent efforts to introduce the study of Sanskrit into his country. However, the authorities did not approve of the teaching of Sanskrit; original translations from Sanskrit and works of Indology did not appear in Rumania until the 1930's.[19] Amongst many other Rumanian scholars who made Sanskrit and Indian culture their intellectual pursuit and formed a literary circle (Junimea), the names of Vasile Pogor, Vasile Burla, and Teohari Antonescu, can be mentioned as more prominent. Antonescu's important work on the philosophy of the Upanishads was the first study in Rumania to deal with such a problem in its entirety.

Information about early Russian awareness of India and Indian culture is at present insufficient. In the South Russian Steppes, some Buddhist images of the pre-Mongol period have been found. Indian fables and stories have long been known in Russia, although it is doubtful if their origins were known. A Russian traveller, Athanasius Nikitin, went to India in the fifteenth century but his diary, a valuable source of information, was unfinished. At the end of the seventeenth century a Russian merchant, Semen Malinkov, was received by Aurangzeb. A small colony of Indian traders and artisans was established in Astrakhan about 1615 and some Indian religious men settled in the region and enjoyed freedom of worship.

The first translation of a Sanskrit text was published in Russia in 1787 by N. I. Novikov. This was not a direct translation from Sanskrit but a Russian version of Wilkins' translation of the *Bhagavad Gita*. Later, a Russian musician, Gerasim Lebedev (1749–1817) who lived in India from 1785 to 1797 and played a significant role in the renaissance of the Bengali Theatre, published his *Grammar of Pure and Mixed East Indian Dialects with Dialogues* in 1801, and *An Impartial Survey of the Systems of Brahmanical East India* in 1805. He also cast the first Devanagari type by the command of Tsar Alexander I.

An Asian Academy was established at St. Petersburg in 1810, and Robert Lenz (1808–1836), who learned Sanskrit under Franz Bopp at Berlin, was appointed the first Professor of Sanskrit and Comparative Philology, but he died at the age of twenty-eight. His work, however, was continued by Pave Yakovlevich Petrov, who taught a number of

Russian philologists and Indologists, including F. Korsch, F. F. Fortunator, and V. F. Miller, and translated into Russian the Sitaharana episode of the *Ramayana* with a glossary and a grammatical analysis.

Once the process had begun, Sanskrit studies expanded rapidly in the receptive atmosphere of Russian intellectual life, and Russia produced famous Indologists, such as V. P. Vasilyev (1818–1900) and V. P. Minayev (1840–1890). A pupil of Minayev, Sergei Fedorovich Oldenburg (1863–1934), founded in 1897 the *Bibliotheca Buddhica*, a series devoted to the publication of Buddhist texts and monographs on Buddhist subjects. The Russian school of Indology had already produced the monumental St. Petersburg Lexicon, between 1852 and 1875. Possibly Oldenburg's greatest achievement was his archaeological explorations of Eastern Turkistan, and his participation in the organization of Russian scientific exploration of Central Asia; Russian explorers were the first to point out the rich archaeological sites on the edges of the Taklamakan Desert. Fedor Ippolitovich Stcherbatsky (1886–1941), who studied under Minayev and Oldenburg in St. Petersburg, Büehler in Vienna, and Jacobi in Bonn, published important works on Buddhist thought and edited numerous Tibetan and Sanskrit texts for the *Bibliotheca Buddhica*. Since the end of the last century, Russian interest and work in Indian studies have become even more comprehensive.

The first direct contact between India and the United States was commercial, and began in the end of the eighteenth century. By the middle of the nineteenth century, American trade with India had greatly increased. Diplomatic and missionary activity followed. American knowledge of India was at first vague, fragmentary, and indirect, acquired through the writings of European scholars. Later, however, the impact of Swami Vivekananda, Rabindranath Tagore, and other visiting Indians was clearly felt.

Since Yale University was founded in 1718 with the help of a cargo of gifts raised in India by Elihu Yale, who was a governor of Madras, it was only appropriate that it was there that Indian studies in the United States were begun in 1841. Edward Elbridge Salisbury (1814–1901), a pupil of Franz Bopp, was appointed the first Professor of Sanskrit. Later, his pupil, William Dwight Whitney (1827–1894), who had also studied with Weber and Roth, filled the Chair with distinction and made the first important American contributions to Sanskrit studies, including editions of the *Vishnu Purana* and the *Atharva Veda*.

Johns Hopkins University was next to set up a Chair in Sanskrit in 1878, within two years of its own foundation. A pupil of Whitney, Charles Rockwell Lanman, the author of the widely known *Sanskrit*

Reader and the editor of the *Harvard Oriental Series,* was appointed to the position, but he moved to Harvard University two years later to set up what was to become an outstanding Department of Sanskrit. Later, several other universities, such as Columbia, California, and Pennsylvania, instituted Chairs of Sanskrit, and America produced many well-known scholars, such as Washburn Hopkins, Maurice Bloomfield, Franklin Edgerton, Arthur Ryder, A. U. William Jackson, and W. Norman Brown. Whilst American scholarship has made notable contributions of its own, Indian thought made its impact on the American mind mainly through European Indology.

Until World War II, American academic interest was primarily confined to the linguistic and literary study of ancient texts. Now, with the independence of India and the role of America in world affairs, the study of India in American universities and colleges has increased and become phenomenally diversified. Research in Indian history, sociology, politics, economics, and many other fields is rapidly expanding, and the recently established American Institute of Indian Studies has given a new impetus to American Indology. Thousands of Indian students are studying at American universities—over one thousand Indian scholars are now teaching there—and countless American scholars, journalists, artists, and tourists have visited India.

Without further straining the patience of the reader, it is not possible to mention here the considerable Indological work done in the other countries of Europe, and the many outstanding contributions made by scholars not already noted; the works of Sten Konow and Georg Morgenstierne from Norway; Jarl Carpentier and Helmer Smith from Sweden; Myles Dillon from Eire; W. S. Majewski, J. Lelewal, D. L. Boskowsk, and S. Schayer from Poland; Hermann Brunnhofer, Ernst Leumann, and Jacob Wockernagel from Switzerland; and Fausboll from Denmark are particularly valuable.[20]

Whilst a good deal of work was thus being done in Europe and America, the study of ancient Indian culture was progressing in India as well, through the efforts of both European and Indian scholars. Amongst the Indians themselves there developed during the nineteenth century a class of scholars who were educated in Western learning and were inspired by the growing spirit of cultural renaissance in India. Of these the works of R. G. Bhandarkar and Rajendralal Mitra are best known. Their tradition gave rise to successive generations of Indian scholars who now do the vast majority of the work in Indian studies.

The initial work of the Asiatic Society of Bengal on written records was soon to lead attention to archaeological remains. Inscriptions in long-forgotten alphabets, coins, etc. were closely scrutinized. Working back from current scripts the older languages were deciphered. One of the most remarkable achievements in this field was James Prinsep's (1799–1840) reading of the Brahmi script in 1837. An erudite scholar skilled in epigraphic techniques, he was able to interpret the edicts of Asoka, giving India knowledge of her noblest ruler, and placing Indian archaeology on a secure chronological basis. His death at the age of forty-one was a grievous blow to Indian studies.[21] A colleague of his, Alexander Cunningham, was an engineer with the British Indian Army and greatly interested in Indian archaeology. He continued Prinsep's work, and in 1862 became the first archaeological surveyor of India. Later his work was carried forward by a number of archaeologists, prominent amongst whom were James Burgess, John Marshall, and R. D. Banerji, who discovered the cities of the Indus civilization in 1922.

Chapter VI

WESTERN RESPONSE TO

MODERN INDIA

WHILST Europe's debt to Greek literature is generally acknowledged, and often overemphasized, it is not always easy for modern generations to imagine the effect Indian ideas have had on European intellectual and cultural progress. The stimulus of Indian literature was such that scholars, exemplified by Macdonell, said: "Since the Renaissance there has been no event of such world-wide significance in the history of culture as the discovery of Sanskrit literature in the latter part of the eighteenth century."[1] Indeed, the impact of Indian thought on the intellectual life of renaissant Europe was so powerful that many European writers have not taken kindly to it. Driven by some strange fear of losing their cultural identity, they endeavoured to minimize or ignore the influence of Indian philosophy, and stretch logic to explain intellectual evolution purely in terms of what they call Western traditions.

India, however, was only one of the several factors which influenced European thought and life. The entire political, social, and intellectual life of Europe at this time was far more active and complex than during any previous age, and perhaps any subsequent one. France led the Age of Enlightenment. Germany was rapidly advancing, asserting its intellectual prowess in literature and philosophy; America and Russia had begun to make important contributions; and science had scored fresh advances. These were far-reaching changes, in which the discovery of Indian literature and philosophy played a limited but significant role.

Inevitably, European response to Indian ideas differed from country to country: indeed, from thinker to thinker. Some received Indian thought more readily and understood it better than others. Others reacted against it almost instinctively. Whatever the response, favourable or unfavourable, deep or fragmentary, it was entirely conditioned by the intellectual climate of Europe and its variations. There was no organized movement to advocate the adoption of Indian ideas. If there were those anxious to underline the virtues of Indian literature, they were the Europeans themselves, acting individually. Seldom were Indian doctrines adopted wholesale—to expect otherwise would be to deny the existence of a powerful indigenous tradition and the intellectual independence of the receiver. Some found in Indian thought reinforcement of their own ideas; others an escape or diversion from their own tradition.

Indian thought and literature had its finest European reception in Germany. In fact, Indology became largely a province of German scholarship, stimulated entirely by academic considerations, as Germany, unlike Britain and France, had no political ties with India or her neighbours. Although Abraham Roger's work, *The Open Door to Hidden Heathendom*, a German translation of two hundred maxims of Bhartrihari, appeared in 1663, it made little impact. Not until the end of the eighteenth century did the Germans come to know some of the famous works of Indian literature.

Europe took *Sakuntala* to heart, and in Germany the popularity of this work ensured that later translations would be welcomed. The first German to recognize the beauty of *Sakuntala* was the poet and critic, Johann Gottfried Herder (1744–1803). Although not familiar with India or its languages, he had already given a somewhat idealized picture of the Indian people in his chief work, *Ideen Zur Philosophie der Menschheit (Ideas on a Philosophy of the History of Mankind)*, in 1787. According to him, mankind's origin was to be traced to India, where the "human mind got the first shapes of wisdom and virtue with a simplicity, strength and sublimity which has—frankly spoken—nothing, nothing at all equivalent in our philosophical, cold European world." He regarded the Hindus, because of their ethical teachings, as the most gentle and peaceful people on earth. His concept of India was taken up by the Romantic movement, and long dominated the fantasy of German poets. The connection which the teachings of reincarnation established between all forms of life opened a new field to Herder and his contemporaries. Herder's *Thoughts of Some Brahmins* (1792), which contains a selection of gnomic stanzas in free translations, gathered from Bhartrihari, the *Hitopadesa* and the *Bhagavad Gita*, expressed these ideals. When George Förster sent him his German translation of the English version of the *Sakuntala* in 1791, Herder responded: "I cannot easily find a product of the human mind more pleasant than this . . . a real blossom of the Orient, and the first, most beautiful of its kind! . . . Something like that, of course, appears once every two thousand years." He published a detailed study and analysis of *Sakuntala*, claiming that this work disproved the popular belief that drama was the exclusive invention of the ancient Greeks.

Herder's letters, published under the title, *The Oriental Drama,* claim that Kalidasa's masterpiece contains a perfection unique in world literature both in poetic substance and the characterization of the heroine. Herder hurriedly passed on his discovery of the Indian drama to his friend, Johann Wolfgang von Goethe (1749–1832), whose own enthusiasm for this play was no less exuberant. He wrote in 1792:

> Wouldst thou the young year's blossoms and the fruits
> of its decline
> And all by which the soul is charmed, enraptured,
> feasted, fed,
> Wouldst thou the earth, and heaven itself in one sole name
> combine?
> I name thee, O Sakuntala! and all at once is said.[2]

Goethe expressed this admiration for *Sakuntala* more than once. Nearly forty years later, in 1830 when de Chézy sent him his edition of the original with his French translation, he wrote to the Frenchman expressing his deep gratitude: "The first time I came across this inexhaustible work it aroused such enthusiasm in me and so held me that I could not stop studying it. I even felt impelled to make the impossible attempt to bring it in some form to the German stage. These efforts were fruitless but they made me so thoroughly acquainted with this most valuable work, it represented such an epoch in my life, I so absorbed it, that for thirty years I did not look at either the English or the German version. . . . It is only now that I understand the enormous impression that work made on me at an earlier age."[3] Goethe goes on to point out the beauties of the work, saying that in it the poet appears in his highest function, as the representative of the most natural state, of the most refined form of life, of the purest moral striving, of the worthiest majesty and the most solemn contemplation of God; at the same time he is lord and master of his creation to so great an extent that he may venture vulgar and ludicrous contrasts which yet must be regarded as necessary links of the whole organization. No wonder he modelled the prologue of his *Faust* (1797) on the prologue to *Sakuntala*. The jester in the prologue of *Faust* is reminiscent of one of the *vidusaka* in the Indian drama, a parallel first noticed by Heinrich Heine.

Goethe's friend, Schiller, who otherwise took little interest in Indian literature, was also moved to enthusiastic praise of *Sakuntala,* which he found in some respects unparalleled in the classical literature of Greece and Rome. He published part of the *Sakuntala* in *Thalia,* and in a letter to Wilhelm Humboldt he wrote that "in the whole of Greek antiquity there is no poetical representation of beautiful love which approaches Sakuntala even afar."

Goethe also admired other Indian poems, such as Jayadeva's *Gita Govinda* and Kalidasa's *Meghaduta* which he read in Wilson's English translation in 1817 and welcomed as "a great treasure." Goethe's second Indian ballad, "Der Paria" (1824), was his best. The plot for "Der Paria" comes from the work of the French traveller, Sonnerat (*Voyage aux Indes,* 1783), who had returned to Europe in 1782 after seven years in India. Goethe's first Indian ballad, "Der Gotund die Bajadere," published in 1797, was also based on Sonnerat.

Whilst Herder and Goethe shared enthusiasm for the *Sakuntala,* their attitudes toward India were very different. Herder was gradually becoming old and moralizing. The *Sakuntala* had captivated him, but it was the rich treasure of Indian gnomic and didactic poetry that appealed to him most. Herder admired India, as did Novalis and Heine, for its simplicity, and denounced the Europeans for their greed, corruption, and economic exploitation of India.

Goethe, on the other hand, reacted to Indian literature as a poet and an artist. Although he was delighted by the harmonious beauty and lyrical intensity of the epics and *kavya,* he did not care for the *Hitopadesa* and philosophy, and he took no interest in Indian mythology and sculpture. He was particularly interested in poetry that expressed human feelings and sentiments in a simple and natural way. Indian sculpture, with its variety and abundance of form, offended his classical ideal of unified beauty. His admiration for India was strong and deep, but it could not compare with his appreciation for Greece. He was fascinated by India, but he understood Greece. Consequently Goethe did not actively participate in the expansion of Indian studies and did not learn Sanskrit, although in the Goethe Archives there are some papers on which the poet tried the Devanagari script. Extreme attraction unaccompanied by proper intellectual understanding was bound to unnerve a thinking, sensitive scholar, such as Goethe. He expressed this feeling to his friend Humboldt in 1826: "I have by no means an aversion to things Indian, but I am afraid of them, for they draw my imagination into the formless and the diffuse against which I have to guard myself more than ever before."[4] However, he consistently acknowledged the tremendous stimulus of Indian thought on Western civilization, and followed the work of German Indologists such as the Schlegel brothers and Bopp with interest and approval.

Inspired by Herder's idealist concepts there developed a belief that the highest form of romantic poetry could be found only in India. The very reason which made Goethe hesitant gave the Romantics a predilection for India. Consequently, they did not content themselves with glorifying it in poetry alone; they laid the foundation for a real science of India.

Until the end of the eighteenth century, French was the language of the German élite and, together with Latin, the language of learning. During the French Revolution and Napoleonic Wars, Germany suffered heavily. After the war, educated Germans became more aware of their own language and heritage, and took an increasing pride in it. At this psychological moment Indian literature appeared in Germany; a certain undoubted cultural and historical affinity between India and Germany probably assumed greater imaginary proportions than it would have at any other time.

Shakespeare on the one hand, and Indian literature on the other, formed the main inspiration of the German Romantic movement. Both were introduced into Germany at about the same time and by the same persons, Friedrich and August Wilhelm von Schlegel. The Romantics found in India that dynamic and synthetic approach to life which they felt was lacking in the formalism and artificiality of the early European Romantic movement, and sought to substitute aesthetic standards for utilitarian ones.

The religions of India also fascinated the Romantics of Germany; throughout the nineteenth century Western religious criticism was inspired by the discovery of Indian polytheism. "If one considers," comments Schlegel, "the superior conception which is at the basis of the truly universal Indian culture and which, itself divine, knows how to embrace in its universality everything that is divine without distinction, then, what we in Europe call religion or what we used to call such, no longer seems to deserve that name. And one would like to advise everyone who wants to see religion, he should, just as one goes to Italy to study art, go to India for that purpose where he may be certain to find at least fragments for which he will surely look in vain in Europe."[5]

Amongst those men of letters who took an enthusiastic interest in Indian literature was the versatile Prussian minister of education, Wilhelm von Humboldt (1767–1835), a brilliant linguist and the founder of the science of general linguistics. He began to learn Sanskrit in 1821 and was greatly moved by Schlegel's edition of the *Bhagavad*

Gita, on which he published an extensive study and which he described as "the deepest and loftiest thing the world has to show."[6] He declared that he was grateful to God for granting him a life so long that he could read the *Gita.*[7]

Ludwig van Beethoven (1770–1827) was also attracted by Indian thought, as is clearly attested by numerous passages and notes referring to Indian ideas and texts found in the Beethoven papers. He was first introduced to Indian literature by the Austrian Orientalist, Hammer-Purgstal, who founded a periodical for the dissemination of Eastern knowledge in Europe as early as January 1809. Beethoven had a deep interest in Indian knowledge long before Indological studies began in Germany. The fragments of Indian religious texts that have been discovered in the Beethoven manuscripts are partly translations and partly adaptations of the Upanishads and the *Bhagavad Gita.* It is not certain if Beethoven himself or his Orientalist friends selected these passages for him.

The German poet, Friedrich Rückert (1788–1866), Professor of Oriental Languages at the University of Erlangen from 1827 to 1841, produced, under the inspiration of August Wilhelm von Schlegel, numerous skilful translations from Sanskrit. His published translations from Indian classical poetry made Indian lyrics and poems widely popular in Germany. Amongst his translations are *Nalopakhyana,* the *Amarusataka,* the *Raghuvamsa,* and the *Gita Govinda,* which lost nothing of its beauty, colour, and atmosphere in Rückert's German version. The Indian poem is such a complex work from the viewpoint of rhyme, alliteration, and allusion that Rückert's version represents a brilliant accomplishment. Of all the German poets, it was he who best understood the character of Indian poetry.[8]

Novalis (1772–1801), one of Germany's greatest Romantic poets, wrote in his essay, *Christendom in Europe,* that poetry, pure and colourful like a beautiful India, stood opposed to the cold and deadening mountains of philistine reason. For him Sanskrit was the most mysterious linguistic symbol of any human expression; Sanskrit took him back to the "original people" who had been forgotten. However, in spite of his emotional enthusiasm for India, Novalis did not really understand Indian thought. Unlike those Indians who believe the objective world is an illusion, Novalis sought to perfect this world. Similarly, when E. T. A. Hoffmann (1776–1822) attempted to create Indian characters in some of his stories, they were magicians who, although traditionally associated with India, were not really representative.

Schelling also accorded India an important position in his *Philosophy of Mythology.* He was a great admirer of ancient Indian literature, especially the Upanishads, which he regarded, like Schopenhauer, to be the genuine wisdom of Indians and of mankind.

Heinrich Heine (1797–1856), a late Romantic lyric poet, whose influence was enormous not only in Germany but in most countries of the Western world, describes the India of his imagination: ". . . in the glass I saw the dear motherland, the blue and sacred Ganges, the eternally shining Himalayas, the gigantic forests of Banyan trees on whose wide shadowy paths quietly walk wise elephants and white pilgrims. . . ."[9] His poem, "Auf Flügeln des Gesanges,"

> Am Ganges duftet's und leuchtet's
> Und Riesenbäume blühn,
> Und schöne, stille Menschen
> Vor Lotosblumen knien.

created a picture of India widely familiar in Germany.[10] Heine's acquaintance with Indian thought, acquired in Bonn under Schlegel and Bopp, remained important to him throughout his life. His approach to Indian works was intimate and sensitive, but it did not lead to uncritical enthusiasm for them. He did not care for the story of the rivalry between Vasistha and Visvamitra, in which he saw a parallel with the investiture contest in mediaeval Europe. However, he had a particular feeling for Indian scenery, as is revealed by his verses in his famous *Buch der Lieder (Book of Songs).* He remarked that if the Portuguese, the Dutch, and the English had carried away ships laden with Indian treasures, Germany would do likewise, but hers would be treasures of spiritual knowledge.

Although Gutzkow titled his novel *Mahaguru* (1832), he shows no evidence of real knowledge of Indian thought. F. Hebbel's attention was drawn to India by Ad. Holtzmann's *Indian Sagas.* In 1863, he wrote the story of King Sibi who by sacrificing his own life saved a dove from a hawk, and his poem, "The Brahmans," gives a moving expression of the Indian concept of the equality of all living beings.

Immanuel Kant (1712–1804) was apparently the first important German philosopher to have some acquaintance with Indian philosophy. Kant's differentiation between the physical world as seen in space and time, and the unknowable thing in itself beyond these concepts, is very similar to the doctrine of Maya. There are certain parallels between Kantian thought and Buddhist philosophy. Like the Buddha, Kant declared a number of questions unsolvable, such as "Has the world a beginning or not?" "Is it finite or eternal?" Stcherbatsky has shown that Kant's doctrine of the categorical imperative has its counterpart in Hindu philosophy, and has pointed out similarities between Kantian thought and later Buddhist thinkers like Chandrakirti. Moreover, according to Hermann Jacobi, Kant's *Aesthetics* had been preceded by Indian writers on poetics.

These are important parallels and strongly indicative of Kant's familiarity with Indian philosophy. But, considering that Sanskrit studies were only beginning to emerge in Europe, and Europe knew very little of Indian philosophy at the time, it seems unlikely that Kant had any direct knowledge of Indian thought. However, the possibility of his acquaintance, as distinct from knowledge, with Indian ideas through earlier Western writings and contemporary travel accounts cannot be ruled out. In his lectures at the Königberg University in East Prussia from 1756 to 1796, he talked about the physiography of India and the customs and manners of the people, and it seems likely that an intellectual of his genius would have gathered other information about India and reflected upon it with utmost care and competence. His observations about Buddhism in Asia and about Hindus appear to endorse the view that he had extensive and accurate knowledge of Indian thought. He said the Hindus were gentle and tolerant of other religions and nations. He was very much impressed by the Hindu doctrine of transmigration, which corresponded in some respects to his own teaching about the destiny of the soul after death. Similarly, Kant's successor, Johann Gottlieb Fichte (1762–1814), includes in his *Anweisung Zu einem selingen Leben* (*Hints for a Blessed Life*) numerous passages which approximate the *Advaita* doctrine.

Whilst Kant and Fichte were not familiar with original Sanskrit texts, Arthur Schopenhauer (1788–1860) knew them, at least in some measure, and openly acknowledged his debt to Indian systems in *Die Welt als Wille und Vorstellung* (*The World as Will and Idea*): "I acknowledge that I owe the best part of my development, beside the impression of the outward world, to the works of Kant and to the holy scriptures of the Hindus and Plato." He believed that if ". . . the reader has also received and assimilated the sacred, primitive Indian wisdom, then is he best of all prepared to hear what I have to say to him."[11] Schopenhauer, who was unusually free from nationalism, and who has been called the philosopher of disillusion and profound pessimism, was introduced to Indian thought in 1813 by one of Goethe's friends, the Orientalist Friedrich Mayer. From then on, Schopenhauer never lost interest. In 1818, he published his most important work, *Die Welt als*

Wille und Vorstellung, in which he put forward the doctrines of pessimism and the subjectivity of will to knowledge. Although his university career had come to an abrupt end at this time, he continued to work on his doctoral thesis privately. He read whatever he could lay his hands on at the Weimar Library concerning Indian thought. Of these, Anquetil du Perron's translation of the Upanishads was his chief source of information. Schopenhauer, although working with an imperfect translation, was extremely enthusiastic about the Upanishads' philosophy and declared them to be "the production of the highest human wisdom." For him no study was so elevating as that of the Upanishads: "It has been the solace of my life, it will be the solace of my death." A few years later when he became acquainted with Buddhism, he regarded it as more profound than Christianity. He did not think that Christianity could ever displace Buddhism in the East: "It is just as if we fired a bullet against a cliff." On the contrary, he thought that Indian philosophy would profoundly alter European knowledge and thought: "The influence of Sanskrit literature will penetrate not less deeply than did the revival of Greek letters in the fifteenth century."[12] Schopenhauer, mainly influenced by the discovery of upanishadic thought, has been called the first apostle of Buddhism in Germany. He was so impressed by Buddhism that he claimed fundamental identity of his philosophy with the teachings of Buddhism, kept a bronze of the Buddha in his study, and occasionally referred to himself and his followers as "we Buddhists." But there are important differences between his philosophy and Indian thought, whether Buddhist or vedantic.

Schopenhauer regarded the Hindus as deeper thinkers than Europeans because their interpretation of the world was internal and intuitive, not external and intellectual. For intuition unites everything; the intellect divides everything. The Hindus saw that the "I" is a delusion, that the individual is merely phenomenal, and that the only reality is the Infinite One "That art Thou."

Another German philosopher, Karl Christian Friedrich Krause (1781–1832) was even more strongly influenced by Indian philosophy. He praised the Vedanta particularly in his *Vorlesungen über die Grundwahrheiten der Wissenschaften* (1829), although he wrote on Buddhism, Jainism, and the Carvakas.

Paul Deussen (1845–1919), a rare combination of a scholar of European philosophy as well as of Indology, was also greatly attracted by the Vedanta philosophy. Works on the Vedanta philosophy and his translation of the *Vedanta Sutras* were published in 1883 and in 1887 respectively. By translating the original texts of the Upanishads into

German and commenting upon them he increased the understanding of Indian philosophy amongst European thinkers. He called the Vedanta system one of the greatest achievements of humanity in the search for eternal truth.

Not all German philosophers were fascinated by Indian thought. Once Europe had recovered from the ravages of the Napoleonic Wars and Indian culture lost its novelty, European intellectuals began to analyze Indian civilization, even if they had no familiarity with original texts. A typical example was Georg Wilhelm Friedrich Hegel (1770–1831), a contemporary of Schopenhauer, who, in reaction to the undiluted romanticism towards India, gave a full chapter to India in his *Philosophy of World History* (1822–1823), and drew some depressing conclusions. With his stress on reason, he criticized the Romantics for idolizing India. He considered the prevailing degenerate condition of Indian society as its natural condition, and maintained it was a society condemned by its own inability to rejuvenate itself. Hegel not only applied erroneous standards but relied on undependable sources—the writings of British administrators and Abbé Dubois' book. How ill-informed Hegel was of things Eastern can best be seen in the brief attempt he makes in his book to define Buddhism. "There is a great dispute going on," he says, "which of the two religions (Buddhism and Hinduism) is older and simpler; for both there are reasons, but one cannot discern it clearly. The Buddhistic religion is simpler, but this may be due either to the fact that it is older, or that it is the result of a Reformation. Probably, however, Buddhism is the older of the two."[13]

Yet it is interesting to notice a likeness between Hegel's famous "dialectical movement," that every idea and every situation in the world leads irresistibly to its opposite and then unites with it to form a new whole, and the Buddhist concept of the "golden mean." Hegel expressly refers to Indian predecessors of his logic of contradictions. Also, his view that man reaches his full stature only through suffering is quite close to the Buddha's declaration that life is dukkha.

Whilst Hegel reacted against Romanticism and against Schopenhauer's enthusiasm for Indian thought, Friedrich Nietzsche (1844–1900) protested as much against Schopenhauer's philosophy as against Deussen's interpretation of the Vedanta. Nietzsche, however, was deeply influenced by Schopenhauer in his youth, and regarded himself as his successor, although superior to him in some ways. He found in *The World as Will and Idea* "a mirror in which I espied the world, life, and my own nature depicted with frightful grandeur." Although he later denounced pessimism as decadent, he remained an unhappy man and under the permanent influence of Schopenhauer's thought. Nietzsche was very appreciative of the Upanishads and, indeed, contemptuous of those Europeans who, devoid of intellectual discernment, wanted to convert and "civilize" the Brahmans. When Paul Deussen told him his plan of translating ancient Hindu texts and expounding their wisdom, he expressed great enthusiasm saying that Indian philosophy was the one parallel to their own European philosophy. In *Thus Spake Zarathustra* (1883–1891), the most revealing and personal of all his writings, Nietzsche propounded his central doctrine, the gospel of the superman, which is his chief legacy to the world. Passionately individualistic, he was a believer in the hero. He found in the *Manusmriti* one of the sources of his own philosophy of superman. He so highly esteemed the Hindu text that he declared all other ethical codes to be imitations and even caricatures of this. He saw the supremacy of the Indian Brahmans as the implicit obedience of the herd to the religious and moral command of the "ruling" caste. Nietzsche was not a nationalist and showed no excessive admiration for Germany; he certainly was not anti-Semitic. He wanted an international ruling race, a vast aristocracy of artist-tyrants. Seldom in Western thought is the difference between man as he now is and man as he might become more emphatically pronounced than by Nietzsche.

During the first half of the nineteenth century, interest was directed towards India as a whole, but in the second half of the century, German scholars were drawn towards Buddhist thought and literature, through the publication of Burnouf's *Introduction à l'histoire du Bouddhisme indien* (1844) and Koppen's *Buddhismus* (1857–1859). Even Nietzsche, who had moved away from Schopenhauer and Wagner, included in his book, *Revaluation of All Values,* a hymn of praise to Buddhism which he found a "hundred times more realistic than Christ's Nativity."

Richard Wagner (1813–1883) was so profoundly influenced by Buddhism as propagated by Schopenhauer and his followers that he confessed he had involuntarily become a Buddhist. He was fascinated by the doctrine of salvation and the ethics of compassion, before which every other dogma appeared to be small and narrow. In his play, *The Victors,* Wagner uses a story from Burnouf's book about a *chandala* (untouchable) female, Prakriti, who was accepted into the monastic order by the Buddha to enable her to find fulfilment in her love for Ananda who had also become a monk, and to make amends for her past sins. Prakriti and Ananda were later transformed into Kundry and Parsifal in his last opera, *Parsifal.* The flowergirls (which Wagner took from Lambrecht's *Alexander Song*) and Kingsor's lance, which hangs above Parsifal's head, have their origins in the story about the Buddha's temptation through Mara. In *Götterdämmerung* (*Twilight of the Gods*), Wahnheim (the abode of illusion) and Wunschheim (the abode of desire), for which the man, delivered from the necessity of having to be born again, strives, are typically Indian concepts. Countless borrowings from India are found in Wagner's work.

In 1881 Hermann Oldenberg (1854–1920) published his brilliant study, *Buddha—His Life, Teachings and Community,* which added greatly to Buddhism's popularity in Germany. Oldenberg also edited and translated the *Dipavamsa* and the *Vinaya Pitaka.* The abundance of new material and the inherent atheism of original Buddhism inspired some German poets of the following decades.

J. V. Widmann created an historically inaccurate picture of the Buddha in his epic, *Buddha,* as the Master who urged pantheism and atheism so that "a new golden age" could be achieved. Karl Bleibtreu's dramas, *Karma* (1901) and *Saviour* (1903), attempted to ease the entrance of Buddhism into Europe, but again it was interpreted inaccurately. The most complete treatment of the Buddha was achieved by Karl Gjellerup in *Pilgrim Kamanita* (1903). He tried to convey some of the nature of Buddhism, and showed much knowledge of Indian customs and Hinduism.

Whilst a general feeling of weariness towards all matters of the world encouraged the influx of Eastern, especially Buddhist, ideas at the beginning of the twentieth century, this impact was considerably increased in the years following because of the intellectual restiveness generated by World War I. Buddhism in Germany was encouraged by the poetry of P. Dahlke and Hans Much. A particularly powerful poetic treatment of the Buddha legend was achieved by Albrecht Schaffer in *The Gem in the Lotos* (1923) which was partly inspired by Sir Edwin Arnold's *The Light of Asia.* Werfel's play, *The Mirror Man,* appeared in 1920. The hero of this play leaves an Indian monastery and through the "mirror man" (the manifestation of illusion) he gradually overcomes maya (illusion) and realizes that dissociation from one's own existence is the highest possible aim.

Most poets at that time no longer believed in the superiority of Christianity. In Josef Winckler's comedy, *Labyrinth of God or the Comedy of Chaos* (1922), the Buddha has only a smile for the twelve Apostles who want to convince him that his time has ended. The hero of Stefan Zweig's *The Eyes of the Eternal Brother* (1921), the Indian *Virata,* attempts to lead a life without guilt. He moves down socially from one step to the other and finally realizes that one should strive to subject one's will but not attempt to live without guilt. The hero in Alfred Döblin's epic, *Manas* (1927), is haunted by the question of where the enemies he has slain in battle will continue to suffer. He therefore goes to the land of the dead in the Himalayas, where he witnesses such terrible things that he suffers a breakdown and dies. His wife who has followed him brings him back to life. The hero then overcomes gods and demons; he no longer rejects the world but worships the forces of nature. Döblin's descriptions of visions belonging to Siva's world show his familiarity with Indian religious literature.

Hermann Keyserling (1880–1946), who found a strong affinity between Christianity and Buddhism, was much impressed by the metaphysical profundity of India. He used Indian thought to measure European standards of conduct and morality. The influence of Keyserling on the European intelligentsia after World War I, especially in Germany, was deep but short-lived. Germany, shattered from the disastrous war, had returned its attention towards India for solace and new inspiration, as is indicated by the publication of innumerable novels and poems with a predominantly Asian background.

Hermann Hesse, awarded the Nobel Prize for literature in 1946, found in Indian thought an answer to his yearning for deliverance from "ego," and from the tyrannical dictates of temporality. Indian thought offered the most radical possibility of undoing the curse of individuation, of annihilating the "idiotic one-after-the-other" by the postulation of the eternal simultaneity of nirvana. The positive attitude of the *Bhagavad Gita* also appealed to Hesse. Yoga and maya are the background to the events portrayed in the *Glasperlenspiel* (*The Game of Glass Beads*). Hesse himself claimed that Yoga had an invaluable effect upon him as a means of improving his powers of concentration. The threefold sequence of sensual love, wisdom, and self-denial experienced by the poet Bhartrihari is interpreted by Hesse as the result of humble and wise humanity. In *Journey to the Orient*, Hesse, whose mother was born in Malabar, says of India that it was "not only a country and something geographical, but the home and the youth of the soul, the everywhere and nowhere, the oneness of all times." It is significant that Hesse, although a Christian, repeatedly substituted the upanishadic *tat tvamasi*, literally "love your neighbour for he is yourself," for Christ's command, "love thy neighbour as thyself." In *Siddhartha* (1922) he tried to reconcile Christian and Indian piety.

Other prominent German writers, such as Paul Dahlke (1865–1928), H. Much, Josef Winckler, Albrecht Schaffer, Franz Werfel, Stefan Zweig, Hermann Kasack, Gustav Meyrink, and Thomas Mann, drew

upon Indian materials. Thomas Mann (1875–1955) gave a new inter-
pretation to an Indian story from the *Vatalapancavimsati* in *The
Transposed Heads,* which Goethe had previously used in his poem,
"Der Paria."

French interest in Indology is also reflected in their literature, especially during the Romantic period. In common with many of his contemporaries, Francois René de Chateaubriand (1768–1848), who deeply
influenced the Romantic movement in France, was an enthusiastic admirer of *Sakuntala.* He had lived in England as a refugee from
Napoleonic France between 1793 and 1800, when Sir William Jones'
translations of Sanskrit works were published.

Victor Hugo (1802–1885) imitated an Upanishad in his poem,
"Suprématie" (1870). He gathered his information from G. Pautheir's
Les Livres Sacrés de l'Orient. Alphonse de Lamartine (1790–1869),
who did for French poetry what Chateaubriand did for French prose,
wrote about Sanskrit epics, drama, and poetry in his *Cours familier de
Littérature* in 1861.

Jean-Jacques Ampère (1800–1864), a friend of Hugo, is reputed to
have said that during the Renaissance Greek works were given the
attention they deserved, but in his day Indian works would be studied
and another Renaissance would be witnessed. Louis Revel went a long
step farther when he remarked that if Greek culture had influenced
Western civilization, the ancient Greeks themselves were "the sons of
Hindu thought." Joseph Mery (1798–1865), who wrote satirical poems
on the French Restoration, could recite the works of Kalidasa and
Bhavabhuti from memory.

In 1825 Philaré le Charles (1798–1873), who did much to familiarize
his readers with the literature of foreign countries, wrote *The Bride of
Banaras* and *Indian Nights.* Paul Verlaine (1844–1896) wrote the
poem, "Savitri," which is a short piece but is indicative that the French
writers had an accurate knowledge of Indian literature. Verlaine became
keenly interested in Hindu mythology during his high school days. His
enthusiasm was such that he said, "Par Indra! que c'est beau, et comme
ca vous dégotte la Bible, l'Evangile et toute la dégueulade des Pères de
l'Eglise." (By Indra! how beautiful this is and how much better than
the Bible, the Gospel and all the words of the Fathers of the Church.)

Louis Jacolliot (1837–1890), who worked in French India as a
government official and was at one time President of the Court in
Chandranagar, translated numerous vedic hymns, the *Manusmriti,* and
the Tamil work, *Kural.* His masterpiece, *La Bible dans l'Inde,* stirred

a storm of controversy. He praised the Vedas in his *Sons of God,* and said: "The Hindu revelation, which proclaims the slow and gradual formation of worlds, is of all revelations the only one whose ideas are in complete harmony with modern science." Anatole France (1844–1924) saw in the Buddha "the best adviser and sweetest comforter of suffering mankind."

English response to Indian culture in the eighteenth century was conditioned by the ostentatious "nabobs," who amassed great wealth through unscrupulousness and deceit. The nabobs "raised the price of Parliamentary seats and made themselves otherwise objectionable to the old-established aristocratic society into which they intruded with their outlandish ways."[14] The image of the epic greatness of India was thus tinctured by the money-making vulgarity of these Englishmen. Consequently, the first reaction of the English was against their own people who were spoiling the good name of Britain in the East. During this period a large number of books were published dealing satirically with the English administration in India: for example, Mackenzie's *The Lounger* (1787), Samuel Foote's *The Nabob* (1772), *Harley House* (1789), and a number of passages in Cowper's poems.

Later, English administration became firm and settled and lost some of its earlier unpopularity, and Indian philosophy and literature came to be known in England. Even before Sir Charles Wilkins translated the *Gita,* or Halhead published *Sanskrit Grammar* (1778), Alexander Dow had published an essay on Hinduism entitled *A Dissertation Concerning the Customs, Manners, Language, Religion and Philosophy of the Hindus* (1768). The first European scholar to produce a real dissertation on Sanskrit learning, he pointed out the vast quantities of Sanskrit literature in existence, plus the fact that the history of the Hindus was older than that of any other people.

Jones had come to India, unlike most of his contemporaries, not to amass a fortune or to seek adventure, but to study Sanskrit and Indian culture in order to transmit Indian learning to the West. Already a master of Greek, Latin, Persian, Arabic, and Hebrew, he had high regard for Western knowledge which had culminated in British achievements. Whilst British culture continued to advance, he believed, because of the free institutions of the West, the Eastern tradition of despotism caused cultural stagnation in Asia. Yet he had great esteem for Indian civilization. He was not a romantic admirer of India but, in fact, a conservative commentator. In assessing Indian heritage he employed his own criteria and Western standards. His initial conclusion was that Europe excelled in the realm of reason; India, in that of reflection. But, as he delved deeper into Indian literature, he modified his earlier opinion to admit the impressive Indian accomplishments in the natural sciences. In 1794, the last year of his life, he declared that ". . . without detracting from the 'never fading laurels of Newton,' the whole of Newton's theology, and part of his philosophy were to be found in the Vedas and other Indian works." His opinion of Indian philosophy was immeasurably high. "One correct version of any celebrated Hindu book would be of greater value than all the dissertations or essays that could be composed on the same subject."[15]

Jones' evaluation of Indian thought attracted the attention of con- temporary British scholars and writers of diverse interests, such as Gibbon, Byron, and George Borrow, who acknowledge their debt to Jones' *Works* and the *Life*. His *Hymn to Narayana*, in which he described the process of creation, inspired Shelley's "Hymn to Intellectual Beauty." Southey and Moore often cite from Jones' writings, and E. Koeppel has recently illustrated that Shelley and Tennyson borrowed from Jones in their *Queen Mab* and *Locksley Hall*.[16]

William Robertson, Principal of the College of Edinburgh and a well-known historian, published his book, *An Historical Disquisition Concerning Ancient India* (1791), describing the knowledge ancient Greeks and Romans had of India, her progress, and trade activities prior to the discovery of the direct sea route between India and Europe. Robertson based his assessment of Indian works on the existing litera- ture, supplemented by his frequent conversations with high British officials in India, whose names he, for reasons of confidence, did not specify. He found both merits and defects in Indian thought and litera- ture.

By the beginning of the nineteenth century, whilst Britain had gained India and Canada, she had lost America. Her industrial revolution was well under way and Britain was emerging as a new type of nation-state combining an industrial capitalist society with an imperialist democratic government. The newly gained prosperity and security from foreign aggression, and the pride of possessing a vast colonial empire, produced a sense of power—a national feeling of implicit faith in her own histori- cal processes and political institutions—which was later to manifest it- self, not infrequently, in racial arrogance. These changes inevitably affected Britain's material and intellectual life. It was during this forma- tive period that words of capital importance in the English language and way of life at present, and which illustrate the changing patterns in culture and ways of thinking, such as industry, democracy, class, art, and culture, came to be used with new meanings.

Between the appearance of William Blake's *Song of Innocence* (1789), in which he first revealed his mystical inclination, and the death of Sir Walter Scott in 1832, the English literary tradition changed its course; the Romantic period, in essence, aimed at liberating human personality from the fetters of social conventions. Whilst English Romanticism largely provided its own momentum, it was deeply influenced by Germany in the beginning of the nineteenth century, and India played a significant part, either directly or through the medium of Germany or Neoplatonism.

William Blake's (1757–1827) belief that human life is a manifestation of eternal being has an upanishadic ring. His idea, quite different from the prevalent one in England, that soul was the true reality and its corporal form a passing shadow, an encumbrance, and his belief that the human was divine, are reminiscent of Indian monism. He declared Jesus Christ "was the only God—and so am I and so are you." He even regarded the beasts as "beings, the Living ones."

Blake's deep concern and preoccupation with fundamental questions of life, his emphasis on complete harmony between art, moral problems, and beliefs, his conviction that the human and the divine are One, and his painstaking study of Neoplatonism, Gnosticism, and the *Bhagavad Gita,* are clearly manifested in his writing. His Four Zoas appear to have a source in the Four Guardians (Lokapalas) of the four quarters of the Hindu mythology. According to Damon, Blake's zoas were derived from the three *Goons, sativa, rajas* and *tamas* described in the *Bhagavad Gita.* Blake's profound emphasis on mysticism, especially in *Songs of Experience* (1794) and his principal prose work, *The Marriage of Heaven and Hell* (1790), was radically out of character with the literary tradition in England at the time, and he was long regarded as an eccentric. In *The Marriage of Heaven and Hell* he vigorously and satirically denied the reality of matter and eternal punishment. In *Songs of Experience,* too, he protested against restrictive codes and exalted the spirit of love. His main poems were written between 1788 and 1820, the period of European discovery of Indian literature, thus Indian inspiration of Blake is plausible. Whilst some attempts to explain Blake's thought as an independent growth away from Indian ideas could have been conditioned by prejudice against alien influences, others are the result of the critics' inadequate knowledge of philosophical thought in general, and of Indian philosophy in particular. Consequently, even some competent recent studies, such as Désirée Hirst's *Hidden Riches,* do not give proper consideration to the Indian inspiration of Blake or of English Romanticism.[17]

Thomas De Quincey (1785–1859), whose qualities as a writer are fascinating despite criticisms of his indulgences as a man, knew something of Indian ideas. In his famous autobiographical narrative, *Confessions of an English Opium Eater* (1822), he describes how in his opium dreams he was hounded by Brahma, Visnu, and Siva.

Thomas Carlyle (1795–1881) found a basis for his doctrine of superiority in the caste system. Carlyle, who was a radical early in life and in the course of years became more and more hostile to democracy and advocated British imperialism, divided humanity into supermen and helots. His way of combatting anarchy by finding heroes who commanded obedience is somewhat reminiscent of Indian brahmanical supremacy.[18]

William Wordsworth (1770–1850), who expressed the deepest aspirations of English Romanticism, endeavoured throughout his writing to communicate his new vision of nature, which was so alien to English tradition that it was not until 1830 that his poetry was given wide public recognition. In intimacy with nature and its beauties, he also found a corrective to his personal despondency. Apart from this, however, Wordsworth seriously attempted to work out a bridge between mental and material worlds. It is impossible for a person familiar with Indian thought not to see the reflections of Vedanta in Wordsworth when he reads:

> And I have felt
> A presence that disturbs me with the joy
> Of elevated thoughts; a sense sublime,
> Of something far more deeply interfused,
> Whose dwelling is the light of setting suns,
> And the round ocean and the living air,
> And the blue sky and in the mind of man:
> A motion and a spirit, that impels
> All thinking things, all objects of all thought,
> And rolls through all things.
>
> ("Tintern Abbey," 1798)

Although Hindu thought is recognizable in Wordsworth's poetry, it is often characterized as "unconscious" or coincidental for he is considered to have been deeply impressed in his romantic ideas by his enthusiasm for France and the French Revolution. This view, however, does not sufficiently account for the fact that, after his return from France at the age of twenty-eight, Wordsworth—together with Coleridge—gave up his dreams of political regeneration for the vision of bringing the greatest possible degree of happiness to the world through proper cultivation of sensibility and imagination in *Lyrical Ballads* (1798).

By the time *Lyrical Ballads* appeared, the works of Sir William Jones had spread some knowledge of Indian thought in England.

Wordsworth's friend, collaborator, and "his spirit's brother," Samuel Taylor Coleridge (1772–1834), was also guided by the same vision. Indeed, he went a step farther in dabbling with the supernatural, as is reflected in "The Rime of the Ancient Mariner" (1798). Although Coleridge did not use Indian material, he was greatly attracted by the words and pictures of old tales, some of which must have come from India. His Eastern inspiration is to some extent attested to by the elusive yet arresting images in "Kubla Khan" (1797). This influence is also displayed in his Circassian love song, "Lewti."

Coleridge emphasized the Neoplatonic tradition and introduced into England the new idealism of Germany, which was influenced by Indian thought. More than any other English Romantic, he was responsible for bringing about the literary revolution which regarded imagination as the most important creative faculty. His cardinal doctrine, reminiscent of the Vedanta, was the wholeness of, and continuity in, self-consciousness as the basis of mental experience which was all absorbed into a single dynamic force, the divine spark in each person, the "I" of every rational being, the free will which was the eventual source of religious faith as well as of genuine perception. Coleridge was well aware of Indian literature, as is illustrated by his letter to John Thirlwell in which he said he often wished to sleep or die, or "like the Indian *Vishnu,* to float about along an infinite ocean cradled in the flower of the Lotus and wake once in a million years for a few minutes."[19]

John Keats (1795–1821), although he knew little about India, was somewhat drawn to her as the passage about the Indian maid in *Endymion* (1818) reveals. Keats was fascinated by the romantic aspect of Greek mythology but *Endymion* was severely criticized at the time for its un-Greek quality. Keats wrote all the poems which brought him such fame within twelve months of *Endymion's* publication.

Percy Bysshe Shelley (1792–1822), who wrote *The Revolt of Islam* and was attracted by an idealized version of the Vale of Kashmir, propounds most magnificently the vedantic doctrine of maya in his elegy dedicated to Keats, *Adonais* (1821), perhaps his finest single poem.

> The one remains, the many change and pass,
> Heaven's light for ever shines, Earth's shadows fly,
> Life, like a dome of many-coloured glass,
> Stains the white radiance of Eternity,
> Until Death tramples it to fragments.

Simultaneously a song of lamentation and a song of triumph, the poem makes no distinction between mortality and immortality. Shelley's passionate conviction that Adonais is not dead, but has "awakened from the dream of Life" and is "made one with Nature," is highly significant.[20] Hindu thought maintains that the end of the journey is to become one with the absolute. Shelley's suggestion that birth interrupts a state of bliss which death restores

> That Light whose smile kindles the Universe,
> That Beauty in which all things work and move,
> That Benediction which the eclipsing curse of
>   birth can quench not. . . . (*Adonais*)

is very close to the Indian concept. Engaged in the pursuit of an un-attainable ideal of beauty, Shelley was inspired by his love for the universe, which included not only the human race or even all living beings, but all elements of nature. His identification with nature—he becomes one with the lark in "To a Skylark," with the cloud in "The Cloud," and with the wind in "Ode to the West Wind"—and penetrating perception of its hidden meaning approximate Indian thought.

In 1810, Robert Southey (1774–1843) published his long narrative poem, *The Curse of Kehama,* drawing upon romantic material from India. Although Southey had studied Indian society and literature and claimed his poem as an authentic picture of India, his knowledge was imperfect, and he graphically endeavoured to show that Hinduism was a false and monstrous religion. Based on a theme from Hindu mythology, this poem conveyed little of India, but added distortion and confusion to the British view of Indian life. Ultimately, Southey himself found the poem unsatisfactory, as did his contemporaries, such as Sir Walter Scott. Southey, neither as famous nor as brilliant as his friends Words-worth and Coleridge, was united with them in the ardour of youthful ideas, and during the years of maturity, in reaction against those same ideas. The foreign influence in his poetry is so prominent that he is remembered primarily for his outlandish settings.

Thomas Moore (1779–1852) was also attracted by Indian material. He showed an insight into Indian society and customs in his poem *Lalla Rookh* (1817), which brought the then huge sum of three thousand guineas for the author. The first edition sold out immediately and during the course of the century it went into innumerable editions. In view of the fact that novels were far too expensive to buy in relation to the average income of the time, the rapid reprints of *Lalla Rookh* reveal more than ordinary attraction for Indian situations. *Lalla Rookh* consisted of four narrative poems woven into the romantic tale of a Mughal princess' love for a Kashmiri poet. Mainly concerned with delighting his readers, Moore presented India as a land of dazzling beauty, full of magnificent palaces, splendid temples, and perfumed gardens. His descriptions of the country, however, merely underlined the prevalent conventionally distorted picture of political India. He relied on rather undependable sources, and occasionally let his imagination get the better of him, as a result of which certain absurd, even nonsensical, descriptions crept into his work.

Many writers used India as a locale for European adventure. For instance, India figured prominently in *The Surgeon's Daughter* by Sir Walter Scott (1771–1832). However, he knew nothing of India, and hinted as much in the introduction to the novel. The story begins in Scotland and ends in the territory of Haider Ali and Tipu Sultan, the famous rulers of eighteenth-century Mysore, which had recently been conquered by the British after a series of prolonged and exacting campaigns. Scott's characters and situations were, of course, fictitious; his knowledge of Indian history inaccurate; and he had a Scotsman's love for fairy tales, fables, and folklore.

Most fiction writers of this period had no personal knowledge of India, and used Indian situations primarily to advance the popularity of their works. But the case of Lord Thomas Babington Macaulay is somewhat different and, therefore, puzzling. He was a well-known man of letters when he came to India in 1834 where he lived for four years. However, he read little of Indian literature and made no serious evaluation of India and her heritage, even though scores of European scholars had revealed the richness of Indian learning, which was available in any number of European languages. If he had done so, the history of the Anglo-Indian relationship might have been different. He wrote one small volume of essays on India, but it was written with such fervour and effect that it was the standard authority on India for many years in England. The revolt of 1857 gave these essays additional popularity as they were easy on the English ear. Despite the abundance of evidence contradicting Macaulay, later English writers continued to echo his ideas again and again, thereby keeping a falsehood alive. Macaulay's India was a distant land across boundless seas and deserts where dusky natives lived under strange stars, worshipped strange gods, and wrote strange characters from right to left.

It is not surprising that India figured in English Romanticism. What does astonish historians is that the Romantic writers found India of

An imaginary scene of the Muslim saint Kwaja Muin al-din Chishti presiding over dancing darvishes during the celebration of a festival at Ajmer. In the foreground sit followers of the Hindu saint Ramananda. Mughal, c. 1660–70 A.D.

Courtesy of the Victoria and Albert Museum, London.

A yogi with a Vina talking to a darvish.
Illustration to the musical mode,
Kedara Ragini. Bundi, c. 1880.
*Courtesy of the Victoria and
Albert Museum, London.*

Humayun's Mausoleum. Delhi.
Courtesy of the Archaeological Survey of India, New Delhi.

A view of the Nalanda Mahavihara.
Courtesy of the Archaeological Survey of India, New Delhi.

ichijo-ten (Mahāsrī). In clay and coloured.
Iokke-dō Todai-ji, Nara. 8th century A.D.
ourtesy of the Hokke-dō Todai-ji Temple,
ara.

Daruma (Bodhidharma) by Bokkei
(Tōrin Anei). Ink on paper.
Shinju-an Daitokuji, Kyoto. 1465.
*Courtesy of the Shinju-an
Daitokuji Temple, Kyoto.*

Panel No. 4, the Siva temple. Bas-relief. Prambanan, Indonesia.
Courtesy of the Archaeological Survey of India, New Delhi.

Head of the Buddha in Angkor Vat style. Khmer art.
Courtesy of the Musée Guimet, Paris.

Head of the Buddha in slate blue limestone. Thailand, 7th–8th century
A.D.
Courtesy of The Trustees of the British Museum, London.

Pediment in Bantei Srei style. Khmer art.
Courtesy of the Musée Guimet, Paris.

Buddha in Bronze. Burma, 16th century A.D. or earlier. Inscribed "Nyaungumin Kuang-mu. *Courtesy of The Trustees of the British Museum, London.*

Gilt-bronze figure of Tara. Ceylon, c. 10th century A.D. *Courtesy of The Trustees of the British Museum, London.*

only passing and minor interest. Perhaps the complexities of a political relationship hampered a better understanding of Indian culture. Britons came to India to govern, acquire wealth, live without interrupting their own habits and customs, and return home in comfort and economic security. Belief in their political ascendancy and material prosperity as evidence of cultural superiority possibly rendered them unreceptive to any but the negative aspects of Indian society. There were, no doubt, some British administrators who made notable contributions to Indology, but most of the traders, as well as the adventurers serving at Indian courts, were hardly men of culture; they were merely interested in "shaking the pagoda tree." Whilst British power was reaffirmed with a certain degree of finality after the revolt of 1857, the uprising left scars on both sides. The British, proud and arrogant with success, still were mindful of how close they had come to total loss and disaster, which made them cautious, suspicious, even afraid. The Indians, on the other hand, smarting under defeat, turned to more organized preparations for their national reconstruction. Each side remembered the savagery and brutalities of the other, without recalling their own part in it. It was in this atmosphere of mutual distrust and fear, later worsened by political crises and conflicts, that cultural intercourse between India and Britain took place. For instance, John Ruskin (1819–1900), whose opinion was coloured by the events of 1857, dismissed Indians and their philosophy as "childish, or restricted in intellect and similarly childish or restricted in their philosophies or faiths."[21]

Ruskin wrote and spoke with equal authority and arrogance on subjects he knew well and those he knew nothing about. However, he was a great teacher—he was Slade Professor of Art at Oxford—and a master of prose. But he was a complex person, at once charming and sinister, righteous and satanic. He inherited a strain of madness and suffered intermittently from insanity. Tennyson expressed sentiments similar to Ruskin's in his *Defence of Lucknow*. But these are extreme examples of English response to India in which reason was subordinated to prejudice.

During the second half of the nineteenth century, Buddhism became better known in Britain, as in Europe. Indeed, since the end of the nineteenth century, many European thinkers and writers have proposed the adoption of Buddhism by the West. Whatever their success, there is no doubt that in recent times Buddhism, because of its rational and realistic character, has gained popularity in the West. Of the three Eastern civilizations, Indian, Chinese, and Islamic, the Indians have influenced the modern West most, especially through Buddhism. In fact, the West— especially Christians—regarded Buddhism as so powerful that it was dangerous.

Sir Edwin Arnold's famous poem, *The Light of Asia* published in 1879, which is based on *Lalitavistara* singing the praise of the Buddha, has become extremely popular. In America it has gone through one hundred editions, and in England between fifty to one hundred. It has been translated into several European languages. Later, scholars like T. W. Rhys Davids (1843–1922), who greatly aided the interpretation of early Buddhism by editing Pali sources, Mrs. Caroline Rhys Davids, Paul Carus, Edward Conze, Christmas Humphreys, and others contributed to the popularity of Buddhism in the West.

In 1881 T. W. Rhys Davids founded the Pali Text Society, which attracted the attention of a number of European scholars to a new and important branch of Indian thought and literature. In addition to two dozen volumes of translations, the Society published one hundred and seventeen volumes of Pali texts and a Pali-English dictionary. The Buddhist Society in London and elsewhere has also played an important role in exposing the West to Buddhist teaching. Looking at the notices of meetings and lectures in any recent issue of the London *New Statesman*, for example, one must get the impression that during the past decade or so interest in Indian thought, especially Buddhism, has been steadily growing in Europe.

Actually, early in the nineteenth century, attempts were made to prove the Buddhistic origins of primitive Christianity. N. A. Notovick's book, *Inconnue Vie de Jesus Christ (Unknown Life of Jesus Christ)*, published in 1834, sought to prove that Jesus had been initiated into his career by a sixteen-year stay with Brahmans and Buddhist monks. Many scholars from different countries later combined in trying to discover cases of Christian dependence on Buddhism, such as Rudolf Seydel (1882), A. S. Edmunds (1909), and Richard Garbe (1914). In 1882 Notovick's book came under heavy criticism. In the English translation of the work he endeavoured to answer the criticism, maintaining that the doctrine contained in the Tibetan verses was the same as that of the Gospels, differing only in outward appearance.[22]

India even partly conditioned English character, for the conquest of India made England a powerful political and military empire. A sense of racial superiority and national exclusiveness, and of a predetermined mission, inverted nationalism which often manifests itself in understatements and in deceptively disguised self-praise for which the British are well known, strict individualism neatly integrated in collective discipline, and ability for endurance under sustained pressure, are natural consequences of the British association with India.

From the early days of the East India Company, Indian words have been continuously adopted into English. Typical words are durbar, bazaar, pukka, khaki, bungalow, divan, pundit, pajamas, baksheesh, begum, chop, chit, cot, fakir, purdah, raj, nabob, darshan, verandah, vakil, zenana, palanquin, mulligatawney, chutney, swaraj, and shikar. "The Oxford English Dictionary," observes Subba Rao "which rejects over half the words noticed by *Hobson-Jobson* and does not contain words which have become familiar only in very recent times, accords recognition to about a thousand words, apart from numerous compounds and derivatives."[23] It is, however, true that this number, large as it is, is small considering the length and intensity of Indo-British contact, and also in comparison to the English words adopted by Indian languages. The assimilation of language over this period was conditioned by the nature and need of the relationship. For instance, in the early phase when contact was predominantly commercial, the words borrowed were mainly from that vocabulary. Later, when Indian thought, literature, and philosophy began to attract the attention of the English scholars, English men of letters began to use terminology from these fields in their writing. Milton, Dryden, Orme, Burke, Scott, Thackeray, and T. S. Eliot are some of the eminent writers who made effective use of Indian words.

In a unique although incidental way, India helped to develop not only British economy and social life, but also political thought. The increasing influx of Indian wealth into England created a new class, whose widening horizon for the deployment and experimentation of political ideas required a setting of India's size. In the East India Company Adam Smith saw an embodiment of the hated "mercantile system." Many English political movements tested their strength and fought their early contests upon Indian questions. A few Englishmen had succeeded in carving out an empire and enforcing an organized, although intensely authoritarian, government. India provided the much needed efficiency in administration and the purpose in government for the dominant English Liberalism of the day, in addition to an operation base for free trade and the missionary activities of Evangelicalism. It was this Indian experience which influenced Utilitarian thought, and caused John Stuart Mill to criticize Liberty, Equality, and Fraternity. He called his book "little more than the turning of an Indian lantern on European problems." One obvious example of Indian influence is the development of British imperialism, another lies in the reform of the civil service. Maine was deeply influenced by India in his study of early societies. He wrote after the publication of *Popular Government*: "If there was an ideal Toryism I should probably be a Tory; but I should wish to win now. The truth is, India and the India Office make one judge public men by standards which have little to do with public opinion."[24]

Echoes of Indian thought could be heard even in lands only remotely concerned with India. For instance, in the works of Mihai Eminescu (1850–1889), the greatest poet of Rumania, Sanskrit and Buddhist influences are found. Eminescu learned of Indian philosophy through Schopenhauer. He also had some knowledge of the Sanskrit language, although it is doubtful that he could read original Sanskrit texts. However, he translated Franz Bopp's *Glossarium Sanskriticum* and a part of his Dictionary. Parts of his poetry appear to be Rumanian versions of well-known Sanskrit texts. For example, in *Letter number one,* his vision of the origin of the world, when the existent and the non-existent were not, is reminiscent of the "Hymn of Creation" from the *Rig Veda.* The idea of nirvana is frequently found in his poems. The Hindu approach to reality and beauty is reflected in many of his verses. Indian literary legends and themes are also found in poems such as "God and Man" and "Looking for Sheherezade." Not only the title of his poem, "Tattwamasi," indicates his familiarity with upanishadic thought, but the content deals with the identity of Atman and Brahman. Hindu monism is reflected in his

> So it is that bird and man,
>   Sun and moon
> Are born and die in Brahma
>   the Sacred—
> Where all things become one.[25]

Eminescu's poetry also contains many erotic themes, such as *Kamadeva,* after the Hindu god of love, the spark of creation. That Eminescu chose an Indian symbol to express one of his intimate sentiments is held as "yet another proof of the deep and wide contact he had with the ancient literature of India."[26]

Russian intellectuals, too, reacting against the increasing mechanization of life, turned towards the East for inspiration. Although this movement was not as powerful as the Romantic movement in Western Europe, especially in Germany, Russia, aided by her rapidly expanding territorial frontiers in Asia, acquired a new Asian awareness in her national disposition. In fact, even before the big Russian advance eastwards, Chadaiev said in 1840 that "We are the darling children of the East.

. . . Everywhere we are in contact with the East, it is from there that we have drawn our belief, our laws, our virtue. . . ."[27] He goes on to claim that as the East is declining, Russia is the natural successor to Eastern wisdom. Maxim Gorki (1868–1936) in a letter to Romain Rolland said that Russia was more Oriental than China. Dostoievsky declared that it would be beneficial for Russia to turn her soul towards the East. In fact, there has always been a sort of gulf between Western Europe and Russia; the former frequently referring to the latter as the East.

Leo Tolstoy (1828–1910) responded to the East with great sensitivity. At Kazan he studied Oriental languages and literature, and came into close contact with Asian people during his frequent visits to Caucasus. He acquired an early reverent interest in Indian culture which he always retained. In 1870 he published a collection of folktales which included some Indian stories. His *Confession,* in which he describes his spiritual struggles, refers more than once to the Buddha with admiration, relates some of the episodes of the Buddha's Renunciation, and seeks to demonstrate the futility of human life on earth in terms of an ancient Indian parable. Ancient Indian literature, Max Müller's series, *Sacred Books of the East,* and later, the writings of Vivekananda made a deep impression on him. He opposed the imposition of what he considered a degenerating Western structure on India, but disagreed with Hinduism on a number of points including Hindu cosmology. Indeed, he looked upon Hinduism through the eyes of a social reformer, yet Indian thought helped him to acquire new standards by which he could revaluate Christianity. Tolstoy corresponded with a number of his Indian friends, including Mahatma Gandhi and C. R. Das. In *Letter to a Hindu,* addressed to Gandhi in 1909, Tolstoy quoted from the Upanishads, the *Bhagavad Gita,* the Tamil *Kural,* and modern Hindu religious writings, including Vivekananda. He urged Indians to adopt what he called "the Law of Love," and not give up their ancient religious culture for the materialism of the West. Tolstoy was amongst the first European intellectuals who reflected on the problems facing India. It is well known that his ideas on resistance to aggression influenced Mahatma Gandhi.

Indian thought made a better impression not only in nineteenth-century Germany than in England but even in distant America. An illustration of this influence is the American transcendentalist movement inspired by Ralph Waldo Emerson (1803–1882). Emerson's central theme is that all that exists is the manifestion of a simple universal spirit. The development of Emerson's thought is revealed in his *Journals* which cover twenty years. India is first mentioned in 1842. It seems that in the beginning Buddhism aroused conflicting feelings in him.

Whilst he admitted the greatness of Buddhist teaching, he was uncertain of its practicability. He was drawn by the concept of the transmigration of soul: "Then I discovered the Secret of the World, that all things subsist, and do not die, but only retire a little from sight and afterwards return again."[28]

The discovery of Hinduism and Buddhism impressed on Emerson that all religions are fundamentally the same. Eighty years later, Romain Rolland came to a similar conclusion which he described as the "predisposition to Vedantism." Repelled by the increasing materialism of the West, Emerson turned to India for solace: "The Indian teaching, through its cloud of legends, has yet a simple and grand religion, like a queenly countenance seen through a rich veil. It teaches to speak truth, love others as yourself, and to despise trifles."[29] As he grew older he became increasingly devoted to Hinduism and Buddhism. Nowhere does Emerson's transcendentalism find more complete expression than in his remarkable poem, "Brahma," which Sencourt suggests is a translation from Kalidasa through a Latin version known to Dr. Morrison of the Indian Institute.[30] The poem may not have been a direct translation from Kalidasa, but it was derived from him. In his essay on Plato, Emerson explicitly acknowledges his debt to India: "In all nations there are minds which incline to dwell in the conception of the fundamental Unity. The raptures of prayer and ecstasy of devotion lost all being in one Being. This tendency finds its highest expression in the religious writings of the East, and chiefly in the Indian Scriptures, in the *Vedas*, the *Bhagavat Geeta*, and the *Vishnu Purana*. Those writings contain little else than this idea, and they rise to pure and sublime strains in celebrating it."

Another American who turned his attention towards India was Henry David Thoreau (1817–1862), a younger contemporary and friend of Emerson. He is chiefly remembered for *Walden*, which much inspired the pioneers of the British labour movement, and for his essay, "On Civil Disobedience," in which he protested the government's interference with individual liberty. In some respect, Mahatma Gandhi's philosophy of life and programme of action were similar to Thoreau's. Both were keen naturalists; both believed in the dignity of human labour and attempted to run self-sufficient farms; both were vegetarians, teetotallers, and non-smokers; both derived their inspiration from the *Bhagavad Gita*; and both were rebels against human injustice.

There is some controversy about Mahatma Gandhi's debt to Thoreau. Thoreau partisans suggest that his "On Civil Disobedience," published in 1849, was Gandhi's source book in his political campaign for civil resistance, because the Mahatma used the phrase "civil disobedience" to describe his resistance to the tyranny of the State. Beyond this use of identical phrases, there is little to substantiate this assertion. In his autobiography, *My Experiments with Truth,* Gandhi lists and analyzes the books that most influenced him during the formative period of his public life when he was experimenting with the political weapon which he called *satyagraha.* In his generous acknowledgement of debts, he does not refer to the work of Thoreau. Some weight has been lent to this misconception by an open letter that Gandhi wrote to the people of America, on the eve of the launching of his Quit India movement in 1942, in which he showed his great esteem for Thoreau, whom he called, in his characteristic humility, his "teacher." This letter, however, also clearly states that Gandhi had found in Thoreau a teacher who, through his essay on civil disobedience, furnished him with scientific *confirmation* of what he was doing, and Gandhi was punctilious in his use of language.[31]

Thoreau was deeply impressed by Hindu thought and his *Journal* contains many comments on his extensive reading of Hindu texts. He wrote in 1850 that the inspiration of the Vedas had fallen on him like the light of a higher and purer luminary, and risen on him like the full moon after the stars had come out. *Walden* contains explicit references to Indian scriptures, such as "How much more admirable the *Bhagvat-Geeta* than all the ruins of the East." He even followed a traditional Hindu way of life. "It was fit that I should live on rice mainly, who loved so well the philosophy of India." Thoreau invokes the language of silence, which is so common in India, in his silent communion with the old fisherman at the pond. Even more significant, perhaps, are the many references to the river and the definite equation of Walden Pond with the sacred Ganges. "To dismiss all of these references as simply part of Thoreau's temperamental affinity for India is to underestimate the extraordinary influence of the Orient on his own thinking and to misunderstand the purpose of *Walden*."[32]

Walt Whitman (1819–1892), who championed American intellectual independence, was amongst those who came under the influence of the Transcendentalists. There are no explicit quotations from Indian literature in Whitman's writings, but he knew of Indian texts. His poems show a strong sense of the brotherhood of man, and it was possibly from the Transcendentalists that he learned an all-inclusive mystical self-identification with all men and all things. In *Song of Myself* he says that "all religions are true"; a doctrine which has always found favour with Hindu thought. In the nineteenth century, this doctrine was powerfully reaffirmed by Swami Ramakrishna. In some of his later poems Whitman shows a definite interest in Hindu mysticism. Most significant of these is *Passage to India* in which he voices the characteristic Hindu doctrine that his own soul is one with the soul of the universe.

The Christian Science movement in America was possibly influenced by India. The founder of this movement, Mary Baker Eddy, in common with the Vedantins, believed that matter and suffering were unreal, and that a full realization of this fact was essential for relief from ills and pains. In *Science and Health* she asserts: "Christian Science explains all cause and effect as mental, not physical. It lifts the veil of mystery from Soul and body. It shows the scientific relation of man to God, disentangles the interlaced ambiguities of being, and sets free the imprisoned thought. In divine Science, the universe, including man, is spiritual, harmonious, and eternal. Science shows that what is termed *matter* is but the subjective state of what is termed by the author *mortal mind.*" The Christian Science doctrine has naturally been given a Christian framework, but the echoes of Vedanta in its literature are often striking.

Late in the nineteenth century, Vivekananda made two trips to the United States, and was received with enthusiastic popular acclaim. There were, however, some critics who were ill-informed of his motives and of the concepts he represented, and who dreaded the influx of alien ideas. Both the devotion and dispute which his lectures evoked stimulated further American interest in Indian religion and thought. As a result, Vedanta Centres and Ramakrishna Missions were established in various parts of the country, and they flourish today as active nuclei of Indian thought. Even before Vivekananda fired the imagination of the American people, Sanskrit philosophy had made an impact on American scholarship by the teaching of Sanskrit at leading American universities.

Later, Tagore visited the United States three times and travelled throughout the country lecturing on Indian art and philosophy and giving readings from his poetry and plays. His writings had already, and have always, received widespread appreciation.

Because of the advance in the mass communication media, the Indian national movement attracted the attention of European peoples who were themselves going through a period of democratic advance, fighting against traditional and aristocratic oppression. Some European intellectuals took a purely academic interest in India during this period, but others were inclined towards a synthesis between East and West. Amongst the latter, Romain Rolland, the French pacifist and author, is outstanding. He was deeply concerned with and championed the cause of Indian thought and culture. He saw a close affinity between the Aryans of the East and those of the West. He met many Indian intellectuals, especially from the Ramakrishna Mission in Europe. He wrote the *Life of Ramakrishna* in which he said, "I am bringing to Europe, as yet unaware of it, the fruit of a new autumn, a new message of the soul, the symphony of India, bearing the name of Ramakrishna. The man whose image I evoke was the consummation of a thousand years of the spiritual life of three hundred million people."[33] He also wrote the world-famous biography of Mahatma Gandhi, which inspired many European thinkers. Having read this biography, Mira ben (Madeleine Slade), the daughter of an English admiral, renounced a life of luxury to live in the ashram of Gandhi. In Gandhi, Rolland saw the embodiment of all that was simple, modest, and pure. Surprisingly, Rolland had never visited India. In close contact on the one hand with Tagore and Gandhi, and on the other with European intellectuals, Romain Rolland was a unique mediator between India and the West. Although a devout Christian himself, he often felt that his Christianity had more in common with the religions of India than with the church in which he was brought up.

Of modern Indian thinkers, M. K. Gandhi (1869–1948) had the most influence on the outside world. Gandhi has often been described as the greatest man since Jesus; he certainly was India's greatest since the Buddha. He represented Indian idealism at its best. All his life he worked on almost all fronts of the Indian revolution, but he combatted evil with good and in the true spirit of love. Satya (truth) was his God; ahimsa (non-violence), his creed. He believed violence to be the antithesis of the spirit of truth. Inflicting physical injury or uttering an unkind word, even thinking ill of others, were serious violations of ahimsa. Indeed, to be truly non-violent meant that one must love his opponent and pray for him even when attacked. No wonder many Christians see in Gandhian doctrines a reflection of Christian thought.

Indeed, Gandhi was a great admirer of Christianity, and often admitted the influence of the Sermon on the Mount which he believed contained Jesus' message of non-violence. Frequently he would read passages from the Bible in his daily prayer meetings. "When I survey the wondrous Cross" and "Lead kindly light amid the encircling gloom" were his favourite hymns. Romain Rolland described Gandhi as the

"St. Paul of our own days." Gandhi was so devoted to Jesus that in the earlier phase of his career many of his Christian friends thought his conversion was imminent. But he was a Hindu to the core. Defining his attitude to a prominent Indian Christian, Kali Charan Banerjee, he said: "Today my position is that, though I admire much in Christianity, I am unable to identify myself with orthodox Christianity. I must tell you in all humility that Hinduism, as I know it, entirely satisfies my soul, fills my whole being, and I find a solace in the *Bhagavad Gita* and *Upanishads* that I miss even in the Sermon on the Mount."[34]

Kropotkin's essays awakened Gandhi's ideas of pacific anarchism. His completely non-violent society was to be stateless, for it was not possible to impose non-violence on a person or society. Tolstoy's *The Kingdom of God is Within You* and Ruskin's *Unto This Last* contributed to Ghandhi's philosophy.

Gandhi, although he belonged to humanity and wielded unparalleled influence over millions of people all over the world, was, in all respects, essentially an Indian. As a London *Times* editorial said on the day after his death: "No country but India and no religion but Hinduism could have given birth to a Gandhi."

Whilst the full reprecussions of Ghandi's influence are still to be seen, there is no doubt they will be unending and inexhaustible. His philosophy has already assumed a self-perpetuating quality. His doctrines of non-violence and satyagraha have not only given Indians a new means of fighting for their rights but have become a source of inspiration to all seekers of justice everywhere. Indeed, non-Indian movements, notably those led by Martin Luther King, Jr. in the American South and Kenneth Kaunda in Northern Rhodesia, might even be regarded as more truly Gandhian in essence than similar movements within India today.

Since the days of the Montgomery bus boycott of 1955–1956, followed by the upsurge of the sit-ins and freedom rides of 1960–1961, the movement for civil rights in the United States has been strongly based on the Gandhian concept of non-violence. The movement, as expected, has assumed a distinctively local character and personality, and has gained notable successes in advancing the Negro revolution in America. Martin Luther King often acknowledged his debt to Gandhian thought and literature.

In Nazi Germany, the real resistance that developed within the country itself was inspired by Gandhian theories of passiveness and non-violent revolution. Its leader, Dietrich Bonhoeffer, was so impressed by the possibility of applying these ideas to Christianity, and employing Gandhian resistance against Hitler's tyranny that he arranged to make a "pilgrimage to India" to visit Gandhi, but political events prevented him from undertaking the journey.

Today, wherever there is a popular people's movement against injustice, it proceeds along lines inspired by Gandhian satyagraha. Indeed, what Marx is to socialism Gandhi is to modern active pacifism. His doctrine of class co-operation and trusteeship inspires hope in those who loathe the prospect of achieving progress only through class conflict. Persuasion, not coercion, is the keynote of polity today. In fact, serious, and in some ways diverse, British writers, such as Sir Stephen King-Hall and Kingsley Martin, suggest that any resistance to nuclear war must be non-violent, organized on Gandhian lines. An Indian Gandhi scholar writes, "Countries distant from India, wherever the field is ready or rather where there are workers in the field, have been influenced by the Gandhian approach to the spiritual and practical fusion. Serious studies in Group Dynamics, group and individual action-therapy are being pursued in great institutions abroad; the Gandhian quantum which stimulates higher loyalties and cohesion rather than spreads negative crowd-infection has stimulated new sociological and applicational research."[35]

Romain Rolland spoke for many of Gandhi's Western admirers when he wrote: "Gandhi is not only for India a hero of national history whose legendary memory will be enshrined in the millennial epoch. He has not only been the spirit of active life which has breathed into the peoples of India the proud consciousness of their unity, of their power, and the will to their independence. He has renewed, for all the people of the West, the message of their Christ, forgotten or betrayed. He has inscribed his name among the sages and saints of humanity; and the radiance of his figure has penetrated into all the regions of the earth."[36] The American missionary, John Haynes Holmes, declared: "If I believe in rebirth, I should—I mention it with due respect—see in Mahatma Gandhi the Christ returned to our world."

Aurobindo Ghose (1872–1950), the modern Indian philosopher, transformed the Hindu spiritual heritage into a dynamic spiritual evolution. He is the only modern Indian thinker known both as a Yogi and as a philosopher. He sought to reconcile the theories of ancient Vedanta with those of modern scientific materialism and vitalism, thus attempting to harmonize spiritual and material demands. He was opposed to scientific materialism that sought to reduce man to the position of an insect.

He believed in the omnipresence of the One and the inevitable culmination of man's evolution into an integral and dynamic union with Him in life. Reality, although manifold in self-expression, is one and indivisible. There is nothing else but Him, and to infuse His unity, harmony, and perfection into worldly life and nature is the mission of every individual human soul. This was the core of Aurobindo's philosophy and the central aim of his Yoga. His Spiritual Realism thus departs from the traditional Indian doctrine of maya. Aurobindo was educated in Europe, and his philosophy was greatly influenced by the theory of evolution and the Western positive attitude to the material world, but he discovered both of these elements in the Saiva and the Sakta forms of the Advaita.[37] Romain Rolland regarded Aurobindo as the highest synthesis of the genius of Europe and the genius of Asia. He was an Indian rishi who had gained a clear insight into the modern scientific mind. Instead of finding a conflict between East and West, he saw the old heritage of the East and the new knowledge of the West as one organized whole. His philosophy, like that of Gandhi, was couched in a language drawn from India's past, but was addressed to problems posed in the modern West.

Whilst Aurobindo's philosophy was rooted in the vedantic consciousness, his Muslim contemporary, Sir Muhammed Iqbal (1876–1938), was deeply committed to Islam. Poet and philosopher, he wrote one of the most popular national songs of India, "Sare Jahan se Acchha Hindustan Hamara." He was well versed in European thought and culture but is better known as a poet than as a philosopher, although he inspired the creation of Pakistan. In Germany, where he completed his doctoral thesis on Persian metaphysics, he became acutely conscious of both the good and the evil of Western scientific materialism, and of the consequent agonizing inner conflicts amongst European intellectuals and nations. He admired the vitality and dynamism of European life but criticized its mechanistic and utilitarian aspects. In his poems and teaching he combined his Islamic beliefs with Western rationalism, and was heavily influenced by Nietzsche.

Although a mystic, he preached the glorification and divination of desire rather than its negation. Somewhat like the *Bhagavad Gita,* he urged man not so much to seek God as to seek his own true self. The essence of his philosophy was the quest for perfect man which could only be achieved through persistent and continuous personal effort. During the last years of his life, Iqbal was increasingly attracted by the progress of Soviet Russia.

Rabindranath Tagore (1861–1941) was a poet, philosopher, educator, and above all, a humanist. Fundamentally inspired by the Upanishads, he did not believe the new India belonged to one race or religion but to humanity. His visits to Western capitals were invariably attended by huge crowds, and he became an object of world-wide adoration. For a poet, especially of a subject-nation, this reception was unique. Despite this, the award of the Nobel Prize in 1913 to Tagore, against the claims of such famous Europeans as Thomas Hardy, Anatole France, Tolstoy, and Zola, drew protests from certain sections of the European and American press because Tagore was not "white." Perhaps in honouring Tagore, the West was endeavouring to show its appreciation of the Indian heritage which he so nobly symbolized.

Tagore wrote in both Bengali and English, and from 1913 onwards his poetry was translated into practically every European language. No other Indian has received greater honour in the West during his lifetime. Such appreciation cannot be altogether devoid of understanding. The West, involved in the conflicts of political and military alignments, on the brink of World War I was frustrated at the futility of material advancement. At this time Tagore brought to them a message which appealed "to their intelligence, their goodwill, their longing for emancipation from the chains of dead matter, speaking to white, black and yellow in the same language . . . with the simplicity of a child and a prophet."[38]

After the war, Europe's response to the culture of Asia took conflicting forms. Whilst some thinkers defended the West, others hailed the East. In this process of European rethinking, India and Tagore played an important role. Numerous Western readers eagerly read Tagore's works, hoping to find mystical solace from the frustrations of life. Many European intellectuals were so firmly convinced that only Eastern ideals could save them that innumerable pseudo-oriental societies were founded all over Europe. Many of these societies had inaccurate knowledge of the East and practiced popularized forms of pseudo-Buddhistic and yogic cults.

Amongst the many European intellectuals and artists Tagore met, William Butler Yeats (1865–1939) was one of his more intimate friends. He dedicated *The Gardener* to Yeats. Yeats' belief that poetry was the product of a mystical experience, a state of trance where worldly conflicts melt away and the subconscious is transformed into artistic creation, had Indian origins. Yeats had discovered India, in fact, long before his intimate contact with Tagore. He had published his essay *The Celtic Element* in 1897, followed three years later by an essay on Shelley in which he compared the ministering spirits of intellectual beauty with the Devas of the East. Impressed in his adolescence by Sinnett's *Esoteric Buddhism*, he was alienated from science; Theosophy, Buddhism, Odic Force, and poetry constituted his world for a long time. In his *Autobiography* he recalls that it was under the impact of psychical research and mystical philosophy that he broke away from his father's influence, and he spent much time in mystical gatherings during his school days. Describing his first meeting with a Hindu philosopher at Dublin, Yeats said: "It was my first meeting with a philosophy that confirmed my vague speculations and seemed at once logical and boundless. Consciousness, he taught, does not merely spread out its surface but has, in vision and in contemplation, another motion, and can change in height and in depth."[39] His appreciation of India, however, in common with many European intellectuals, was more romantic than academic. After his contact with Tagore and his discovery of the English version of the *Gitanjali*, he turned more towards the East for inspiration. When Sir William Rothenstein, the celebrated English art critic and painter who was chiefly responsible for introducing Tagore to English intellectuals, gave Yeats the manuscript of the *Gitanjali* to read before it was published, Yeats was so deeply moved by it that he carried it with him everywhere. He records in his preface to the first edition of *Gitanjali:* "The lyrics . . . display in their thought a world I have dreamed of all my life long. The work of a supreme culture, they yet appear as much the growth of the common soil as the grass and the rushes."[40] He continues: "A whole people, a whole civilization, immeasurably strange to us, seem to have been taken up into this imagination; and yet we are not moved because of its strangeness, but because we have met our own image, as though we had walked in Rossetti's willow wood, or heard, perhaps for the first time in literature, our voice as in a dream."[41] Yeats wrote some poems which had an Indian setting, such as "Jealousy." "Kanva on Himself" is based on a Hindu prayer: "I have lived many lives. . . . Everything that has been shall be again."

The quality Yeats valued most in Tagore's poetry was his union of sensuous images and deep spiritual appreciation of life. Yeats also aspired to what he called the "unity of being," to bring together the natural and the spiritual world in his poetry. In his conception, nature and God were not separated by thought, and the constricting sense of guilt was banished by gaiety and joyfulness in which the creative mind of the artist had been freed. According to Yeats, European writing, despite its familiar metaphor and general structure, was no longer acceptable because spirit and matter were irrevocably separated and as a result nature had become evil. Yeats could not forsake nature which was so full of art, beauty, and music. In Tagore he found a saint who sang of the joy in life without disturbing its deep sense of sanctity. Unlike Tagore, however, Yeats was keenly interested in the Yoga system and the Tantra. The authoritative texts of these two systems had reached Europe at about the same time and they made a further impact on Yeats.

Towards the end of his life Yeats moved away from Tagore a little, but he continued to draw inspiration from India, which contained for him the vision of the final harmony in human life. Like another Irish poet, George William Russell (popularly known as A. E.) who had also come under the influence of the Upanishads and Theosophy, Yeats discovered an identical spirit underlying both Gaelic and Indian civilizations.

In his "Meru" (1935)—Meru is the central mountain of the world in Indian mythology—Yeats contrasts the peaceful life of the mystic, despite the hardships of nature, with the transitory cycle of creation and destruction exemplified in the world of man. Yeats was influenced not only by Indian mysticism, but also by the secular aspects of Indian classical literature and art.

Traces of the influence of Indian secular thought are also noticed in the works of other writers, such as Edward Carpenter, Havelock Ellis, and D. H. Lawrence, who found support in the *Kama Sutra* for their revolt against the rigid sexual ethics of an earlier period. This text, widely read despite restrictions on it of various kinds, has had a far more subtle effect on Western people than is often realized.

The mysticism of T. S. Eliot, Aldous Huxley, and W. H. Auden clearly stems from Hindu roots. Aldous Huxley, an exacting critic, a brilliant novelist, and a satirist of his age, was deeply concerned with Indian religions and philosophy. He was, however, a highly sophisticated European with scientific training. He tested both aesthetic enjoyment and mystic experience by what he saw in conduct and behaviour, both in himself and in the world around him. He found many faults with the Indian attitude towards life. Yet he was convinced, after prolonged reflection, that society could not be changed unless the individual sensibility, cleansed of all passions, proceeded towards self-realization through selflessness. In *Beyond the Mexique Bay* (1934) and *Ends and Means* (1937) he suggests that the flux of time is an illusion caused by man's preoccupation with his personal affairs, and it is through contemplation that man can merge into the timelessness of reality. For the first time in *Ends and Means*, a pacifist manifesto,

Huxley almost reverentially mentions Gandhi, in whose achievement means and ends are inseparable. In *Ape and Essence* (1948) he regarded Gandhi's assassination as a cosmic tragedy. *The Perennial Philosophy* (1946) is yet another illustration of his knowledge of Indian thought, especially the Vedanta.

T. S. Eliot shows considerable knowledge of and sympathy with Hinduism and Buddhism in his writings. *The Waste Land*, for instance, contains references to a sermon of the Buddha and to a famous passage of the *Brihadaranyaka Upanishad*, and concludes, like an *Upanishad*, with the Sanskrit words *Shantih shantih shantih* (Peace! Peace!! Peace!!!!). *Four Quartets* reaffirms his familiarity with and interest in the Hindu and Buddhist texts. In "The Dry Salvages," which treats time and eternity, he makes an explicit reference to the *Bhagavad Gita* and to its cardinal doctrine of *niskama karma*—that all man's actions should be motivated by rightness and goodness, not by expectation of gain or merit.

Indian influences can easily be seen in Somerset Maugham's *The Razor's Edge*, and in the writings of Edith Sitwell, Christopher Isherwood, and Gerald Heard. C. G. Jung interpreted Hinduism and Buddhism in terms of his psychological system, and pointed out the great significance of Indian thought for the modern West: "We do not yet realise that while we are turning upside down the material world of the East with our technical proficiency, the East with its psychic proficiency is throwing our spiritual world into confusion. We have never yet hit upon the thought that while we are overpowering the Orient from without, it may be fastening its hold upon us from within."

Many other Western scientists have been profoundly attracted by Indian thought, causing them to revise their own intellectual pre-suppositions and inheritance. The relationship between the body and the mind is as much a concern of the Western psychologist as it was of the ancient Indian philosopher. Kenneth Walker, a famous British surgeon, has devoted a good deal of time and writing to the study of Indian thought and literature in search of an answer:

From the point of view of science we see man as an elaborate piece of mechanism, his actions determined by man's endocrine glands, his central nervous system, his hereditary endowments, and his environment. From philosophy we learn that his capacity for knowledge is strictly limited, so that by means of the sense organs alone he can never know reality. This is confirmed by Eastern philosophy, but a new idea is added. Man, as he is, can see no more and do no more, but by right effort and right method, he can gain new powers, understand more, and achieve more. Finally we have the

264

confirmation of this idea by religion. Whatever may be the differences in their creed, whatever may be the variations in their philosophy, all religions, without exception, contain this idea of the possibility of change, so that a man may become other than he is. From the point of view of all religions man is a being in whom are lying latent higher powers.[42]

Amongst contemporary interpreters of Indian culture and philosophic thought, S. Radhakrishnan (1888–   ) is the best known. His many works, almost thirty, written in superb English with arresting original-ity, his long period of teaching Indian philosophy at Oxford Univer-sity, and his eloquent, lucid lectures, have made him the representative Indian philosopher for most foreigners. His scholarly status, no doubt, has been aided by his pre-eminence in Indian political life; he served a term as India's Rastrapati, President.[43] In fact, well before Rad-hakrishnan's work became widely known, he had made such an impact on the West that more than thirty years ago C. E. M. Joad published a book entitled *Counter-attack from the East. The Philosophy of Rad-hakrishnan.*

Generally, Radhakrishnan is regarded as the philosopher of a dy-namic idealism characterized by a deep spiritual note, a catholic outlook, an appreciation of the eternal values of all cultures and religions, and an abiding, confident optimism as to the future of human civilization. His idealism contains certain influences of Western thinkers such as Plato and Hegel, but it is essentially upanishadic in its comprehensive-ness. He accepts the monistic and the theistic view of the Upanishads, and does not subordinate the one to the other. The essence of his ideal-ism is the primacy of the spirit and its manifestation in matter, life, mind, and self. It is not the substance of Hegel, for it is not immobile but dynamic and real. It is felt everywhere, although seen nowhere. The spirit is the absolute, and is not only imminent but also transcendent. He is a follower of Samkara, but does not regard the world as an illu-sion (maya), as most other Advaitins do. Although the creation of the world is inexplicable, the world is not devoid of value and importance. He would prefer to treat the world as a combination of being and non-being.

Of the other interpreters of Indian culture who have made substan-tial impact on Western thinking, Ananda Coomaraswamy (1877–1947) is unique. Born in Ceylon of a highly successful Ceylonese barrister and a British mother, and originally trained as a geologist, he became a scholar and philosopher wholly wedded to the Indian tradition. His masterly analysis of Indian culture exhibits a rare combination of

265

INDIA AND WORLD CIVILIZATION

scientific investigation and artistic formulation. His researches include work on archaeology, philology, iconography, metaphysics, and religion. For the last thirty years of his life he worked at the Boston Museum of Fine Arts. His writing reveals a devoted, painstaking, and erudite scholarship, encyclopaedic intellect, and sensitive insight. His works have acquired such a high degree of authority that it is virtually impossible to pick up any significant modern work on Indian art which has not drawn upon Coomaraswamy.

He wanted India to remain Indian and continue to demonstrate that a pattern of life rooted in religion and philosophy can also be elegant, graceful, and fully satisfying. In India philosophy has been the key to the understanding of concrete life, not a mere intellectual exercise in abstract thought.

In Jagdish Chandra Bose (1858–1937) can be seen a remarkable Indian response to Western impact. Bose, a pioneer of modern Indian science, combined ancient Indian introspective methods with modern experimental methods to demonstrate "the universal livingness of matter" or "the omnipresence of Life in Matter." He demonstrated by laboratory tests, using special scientific instruments of extreme delicacy and precision, that plants possessed life. Modern science thus endorsed the ancient upanishadic truth that the entire universe is born of a life-force and is quivering with a touch of animation. His work represents the triumph of spirituality over extreme materialism.

In 1897, two disciples of Sri Ramakrishna, Swami Vivekananda (1863–1902) and Swami Brahmananda (1863–1922), founded the Ramakrishna Mission with its headquarters at Belur near Calcutta. Whilst Brahmananda remained in India as head of the organization, Vivekananda pioneered the establishment of Ramakrishna Missions in America and other Western countries. However, when Vivekananda first visited the United States in 1893 to attend the World-Parliament of Religions at Chicago, he did not come as a missionary of the Ramakrishna cult but as an exponent of Vedanta philosophy. Hence Vedanta philosophy got further circulation before the Ramakrishna movement gained currency. In any case, the distinction between the two is small.

Vivekananda boldly proclaimed that Vedanta was destined to be the religion of mankind. He received a spontaneous ovation at the Chicago meeting when he gave his remarkable presentation of the Hindu religion. He won popular recognition abroad for India's ancient civilization, for the Vedanta philosophy, and for India's newborn claim to nationhood. Such was the impact of his personality that wherever he

266

went, whether in Europe, China, or Egypt, he created a minor sensation; in America he was called the "cyclonic Hindu."

The influence of Vivekananda and the Ramakrishna Missions, through their *maths* in almost every Western capital, is considerable. Although essentially Hindu, they advocate the oneness of all religions and the doctrine of "one goal of the many paths." This extreme religious tolerance has a natural appeal to many in the West. There are some, however, who dread a deeper challenge in this "live and let live" approach.

How deeply Indian ideas have impressed the Western mind through Theosophy can be gauged by the great popularity of the works of J. Krishnamurti (1895–   ), who was acclaimed in his youth as "Messiah." The central theme of Krishnamurti's teaching is that it is through self-knowledge that man comes to eternal reality.

The term Theosophy is a translation of the Sanskrit term, Brahmavidya. First used in the third century by the Greek philosopher, Iamblichus, it meant the inner knowledge concerning the things of God. In its modern sense, Theosophy was a movement founded by Madame H. P. Blavatsky in 1875 in New York. The Theosophical Society is a nonsectarian body whose creed is that there is no religion higher than truth. It seeks to form a nucleus of the universal brotherhood of humanity, without distinction of race, creed, sex, caste, or colour; to encourage the study of comparative religion, philosophy, and science; and to investigate unexplained laws of nature and the powers latent in man.

Theosophy, signifying a knowledge of Brahman or the Absolute, closely follows the concepts propounded by the Upanishads and Indian philosophies. For example, the doctrine of the one transcendent, eternal, all pervading, all sustaining, self-existent life, and of the reincarnation and liberation of soul bear deep affinity to Hindu ideas. Theosophists regard India as the guardian of secret wisdom and esoteric science, and the chief exponent of the transcendent unity of all religions.

In addition to the influence of the Theosophical Society in the West, Theosophy has also had a notable impact in the countries to the east of India. In Indonesia, for instance, early nationalism came under Theosophist influence through *Taman Siswa*, literally garden of pupils, and Sukarno at one time subscribed to Theosophy. Madame Blavatsky founded a branch of the Theosophical Society in Java in 1883; by 1910 it had a membership of over two thousand, about half of which were Europeans, and the rest Indonesians and Chinese. The Theosophical movement in Indonesia also ran its own schools, called the Arjuna Schools.

Yoga, which seeks to join the unenlightened nature of man to the enlightened and divine part of himself through knowledge and discipline of mind and body, is becoming increasingly popular in the West. The Western world is best acquainted with Hatha-yoga (the yoga of body control), as is indicated by a flood of publications on the subject and the rapidly growing number of Yoga schools. Paul Brunton's *The Hidden Teaching Beyond Yoga,* published in 1941, has gone through eleven printings. The first official recognition by a British local authority was given recently when the Birmingham City Council introduced courses in Yoga, for which there had been a growing demand for some years. Reporting on the Birmingham Yoga Schools, the *Times* (London) on 23 February 1965 observed: "The attractions are often relaxation and gentle exercise, and the air of Oriental mystery which surrounds the classes. The long list of pleasures from which a fulltime yogi should abstain seem not to be observed by night school students. Many of them say they would not want to 'go in any deeper,' but in subtle ways the classes have changed some of their beliefs."

The father of the Yoga philosophy, Patanjali, defined it as "restraining the mind-stuff from taking various forms." Based on psychological conception by the proper training of mind, Yoga aims to reach the higher levels of consciousness. It is a method of finding things out for oneself rather than a preconceived metaphysical theory of reality or of universe. Yoga aims at removing suffering, sin, and all imperfections caused by *avidya* (ignorance), egoism, attachment, aversion, and clinging to life, which belie the true nature of self. By eliminating these obstacles through knowledge or illumination, and by controlling the flow of ideas in one's mind, one can become a true man. It is only natural that such a widely known system should be wrongly interpreted and even denounced at times for its quaint practices. Apparently its influence perturbed a widely read naturalized British writer so deeply that he venomously attacked Indian thought, about which he knew, by his own confession, but little, and reiterated the prejudices of those who are convinced that Western philosophies are the unfailing standards of all truth.[44]

The growing influence of Indian thought in recent years has indeed frightened some Western religious writers, such as Hendrik Kraemer (*World Cultures and World Religions*), who have designated it as the "Eastern invasion of the West." Perhaps excessive anxiety to defend the Western Christian tradition may have led Kraemer to over-rate Indian influence. But there are many European scholars who have denounced Indian thought in unmistakable terms. Whether response or resistance, admiration or denunciation, all are equally indicative of impact and stimulus.

In a limited way the migration of Indian labour to other countries provided yet another link between India and the outside world. Indian settlers began to move to other countries in 1830, mainly to work on British plantations. This made the abolition of slavery commercially possible a few years later, when the notorious indenture system was introduced in the British Empire. Indian migration, enforced or voluntary, has possibly been second only to that of the Europeans. Whilst it does not come anywhere near the combined migration of all the European countries, it exceeds—in absolute numbers, not in the proportion of population—the recorded overseas migration of any single country. According to one estimate, twenty-eight million Indians migrated to various countries between 1834 and 1932. Today there are said to be more than four million Indians in forty countries all over the globe, in some of which they form a majority, such as British Guiana, Fiji, and Mauritius. In some they constitute strong minorities; in Britain, a recent estimate would show them to be over forty thousand. Their economic and political importance is considerable, and there must also be a significant cultural impact.

An important social survey, carried out in Britain about ten years ago, produced some surprising results. A representative sample of five thousand persons, of both sexes and all ages and classes, was chosen for questioning. Nearly a quarter of the population of England did not consider that they belonged to any religion or denomination. About half the population—forty-seven per cent—expressed a positive belief in a future life; a third—thirty per cent—stated that they were uncertain. What is most significant, however, is that a quarter of all those who professed belief in an after-life—an eighth of the population—did not believe that this after-life would be eternal; eleven per cent of the believers actually declared their faith in transmigration. This was "perhaps the most surprising single piece of information to be derived from this research."[45] Belief in reincarnation is a typically Indian doctrine and is contrary to the creeds of Europe and western Asia.

Politically and intellectually it was inevitable that there should have been some reaction in Europe against an invasion of Indian learning. Reaction against alien ideas appears to be a common human irrationality. Certainly, the nature of political relationships and nationalistic pride understandably played a significant role. European nations generally were more receptive to Indian ideas during the early period of their relationship which was based on relative equality. But as European political, technological and economic supremacy over Asia came to be recognized, an attitude of superiority crept into the European—and particularly the British—outlook. The influence of political relationships on cultural intercourse is further illustrated by the fact that, once the British became overlords of India, Indian learning drew more sympathetic and imaginative understanding from other European countries than it did from the British.

The discovery of Indian thought by European scholars in the eighteenth and nineteenth centuries led to an outburst of admiration and enthusiasm, mainly because they felt that Indian thought filled a need in their European culture. Neither Christianity nor the classical cultures of Greece and Rome were considered satisfactory any more and the European intelligentsia sought to apply the new knowledge, brought in increasingly by Indologists, to their own spiritual preoccupations. Upon closer examination of Indian thought, whilst some of the deeper ideas were revealed, illusions were exposed. Even some admirers became critical and sceptical. Both reactions were based on insufficient knowledge. Goethe himself moved from one opinion to the other, although he continually acknowledged the tremendous stimulus of Indian thought. This conflicting approach is in fact characteristic of the modern European attitude towards India. Although in recent years some European writer's have made a thorough and understanding study of Indian thought, India still conjures up conflicting images in Western minds, and evokes a variety of responses ranging from Kipling's caricatures to Max Müller's "the very paradise on earth."

It is significant that, with notable exceptions, India appears to have been most attractive to those Europeans who did not visit the country personally. In other words, Indian thought made a better impact on the European mind than did contemporary Indians.

Although it was uneven, intermittent, and in many ways limited, the stimulus provided to the West by Indian thought was timely and invaluable. Of all the European nations Germany's response to India was most enthusiastic and open-hearted. Perhaps the similarity between the German and the Indian mind, in the sense that both are given to contemplation, abstract speculation, and pantheism, and both have a tendency towards formlessness, inwardness, and transcendentalism, contributed toward German understanding of Indian literature. Leopold von Schroeder says: "The Indians are the nation of romanticists of antiquity: The Germans are the romanticists of modern times." He even concludes that all the romantic minds of the West turn towards India because of the deep-rooted similarity between romanticism in Europe, and, what he considers to be, romanticism in India. Sentimentality and feeling for nature are common to both German and Indian poetry, whereas they are foreign, for instance, to Hebrew or Greek poetry. The similarity between the two peoples is further illustrated, in a different area, by the Indian tendency to work out scientific systems; India was the nation of scholars of antiquity, in the same way as the Germans are the nation of scholars of the modern times.

Even if suggestions of parallels between the Germans and Indians are discounted as being over emphasized, if not altogether misleading, it cannot be denied that German response to Indian literature and philosophy was prompt and profuse, which must have been considerably conditioned by some intrinsic appeal of Indian thought for the German mind.

The French were not amongst the first Europeans to come into contact with India. But, as soon as French travellers, who are known for their literary taste, visited India and reported on their travels, French literary circles responded enthusiastically. French interest in Indian studies, which was much anterior to that of the English, was distinctive for its imaginative understanding of Indian literature and thought. There have been many eminent French Indologists, and both the volume and quality of French contributions to Indian studies are remarkable. In fact it is a matter of some surprise that Indologists working in the English speaking world have not made full use of these French contributions.

The British response to Indian learning was most mixed. Whilst India remained a trying political problem, she was a symbol of British power and achievement, as well as a major source of her economic wealth. India as a national political problem required collective reaction, but intellectual response was a personal matter. Individual thinkers studied India closely and whilst some were fascinated, others were repelled. In both cases, Indian ideas stimulated British imagination and exercised influence in a variety of ways, which at times were conflicting. Often for political expedience—for instance the need to justify domination of India to the British public—British administrators were compelled to interpret Indian culture as degenerate and decadent. Even the Utilitarians, who advocated liberty and democracy, supported the continued rule of the Company so that Indian society could be rejuvenated.

Another barrier between Indian and British cultural co-operation was the Englishmen working in India. The early administrators were indifferent to anything except trade and profits; the later ones, after 1830, suffered from a sense of cultural inferiority, which, compounded with political superiority, manifested itself in self-righteousness, prejudices, and arrogance. They often came to India for only a few years, invariably lived an exclusive life, and returned home to condemn Indian culture and traditions with gusto. Their callous indifference to Indian art is well reflected by the fact that the liberal William Bentinck, who initiated social reforms in India, seriously considered the possibility of dismantling the Taj Mahal and selling the marble to meet the shortage of money in the Company's treasury. He was prevented because "the test auction of materials from the Agra palace proved unsatisfactory." Fed on Macaulay, Mutiny, and Kipling, the English, no wonder, did not appreciate India.

In spite of these handicaps, Indian literature captured the imagination of a few British scholars and writers. This unknown land of romantic dynasties, luxury and exotic beauty, and mystic religions and developed philosophies became a source of inspiration for romantic literature. Indian peoples, scenery, costumes, courts, religious ceremonies, folk songs, tiger hunts, hermits, and buildings presented a kind of fairytale picture, which increasingly captured popular interest.

It is a pity that Europeans did not press on with their advantage and make better use of Indian knowledge. If Indian philosophy, literature, and art had received a fuller and less inhibited appreciation in Europe, some new form of all inclusive civilization or European renaissance, more comprehensive than a mere technological and industrial revolution, might have emerged. However, a British-Indian civil servant and historian, Garratt, considered that the British rulers of India were not a good channel for cultural intercourse, for they had "failed to achieve a 'union of Hindu and European learning' or to give any scope to the technical skill and knowledge inherent among the people."[46]

Chapter VII

INDIAN RESPONSE TO
MODERN EUROPE

WHILST Europe sought ancient Indian learning, India focused her attention on modern European knowledge. In this cultural encounter, initiative remained for the most part with Europe, for she was a young developing society with an inquisitive mind and the material resources to obtain easy access to what she fancied. In contrast, Indians even if they knew what they needed, could not get at it at will. As a result, Europe absorbed Indian wisdom within a much shorter period than Indians took to gain Western knowledge. Indeed, some Western scientific theory and technological know-how has only been acquired since Indian independence.

Once the initial period of romanticism and disillusionment had been overcome, and the Indo-British political relationship was firmly established, a new phase of cultural interaction between India and the West began. With the increasing Western domination of Asia and the advance in science and technology, the process of cultural exchange gained speed and momentum. The traffic of people and ideas between India and Europe grew correspondingly, and numerous Indian intellectuals, students, officials, soldiers, tourists, princes, and merchants began to visit Britain and Europe. The cultural encounter between India and modern Europe hardly has a parallel in history.

Western tradition is a highly generalized, extremely vague, and ill-defined concept that is often stretched to include or exclude anything at will to suit the purpose in hand. It is not a unitary system of thought, nor has it an unbroken historical continuity. There are deep controversies as to its exact nature and value, and it is a complex of diverse, even contradictory, ideologies and traditions. For instance, it is equally proud of the imprints of early Greek and Christian traditions which were relentlessly opposed to each other.

273

Even a casual investigation reveals the inherent contradictions of Western tradition. Western tradition is often characterized as one of material progress and scientific advancement, yet Christian mystical thought is superbly well developed, and until recently science was positively denounced in the Christian West. In most respects scientific inquiry was much more highly developed in the Hellenistic period than it was in mediaeval Europe. In fact, exactly why Hellenistic science declined needs an explanation. Again, it is repeatedly pointed out that Western tradition stems from the enlargement of individual liberties, and that individual liberty is the essence of Western civilization. Some Western scholars go much farther and assert that the West has regarded "a denial of freedom as a denial of the value of the individual and therefore as a sin against the soul of man." Yet it is not possible to completely ignore the Western institutions of slavery, feudalism, colonialism and imperialism, and racism. Western liberalism, of which the West can be justly proud, was born in the seventeenth century as a reaction against the violence and hatred that had prevailed during the almost unbelievably atrocious religious wars. But even since then, liberalism has not remained unchallenged in the West. Indeed, totalitarianism and suppression of freedom of thought and person appear to be the unbroken trend of a Western tradition that can claim most of the great despots of world history, including Alexander, Julius Caesar, Nero, Napoleon, Hitler, and Mussolini. This fact is even more startling when these dictators and conquerors are contrasted with the prophets of non-violence and peace, such as Jesus Christ, Gautama Buddha, Asoka, and Mahatma Gandhi, who were all born in Asia. Even the concept of the divine right of kings found far more serious advocates amongst Western monarchs—the Greek Alexander, the Roman Caesars, Russians Czars, French Bourbons, and British Stuarts. It is true that the Western world has continuously fought for liberty, but this only serves to illustrate the existence of anti-freedom forces and a totalitarian current in Western tradition.

Again, it cannot be claimed, as is often done, that the rise of Christianity did much to improve the position of the individual, for religious persecution has been a common feature of Western Christianity. The once persecuted Christians, having gained power, themselves became persecutors; Caesar was more, not less, divine when he became the sword of Christianity. The terrible struggles between Church and State were not fought for individual, or even religious, freedom; the Church sought to compel the secular power to serve its own purposes. Any individual who did not subscribe to the Church's belief was at once denounced as a heretic. Crusades and religious wars of extermination were often as bloody as Hitler's slaughter of the Jews and Gypsies. The Church even persecuted the mediaeval minstrels and Gypsies because they loved freedom. Once the so-called heretics came to power they were no less tyrannical and no more tolerant than their erstwhile persecutors. It was Calvin, an apostle of Protestantism, who managed to bring secular and religious life under a single authority, and thus to direct thought and action alike by "the rule of the saints." His was the first monolithic party of the Western civilization, from which all totalitarian states have learned. "Toleration, when it came did not spring from deep-rooted conviction; it originated in the boredom and weariness of the mass of ordinary men with the conflict of totalitarian rulers who had struggled to tear Europe apart."[1]

Christianity, which is in practice a unique combination of beliefs and clergy, whilst owing its religion to Jesus and his early Asian disciples, is, in strict ecclesiastical hierarchy, an essentially Western movement. Whatever may have been the value of the Church in religious practice, it has inhibited freedom of thought and individual liberty by relentlessly enforcing its presuppositions as eternal truths. It is the Church which sets moral standards for the individual and prescribes his belief. The organization of the Church is unparalleled in history. No federation of states has been as comprehensive and universal in taking hold of the minds of people, and no monarch or dictator has been given the complete and willing obedience of such a wide and vast body of peoples as has the Church. The Islamic Caliphate and Buddhist monasticism were, in this respect, no way comparable to the Christian Church. The former was too often divided, and was always too temporal to command any control of minds, and eventually was abolished. The Buddhist Sangha was, at best, a collection of autonomous monasteries.

Communism, with all its scientific reason, humanism, and economic equality, is essentially a totalitarian doctrine, negating individual liberty, and is a typical, almost exclusive, Western concept. Communism stresses the primacy of reason, but, like a missionary religion, it has a sense of its own infallibility and an obligation to world-wide expansion. Its greatest exponents have mainly been Western or Western-trained.

Even British thought, which was more directly and closely linked with India than that of other European countries, had its own inner conflicts and contradictions in respect to India, ranging from Edmund Burke's liberalism and John Stuart Mill's utilitarianism to John Bright's radicalism. Burke desired India to stay Indian; in fact, he was rather anxious to reform the disreputable English trustees in India. He strongly condemned the facile and much used aspersion of "Oriental Despotism" and warned his countrymen against passing judgement upon a people, for ages civilized and cultivated, who formed their laws and institutions prior to "our insect origins of yesterday." The Utilitarians and Evangelicals, on the contrary, saw little good in Indian society and desired to Westernize it completely by denying individual liberty to the Indian. The Utilitarians, whilst not denying the abstract right to liberty, could see no alternative to a benevolent British despotism in India, conducted from London. India exposed Utilitarianism's paradox between its principle of liberty and that of authority. The Evangelicals' viewpoint was religious; they believed that only through Christianity could temporal welfare and spiritual salvation be achieved. Hence, they looked upon the British conquest of India as a divine act of punishment for Indian paganism, and an opportunity for Indians to redeem themselves from their depraved system of superstition. Thus they sought the rapid conversion of the peoples of India to Christian ways, as interpreted by Western clergy. If Utilitarianism provided a justification and a practical basis for British imperial rule in India, Evangelicalism gave it a sense of urgency and intense zeal.

Each diverse current of thought or tradition had its corresponding influence on India, and the Indian response, consequently, was as varied as Western tradition itself.

The Portuguese were the first European power to expand into India. Their activities were essentially an extension of the Christian crusade against Islam, and a search for trade. Although they were the last of the colonial powers to leave Indian territory (in 1961), their imprint on Indian culture is negligible.

Whilst the seventeenth century marked the zenith of India's mediaeval glory, the eighteenth century was a spectacle of corruption, misery, and chaos. The glory of the Mughals had vanished, life had become insecure, the nobility was deceitful and oppressive, and intellectual curiosity had given way to superstitious beliefs. The country was in a state of military and political helplessness. In this atmosphere, literature, art, and culture could barely survive. The malaise of India was aggravated in full measure by the East India Company with its indiscriminate exploitation, corruption, and bribery.

In contrast, Europe was robust and vigorous. This was the Age of Enlightenment, and Europeans had gone through a process of rebirth during which religion was detached from state, alchemy from science, theology from philosophy, and divinity from art. A Western scholar recently asserted that "Western science and philosophy as they have developed in the last three or four centuries, are the most sustained, comprehensive, and rigorous attempt ever made by man to understand himself and his environment, physical and social. . . ."[2] Even if the achievement of the modern West is not as unprecedented as is claimed, there can be little doubt that the cultural vitality, the variety, and the spirit of scientific inquiry displayed by Europeans in the seventeenth and eighteenth centuries mark the rise of a civilization more dynamic than anything seen in the West since Alexandria's heyday. Thus, the impact of Western culture on India was that of a dynamic society on a static one. It is a cruel irony of history that whilst two major revolutions —the French and the American—upholding the human rights to liberty and equality were taking place in the West, India was in the throes of losing her own freedom to Western mercantile imperialism.

The West provided India with the necessary impetus for a real stock taking and reform. The introduction of Western culture, education, and scientific techniques gave traditional Indian life a jolt, shocking Indians into a new awareness and vitality in thought and action. Long dormant intellectual impulses emerged and a new Indian spirit was born. During the period of Western supremacy in India, the conflict of two civilizations certainly produced unrest, but it also sustained and stimulated intellectual life.

Western influences became effective in India mainly through the British, who were the pioneers of a new technological and industrial civilization. They represented a new historic force which was later to change the world, and thus were the forerunners of change and revolution. Although Indian and Western civilizations were at approximately the same level at the time, they were tending in different directions: the former was declining, the latter progressing. India lost to Europe because it lacked political organization, including a central government, and a progressive outlook.

The British domination of India has been described as a "political and economic misfortune," and in some respects it was indeed enervating and devitalizing. Dadabhai Naoroji, whilst pointing out the many blessings of law and order it had conferred on India, called the despotic system of government in British India "un-British," for it was as destructive to British ideals and honour as it was to India. In 1937, a distinguished British civil servant, G. T. Garratt, declared that the period of Indo-British civilization of the previous one hundred and fifty years had been most disappointing, and "in some ways the most sterile in Indian history."[3] This must come as a shock not only to those who

277

have been brought up to believe in British virtue but also to those who do not take an uncritical view of British colonialism. Garratt was no Indian nationalist charged with exaggerated patriotism. He had scrupulously analyzed the problem and advanced some impressive arguments in support of his assertion, although he no doubt overstated his indignation at "what could be done but was not done." Whilst it may be irrelevant to dwell here upon the merits and demerits of British colonial policies, there can be no doubt that British impact led to such a transformation of Indian society that Indians, in retrospect, may even be thankful for what the British did, regardless of what they did not do.

Western influences were very different from any India had received before. This time the newcomers not only had a different religion but also a different outlook on life, and an economic system which was the result of new scientific and technological advances. They had firm political values, well-developed cultural traditions, and superior technical skills. Above all, their organization in all respects—military, religious, economic, and political—was remarkable and iron-cast. Whilst India has always held her own in the realm of thought, broadly speaking, organization and co-ordination have never been her strong points. Indeed, in India, as in no other civilization, except with doubtful and partial exceptions in ancient Greece and modern France, extreme intellectual individualism has been a dominant, zealously guarded characteristic. Complete freedom of individual thought, academic disputes, and philosophical debates led to an enriched Indian cultural heritage. But individualism caused frequent clashes, frustration, and indifference in political and military spheres. No serious attempt was ever made by Indian states to direct and superintend the dissemination of Indian culture. It is indeed surprising that whilst intellectually so independent and individualistic, Indians followed for centuries a caste system almost unparalleled in its rigidity. That they were unable to suppress its ugly features, and paid for it heavily in terms of social suffering and cultural decline, would further emphasize the Indian lack of collective discipline and organization.

It is not a rarity that intellectual perseverance and thoroughness of analysis add to the infirmity, rather than to the clarity, of conclusions. Having searched into all aspects of a problem, Indians do not necessarily feel the need to opt for one view or the other. They are quite content to accept the reality of contradictions in a given situation, a quality which baffles most people but is easily acceptable to the Indian mind. Indians accept reality as it is, which may or may not be unitary, and their decisions and beliefs are generally tentative, for the finite mind cannot always comprehend totality. Contradiction, not compromise, has been the keynote of Indian intellectual and political strengths and weaknesses, and even conditions her present-day revolution. Compulsion to make a firm choice in cases of conflicting views often results in merely selecting a preference for the one against the other. There is no fervour of conviction in it. Whenever there is fervour in Indian convictions it is generally emotional and indecisive; belief based on pure emotion is passion, not conviction.

Consequently, upon being confronted with British power, India could neither penetrate the steel ring of British organization nor could she absorb their culture into her own pattern. Intellectually indifferent, spiritually subdued, and physically weak at the time, Indians found an adjustment with the newcomers not only practical but essential.

Indian response to Western impact was first noticed in religion. Indians were not unfamiliar with Christianity, nor were they ill-disposed towards it. Christianity dated to the first century A.D. in India, long before Britain had even acquired the necessary degree of cultural sophistication to be able to appreciate Christian doctrines. Whilst Indians were attracted by the practical ethics of Christianity and the social welfare activities of Christian missionaries, they were repelled by their excessive zeal, their religious arrogance, and their harsh criticism of Indian religious practices and social customs. Indians could not understand the narrowness and intolerance of the Christians, in marked contrast to India's inclusive and tolerant religion. They were prepared to admit Christ as one of the prophets of God, but not as the only son of God. Despite their indignation at the new heralds of Christianity, Indians became acutely conscious of their own inadequacies and intellectual inertia.

Even though Christian missionary activity in India became widespread during British rule, the East India Company was disinclined to mix trade and religion. From the beginning it set its face against all missionary activities, and after 1757 it decided to exclude missionary propaganda in the territories under its control. However, the Company's attempts to restrict missionary work within its territory were frustrated in 1808 by Spencer Perceval, who has been called "the Evangelical Prime Minister" because of his zeal for Church reform. He was assassinated in 1812, but by then his efforts, in combination with those of Wilberforce and the Evangelicals, had already broken the Company's resistance to missionaries. The Charter of 1813 required the East India Company to allow missionaries to travel on its ships, and to admit a British bishop at Calcutta. By this Act, however, the Company's trade monopoly was abolished and its commercial opposition to missionaries weakened.

In any case, the Company had never successfully controlled missionary activity in India. Several Christian missions had been at work in various parts of India for a long time. Catholic missions had been active since the arrival of the Portuguese, and in 1780 the Serampore Mission was established in Bengal. By 1792, the spirit of evangelism had permeated Protestant churches deeply enough to move the English Baptists into organizing the first Protestant mission. Three years later the London Missionary Society was formed, and a powerful evangelical movement began in Britain, the vibrations of which, under the direction of William Carey, were felt in British India. Whilst the Company itself, as a mercantile corporation, could not lend its support to Christian missionary activity, many individuals in the administration felt deeply convinced of the need for evangelical work in India, and gave their active cooperation to the missionaries.

Although the Christian missionaries intensified their activities under the stimulus of the Act of 1813, they met with only limited success through conversions. The impact of Christian thought itself, however, was considerable, culminating in a revival, reinterpretation, and reorientation of Indian thought. Just as the impact of Islam had given encouragement to the Bhakti movement in mediaeval times, the advent of Western civilization caused the growth of numerous reform movements in modern times.

Bengal, where British power was concentrated at the time, and which had felt the worst of the East India Company's early misrule, took the lead in both cultural and political advances. The earliest stirrings of the Indian cultural renaissance appeared under the leadership of Raja Ram Mohan Roy (1772–1833) who made the first organized efforts to adapt Hinduism to the new situation. He made a clear distinction between good and bad traditions, and reasserted the wisdom of welcoming a good concept, regardless of its nationality.

He was a scholar of Sanskrit, Hebrew, Greek, Persian, English, and Arabic. A devout Hindu inspired by the vedantic philosophy, he was also deeply influenced by Sufism and was an admirer of Christianity and Western thought, especially the writings of Montesquieu, Blackstone, and Bentham. Towards the end of his life, he was also attracted by the revolutionary movements of America and Europe.

He was perhaps the first earnest modern scholar of comparative religion. Making a clear distinction between Western virtues and Western failings, he defended Hinduism against the attacks of missionaries as stoutly as he challenged the orthodoxy to abandon its ritualistic conventions. He kept in close touch with Oriental research and interpreted the ancient Indian texts in the light of Western doctrines and ideas. Consequently he became an uncompromising and vehement opponent of idolatry and of all rituals connected with it. At the age of thirty-one, he published a book in Persian, denouncing idolatry and advocating belief in one god and a universal religion. He conceived the idea of a universal church, somewhat in the tradition of Akbar's Din-i-ilahi, combining the best spiritual traditions of Hinduism, Christianity, and Islam and accepting equally the teachings of all religions. He looked beyond dogma, ritual, and philosophical dialectics to seek the fundamentals of each faith, and found them identical.

Although willing to join in Christian worship, Ram Mohan Roy was an ardent Hindu who found Hinduism's defence against Christianity in Vedanta, which supported his ideas on the unity of God, the futility of idolatry and pilgrimages, and the doctrine of Karma and incarnations. In an exposition on Christianity, *The Precepts of Jesus, the Guide to Peace and Happiness,* he extolled the ethical teachings of Christ but rejected the miraculous legends about his life which he said were due to a misinterpretation on the part of his followers. Moreover, he did not believe that man could atone for his sins simply by repentance. This was, in fact, a reply to missionaries rather than a call to Indians. He regarded a bigoted Christian to be as conceited as a bigoted Hindu, and ignored both. He accepted the humanism of European thought. Whilst his denunciation of Hindu orthodoxy antagonized Hindu traditionalists, his discriminating approach to Christian doctrines displeased Christian diehards. Despite strong opposition from a superstitious and indifferent people, aggressive missionaries, and a mercenary government, he persisted in his endeavours. As a result he set India on a course of cultural reformation, which gradually gathered momentum and support, and eventually made it possible for modern India to emerge.

In his attempt to bring about harmony between faiths, Roy founded the Brahmo Samaj in 1828. Brahmo Samaj was not an entirely new religion, for it was based on the vedanta philosophy, but its outlook was European, and it derived its inspiration from the intellectual movements of the eighteenth century. Doctrinally somewhat similar to Unitarianism and attempting to synthesize the cultures of East and West, it encouraged rationalism and social reform.

Ram Mohan Roy, however, was much more than a religious reformer. He was a patriot who represented Indian nationalism on the defensive;

its leaders at this stage were cautious, and apprehensive. He commenced the task of national reconstruction on several fronts with vigour and industry. In 1823, twelve years before Macaulay wrote his famous minute on education, Ram Mohan Roy had petitioned the British Government to introduce English rather than continue traditional Indian education. A few years earlier he had founded a Hindu college at Calcutta, where Western learning was taught. Macaulay, who is credited with having forced the issue in favour of English education, not only followed the arguments advanced by Ram Mohan Roy, but even borrowed some of his language.

Roy relentlessly battled the ugly but hallowed custom of sati to save women from cruel deaths. This custom, for some unknown reason, increased in Bengal during British expansion. Ram Mohan filed petitions for its abolition before the British, and ten years later, when William Bentinck did abolish sati, Roy was profoundly moved. When a group of reactionary Indians petitioned the Privy Council in London to reverse the abolition, he appeared before the Council personally and successfully defended Bentinck's measure. Many sincere leaders before him had exposed the evils in Indian life and religion, but none had grasped with as much clarity the passivity which had come to paralyze the Indian mind, and none had worked with such devotion, perseverance, and conviction to revitalize Indian thinking.

Ram Mohan Roy was received enthusiastically in Europe, and exercised a considerable influence upon liberal Protestants, especially Unitarians. He went to England ostensibly as the ambassador of the Mughal king to recover Mughal authority from the British Company. He did not succeed in his political mission, but he helped to bring India a good deal closer to the West. During his stay, he met leading British statesmen, philosophers, and historians, such as Jeremy Bentham and James Mill. So highly did Bentham hold Ram Mohan Roy in his esteem that when the Indian scholar arrived in London in April 1831, Bentham was the first man to call on Roy at the Adelphi Hotel. Bentham was eighty-three years of age at the time and fastidious—he refused to see Mme. de Staäl in 1813 because he thought she had nothing of interest to say. In welcoming Roy at the British Unitarian Association's reception, Sir John Bowring placed Ram Mohan in the same class as "a Plato or a Socrates, a Milton or a Newton." Bentham even actively agitated to secure Roy's election to the British Parliament.

The new spirit of humanism and rationalism stimulated Indian thought and literature enormously. No longer was Indian writing appended to theology, mythology, and scholasticism. No gods and goddesses descended from heaven and played a part in human life. Man now occupied the foremost place, steering his course of life without divine help. This concept of the world was somewhat similar to that which had existed in the ancient past, of which only a dim recollection had survived. Soon new ideas began to fill old patterns and Indian writers and thinkers were inspired not only by the renewed spirit of humanism but also by the French revolutionary spirit of liberty and equality.

After the death of Ram Mohan Roy in Bristol in 1833, the Brahmo Samaj remained the focus of the Hindu renaissance. Debendranath Tagore (1817–1905), who had been in intimate contact with Roy, continued the monotheistic tradition. In 1839, he founded the Tattvabodhi Sabha, which played a significant role in the cultural revival of India, especially in Bengal. Unlike Ram Mohan, however, his ideas reflect little Christian influence. In spite of his impressive missionary activity, Debendranath, who became an ascetic, seems to have embraced Brahmoism primarily out of an intense spiritual craving, not out of any inclination for social reform.

After him came the dynamic, although somewhat erratic, Keshab Chandra Sen (1838–1884), under whose direction the eclecticism of the Brahmo Samaj gathered momentum. His enthusiasm was infectious and he wielded tremendous influence upon his contemporaries. Widely read in Western philosophy, he was especially attracted by Carlyle and Emerson. His own backgorund was vaisnava, and Ramakrishna's idea of the harmony of all religions captured his imagination. He wanted the Samaj to maintain not merely that there were truths in all religions but that all religions of the world were true. Not a Christian, he was nevertheless a great admirer of Christ. Indeed, his teachings were so close to Christianity that at one time his conversion to the Christian faith was thought imminent. But he was deeply saturated in Hindu thought and often, especially in his later life, would stress the validity of many vedantic ideas. He believed that many Hindu rituals and usages could be reinterpreted and restored with new symbolic meaning to suit the Brahmo Samaj. Consequently, he retained many Hindu practices in Brahmo worship but turned to Christianity for ethical guidance. Despite his mental prowess and unquestionable integrity, clarity or consistency of thought was not his strong point. In his *New Dispensation,* published in 1881, he set out to create a third dispensation—the Old Testament being the first and the New Testament being the second—and declared himself the centre of it, as Christ was of his dispensation. But immediately he felt he was a sinner; a slave of Christ, *Jesudasa.* He called himself "a child of Asia" and loudly claimed Christianity to be an Asian religion.

He asserted that Jesus was akin to his Asian nature and ways of thinking, and that Christianity was more comprehensible to the Asian mind
than to the European. He made a clear distinction between the spirit
of Christianity and the fashions of Western civilization. He was a relentless opponent of hypocrisy, insisted on social purity and upright individual conduct, and preached his views throughout India with
unsparing energy. In some ways he was ahead of his times. He was the
first Brahmo Samaj leader to advocate the welfare and rights of men, to
attempt a new interpretation of history, and to evolve a modern prose
style in Bengali. He took radical positions on social and religious issues
which may not have endeared him to some of his contemporaries but
undoubtedly left an impact on them. After his death, the Brahmo Samaj
ceased to be a living force, but by that time it had served its extremely
vital purpose of national awakening.

The Brahmo Samaj was an attempt to achieve a synthesis of East and
West by some educated and restive men of Bengal. It did not become
a mass movement, but impressive leaders gave impetus to a chain of
religious reforms and social consciousness which gradually bound the
whole country together. Not all of these movements were kindly dis-
posed towards Western culture, but they all created a new spirit and the
face of the country began to change. Later religious movements were
mainly concerned with asserting the pure and original form of Hinduism
and returning to it.

Under the stimulus of renascent Hinduism in Bengal, the Prarthana
Samaj society was founded in Maharastra in 1867. Bengal and Maharastra had divergent historical experiences during the Mughal period,
but they had much in common in the nineteenth century. Both had for
some time been the scene of European activities and both had developed
the urge to reform traditional society in a reaction against foreign
domination. Eminent persons joined the Prarthana Samaj, such as M.
G. Ranade (1842–1901) and Sir R. G. Bhandarkar; the former being
its most outstanding leader. Somewhat milder in policy than the Brahmo
Samaj, the Prarthana Samaj believed in the fatherhood of God and the
brotherhood of man, but their theism rested largely on ancient Hindu
thought. The Vedas, however, were not their source of inspiration, and
transmigration was left an open question. The Prarthana Samaj opposed
idolatry, child-marriage, prohibition of widow remarriage, and caste,
but membership was not forfeited if these practices were continued. The
Prarthana Samaj did for Maharastra what Brahmo Samaj did for
Bengal.

Through the efforts of these cultural movements, the spread of English education, the study of Indian culture, and the increasing order-liness of political organization, there had awakened in India a deep sense of nationality and cultural pride. The emergent India demanded a more militant defence of its own inheritance, and the growth of national, as opposed to regional, movements. Soon the initiative passed to Swami Dayananda Sarasvati (1824–1883), who based his teachings entirely on the Vedas, "the primeval scripture of humanity," which he regarded as the revealed word of God. He thought the amorphous nature of Hinduism exposed it to much weakness, which could be repaired by possessing, like Islam and Christianity, a revealed work of unquestion-able authority.

Born in 1824 in Kathiawar in western India, Swami Dayananda spent many years in the quest of truth. He began his public life in 1868. After an extensive lecture tour severely criticizing certain weak-nesses of Hinduism, as well as those of Christianity and Islam, he founded the Arya Samaj in 1875; it has since been an active movement in Hindu life, especially in the Punjab.

Untutored in English but a profound Sanskrit scholar, Dayananda, in his most important work, the *Satyartha Prakash,* made a brilliant attempt to discover in the Vedas the bases of the Christian and Muslim religions. His chief convictions were that there was only one God to be worshipped, without the aid of idols. The many divine names which occur in the Vedas were all epithets of the one true God. Many other Hindu texts were of value but they were not to be followed where they contradict the Vedas. Swami Dayananda relentlessly opposed priests, who he believed had caused discord and disunion, in marked contrast to prophets of other faiths who had attempted to unite humanity. He emphasized the fundamental purity of Hinduism, as he conceived it, which was to him the original vedic religion.

Fearless and overpowering, Dayananda aimed at giving self-confi-dence back to Hindus, although he ruthlessly denounced the deplorable practices prevalent in contemporary Hinduism. He asked Hindus to adopt modern ideas that impressed him, and he introduced militancy into Hinduism. His strong urge to assert Hindu nationalism found expression in the Shuddhi movement to take Hindus who had been converted to Islam or Christianity back into the fold. This was a novel experiment which was resented by Muslims and Christians. However, belonging to proseletyzing religions themselves, they really had no logical argument against this practice, even if it were a new one for the Hindu.

As there is no sanction in the Vedas for caste and other taboos that had gripped Hindu society, the Arya Samaj vigorously advocated drastic social reform. For example, it spent large sums of money on sacred thread for millions of untouchables, thus making them equal to other members of the Hindu society. However successful the Arya Samaj may have been as a militant organization, its appeal was mainly confined to the Punjab, chiefly for two reasons. By exclusively emphasizing the Vedas, it ignored the rich tradition of Hindu culture which had followed them for over two thousand years. The concept of Arya and Aryavarta, inherent in vedic supremacy, excluded South India, which has been in many ways the real repository of Hindu culture in later times.

Swami Dayananda and his followers disclaimed any indebtedness to Western ideas, but this would appear rather an assertion of national pride than a statement of fact. A distinctive feature of the Arya Samaj has been its remarkable contribution to the spread of English education, through its numerous Dayananda Anglo-Vedic schools and colleges throughout the country. It is significant that a movement which superficially seemed inward-looking and which raised the cry of "back to the Vedas" should have done more than any other single Indian public organization to spread Western knowledge in India.

Dayananda's contemporary, Sri Ramakrishna Paramahamsa (1834–1886), in preaching selfless devotion to God and seeking self-realization, approached Muslim and Christian mystics. He emphasized that different religions are but different paths to reach the one God, and that if one religion is true, then by the same logic, all other religions are also true.

Ramakrishna, who lived at the temple of Dakshineshwar near Calcutta, was a poor priest without any formal education. It has been claimed that what Socrates was to the Greek consciousness, Ramakrishna was to the modern Indian renaissance. Max Müller said that in comparison to the illiterate Ramakrishna the brightest intellects of Europe were mere gropers in the dark. In a recent study, Christopher Isherwood has called Ramakrishna the incarnation of Siva.

Ramakrishna never claimed to be the founder of a new religion. He simply preached the old religion of India, founded on the Vedas and the Upanishads, and systematized in later commentaries. He was not an original thinker in the true sense of the word, but he could recognize many things, including the divine presence, which others could not. He never wrote a philosophical treatise, but his pithy sayings and simple, commonplace illustrations are marvels of lucid exposition. Not urbane, and often even devoid of grace, he was utterly genuine, sincere, and forthright.

His dynamic disciple, Swami Vivekananda, preached the teaching of his guru to India and to the world in somewhat the same manner as

Saint Paul preached the gospel of Jesus. Whilst Ramakrishna was a mystic, depending upon intuition and vision, Vivekananda was an intellectual, relying mainly upon reason. In India he pioneered rationalism in religion and philosophy, as Ram Mohan Roy had done in the field of social thought. He preached the "oneness of all religions," asking Hindus to become better Hindus, Muslims to become better Muslims, and Christians to become better Christians. He impressively interpreted Indian thought to Western peoples and provided a bridge between the East and West, both of whom needed reform; the former lacked food and education, the latter, spirituality. Through his forceful and logical speeches, he established the inherent virtues of the Hindu religion. The period of apologies was over; his was the voice of the self-confident Hindu who expounded his faith with the fullest conviction and righteous pride. Rooted in the past and full of pride in India's heritage, Vivekananda was modern in his approach to the problems of life, providing a bridge between the past of India and her present. He foreshadowed Mahatma Gandhi in his burning enthusiasm for the uplifting of the masses. He regarded India, in spite of her degradation, as the home of spiritualism and enlightenment, but he attacked Indian inertia, disunity, and lack of national pride. He was impressed with American efficiency and equality, and British tenacity, law-abidingness, and sense of loyalty. In 1897 he founded the Ramakrishna Mission at Belur, near Calcutta, and the new institution adopted a comprehensive programme of social service. It started schools, colleges, hospitals, orphanages, and libraries, and has remained a leader in rendering humanitarian services in India.

Although Vivekananda died at the age of thirty-nine, he left a permanent mark on Indian life and thought. The great national leaders, such as Gandhi, Tagore, and Nehru, often acknowledged their debt to him. Towns, streets, bridges, and institutions are named after him in all corners of India, and it has been said that to understand India an understanding of Vivekananda is essential.

The Theosophical Society moved its headquarters from New York to India in 1879. At first the Society aimed mainly at the investigation and propagation of the belief in life beyond death, but later the scope of its inquiry was broadened considerably. Today it is a blending of the wisdom of the East and the West. Theosophists, whilst seeking liberation, are pledged to lead a life of sacrifice. They are encouraged to act according to their oft-quoted maxim, "Light on the Path," and to "try to lift a little of the heavy Karma of the world." The members of the Society are required to lead highly ethical and moral lives and oppose the increasingly materialistic outlook on life. Religious fanaticism is not allowed and the followers of any religion can become members, adhering to what is best in their own religion.

At a time when Hinduism, Christianity, and Islam were competing with each other, this stress on the unity of religions served a very useful purpose. Although not a mass movement, the Society significantly affected the outlook of the emerging nation. For a while, at least, it accommodated the urge of educated Hindus to find a common denomination for their various sects.

Annie Besant (1847–1933), who came to India in 1893, was the Society's most forceful leader. She was at one time a British socialist leader and an atheist. She said that she remembered India from her past incarnation and looked upon it as her "motherland." She adopted the Indian way of life, and translated various important Hindu texts into English. A persuasive speaker, she advanced the popularity of Hinduism and Indian culture through her widely attended public lectures. She took an active part in the Indian national movement and became the first woman President of the Indian National Congress. However, she disagreed vigorously with her contemporary Indian nationalism leaders, Lokamanya Tilak and Mahatma Gandhi.

Indian Islam also felt the impact of the West, but its response was somewhat different from that of Hinduism. Whilst many educated Hindus were eager to reconcile Western ideas to their own inheritance, Muslims remained markedly disinclined for some time to accept the validity of any knowledge not blessed by the Quran. The Muslims refused to give up Persian and Arabic to learn English. Typical of early Muslim response was Mirza Abu Talib Khan (1752–1807), who was one of the first Indians to visit Europe where he was lionized by English aristocracy. In *The Travels of Mirza Talib Khan*, he described the peculiarities of European customs and the evils of Western materialism, and advised his fellow Muslims to continue to ignore Western learning out of "zeal for their religion." In 1835, when Bentinck decreed the introduction of Western education, a number of Muslim notables of Calcutta presented a petition to the British Government asking them to rescind the decree. They felt it was a slight on their own learning and feared that it was aimed at the Christianization of India. The centuries' old rivalry between Islam and Christianity also contributed to Indian Islam's hostility.

In 1837, Persian was dicarded as the official language, Muslim laws and Muslim courts were abolished, and high positions in government and the army were closed to Muslims in the same way as they were to other Indians. The loss of political ascendancy and the secularization of government produced discontent, resentment, and resistance to the West. Many Muslims even felt, like the Arabian Wahhabis, that British India was no longer a suitable place for the Muslim community, and some of the more zealous ones, under the leadership of Sayyid Ahmad of Rae Bareli, preached the need to emigrate to other Muslim countries. The inevitable consequence of this self-imposed isolation and resistance to modernization was that by the middle of the century Muslims were left well behind the Hindus in progress.

In 1857, the Mughal Empire was irrevocably ended, and with it Muslim hopes of political supremacy in India. Not only were the Mughals dislodged but the Muslim political superstructure built upon Indian society over a period of centuries was shattered.

In 1867, the Muslim intellectuals and nationalist leaders who had taken a prominent part in the Indian revolt of 1857, set up the *Darul-Ulum* at Deoband, professing loyalty to Islamic law and religious orthodoxy. The Deoband School derived its doctrines from Shah Walli Allah Dihlawi (1703–1762), who envisaged Islam as an unfinished social movement begun by Muhammad, and who aimed at purifying the faith. The school made a vigorous and determined effort to resuscitate classical Islam. It accepted the old order but tried to revive and purify it. The Deoband School became the most important and respected theological academy of Muslim India, indeed of the entire Islamic world next to Al Azhar of Cairo. It produced some brilliant Muslim leaders and developed a strong tradition of vitality and quality.

The first concrete efforts to adapt modern thought to Islamic culture were made in the second quarter of the nineteenth century at Delhi, where a group of able men set out to revive Urdu by publishing Western works in that language. Later, in 1863, under the leadership of Nawab Abdul Latif, some liberal Muslims founded the Muhammadan Literary Society at Calcutta whose main objective was to emphasize the increasing importance of Western learning and culture. In trying to assimilate Western knowledge, leaders of this movement leaned too heavily on the British for support, and primarily attracted loyalist Muslims. Even theologically the movement distinguished itself by being thoroughly pro-British. It opposed the popular Wahhabi *jihad* agitation against the British "infidels" and by this denunciation, the Society gained the gratitude of both the British Government and the well-to-do Muslims.[4]

Continuing somewhat in the same tradition, Sir Syed Ahmad Khan (1817–1898) attempted to persuade Muslims to change their religious outlook and reconcile themselves to the changing environment. Sir Syed, convinced of the futility of fighting the British, "remained faithful to the British and helped them by saving the lives of those in danger" during the revolt of 1857.[5] He sought to improve the position of Indian Muslims through co-operation with the British authorities.

Anxious to draw the Muslims out of their shell of orthodoxy and to reconcile modern scientific thought with Islam, he actively pursued a policy of social and educational reform. He pointed out the basic similarities between Islam and Christianity, attacked the purdah system which segregated women from men, advocated the emancipation of women, opposed allegiance to the Turkish Caliphate, and, above all, advised his fellow Muslims to accept English education. He founded the Anglo-Oriental College at Aligarh in 1877; the College gained university status and played a vital role in the movement for Pakistan. He published a multi-volume commentary on the Quran in which he tried to prove that the teachings of Islam were in complete harmony with modern scientific theories, and sought to assimilate the best of Western thought into the Islamic faith. He was consequently severely criticized by the orthodox section of the community and his interpretation of Islam has generally been ignored. But his religious writings and advocacy of social reforms have made a lasting impression on Indian Islam.

Maulana Abul Kalam Azad (1888–1958) was also influential in helping modernize Indian Muslims. Unlike Sir Syed, Azad was an uncompromising adversary of the British imperial rule, and an important leader of the Indian National Congress. He was an even greater Islamic scholar than Sir Syed and a versatile litterateur, combining religious knowledge with scientific research. Azad's commentary on the Quran is universally acknowledged as an outstanding contribution to Islamic studies. Although educated entirely in the orthodox tradition, he imbibed the spirit of the modern West. He interpreted Islam as a universal religion which could embrace the diversity of all creeds. A brilliant theologian, his work is distinguished by a spirit of free inquiry. His interpretation evoked criticism from the orthodox, and admiration from liberal thinkers. A progressive revolutionary dedicated to true freedom, he is included amongst the *Ulama* (learned men) because of his religious learning, in which he was unsurpassed.[6]

There was bitter rivalry between Deoband and Aligarh. The achievement of Pakistan may be regarded as Aligarh's success, but the cultural response goes on, and it is yet to be seen which of the two schools will finally triumph in reconciling Islam to modernity. It seems likely that the uninhibited cultural response of the Muslims of India and Pakistan may well proceed along the lines of Deoband, resuscitating the purity of classical Islam with the assistance of modern concepts and needs.

Looking at what has happened in these two countries since the partition, it would appear that Islam in Pakistan is primarily a political consideration, whilst in India it is more concerned with cultural and religious advancement.[7]

Whilst the Deoband and Aligarh movements represented the two divergent Muslim responses to Western impact, Muslim response generally was significantly different from that of the Hindus. The Hindu reform movements were ruthlessly self-critical, often questioning the very validity of some of their sacred texts and eager to absorb or adapt Western knowledge, and all—orthodox and unorthodox—were nationalistic in varying degrees of intensity. In contrast, the Muslims on the whole were not so anxious to accept new ideas. Whilst the orthodox movement, attempting to resuscitate classical Islam, was intensely opposed to British rule in India, the unorthodox movement, seeking to carve a new image of Islam, advocated loyalty to British power. The orthodox saw the security of Islam in a free and united India. The unorthodox, fearful of Hindu supremacy, eventually sought the partition of the country. In other words, the cultural and religious response of the Indian Muslim community to the West was largely conditioned by economic and political factors, as a result, the orthodox dreaded European Christian domination, the unorthodox dreaded Indian Hindu domination.

The British established an orderly and centralised government in India, although it was unwieldy and extremely bureaucratic. The British administration in India, by its very nature, first demolished the traditional personal rule and later brought about the development of the rule of law. In contrast to the older Indian system, the fundamental feature of the British administration was its impersonal character, which had its merits as well as its demerits. The multiplicity of governmental functions gave rise to a highly graded paternalistic bureaucracy which eclipsed the self-governing village Panchayats and at times discouraged individual initiative. But a somewhat democratic control served as a continual reminder of the superior value of parliamentary democracy.

Although independent India has borrowed profusely from other Western political systems, such as the United States and Ireland, and is inevitably developing its own body of parliamentary experience, her political values and institutions are based principally on British experience. Broadly speaking, Indian political organization is Western in its aims, assumptions, and techniques. The concepts of human rights and of human equality, implied in the ideal of democracy, are a Western legacy. These concepts are so inseparably grafted onto the Indian body-politic and appear so natural that many scholars have tried to trace their origins to early India. Democracy is working most satisfactorily in India today but not in most other countries of Asia and Africa, many of which were also ruled by the British. These facts lend considerable weight to the view that democracy was not altogether alien to Indian temperament and tradition.[8] Again, if Indians were borrowing from the British, irrespective of their own values and national considerations, they would have sought to set up a typically British, monarchical democracy, but instead they worked frantically to abolish the princedoms left behind by the British. Whilst it is possible to trace prototypes of some modern political ideas in ancient Indian tradition, such as democracy and individual liberty, it is difficult to find approximate parallels of such Western political institutions as parliamentary democracy or the cabinet system. Whatever Indian precedents there may be, there is no doubt that in contemporary India these concepts and institutions are of Western inspiration.

The Indian civil service, now called the Indian Administrative Service, was carefully built up during the British rule into a powerful and efficient, although impersonal and bureaucratic, force. Once the much criticized patronage system of recruitment was replaced by competitive examination in 1855, the service acquired a unique reputation for skill, experience, and devotion to duty. The core of the service consisted of the District Officers, modern variants of Asoka's *Rajukas,* whose duties were, similarly, to collect revenue and keep peace. Many members of the I.C.S. became deeply interested in historical research, and much of Indian historiography was pioneered by these administrators.[9]

More important, however, was the British impact on law, which has been described as the finest and the most abiding British contribution to India. Before the British period, both Hindus and Muslims merely applied, at best, the sacred law and, at worst, the will of the ruler; often there were different laws for different regions and castes. A Brahman could sometimes go free, or escape with relatively light punishment, where a sudra incurred heavy penalties for the same offence; often the former could not be punished on the evidence of the latter. In many cases Muslim law was based on religious partisanship and privileged birth. The Mughal Emperor regarded himself as the earthly Shadow of God and the source of all law and justice. The British made the law applicable to all alike, and detached it from religion.

Neither in Hindu nor Muslim India was there a law-making body. The former relied on ancient codes, as interpreted by the learned Brahmans, to regulate life and society. For the Muslim, Prophet Muhammad had revealed once and for all the divine law which was above modification. Islamic law, derived from the Quran and the *Hadith*, was all comprehensive, compulsorily regulating the public and private life of society and the individual. Thus, law was an appendix to religion until British impact liberated it and made it an instrument of social advancement. It was this changed character in Indian legal attitudes that made it possible for free India to enact laws abolishing untouchability, unequal status of women, and other social evils.

It must, however, be pointed out that law did not become fully independent of faith. During the British period it remained largely restricted by firm religious conventions and susceptibilities, especially in the social sphere. Even in India today the social life of Muslims is regulated by law based on Islamic beliefs; for instance, their marriage customs and property and inheritance rules are yet to be secularized.

With this new legal system and the monolithic administration, came a complicated structure of high and low courts, giving rise to litigation, often unnecessary and always prolonged. A poor man found justice remote and beyond his reach, for it became expensive and too technical. What was previously "known" locally now had to be "proven" in distant courts, through a tedious procedure and an often unfamiliar law. The lawyer, with his skill to convince the judge of the validity of evidence but not necessarily of the actuality of crime, assumed paramount importance. There developed a long hierarchy of judicial officials whose ranks had first to be penetrated before the case could be heard. The familiar and ancient system of the Panchayati Raj was suppressed. Whilst some of these undesirable features were inherent in the system, many were the result of misguided and ill-controlled practice.

Pre-British Indians were not litigious. Numerous authorities of the contemporary scene have amply testified to the general truthfulness and honesty of Indians, and to the integrity of Indian merchants. Typical was the comment made in 1852 by Sir Erskine Perry, who had been the Chief Justice of Bombay, that "the sanctity of mercantile books was such that in the Native Courts of justice, the production of the books was quite conclusive as to the veracity of any transaction in dispute."[10] Similarly, Colonel Sleeman reported that he had witnessed innumerable cases in which a man's property, liberty, and life had depended on his telling a lie, and he had refused to do so.

Whilst the British impact discouraged economic progress it proved beneficial in social life, despite hesitant and uncertain policy. The prohibition of sati, the abolition of child-marriage, and the undermining of caste or sex distinctions were commendable measures which, if taken to their logical end, could have purged India of its social evils long before the enactments of independent India.

The economic consequences of British rule, looking at both the credit and debit sides, leave much to be desired. Indian economy, on the eve of British expansion, was not backward for the time, and India had a flourishing export trade in silk, cotton, brocade, salt, and sugar, but economic exploitation by the new rulers led to its rapid impoverishment. Indian rural economy was transformed to suit the new modes of industrial Britain. This transformation led to drastic changes in the Indian way of life, the most fundamental of which was the disintegration of the old village community structure, partly as a result of the spread of commercial agriculture. Pre-British Indian agriculture was, by the standards of the period, robust, rich, and well provided for by widespread irrigation systems which had a history stretching back to pre-Mauryan days. The entire country was carved by an extraordinary labyrinth of canals, tanks, and dams, constructed by the state at prodigious expense. Bernier marvelled at the extent and size of the engineering works he saw in India, and in 1800, Francis Buchanan, who travelled extensively in India between 1800 and 1810 collecting agricultural data for the British Government, saw several large reservoirs which were still functioning.[11]

Indian manufacturing skills and economics were well advanced; spinning and weaving were national industries. Indian industry suffered severely because of the partisan and protective policy favouring British manufactured goods. Indian textiles, ivory works, brassware, gold and silver, filigree and luxury goods, which were once famous abroad, gradually fell into disuse, reducing millions of the artisan class to unemployment, poverty, and many to death. Vast numbers of these displaced artisans were forced to go back to their villages to live on the already fully occupied land. The crisis in industry led to a crisis in agriculture. Land holdings became smaller, the number of landless labourers increased, and villages became overcrowded. Poverty thus multiplied, famines became common, and rural India became progressively more ruralized.

Famines were not unknown in Indian history but the frequency and intensity with which they occurred during the British period were unprecedented and disconcerting. It has been estimated that in earlier times a major famine occurred, on an average, once in fifty years, and that between the eleventh and the seventeenth centuries, there were fourteen famines, almost all of which were confined to small local areas. But, from 1765, when the British took over Bengal, to 1858, when they quelled India's first major revolt, twelve famines and four "severe scarcities" occurred. This frequency increased in the latter part of the nineteenth century. Although there is no accurate record, a conservative estimate suggests that in the nineteenth century alone more than twenty-one million people died of starvation. In 1943, four years before British withdrawal from India, more than three million people perished in the Bengal Famine. It is significant that those parts of India which had been longest under British rule were the poorest at the time of Indian Independence.

Although India remained predominantly agricultural, the inflow of British capital, the development of a modern banking and communications systems, the establishment of textile, jute, sugar, and cement factories, and the European demand for tea and coffee led to the beginnings of industrialization. However, it remained extremely limited until the withdrawal of British power. Towards the latter part of British rule, the changed nature of the British economy and the demands of war rendered Indian industrial development a little more necessary, and after the British industrial revolution had reached the height of safety, it not only allowed but even required Indian small-scale industrialization in certain specified spheres.

The growth of modern commerce and industry brought urbanization. Old towns, located in religious, political, or trading centres, were now replaced by large metropolitan cities, such as Bombay, Madras, and Calcutta, and by purely industrial towns, like Ahmadabad. The densely populated cities were an inevitable source of slums, but they also became dynamic political, cultural, and economic centres of a type unknown in India before. The cities and traditions of civic life later played an important role in developing the national consciousness and progressive aspirations of India, as they had done elsewhere. Rome introduced the city into most of continental Europe, and with the city came citizenship and the civic tradition, the greatest contribution of Mediterranean culture.[12] When Rome declined, the Romanized cities upheld the Roman tradition. Later, the rise of the mediaeval city in Europe led to far-reaching changes in the intellectual life of Western society. In India, urbanization attracted landless labour from the village, which weakened the joint family system and the traditional social structure.

The growing complex of new occupations could not be accomodated within the caste system. Industrialization, secular education, and improved means of transportation and communications all operated against the institution of caste. Untouchability and caste discrimination can only survive in a small village community where everyone's caste is known. Wherever crowds of people were thrown together, caste was not visible, nor was it possible to follow all the rules of caste in modern urban surroundings. The need to survive in new conditions, the increasing knowledge of the irreligious character of caste, and crusades by national leaders, especially Mahatma Gandhi, shook the foundations of the caste structure. Consequently, when India became independent, there were, except for the inevitable orthodox, no mental reservations against the abolition of caste.

During the British period, India developed considerable interest, if not competence, in science and its application to human affairs, even though Indian technological development was still in its infancy. Scientific thought was a major part of the Indian inheritance but modern technology was a Western innovation. The British mainly encouraged humanistic and literary education in India, and neglected technical studies and sciences. Whilst there were many liberal arts colleges in India, there were only a few engineering or medical colleges. But the enthusiasm with which the Indians have taken to science and the rapid progress made in recent years is instructive, especially to those who think of them as unworldly recluses, levitating in forests and holy places.

Modern education, in which aesthetic values seldom find a place, is not conducive to artistic development, in India or elsewhere. Indian artists, however, managed to retain their traditional values and forms, partly because the modernists neglected them, and partly because of pride in their rich heritage. Consequently, the old canons are still systematically applied in every form of popular art in India, and modern Indian art, on the whole, retains the spirit of its exceedingly rich past. But it has been influenced by artistic developments in Western countries. Reflecting the new technical civilization and expressing the spirit of its time, modern Indian art has become no less experimental than that of Europe or America.

The Portuguese were the first to introduce late Renaissance and Baroque art into their Indian possessions. It had limited effect. It was with the British, and their need to build bungalows, factories, forts, cathedrals, and cities, that Indian art came under a major European influence; Bombay government offices, the Lahore railway station, the palaces of Gwalior and Baroda, and the Victoria Memorial in Calcutta are but a few examples of various European architectural styles.

Later in the nineteenth century, a reaction against imitating Europe set in, and Indian art took a new turn under Englishmen, such as E. B. Havell, and Indians, such as A. N. Tagore. For a while, an art revival persisted which attempted to recreate a national style of painting. But, as in other spheres of cultural life, a process of synthesis commenced. New schools began to arise, and there is no doubt that a fully developed Indian art will be an integration of past and present, a synthesis of East and West. Modern Indian artists are expressing themselves in all the modern idioms of Europe and America, accompanied by the modes of art practiced in India. Whilst Indian painters follow the styles and techniques of modern Europe, especially of France, they depict scenes and people in recognizably Indian manner.

British-built structures guided Indian architects. The importation of European styles was soon followed by a period of blending the rich Indian tradition with European design. An example of this was the capital of British India, New Delhi, built by Sir Edwin Lutyens and his associate, Sir Edward Baker, in the 1930's. Their first designs were a type of neo-Roman style but, under severe criticism from innumerable people in England, including such outstanding names in literature and art as George Bernard Shaw and Sir William Rothenstein, the plans were revised to incorporate Indian motifs. But the product did not turn out to be a synthesis of styles but an assortment of patterns, hybrid and uninspired, partly because New Delhi was built at a time when the old style had lost all virility, and the new style was yet to be developed. However, further changes have taken place since and a composite style may well be on its way, blending elements of Hindu, Mughal, and Victorian Gothic architecture.

Dance and music remained almost uninfluenced by European styles. Certain modifications, however, are noticed in popular music, especially in Indian cinemas, and in modern musical compositions which have adopted Western techniques. Some Indian composers, such as Sarabji, have written music in Western styles, sometimes using Indian motifs. Ali Akbar Khan occasionally incorporated a certain amount of harmony and Western melodies into his improvizations.

Direct British impact on Indian social and cultural life may not have been as decisive as it was on Indian economic and political organization. But the revival of the tradition of learning and the introduction of English secular education illuminated the path of Indian modernization, just as the Indian appetite for knowledge had sustained India's greatness in the past.

Education in ancient India, though somewhat limited in scope, was not commercial; teachers were generally not paid, nor did students race through examinations to pick up lucrative jobs. It was a voluntary partnership in pursuit of truth. Standards were too demanding and academic freedom so firm that even the strongest ruler could not tamper with universities. On the whole, the system of learning was exceedingly effective. Emphasis was on philosophy but science was also studied, and in all subjects an attitude of criticism and a spirit of inquiry and reason were encouraged. However, this tradition of learning declined during the long period of changing political patterns in India.

The mediaeval rulers remained indifferent to scientific and secular education, and whilst the Western countries were making rapid scientific progress, India allowed her intellectual heritage to go unused. The spirit of inquiry was replaced by a sacrosanct attitude towards authority, and an uncritical acceptance of opinions discouraged rational analysis.

The rise of Muslim power in India did not help matters much. Islam, which had stirred Indian intellectual and cultural life into a burst of activity, did not subscribe to the absolute supremacy of the human intellect; it was decisively restricted by the holy scriptures as interpreted by the Ulama. Islam had begun as an assertion of intellectual freedom, but the initial urgency for this freedom was soon lost. Once Islam's earlier democracy was replaced by authoritarianism, Muslim education also became subject to state authority, even in the most creative centres of Islamic civilization. It is no small wonder that Muslim education in India also became increasingly dogmatic, inward-looking, and stereotyped. There was, no doubt, a wide network of schools, but the system of education, consisting chiefly of the study of theology and scripture, was not conducive to the sustained growth of higher learning. Neither science nor technology was taught, although during the reign of Feroz Shah Tughlaq an unsuccessful attempt was made to introduce a simple form of technical education.

Indian education was in an especially neglected state on the eve of British supremacy in India. Whilst the Hindu system of learning was jealously guarded in Brahman caste interests, Muslim education, although open to all, was dominated by theologians and confined to the faithful study of the Quran. Both systems neglected literary and scientific education, critical analyses, and women's education.

The East India Company was reluctant to take responsibility for expensive programs, such as religion, public welfare, and education; although there were notable individual exceptions, for example, William Carey and Sir William Jones. Until compelled to act otherwise, the British Company's rule was like that of a mediaeval police state, anxious to extract revenue and keen to maintain internal and external security with no sense of obligation and responsibility for public welfare, health, and education. Under the Act of 1813 the Company was required to promote public education, and to make a ridiculously inadequate annual grant of one lakh of rupees for educational purposes.

Many Indians were already somewhat familiar with Western education through the activities of Christian missionaries. Danish missionaries had taken the lead in starting English education in India from the middle of the eighteenth century. Ram Mohan Roy even founded an English school, the Hindu College—now known as the Presidency College—at Calcutta in 1817. Starting with a hundred students, the College soon became the leading educational institution of Bengal. In other parts of the country, English schools and colleges had been established through private efforts.

Although Ram Mohan Roy wanted Western knowledge, he wanted to use education to promote the moral and rational development of the individual. He was as much distressed at the secularism of the Hindu College as at the orthodoxy of the pundits. Whilst Roy believed that the new learning "was indispensable for the progress of the nation," he never lost his admiration for the Hindu *Sastras* which he sought to study in the light of modern thought.

After years of agitation, in 1835 Macaulay's minute was written and Governor General Bentinck took a definite decision in favour of English. However, it was not until 1853, forty years after the Act of 1813, that East India Company officials seriously investigated Indian education, as a result of which the modern system of education in India emerged. The universities of Bombay, Calcutta, and Madras, modelled on the lines of London University, were founded in 1857. For a long time these universities continued to be staffed by Europeans and taught a Western curriculum. The British were not very generous with expenditures on education; at the turn of the century, after more than a century of rule, they provided little more than a million pounds a year for the education of about 240 million Indians—a penny a head.

Widespread progress of Western education, however, was made possible by the open-door policy introduced by the British, and by the vast sums donated by Indian philanthropists. Learning, hitherto mainly confined to Brahmans, rulers, or aristocrats, was now available to all those who cared for it, although the expense involved made it still the privilege of the well-to-do few. However, the multiplication of presses meant greater production and wider circulation of books and, in turn, education. (The art of printing had been introduced by Portuguese missionaries in the sixteenth century but it made progress only after the establishment of the British rule.)[13]

Western education was like an explosive force as it shattered dogma and superstition. The Indians were compelled to reflect upon the bases of their beliefs and institutions and to measure them against European standards. If this new thinking helped the modernization of India, it also gave rise to a class of Indian thinkers who shared Macaulay's contempt of Oriental learning and, like Macaulay, without bothering to study it.

Indians took to Western learning so wholeheartedly and uncritically that many of these newly educated men became comic imitators, without any enduring contact with either West or East. They were overawed by Western knowledge and in their eagerness to profit by it, missed its very essence—intellectual scepticism and scientific investigation. Without a critical understanding of Western learning, they made no effort to learn their own. Even competent Indian scholars acquired, at best, a high level of scholarly knowledge, but made no creative contributions to learning. With great expertise they either elaborated Western concepts or sought endorsement of their ideas in Western literature. Whilst Western learning opened up new vistas of knowledge for the Indians, in some ways it blunted the edge of their intellectual scepticism. Consequently, English-trained Indian scholars were generally inferior to European authorities. Their intellectual subservience had been so intense that even at present, despite political independence, Indians have yet to assert their intellectual freedom.

Some effects of English education were quite ugly, for it gave rise to a cultural minority with its own distinct features and interests. Although the English-educated Indians were a very small minority in the country (less than one per cent), they were numerous enough to constitute a class of their own. Patronized by the British Government, this class soon dominated the top levels of Indian life. It became a kind of middle class interposed between the masters and the masses, often acting as an insulator protecting the former against the latter. Whilst peasants, workers, and petty tradesmen did not speak English, those above them, from clerk to councillor, did. Spurred by the class-preservation instinct, the Westernized Indian was led to rather indiscriminately adopt Western forms in speech, dress, and manners; and to isolate himself from the "illiterate" and "uncouth" masses of his own people. At best, he was a laboriously cultivated English gentleman. At worst, he was clumsy if not ludicrous, and often crude, pretending to enjoy European food, music, and painting, at times even speaking his own native language with an English accent.

The snob value of English degrees was so great that those who had any kind of degree would take care to display it meticulously, and those who could not pass their examinations would be anxious to let it be known that they had reached the take-off point, even if they could not take off. As a result, there grew up not only a class of B.A.'s, but also a class of "B.A. failed" or "Intermediate passed."

The English-educated had a hierarchy of their own; the Brahmans of this class were those who returned from England, preferably with a degree—any degree—but without it if necessary. Those Indians who desired a Western education other than English flocked to Germany and other Western centres of learning. History does not offer a parallel to this phenomenon where efforts for learning produced such a pathetic class of self-complaisant and servile scholars. The nearest example, perhaps, may be that of the English themselves during the Norman period, when it was fashionable to be French in speech, appearance, and behaviour, and English was the language of the vulgarian.

Reaction against this kind of English education inevitably set in. A number of "national" institutions which imparted both Indian and Western learning, such as the Kashi Vidyalaya, the Jamia Milia, and the Gurukula, were established. In contrast, the Anglicized schools and colleges strongly emphasized English education—not even European learning—and students learned a good deal of England, its birds, countryside, and flowers, and of English literature and history. The national institutions did not, as expected, gain widespread support in the absence of government patronage. They were not assisted financially or otherwise by the state, nor were their degrees recognized. On the contrary, the British Government looked upon them with distrust as centres of "subversive" propaganda. Indeed, these institutions did seek to inculcate a sense of nationhood and Indian-ness and therefore attracted students with nationalistic inclinations. As their degrees did not originally entitle them to government or other positions, they did not draw a response from the practical-minded. Despite their limitations and small numbers, they have produced quite a number of competent and successful national leaders, such as Acharya Narendra Deva, a much respected Indian patriot-scholar, Lal Bahadur Sastri, who succeeded Jawaharlal Nehru as India's Prime Minister, and Zakir Hussain, who was the first Muslim president of India.

The influence of English literature on the literature of Indian languages was intensive. Poetry had been composed in India since the days of the *Rig Veda,* but prose began to be written for the first time after a break of more than a thousand years. Begun as polemics for and against religious and social reform, prose forms rapidly reached maturity. Novels, short stories, essays, and modern drama developed in Indian writing—the short story particularly in the twentieth century.

Shakespeare became an integral part of Indian studies, exercising an almost hypnotic influence on Indian literature and drama. Shakespeare was not known to Indians until the beginning of the nineteenth century, although he was writing his great tragedies around the time the East India Company was founded in 1600. Once, however, English education was begun and a knowledge of Western literature and thought became a status symbol and an essential prerequisite for professional and pecuniary gain, Shakespeare became familiar reading in Indian literary and dramatic circles. For most English-educated Indians, Shakespeare's characters, the situations in his plays, and significant quotations, became almost as intimate a part of their lives as those of their own best writers.

Most of Shakespeare's better plays have been translated into Indian languages. First to appear, in 1853, was a Bengali translation by Harachandra Ghosh called *Bhanumati Chittavilasa,* an adaptation of the Portia-Bassanio theme from *The Merchant of Venice.* Since then all of Shakespeare's comedies have been translated, with the exception of the "dark comedy," (in fact unclassifiable as a kind of drama) *Troilus and Cressida.* The Marathi version of the minor comedy, *The Taming of the Shrew,* rendered by V. B. Kelkar in 1891 has been "acclaimed to be such a perfect stage version that even if Shakespeare were a Hindu, he could not have improved on it." P. Sambanda Mudaliar's Tamil adaptations of Shakespeare are well known. The four best known tragedies have been translated with alterations to suit the Indian taste, which prefers a happy ending. For instance, Hamlet and Ophelia are reconciled at the end; Desdemona is not really dead; a daughter is provided for Macbeth in answer to the famous question, "How many children had Lady Macbeth?" to make it possible for her to be married to Malcolm at the end.

However, it is doubtful if Shakespeare will continue to attract Indian universities as before, and the modern scholar's image of Shakespeare— emphasizing the technical, social, source-hunting, and temporal aspects of his work—does not appeal much to Indians, who prefer to look at him from literary and human viewpoints, as did the romantic poet-critics during the last century.

The continual growth of secular and scientific knowledge affected the whole Indian attitude towards life. Indians were overpowered by the ideas of Western liberty, parliamentary government, and nationalism. Later, Marxism and socialism also permeated Indian thinking. Early Indian nationalists even drew their inspiration from European patriots. In the 1870's, Italian nationalist leaders, such as Mazzini and Garibaldi, were popular idols of Indian patriots. The Irish movement for self-rule was closely watched and admired by many Indian leaders, for whom the Irish patriots were models of devotion and sacrifice. De Valera was as much an Indian as an Irish hero, and Subhas Bose was often called the Indian De Valera.

Two major political ideologies have dominated Indian life for about a century—nationalism and Marxism. Indian nationalism has long assumed its own individual personality, and there is every likelihood that Indian communism may well become distinctly Indian before gaining any widespread adherence in India. Indian communists already look more to Gandhi and Nehru than to Marx and Lenin. Nationalism was, no doubt, primarily a reaction against British imperialism, which gave it the consciousness of a common political community, the urge to organize, and the power to attract widespread attention. It was further strengthened by territorial unification, a uniform educational system, the establishment of a communication network, and a highly centralized administration. But its ideological rationalization and form came from the influx of Western liberal ideas and a growing pride in its own cultural past.

How much Indian nationalism owes to the direct impact of European liberalism would be extremely difficult to ascertain. The force of liberal ideas certainly made British imperialism more humane and receptive to Indian demands, although the growing power of commercial interests in an era of industrial revolution invariably counselled authoritarianism. Democracy at home was to "co-exist with despotism abroad." The conflicting principles of liberty and empire were to be blended into a new and unique doctrine of "domination for the dominated."

Many of the prophets and leaders of Indian nationalism were, no doubt, greatly influenced by European liberal thought, but their main inspiration was India's cultural renaissance, which was almost contemporary with Western liberalism. Ram Mohan Roy implored the British to introduce colleges of Western, not Oriental, learning to India. He saw no contradictions between the freedom of liberalism and the intrinsic values of Hinduism. Roy was not a product of the West, and did not visit there until the end of his life. Even Jawaharlal Nehru, who adopted British habits and thought-processes "more than even the British themselves," regarded Indian cultural heritage as the driving force behind unity and progress. Bal Gangadhar Tilak, the "Father of Indian Unrest" and the first man to suggest to Indians the goal of "swaraj (freedom) is my birth-right," did not visit England until almost the end of his career. He was deeply inspired in his political philosophy by the *Bhagavad Gita*. However, it would not be correct to assume that Western ideas did not influence their thinking.

The common people, who formed the great bulk of the Indian national

303

movement, knew little of Western liberal ideas. The only impact they felt directly was Western imperialism. To them, Western concepts of rights and freedom were vague, hypothetical, and even hypocritical. They could see the value of these concepts only when they were presented in Indian terms. Thus, Aurobindo Ghose, a completely Westernized and English-educated intellectual, who renounced politics to retire to Pondicherry in the pursuit of Divine consciousness, spoke of nationalism as an *Avatar* (an incarnation of God), which must emancipate humanity from demonic oppression. Nationalism, being God, was immortal, and therefore no government could destroy it. Aurobindo Ghose, despite his too brief incursion into politics from 1905 to 1910, was able to introduce into the Indian nationalist movement an esoteric philosophy which proved to be of immense political value both at home and abroad. The divinity of "Mother India," long cherished as an abstract and ethical conception by many generations of Indian nationalists, became a political weapon of unquestionable efficacy in his hands. He preached that the sanctification of patriotism was the dedicated worship of India personified as the Great Mother. Much later, Mahatma Gandhi spoke along the same lines to "the teeming millions of India," who followed him. His concept of political freedom was translated into "Ramarajya," the kingdom of Rama, which was based on principles of universal morality, and in which justice, righteousness, and the will of the people were supreme.

It was this alliance between the imported concepts of liberty and unity, and the developing ideals of renascent Hinduism which gave Indian nationalism not only a distinctive character but also a worthwhile meaning and force. The concept of nationality, that is, the existence of a community within a defined territory, and patriotism were both known to Indians throughout their history. Ancient literature testifies to a well-defined image of Mother India and to a clear consciousness of national solidarity called Bharatavarsha, or just Bharat, a name now reinstated in the republican constitution of India. Deep sentiments of love and service for India were voiced in the vedic and epic literature. The *Manusmriti* contains passages of extreme patriotic fervour such as "Mother and Mother-country are greater than Heaven." The protective natural frontiers of India helped to weld all Indian peoples into an Indian oneness. The resuscitation of this image gave a definite meaning to Indian nationalism, and Indians responded with intense feeling.

Indian leaders visualized political and social development as going hand in hand, and considered social rejuvenation essential for political and economic progress. Consequently, Indian nationalism in its early phases was closely linked with cultural renaissance. Later, it became more virile and political in character. It was not only the pride of the old, but the vigour of the new which agitated for change (*inqilab*). Liberation from alien rule was not sufficient; the nationalist movement was to be the comprehensive crusade against all kinds of oppressions—including social and economic. In the final phase, the cry for change almost subordinated the demand for political independence (*swaraj* or *azadi*).

The fact that Mahatma Gandhi, who was typically representative of the Indian synthesis of contradictions which baffles logic, was able to gain leadership of the national movement with little resistance and held it almost unchallenged until his death, would further illustrate the syncretic nature of Indian nationalism. Mahatma Gandhi, however, made a distinction between Western and modern civilizations. Although both were equally good, he believed the latter had taken a wrong turn in the West. He, therefore, asked India to keep clear of that kind of modernized West. His position was somewhat similar to that of Tolstoy—a moral man in an immoral world, which had been brought about by a materialist, militarist, and imperialist way of life. He called upon his countrymen to select those elements from Western culture, as from any other, which were essential for their own progress. The spirit of the century was to be reconciled with that of the country.

In an era of intense nationalism, cultural pride, and racial prejudice, Rabindranath Tagore sought to broaden India's outlook to one of worldwide humanism. Truly a world-citizen, he consistently warned his countrymen against the evils of nationalism, and, like Gandhi, spoke of India's self-purification and constructive work. For him, the ideal of humanity transcended the love of country. Political freedom was not necessarily real freedom but might merely be a means of becoming more powerful. Real freedom was of the mind and the spirit, and this could not come to India from outside. Tagore was not against any one nation in particular but the idea of nationalism in general. He was, however, very proud of Indian culture, and called upon the West to understand its good qualities. Tagore's influence over the Indian mind has been incalculable; more than any of his contemporaries, he helped to harmonize the ideals of East and West, and to broaden the bases of Indian nationalism. He was one of the world's great internationalists, believing in and working for international co-operation, taking India's culture to other countries and bringing theirs to India.

Jawaharlal Nehru's greatest gift to renaissant India was to underline the intrinsic merits of Western culture. Although influenced by his

Indian heritage, Nehru was completely Western in his outlook. Scientific rationalism, humanism, and socialism had a profound influence on him, enabling him to fill a gap in Indian political life, a gap that could otherwise have proven very costly. Western individualism was essential in order to give the Indian a feeling of self-reliance. Contemptuously discarding traditional self-effacement, he preached and practiced self-assertion, even at the risk of appearing arrogant; competent arrogance was preferable to empty humility in a society ridden with multiple social and economic inequalities.

Nehru was the living symbol of what was best in the West. Most Indian intellectuals saw in Nehru the ideal expression of their Westernization, and a bridge between tradition and modernity. Even at a time when Nehru lay in a British prison, he recorded in his *Autobiography,* "in spite of my hostility to British imperialism and all imperialisms, I have loved much that was England. . . ." Yet, he spoke the Gandhian language of India: "Do away with evil, put your faith in goodness— in your goodness and the goodness of your opponent."

Influenced by the ethical norms of Western humanism, the precepts of the Upanishads, and the rationalism of the Buddha, Nehru had been attracted by Marxist theory, during the late 1920's. He was generally regarded as the patron of democratic socialism in India, although he was never a member of any socialist party. It was mainly through his efforts that Marxism, a completely Western product, was admitted to Indian political life, and it has since considerably influenced modern Indian thought, politics, literature, economic life, and social outlook. It was mainly Gandhi's moral influence and Nehru's admiration for Gandhian satyagraha that restrained Nehru from becoming a Marxist socialist. During his visit to Europe in 1926–1927, he came into contact with numerous Marxist intellectuals and leaders, especially at the Congress of the League of Oppressed Peoples at Brussels. Later, he went to Russia and was greatly impressed by the achievements of Socialist Russia. Since then he always advocated a socialistic society for India, based on democracy and individual liberty.

From the declaration of Indian independence until his death in 1964, Nehru dominated Indian life and politics blending modern values into Indian tradition with a skill that hardly has a parallel in history. Throughout his life, despite frequent criticisms of his policy of non-alignment, he remained a key man in world politics. A leader of an anti-imperialist revolution, he embodied the hopes of peace of men all over the globe. Others looked upon him as the architect of a unique democracy, struggling between divergent forces to acquire economic prosperity and social justice. The Indian revolution, although rooted in Gandhian ethics, could be described as "Nehruesque," for it is to Nehru that it owes its present form, reflecting his typical combination of Indian idealism and Western materialism.

Nehru was not a philosopher in the sense that Gandhi was, but without him much of Gandhism would have remained in disuse, somewhat in the same way as Marxism would have without Lenin. He commanded both the respect of the intelligentsia and the love of the common man. He was not only an exponent of the cherished ideals of his people but an expression of human conscience. Few statesmen could claim his empiricism without opportunism, and doctrinism without dogmatism. He could win the personal affection of his political adversaries without compromising either relationship. He believed that the "creative mind," with its social sensitiveness, could alone solve the crisis of the human spirit. It is this humanism which made him a representative of the West in the East and of the East in the West.

A major consequence of the West's impact on Indian tradition has been in psychological attitudes. Being a self-contained, rich, agricultural community, India was conservative, hospitable, tolerant, and somewhat fatalistic. But all this changed, first under prolonged foreign domination, and later under the pressure of the newly developing competitive society. India's natural contentment has given way to a spirit of rebellion and self-reliance which, under the excessive zeal of new converts, often inclines Indians to self-deprecation and lack of collective discipline. Highly individualistic, Indians have always resisted any regimentation of thought. Extrovert, nonconformist, and informal, they express themselves uninhibitedly, and indulge too often in reflection and introspection. Whilst these qualities gave India a distinctive character, and advanced her learning and democracy, they have often enough in the past, as in the present, reached a point where they hinder organization, team work, and discipline, the essential virtues of material transformation. It is curious, for the Indian does not lack in self-discipline, or even in self-denial. In fact, self-discipline to the Indian is not denial of one's liberty but an aid to individual spiritual perfection. However, any collective political discipline is regarded as an abridgement of individual liberty. Despite exemplary devotion and the spirit of self-sacrifice, conspiracies, mutinies, and underground revolutionary movements failed in India because of poor co-ordination and the inevitable leakage of information. Mass movements, such as Mahatma Gandhi's satyagraha, succeeded because they were open, and required essentially individual effort. Whilst crowds of people participated in satyagraha, in effect, each individual was a self-contained movement, and as an individual he could successfully protest against what he thought was unjust. Gandhi often did, alone.

Indians have yet to strike a balance between these two opposites and learn to blend individual liberty with social discipline in order to speed national advance. The value of compromise and discipline in a collective effort cannot be overestimated. No chapter of history is more instructive in this respect than that of Western activities in Asia. Western domination was, in fact, the triumph of organization and team work over personal valour and an unco-ordinated approach to politics. It is this Indian inability to integrate individual qualities into a collective pattern which, more than any other, finds its expression in a variety of meaningless disagreements, consuming national effort and morale. It seems sometimes that every Indian is a walking Lok Sabha as well as a moral preceptor. What India needs, and has often stood in need of, is not so much sound advice as sustained endeavour.

Reflection and criticism are, no doubt, indispensable for both the political and spiritual health of a nation, but they can be overdone. Democracy after all consists of both criticism and effort. In India, they sometimes part company. Excessive self-criticism soon leads to loss of self-confidence, and thoughtless and irresponsible expression creates an atmosphere of general frustration. Together they drain national energy. Today, India's most severe criticism comes from thinking Indians, especially from perfectionists and those whose expectations far exceed their competence. As perfection is unattainable, and undeserved expectations remain unfulfilled, frustration is inevitable, with the result that the very class of people who should be in the vanguard of an Indian revolution are its great liability. One often finds on the one side the educated Indians, extremely critical of everything and exuding gloom, and on the other the common people solemnly engaged in the tasks of national reconstruction. Irrespective of what awaits them—although it is prosperity they expect to find—and unmindful of the urgency of their job, the common men in India evidently find honest work for honest ends inspiring and satisfactory in itself.

The frustration of educated Indians is in no small measure conditioned by Western criticisms of Indian achievements, which are not always valid. Indians cannot shut themselves away from criticism, valid or invalid, for they respect their own right to criticize. Often Western critical analysis is more effective than it should be because it is couched in English, a language in which the Indians are at a disadvantage. Indians, however, are often reluctant to confess to this inadequacy for they still confuse knowledge of English with knowledge itself and unconsciously tend to measure the degree of a person's learnedness by his command of English.

But even well meaning critics of India, who would like to see India progress, quite often inadvertently measure India in Western terms and confuse a difference of values and emphasis with unsoundness of policy and practice. In any case, in their anxiety to achieve rapid results they have imposed a sense of urgency on the Indian experiment. Delay might explode India, they fear, and may even disrupt world order. Indisputably, the sooner Indian poverty is banished the better. But it would be imprudent to lose balance for speed. It is better to reach the goal late on one's own feet than to arrive soon on a stretcher.

India is not racing against either time, economic poverty, political rivalry, or alien criticism. She is fighting herself. If, during this period of development, she cannot keep up national morale, avoiding the frustrations inherent in partial successes or failures, and stand firmly optimistic against the unsolicited flood of gloomy prophecies, no amount of her past glory or professions of noble faith can lead her to the desired goal.

If the British brought out the best in Indian society, they also emphasized its hitherto dormant weakness. One such influence was on the social and political relationship between Hindus and Muslims, which finally destroyed the political unity of India. Before the advent of the British in India, Hindus and Muslims had lived side by side for about a thousand years in distinct social compartments, accommodating each other's religious beliefs. In political spheres, there were, as anywhere else, divisions within each community as dictated by the politics of power. Political relationship was not hinged to religious beliefs. Socially, Muslims were yet another caste in India. Just as the caste system separating Hindus from Hindus came under condemnation, so did the exclusion of Muslims from Hindu society. But Hindu-Muslim social assimilation was a very different problem because of their diverse faiths and traditions. Later, the development of modern politics, involving a relentless struggle between Indian nationalism and British imperialism, gave rise to Muslim nationalism. Whilst the ruling power remained alien, both Hindus and Muslims were equally deprived of authority, but once the prospects of democratic self-government began to emerge, the numerical superiority of Hindus caused a natural concern to Muslims.

Whether the British deliberately introduced the policy of "divide and rule" or not, they did little to maintain the separation of religion and politics, and still less to tone down the consciousness of communalism. They certainly did make positive efforts to accommodate the problems and to allay the fears of minorities. But their attitudes and statements, made either in genuine ignorance of the effect of their policy or in conscious effort to profit by it, overemphasized the problem, and even inflamed fears. Practically every Secretary of State and Viceroy kept notes for a stereotyped statement, which was repeated with necessary but minor variations on every public occasion, stressing the manifold divisions in Indian society. Referring to India's many languages, races, and creeds, it sought to mobilize all the interests opposed to Indian nationalism and unity. It paraded minority statistics, not always quite accurate, and invariably dwelt on the opposed religions and depressed classes. Sometimes this was done in a tone of fatalistic regret, sometimes with an air of polemical triumph, but always the stress was on the divisions of India. This was surely the wrong way to try to bridge such divisions. The reverse would have been more appropriate. The British might have emphasized the fundamental unity of the two religions and their common historical past.

It must, however, be pointed out that Western thought is, unlike Indian, permeated with the consciousness of religious differences and antagonisms, even amongst denominations of the same Christian faith. Religion was the keynote of British politics and education until the end of the nineteenth century. The British could have recalled that it was only in 1829, after a period of prolonged opposition, that the Catholic Emancipation Act was passed in Britain, even if they chose to ignore the terribly bitter Catholic-Protestant conflicts and other religious struggles. It was in 1836 that the Marriage Act of 1753, under which no one could be legally married except by a Church of England parson, and which was an intolerable insult to Catholics, was remedied. Religious bigotry was intense in education. Catholics could not enter the Universities of Oxford and Cambridge until 1871, after the working class of the towns had been enfranchised by the Reform Act of 1867, and long after the rise of liberalism and concepts of individual freedom.

The treatment of the Jews was no better; indeed, the Jews did not get full and equal citizenship rights until 1866. Charles Bradlaugh was not allowed to take his seat in Parliament because he was an atheist, and it took six years of painstaking struggle before he could enter the House and voice the views of his constituents. Indeed, religion in England was more than a matter of personal preference, and the Anglican Church was more than an ecclesiastical choice. Protestant ascendancy was an integral part of the British Constitution; the Coronation oath pledged the monarch to defend Protestantism by law and power, and the Act of Settlement ensured a Protestant succession.

Yet the British might have communicated to Muslims and Hindus the Western discovery made long ago, that creed was an irrelevance in modern politics, and emphasized the significance of economic and social issues. "If every day and in every way, each according to his temperament and opportunities, using the press and the wireless, schoolbooks and white papers, the officials and spokesmen of this mighty government had sought to minimise religious differences and promote an outlook of secular commonsense, and done this steadily for fifty years, is it certain that this feud would rage as it does today? They chose to make the other speech."[14]

The influx of Western culture was a gradual, persistent, and unpremeditated process, brought in by a motley crowd of Europeans ranging from unscrupulous adventurers to devoted intellectuals, missionaries, and administrators. As a class, these heralds of change, however, made no conscious effort to hasten the process. This part of Indian cultural transformation is a fascinating period of physical endurance, intellectual interaction, and social rejuvenation. Indian response to the West was ambivalent. It endeavoured, on the one side, to reassert India's great cultural past and, on the other, to purge its traditional character. Consequently, India sought to strike a delicate balance between the two.

As might be expected in any cultural encounter between two powerful civilizations, Western impact on India highlighted both the virtues and evils of Indian society and culture. Whilst the British industrial revolution inaugurated a new material era that transformed Indian economy, it also gave rise to poverty, overpopulation, and famine. Whilst it stirred the depths of the Indian mind, awakened its dormant spirit of scientific inquiry, and made new contributions to Indian life, it also compelled Indian society to defend its traditional inheritance, causing a cultural revivalism. In its totality it acted as a catalyst, setting in motion cultural processes which gradually led to an organized national consciousness and unity, and eventually to the modernization of traditional India.

Western influence on modern India, transmitted through English education, Christian missions and, mainly, British domination, has indeed been both extensive and varied. Although Christian missionaries initiated cultural exchange in India, it was not until the British colonial administration began to train Indian personnel for utilitarian ends and the Indians themselves felt the pressure for change, that India began to break away from tradition to enter modernity. Despite many commentaries on the subject, the process and all its implications are yet to be evaluated dispassionately. Perhaps its full magnitude can only be seen after it has stood the test of time. India today is both old and new, and this makes her at once distinctive and complex. That Indian modernization began under Western impact is not denied, but how much of it is her own renewed vitality is often a subject of intense, if not acrimonious, debate. The two views are not really contradictory or even incompatible; the differences mainly arise when too much is claimed on one side and too much discounted on the other.

Historians have achieved no consensus, nor are they expected to, on the nature and consequences of the British impact on India. British rule of India was a long process with several clearly marked phases. Inevitably, cultural processes during this period proceeded in various directions and at various levels. In some respects, the British influence was positive; in others, negative. Again, some influences were the outcome of a conscious policy, whilst others were unintentional and incidental. But in all respects it was a stimulant on a stagnant society, with reactions ranging from imitation and assimilitation to rejection.

The restoration of law and order, the unification of the country under one central authority, the emergence of the middle classes, the development of transport and communications, the revival of international consciousness, in themselves are praiseworthy contributions. But what is more important is that because of these it was possible for Indians to pursue other cultural and intellectual activities. It is not for what the British actually contributed that they should be judged, but for making it possible for Indians to rejuvenate the best of their culture and determine their own destiny. By making them conscious of both their weaknesses and of their strengths, the British gave the Indians objectives and methods to approach these objectives. Knowledge of Western thought and method, and especially Western experience, gave Indians hope for the success of their new ideals. Without the awareness of the modernization processes which the West itself had gone through, it is extremely unlikely that Indian society could have been stirred into action. Precept without precedent seldom appears attractive.

The spirit of modern India is something like the spirit of nature itself. It is ever new, constantly changing, yet old. Whilst they are actively engaged in the pursuit of scientific achievements, the Upanishads will continue to fascinate and inspire Indians, who will retain their search for the ultimate, without sacrificing material prosperity. Meanwhile, they will bear the weight of poverty with their characteristic quietness and happiness. Gandhi will always inspire them more than

312

Marx, and their means will be as important as their ends. Yet what India represents today is the emergence of a new civilization, not merely the continuation of an old one.

India was in need of modernization, and the West introduced it to her. Modernism, however, must not be confused, as is so often done, with materialism or even Westernism. There is nothing inherently Western about modernism because it does not emanate from space but time. The modern Indian man, for example, may be agnostic, atheist, religious, or mystical. He is quite capable of experimenting with dangerous microbes or exploring outer space in search of truth. His motivation may be the spiritual conviction that man must know the truth about all things, or the faith that human suffering will be reduced if not eliminated. A modern saint, like a Karma Yogi, is often seen with hospital instruments or laboratory test-tubes praying inarticulately to an impersonal God called science or humanity. Modernism may have begun in the West but it is a universal and common human heritage. Even if there had been no British rule in India, modernism would still have come, as it came, for instance, to Japan. In an era of increasing scientific and technological advancement, the cultural isolation of one region could scarcely be possible. Without the impediment of colonial rule, Indian response to the West might have been even more unrestrained. Even so, although her choice of Western learning was somewhat limited by British imperial needs, the initiative to select from what was offered was mainly her own. India elected to absorb voluntarily. She resisted Western domination, but not Western learning.

Notes

Notes to Chapter 1

1. It is from the name of this dynasty that the name of the country, Korea, is derived.

2. D. Bethune McCartee, a well-known American scholar, writes: "The art of spelling was invented neither by the Chinese nor by the Japanese. Its introduction into both these countries (and, as we are convinced, in Corea as well), was the result of the labours of . . . the early Buddhist missionaries. In all the three countries . . . the system of spelling is most undoubtedly of Sanskrit origin." Cited in W. E. Griffis, *Corea— The Hermit Nation*, p. 338.

3. In 607, a Japanese mission visited China, and a year later the Chinese sent a return mission. The Japanese Emperor addressed the Chinese Emperor Tang-ti of the Sui dynasty as "the Emperor of the East respectfully greets the Emperor of the west," but the Chinese Emperor returned "the Emperor greets the sovereign of Wa." Wa was the old name of Japan.

4. The ancient religion of Japan did not have a name, but after the introduction of Buddhism, it was called Shinto to distinguish it from other creeds.

5. Yamato is now a province in central Japan, but at the time it meant the whole of central Japan. Until Tokyo was made the capital of the country in 1869, the seat of government and the Imperial residence were always in that part of the country.

6. In Japan the reigning Queen in her own right is designated as "Emperor" to distinguish her from the Queen consort, who is addressed as "Empress."

7. The present temple is not really the original since it has been rebuilt many times on the original plan.

8. He died at Kongobuji, the leading monastery of the Shingon sect, but his followers believe he did not die but merely entered into *hyuji*, eternal *samadhi*. At a fixed time a properly qualified high priest comes and changes Kukai's gown in the inner sanctuary where he is believed to be staying in meditation.

9. D. C. Holtom, *Modern Japan and Shinto Nationalism*, p. 129.

10. H. Nakamura, *Japan and Indian Asia*, p. 8.

11. D. Suzuki in Chaman Lal (ed.), *India and Japan*, p. 11.

12. Nakamura, *Japan and Indian Asia*, p. 3.

13. The *Abhidharmakosa* of Vasubandhu and the *Vijnaptimatratasiddhi* of Dharmapala have become known to the West only through the French translations by L. de La Vallée Poussin, whereas in Japan numerous treatises have been composed upon them.

14. Even the bibliography appended to the *Immyo Zuigenki* (The Origin of Buddhist Logic) written by Hotan in the first half of the eighteenth century includes eighty-four Japanese works of logic.

15. The Sanskrit original of the poem runs as follows:

> Sarve Samskarah anityah
> Utpadavayadharminah
> Tesam vyupasamah sukham,
> Avadad mahasramanah.

The Sanskrit verse is based on the last words of the Buddha in the *Sutra,* and its English rendering would be:

> The flowers, however fragrantly blooming
> Are doomed to wither, and who in this world
> Can hope to be permanently living?
> The remotest mountain path of existence is crossed today.
> Awakening from a dream so evanescent,
> I am no more subject to intoxication.

One of the popular Japanese games played at New Year festivities is played with cards called *ihora karuta.* A pack consists of forty-eight cards —each with a short saying beginning with one of the forty-eight letters.

16. See Johannes Nobel, *Central Asia: The Connecting Link Between East and West,* Ch. V, for a brief account of this theme.

17. The print appears to have been made from a metal plate in the middle of the eighth century. The regular printing of Buddhist books from wooden blocks did not begin until later, during the early Kamakura period.

18. Sakira is an old name of Indra by which he is chiefly known in Japan.

19. Shinto mythology is founded on legendary stories that appear in two ancient collections: the *Nihongi* or *Nihonshoki* (Chronicles of Japan), and the *Kojiki* (Records of Ancient Things). The former, written in Chinese, was published in 720 by imperial order and is an official history. The latter, also written in Chinese characters but in a syntax which is purely Japanese, is a compilation of older stories put together in this collection between 704 and 714. Three other collections of stories and myths deserve mention: the *Kogoshui,* composed in about 807, the *Fudoki,* composed in the early eighth century, and the first ten books of the *Engishiki,* a ceremonial dating from 927. The last of these contains not only Shinto mythology, but more particularly Shinto religion. Before these collections were compiled, Shinto religion and mythology had already come under foreign influences, for example, Buddhism in Japan had been firmly established for a long time.

20. Gino K. Piovesana, *Recent Japanese Philosophical Thought,* p. 103.

21. Sir Charles Eliot, *Japanese Buddhism,* p. 191.

22. Coomaraswamy, however, does not subscribe to the the view that there

exists a very close connection between Horyuji and Ajanta, and believes that the sources of the Japanese work are to be sought in Khotan rather than in India. But it seems as though the Japanese must have depended in some degree directly upon Indian sources; it would be impossible otherwise to explain such remarkable iconographic parallels as the Jikoku Ten (Dhrtarastra) of the Kondo standing on a crouching demon, with the Kubera Yaksa of Bharut; and difficult to account for the great admixture Brahmanical, especially many-armed, forms so characteristic of the mixed Shinto-Buddhist pantheon. A. K. Coomaraswamy, *History of Indian and Indonesian Art*, pp. 154–55.

23. H. J. R. Murray, *A History of Board Games*, p. 36.

Notes to Chapter II

1. Ancient Americans are popularly referred to as Red Indians, and by archaeologists as Amerindians. Whilst these two designations have the advantage of common usage and currency on their side, they often produce confusion, particularly for students of comparative history and civilization. Ancient Americans are neither red nor Indians; they have lived in America, having originated from Asia, for a much longer period than Indo-Europeans have in Europe. Hence, it is perhaps more appropriate to call them Asiomericans rather than Amerindians. There seems little justification to perpetrate a mistake made by Columbus centuries ago.

2. Recently a Welsh writer, Mr. Richard Deacon, has claimed a Welshman, Madoc, son of Owain, King of Gwynedd, reached America three centuries before Columbus. An American scholar, Dr. Cyrus Gordon, believes that the Phoenicians discovered Brazil about two thousand years before Columbus reached the Bahamas. His conclusion is based on a new interpretation of an inscription found at Parahyba in 1872, and long regarded a forgery.

3. Bernal Diaz's is one of the two very personal accounts of what befell pre-Columbian civilization that have survived. He wrote the story of the conquest of Mexico late in life, less to vindicate or extol his own part in it than to correct the misrepresentations of others. The other account is about the Incas, written by Garcilaso de la Vega, son of a Spanish captain and the Princess Chimpu Occlo (first cousin of the last Inca monarch). He wrote down, also late in life, all he knew of the history and customs of his mother's peoples and of how their empire, the Tahuantinsuyu, collapsed. As he was of mixed descent and a devout Roman Catholic, he sought to reconcile Incas and Spaniards, and to contrast the horror and devastation caused by the Spaniards with the salvation they brought in the Christian religion.

4. Calder, *The Inheritors*, p. 151.

5. Honore, *In Quest of the White God*, p. 17.

6. For example, Hiram Bingham, Waldeck, Brasseru de Bourbourg, Le Plangeon, Alfred Maudslay, Ruz Lhullier, S. G. Morley, Edward Herbert Thompson, Tello, Zelia Nuttal, Manuel Gamio, Garcia Payon, and many

others. These names are mentioned without any consideration of priority of work or importance.

7. *The Conquest of Mexico* (1843) and *The Conquest of Peru* (1847).

8. According to Emerson, Humboldt was one of those wonders of the world, like Aristotle, who appear from time to time as if to show the possibilities of the human mind.

9. Von Humboldt, *Research Concerning the Institutions and Monuments of the Ancient Inhabitants of America*, I, Part XXX, 22.

10. John Lang published a second edition of his work in 1877, in which he claimed that two missionaries, John Williams and William Ellis, of the London Missionary Society had literally *stolen* his theory and had incorporated it into their respective publications, *A Narrative of Missionary Enterprises in the South Sea Islands* (London, 1837), and *Polynesian Researches* (London, 1831) without acknowledgment to him. See Lang, *Origin and Migration of the Polynesian Nation*, pp. 305–28.

11. Analyzing the development of societies, Gordon Childe remarks ". . . it is not in the least surprising that the development of societies observed in different parts of the Old World, to say nothing of the New, should exhibit divergence rather than parallelism. . . . But a comparison of the sequence summarised discloses not only divergence and differentation but also convergence and assimilation. To the latter phenomena it is hard to find an analogy in organic evolution." *Social Evolution*, p. 166.

12. R. Heine-Geldern and G. F. Ekholm in Sol Tax (ed.), *The Civilizations of Ancient America*, p. 301.

13. B. Rogers, "An Archaeological Pilgrimage to Santiago de Compostela," *Science*, Vol. 131, 1180.

14. Heine-Geldern and Ekholm in Sol Tax (ed.), *The Civilizations of Ancient America*, pp. 308–09.

15. Paul Kirchoff, "The Diffusion of a Great Religious System from India to Mexico." See *Sobretiro del XXXV Congress International de Americanistas*, p. 88.

16. *Ibid.*, p. 73.

17. D. A. Mackenzie, *Myths of Pre-Columbian America*, p. 58.

18. E. B. Tylor, "On Diffusion of Mythical Beliefs as Evidence in the History of Culture." See *Report of the British Association*, 1894, p. 774.

19. Scholars such as Laurette Sejourne, however, definitely accept his historical reality because his qualities of leadership are often mentioned. Laurette Sejourne, *Burning Water—Thought and Religion in Ancient Mexico*, p. 25.

20. Some scholars see in Quetzalcoatl a Christian missionary who had reached America by accident.

21. Miguel Leon-Portilla in S. N. Kraemer (ed.), *Mythologies of the Ancient World*, p. 449.

22. M. Leon-Portilla, *ibid.*, p. 468.

23. M. Leon-Portilla, *ibid.*, p. 468.

24. M. W. De Visser, *The Dragon in China and Japan*. p. 5. Visser goes on

to say that the Indian serpent-shaped Naga was identified in China with the four-legged Chinese dragon, because both were divine inhabitants of seas and rivers, and givers of rain. Whilst it is certain that the cult of Naga was one of the most popular cults in ancient India, it is a subject of scholarly debate as to whether it is of Aryan of pre-Aryan origin. There was a form of Naga-worship prevalent in the Indus Valley period, but others argue that the form of Naga-worship, as it is known, dates from the vedic period. They refer to "Ahi-Budhnya," the serpent of the deep, mentioned in the *Rig Veda,* who was an atmospheric deity, and who, in some texts, is mentioned as a divinity of middle or aerial region.

25. Some writers have described the Maya elephant as a badly drawn bird. This confusion appears to have been caused because the Mayan sculptor apparently had never seen an elephant and must have used a manuscript picture as his model, which, in its turn, may have been drawn from memory.

26. "It would be ridiculous to assert that such a strange doctrine was of spontaneous origin in different parts of the Old and New worlds." D. A. Mackenzie, *Myths of Pre-Columbian America,* p. 70.

27. Heine-Geldern and Ekholm in Sol Tax (ed.), *The Civilizations of Ancient America,* p. 307.

28. W. H. Prescott, *Conquest of Peru,* p. 118.

29. Miles Poindexter, *The Ayar-Incas,* Vol. 11, 211–15.

30. *Ibid.,* pp. 271–87.

31. The chromosome complement in *Gossypium* is basically $N=13$; all the wild species except one are diploid. The tetraploidal form has twice $(2N=26)$ the number of the original number of chromosomes.

32. Hutchison, Silow, and Stephens, *Evolution of Gossypium,* p. 98.

33. "The genetic and cytological data justify the assumption of closer homology between the New World cottons and their nearest diploid relatives, and a more recent origin for allopolyploidy, than the proponents of the land bridge theory supposed. Firstly, all the allopolyploid species bear lint, and the only other lint-bearing species are the Old World cottons, carrying the A genom. Since the differentiation of the A genom has been shown to be bound up with the improvement of lint by civilized man, A-bearing, linted allopolyploids can only have arisen since the origin of human civilization. Secondly, on cytological, morphological, and phenogenetic behaviour, *G. raimondii* is more closely related to the New World cottons than any other species carrying the D genom. This also indicates a recent origin for the New World cottons, since it suggests that the American diploid species were differentiated *inter se* before the occurrence of allopolyploidy. Such a recent origin rules out any theory of natural spread to account for the meeting of the diploid parents, solely on the inadequacy of the time available. Only one alternative remains, that they were carried across the Pacific by man among the seeds of his crop plants and with the tools of his civilization." Hutchinson *et al, Evolution of Gossypium,* p. 76.

34. Sir Joseph Hutchinson, see *Endeavour*, XXI, 14.

35. C. R. Stonor and Anderson, "Maize Among the Hill Peoples of Assam," *Annals of the Missouri Botanical Garden*, XXXVI (3), 356.

36. G. F. Carter, "Movement of People and Ideas across the Pacific" in J. Barrau (ed.), *Plants and the Migrations of Pacific Peoples*, p. 9.

37. Suggesting the most likely itinerary of early Buddhists sailing to America, Arnold and Frost say: "They followed the course of the current to America and would be thrown on the coast where it struck in it greatest force. The Pacific Counter Current turns off into two branches on nearing the coast at about 10 degrees north latitude, part going to the south and part north. If they took the southern branch they would come in contact with the Equatorial Current coming up from Peru, and inevitably be carried out to sea again. On the other hand, if they took the northern branch, they would be carried for some miles along the coast until about latitude 13 degrees, where the current runs in close, and there would be the most probable spot for them to land." Cited in R. Wauchope, *Lost Tribes and Sunken Continents*, p. 95.

38. *Journal of Royal Asiatic Society*, I, p. 2. Paper written by John Edye, and communicated by Sir John Malcolm.

39. Wauchope, *Lost Tribes and Sunken Continents*, p. 92.

40. Hawaiki and its dialectal equivalent is an ancient traditional term for a homeland throughout Polynesia, New Zealand, and Hawaii.

41. Recently, an Indian scholar, Chhabra, has noted certain resemblances between the symbols found in the petroglyphs from the Hawaiian Islands and those on the Harappan Seals. Some of the symbols in the petroglyphs are described as akin to early Brahmi script. B. Ch. Chhabra, "Vestiges of Indian Culture in Hawaii," *Vishveshvaranand Indological Journal*, I, part 11, 335–37.

42. D. A. Mackenzie, *Myths of Pre-Columbian America*, p. iv.

43. Heine-Geldern and Ekholm in Sol Tax (ed.), *The Civilizations of Ancient America*, p. 306.

Notes to Chapter III

1. The terms Further and Greater India are not of Indian, but of French or Dutch, coinage.

2. Cited in G. Coedès, *Journal of South East Asian History*, September, 1964, p. 1.

3. *Ibid.*, p. 4.

4. P. C. Bagchi, in K. A. Nilakanta Sastri (ed.), *A Comprehensive History of India*, II, 772.

5. B. P. Groslier, *Indo-China*, p. 47.

6. The author of the Periplus even mentions flourishing trade, including malabathron (cinnamon) from which the well-known Roman unguent

was extracted and which doubtless is a corruption of tne Sanskrit *tama-lapatra* (the dark leaf), between China and India through the unconscious mediation of the wild Sesatai people, who possibly lived in the north of Burma.

7. Paul Wheatley, *The Golden Khersonese*, pp. 185–86.

8. Arthur Waley, *The Way and Its Power*, p. 114, also see B. P. Groslier, *Indo-China*, p. 48.

9. The stupa as it is at present is an enlargement of the original Asokan one.

10. H. G. Quaritch Wales, *The Making of Greater India*, pp. 29–31.

11. Robert Heine-Geldern, cited in K. A. Nilakanta Sastri, *South Indian Influences in the Far East*, pp. 1–2.

12. *Ibid.*, p. 3.

13. This subject also raises the question of the existence of the many parallels between the ancient American civilizations on the one hand and those of East Asia and Southeast Asia on the other.

14. Groslier, *Indo-China*, p. 41.

15. G. Coedés, *Journal of South East Asian History*, pp. 1–26.

16. Groslier, *Indo-China*, p. 50.

17. There are historians who identify places all over the central uplands of Ceylon which are closely associated with the stories of Rama and Ravana. See M. D. Raghavan, *India in Ceylonese History, Society and Culture*, pp. 1–8.

18. On a full moon day in December the Buddhists of Ceylon commemorate the arrival of the tree. The sacred Bo-Tree, reputedly 2300 years old, is in a state of decline. The original branches are dying and it is feared that in the course of time will wither away. At present the entire tree and its branches are supported by long poles and it is chemically treated to keep it alive.

19. The earliest known alphabet in Ceylon is substantially Asokan Brahmi.

20. The beautiful Buddha statue of Anuradhapura, draped in the Amaravati style of thin clinging material without folds, moved Jawaharlal Nehru so greatly that he carried a picture of the image with him for many years. Cited in Raghavan, *India in Ceylonese History, Society and Culture*, p. 93.

21. *Ibid.*, pp. 108–09.

22. G. H. Luce in Burma Research Society, *50th Anniversary Publication*, No. 2, p. 307.

23. R. C. Majumdar (ed.), *History and Culture of the Indian People*, III, 648.

24. It is only in this century that the history of the Pagan Period, as well as the earlier history of Burma, has come to be systematically studied. The main credit for pioneering the study is due to G. H. Luce and Pe Maung Tin who edited the *Inscriptions of Burma*.

25. The theory that Nanchao was the home of the Thais, who had been driven out of their original homeland by the Mongols, was first put forward by Terrien de Lacouperie. A modern writer, Hsu Yun Tsiao, has questioned it. See *The Journal of South Seas Society*, IV (2).

26. Walter Liebenthal, while subscribing to the theory of Indian influence on Nanchao, is of the opinion that it reached Tali, Nanchao, in the second half of the eighth century via Kamarupa and Tibet routes, for he holds the view that the Burma road was not opened to traffic "until between 791 and 858." *Journal of the Greater India Society*, XV (1), 8.

27. Majumdar, *History and Culture of the Indian People*, III, 648.

28. R. C. Majumdar, *Hindu Colonies in the Far East*, p. 257.

29. Cited in R. Le May, *Buddhist Art in Siam*, p. 10.

30. Le May, *The Culture of South-East Asia*, p. 63.

31. There has been some controversy about the exact location of this state. According to the Kedah annals it was on the west coast. But the evidence favours the east. For a discussion of the point, see D. Devahuti, *India and Ancient Malaya*, pp. 22–31.

32. A modern writer on Buddhist art describes somewhat graphically the various waves of Buddhist influence protruding out of India in divergent directions but converging upon Indo-China: "If we consider the development of Buddhist art and culture in general, there is, on one hand, a movement from north-eastern and south-eastern India towards south and south-east Asia, which makes a slight turn to the north-east and so reaches the border-line we have mentioned; here in Indochina it encounters another branch coming from the north, by way of Burma. On the other hand, from the northern and north-western part of India there is a great migration right across Central Asia as far as China, where it divides: one line continues eastwards to Japan via Korea; another turns southwards until it reaches the Indian sphere of influence along the Annamese-Cambodian border. Thus the two jaws of a giant pincer movement meet in this area." See D. Seckel, *The Art of Buddhism*, p. 51.

33. Groslier, *Indo-China*, p. 41.

34. It has been suggested that the name Mekong has been derived from Ma-Ganga, Mother Ganges.

35. The Mison Stele inscription of King Prakasadharma dated 657, dealing with the foundation of Bhavapur, the capital of Kambuja.

36. Kaundinyas were a well-known class of Brahmans in South India during the first centuries A.D.

37. K. A. Nilakanta Sastri, *South Indian Influences in the Far East*, p. 48.

38. *Ibid.*, p. 36.

39. See *Journal of Indian History*, XLI (2), 415.

40. Groslier, *Indo-China*, p. 89.

41. Cited in Le May, *The Culture of South-East Asia*, p. 133.

42. Groslier, *Indo-China*, p. 170.

43. Devahuti, *India and Ancient Malaya*, p. 26.

44. Sir Richard Winstedt, *The Malays: A Cultural History*, p. 26.

45. Cited in Sastri, *South Indian Influences in the Far East*, p. 81.

46. This view, however, is disputed by Quaritch Wales, although Sastri seems to favour the interpretation of Evans.

47. Winstedt, *The Malays: A Cultural History*, p. 27.

48. Yavadvipa, to which Sugriva sent search parties looking for Sita, is a Sanskrit name mentioned in the *Ramayana*. Toward the end of the fifth century, Aryabhata, the Indian astronomer, wrote that when the sun rose in Ceylon it was midday in *Yavakoti* (Java) and midnight in the Roman land. In the *Surya Siddhanta* reference is also made to the *Nagari Yavakoti* with golden walls and gates.

49. Indonesians, mixed with Negroids, are found in Madagascar, where Mongoloid features are strongest in the interior of the island. It is therefore suggested that there was migration from Indonesia to Madagascar, probably in the first century. A recent writer has even suggested that in the early centuries of the Christian era Africa was the scene of Indonesian colonization on a fairly large scale, influencing her culture. This is illustrated by reference to Madagascar both in regard to vocabulary and musical and cultural practices. Certain African instruments and practices are compared with their Indonesian equivalents, including the drum-xylophone, clapperless bells, the *sese*, chorus-singing, *oriki* (Yoruba praise-songs), the *klama* songs of Ghana, and the vocabulary associated with the national *tshikona* flutes of the Venda in South Africa. It is the musical evidence which the author finds most convincing. See A. M. Jones, *Africa and Indonesia*.

50. R. C. Majumdar, *History and Culture of the Indian People*, II, 650.

51. It was during his reign, according to Lineham, who relied on the *Malay Annals*, that Singapura, modern Singapore, was founded. But Winstedt disputes it. See Sir Richard Winstedt, "A Note on the founding of Singapore," *Journal of South East Asian History*, September 1964.

52. Jules Leclercq, *L'île de Java*, p. 147, cited in B. R. Chatterjee, *India and Java*, p. 37. At a very popular shrine of the Buddha in Surabaya, East Java, where Indonesians come in large numbers to worship the image of the Buddha and to offer gifts—the popularity of this Buddha as a generous dispenser of boons is very high in the area—the caretaker when asked how he, as a Muslim, could make his living out of image-worship, simply replied that he was asked to do so by the Muslim priest.

53. Sastri, *South Indian Influences in the Far East*, p. 100.

54. F. A. Wagner, *Indonesia*, p. 126.

55. Heinrich Zimmer, *The Art of Indian Asia*, I, 300.

56. This example has been taken from the writing of a contemporary Indonesian historian who uses it as an illustration for the same purpose. R. M. Sutjipto Wirjosuparto, *A Short Cultural History of Indonesia*, p. 22–23.

57. Gregorio F. Zaide, *Philippine Political and Cultural History*, I, 36.

58. Alfred L. Kroeber, *Peoples of the Philippines*, p. 11.

59. The three figures include Lao-tzu from China and two others representing Anglo-Saxon law and justice, and Spain.

60. Sastri, *South Indian Influences in the Far East*, p. 144.

61. An eminent historian of the Philippines suggests ethnic affinity between Indians and Filipinos, because of which certain racial qualities of the Filipinos—their dignity of bearing, their stoical outlook on life, and their indifference to pain and misfortune—were inherited from the Hindus. Zaide, *Philippine Political and Cultural History*, I, 45.

Notes to Chapter IV

1. Edward C. Sachau, *Al Biruni's India*, pp. 22–23.
2. It is one of those strange coincidences of history that when the Indo-European world was in a state of decline, with flashes of intermittent brilliance, the rest of the world was well on the path of progress.
3. It is also suggested that the Rajputs, especially the Gurjaras, are the Huns or peoples who came in their wake.
4. Many Rajput rulers, however, cared a lot for social welfare. Some of them carried out great irrigation schemes, and most encouraged religion and learning.
5. There is evidence to suggest that there were larger and finer temples at centres such as Kanauj, Banaras, Prayag, and Ujjain. Khajuraho and the Orissan temples survived because they were not in the path of the Muslim conquerors, who destroyed almost all the ancient temples of northern India.
6. Syed Mahmud, *Hindu Muslim Cultural Accord*, p. 18.
7. *Ibid.*, p. 21.
8. *Ibid.*
9. The Christians in the area were also honourably named, but to distinguish them from the Muslims they were called *Nussarani Mappidas*.
10. Elliot and Dawson, I, 115–86.
11. Nominally though, the Mughals remained sovereigns of India until 1857 when the last ruler, Bahadur Shah II, was deported to Burma by the British. The East India Company ruled as an agent of the Mughal Emperor.
12. In South India, however, there arose the Vijaynagara Kingdom of which visiting foreigners, Persian, Italian and Portuguese, have left glowing accounts. It was constantly at war with the neighbouring Bahmani Kingdom and collapsed in the middle of the sixteenth century, under the attacks of a coalition of Deccan Sultans.
13. Today, at most, ten per cent of the Muslims of India and Pakistan are descended from foreigners. Even in these cases this means only that one of their many ancestors several centuries ago was a Turk or Arab or the like.
14. The date of Sankara is a matter of controversy: "According to Telang Samkara flourished about the middle or the end of the sixth century A.D. Sir R. G. Bhandarkar proposes A.D. 680 as the date of Samkara's birth, and is even inclined to go a few years earlier. Max Müller and Professor Macdonell hold that he was born in A.D. 788 and died in A.D. 820." S. Radhakrishnan, *Indian Philosophy*, II, 447.

15. Bhakti, however, began in South India (Tamilnad) long before Sankara. The earliest Tamil bhakti hymns are older than the Quran, and the cult reached Maharastra before Islam had made any impression there.

16. The accuracy of his dates is uncertain. In Arabic the word *Kabir* means great, and in the Quran it is one of the names of Allah.

17. Babur once visited Nanak and said: "In the face of this *faqir* God is coming into sight."

18. Recently W. H. McLeod has put forward the view that the religion of Guru Nanak, and so of Sikhism as a whole, is basically Hindu in origin, and that Muslim influence, although evident, is not of fundamental significance. Sikhism is firmly embedded in the Sant tradition of northern India, in the beliefs of the so-called *Nirguna Sampradaya*. See W. H. McLeod, *The Influence of Islam upon the Thought of Guru Nanak* (a paper read at a seminar held at Simla in September 1966).

19. There are about ten million Sikhs in India at present, who are reputed for their enterprise and valour. Their main scripture is called the *Granth Sahib* or the *Granth*. *Granth* is a Sanskrit word meaning a treatise or book. It contains about twenty thousand hymns and verses, which were mainly compiled by the fifth Guru of the Sikh religion, Arjun, who was the head of the order from 1581 to 1606, until his execution by the Mughal Emperor Jahangir.

20. Despite much greater efforts and vastly improved technological facilities, even English has not become the language of the masses in modern times.

20a. A modern writer however refuses the view that the various styles of North Indian music were invented by the musicians of the Muslim period. A. Danielou. *Northern Indian Music*, p. 39.

21. Some of the better known artists were Mir Saiyid Ali and Khwaja Abdus, Samad of Shiraz, Biswanath, Basawan, Farrukh Beg, Jamshid, Khusrau Quli, Miskin, Zal, Tara, Mahesh, Jahan, Haribans, Makhu, Kesu, Khemakaran, Ram Lal, and Mukund.

22. The same is equally true of the influence of Western dress on India in modern times. Whilst men have adapted the European suit to their style, Indian women have retained their traditional sari.

23. Such as the *sayyid, shaikh, pathan, malik, momin, mansoor, rayeen, qasale, raki, hajjam, dhobi, teli,* and *bhat* which divide Indian Muslims.

24. Murray T. Titus, *Islam in India and Pakistan*, p. 173.

25. R. C. Zaehner, *Hindu and Muslim Mysticism*, pp. 93–94.

26. "Thus the evidence for Vedantin influence on Abu Yazid is not merely the fact that his master was a man from Sind, but the inexplicability of many of his utterances except against a Vedantin background." *Ibid.,* p. 100.

27. Murray T. Titus, *Islam in India and Pakistan*, p. 156.

28. D. M. Lang, *The Wisdom of Balahvar*, pp. 24–29.

29. Sir Charles Eliot, *Hinduism and Buddhism*, III, 462.

Notes to Chapter V

1. W. Robertson, *An Historical Disquisition Concerning the Knowledge which the Ancients Had of Ancient India*, p. 173.
2. Sasetti, who was in India from 1578 to 1588. Cited in Robert Sewell, *A Forgotten Empire*, p. 211.
3. C. M. Cipolla, *Guns and Sails in Early Phase of European Expansion, 1400–1700.*
4. A. A. Macdonell, *India's Past*, pp. 237–38.
5. M. Winternitz, *A History of Indian Literature*, I, Part 1, 8.
6. "Gentoo" was derived from the Portuguese term "gentio" meaning heathen.
7. Forbes, *Oriental Memoirs*, II, 212.
8. Cited in A. J. Arberry, *Oriental Essays*, p. 83.
9. Jones made his translation from the "Bengali recension," which is regarded by scholars as less pure than the Devanagari recension. Boehtlingk was the first to edit the Devanagari recension of this play at Bonn in 1842. No other edition of the text of this recension was published until M. William's first edition in 1853. An edition of the same recension was published at Bombay in 1861, and one at Breslau in 1872 by Burkhard.
10. Prior to Jones' discovery of the linguistic affinity between the Indo-European languages, and independently of the English tradition in Indian studies, the French Orientalist, Joseph Deguignes, had published a paper in the *Memoires de l'Academie des Inscriptions et Belles Lettres* identifying the Sandrokottos of the Greeks with the Chandragupta of the Indians and thus producing the basis of Indian chronology and suggesting common linguistic origins.
11. G. T. Garratt (ed.), *The Legacy of India*, p. 31.
12. M. Müller, *Chips from a German Workshop*, IV, 379.
13. F. Egerton regarded *Meghaduta* as "a glorious love-poem, surely one of the most beautiful known to man." Britain, however, continued to produce Indologists, many of whom, such as G. A. Grierson, Sir Monier Williams, A. A. Macdonell, R. T. Griffiths, F. W. Thomas, Rapson, A. B. Keith, Sir Ralph L. Turner, Sir Harold W. Bailey, and T. Burrow, have made notable contributions.
14. Jean Filliozat in *Indian Studies Abroad*, p. 8.
15. Other texts were discovered by the missions of Sir Aurel Stein, Germany's Von Le Coq and Grundwedel, and Japan's Tachibana. A fragmentary Sanskrit text was accompanied by its Kuchean version.
16. For example, Hermann Oldenberg's *Das Mahabharata—seine Entstehung, seine Inhalt, seine Form (The Mahabharata—its Origin, Contents and Form)*, published in 1922. This work is the most comprehensive and striking of its kind.
17. Whilst Max Müller was engaged in bringing out his series of volumes of the *Rig Veda*, another German scholar, Theodor Aufrecht (1822–1907), Professor of Sanskrit at Edinburgh, published an edition of the complete text of the *Rig Veda* in Roman characters in 1861–1863.

18. *The Infinitive in Vedic, with the Verb System of Lithuanian and the Slav Languages,* published in 1871.

19. Arion Rosu, *Indo-Asian Culture,* January 1960, pp. 189–91.

20. For a fuller appraisal of Indological studies in the West, see V. Raghavan, *Sanskrit and Allied Indological Studies in Europe.* Also see *Indian Studies Abroad,* Bombay, 1964.

21. It was the occurrence of the word *Piyadassi* in the *Mahavamsa* that helped Prinsep and other scholars to identify King Piyadassi of the edicts with King Asoka.

Notes to Chapter VI

1. A. A. Macdonell, *A History of Sanskrit Literature,* p. 1.

2. M. Williams (ed.), *Sakuntala,* trans. E. B. Eastwick.

3. Marianne Von Herzfeld and C. Melvil Sym (trans.), *Letters from Goethe,* p. 514.

4. Alex Aronson, *Europe Looks at India,* p. 61.

5. *Ibid.,* p. 54.

6. Winternitz, *A History of Indian Literature,* I, 15.

7. There have been other German statesmen, such as Von Thielmann, Rosen, and Solf, who devoted their leisure to reading Indian literature.

8. Johanne Novel, *Central Asia: The Connecting Link Between East and West,* p. 95.

9. Alex Aronson, *Europe Looks at India,* p. 56.

10. An English rendering of this verse would be:
    At the Ganges the air is filled
    with scent and light
    And giant trees are flowering
    And beautiful, quiet people
    Kneel before lotus flowers.

11. Arthur Schopenhauer, *The World as Will and Idea,* trans. R. B. Haldane and J. Kemp, pp. xii–xiii.

12. Will Durant, *The Story of Philosophy,* p. 339.

13. Aronson, *Europe Looks at India,* p. 86.

14. G. M. Trevelyan, *English Social History,* p. 391. The other wealthy class of Britons from overseas at the time were the British owners of West Indian slave plantations, known as Creoles.

15. George D. Bearce, *op. cit.,* p. 23.

16. A. J. Arberry, *Oriental Essays,* p. 82.

16a. S. Foster Damon, *William Blake—His Philosophy and Symbols,* p. 365. "Tharmas, the western Zoa, represents the Body and the senses. His name was undoubtedly derived from Tamas (Tama, or Tamasee), the Hindu name for Desire. Blake had been reading the *Bhagvat-Geeta* (London, 1785), and had been so impressed by it that he made a water-colour drawing of *The Brahmins—Mr. Wilkin translating the Geeta* (No. 84 in Rossetti's list of Blake's paintings). In Lecture XIV of this book is a description of the three 'Goon': *'Satwa* truth, *Raja* passion, and *Tama* darkness; and each of them confineth the incorruptible spirit in the body' (p. 107). From other references to the Goon, it appears that they correspond almost precisely to the three lower Zoas: Satwa being Urizen, Raja being Luvah, and Tama being Tharmas. The fourth and highest Zoa, Urthona, is the 'incorruptible spirit' in the passage quoted above. Needless to say, Blake thought more highly of the Goon than the Brahmins: he desired a harmony of the four Zoas; they sought the subjection of three to Urthona." Considering however that Tharmas is close to Greek Thaumas, both verbally and in symbolic properties, Harper suggests that Blake possibly borrowed from both the Neoplatonic (through Taylor) and Indian (through Wilkins) sources. George Mills Harper, *The Neoplatonism of William Blake,* p. 181.

17. See the *Times Literary Supplement* (London), 9 April 1964, for a review of Désirée Hirst's *Hidden Riches.*

18. Carlyle who preached the gospel of stern manliness was, it is strongly suspected, in fact impotent.

19. L. G. Salinger in Boris Ford (ed.), *From Blake to Byron,* p. 193.

20. G. T. Garratt (ed.), *The Legacy of India,* pp. 33–34.

21. John Ruskin, *Lectures in Art,* p. 158.

22. N. Notovick, *The Unknown Life of Christ,* p. xxx.

23. G. Subga Rao, *Indian Words in English,* p. 100.

24. John Roach, "Liberalism and the Victorian Intelligentsia," *The Cambridge Historical Journal,* XIII, No. 1 (1957), 64.

25. Sergiu Demetrian, *Indo-Asian Culture,* July 1965, p. 186.

26. Tudor Vianu, *Indo-Asian Culture,* October 1957, p. 189.

27. Aronson, *Europe Looks at India,* p. 127.

28. *Journals of Ralph Waldo Emerson,* VI, 494.

29. *Ibid.,* IX, 197.

30. Robert Sencourt, *India in English Literature,* p. 224.

31. S. D. Kalelkar, "Thoreau and Mahatma Gandhi," *The Modern Review,* June 1963, p. 460.

32. Frank Macshane, "Walden and Yoga," *The New England Quarterly,* XXXVII, No. 3 (September 1964), 323.

33. Romain Rolland, *Life of Ramakrishna,* pp. 12–13.

34. S. D. Kalelkar, "Thoreau and Mahatma Gandhi," *Gandhi Marg,* January 1964, p. 57.

35. Amiya Chakravarty in *Gandhi Marg,* January 1964, p. 67.

36. Romain Rolland in Radhakrishnan (ed.), *Mahatma Gandhi: Essays and Reflections,* p. 197.

37. R. S. Raju in S. Radhakrishnan (ed.), *History of Philosophy: Eastern and Western,* I, 534.

38. A. Aronson, *Rabindranath Through Western Eyes*, p. xii. Tagore's works were so popular in Europe that the librarians would receive requests for his works from all sections of people, many of whom did not even know his nationality. A well-known London library was once requested in a letter, "Please send me a copy of the Jewish writer's book *Gitanjali;* his name is Tagore, I think." Another reader asked, "Have you got the Russian Tagore's latest volume." A third one asked for "a copy please of that Arab poet's new volume of songs." Reported in *Hindu*, 23–29 March 1914; reproduced in 30 March 1964 issue. Yet there was the American Customs official who seriously asked Rabindranath Tagore if he could read and write.

39. W. B. Yeats, *Autobiography*, pp. 91–92.

40. Rabindranath Tagore, *Gitanjali*, pp. xiii–xiv.

41. *Ibid.*, p. xvii.

42. Kenneth Walker, *Diagnosis of Man*, p. 248.

43. Despite his having gained the highest office in the Indian State and despite his many great services to the nation, he had never been a professional politician. It is a tribute to Indian respect for learning that they should have chosen a philosopher, rather than a politician, to this supreme office. The late President of India, Dr. Zakir Hussain, was also principally an academician.

44. Edward Conze, "Dr. Koestler and the Wisdom of the East," *The Hibbert Journal*, LIX (1961), 178–81. It is a review of Koestler's widely read book, *The Lotus and the Robot*.

45. Geoffrey Gorer, *Exploring English Character*, p. 259.

46. G. T. Garratt, *op. cit.*, p 394.

Notes to Chapter VII

1. A. J. P. Taylor, *The Eastern Tradition*, pp. 62–63.

2. John Plamenatz, *On Alien Rule and Self-Government*, p. 16.

3. G. T. Garratt (ed.), *The Legacy of India*, p. 394.

4. W. C. Smith, *Modern Islam in India*, p. 15.

5. I. H. Qureshi in W. Th. de Barry (ed.), *Sources of Indian Tradition*, p. 740.

6. Mohammad Habib in Hamayun Kabir (ed.), *Maulana Abul Kalam Azad*, p. 91.

7. Comparing the progress of Islamic learning in India and Pakistan of today, a Pakistani professor of Arabic at Karachi University commented: "India is far ahead in this respect. . . . The stark fact is that Arabic-Islamic learning is simply neglected in our country. . . . How unfortunate that in our schools and universities Islamic studies is not an academic study but an empty slogan . . . just part of the Islam-mongering rampant everywhere." S. M. Yusuf, "The World of Islam," *Pakistan Times*, 19 June 1964.

8. Whilst there were democracies of an early variety in India and each in itself was small in size, they were spread over a much wider area and survived for many centuries. Hindu India, in any case, knew "government by discussion" at all levels, right down to the family council.

9. Some of the more famous of the many outstanding works are: Mount Stuart Elphinston's *History of India;* Vincent Smith's *Oxford History of India, Asoka,* and *Akbar;* Sir George Grieson's *Linguistic Survey of India;* Colonel Tod's *Annals and Antiquities of Rajasthan;* Romesh Chandra Dutt's *The Economic History of India.*

10. Cited in Romesh Dutt, *The Economic History of India,* II, 194.

11. Francis Buchanan, *Journey From Madras.*

12. Christopher Dawson, *Making of Europe,* p. 6.

13. The Spanish lay-brother, Joannes Goansalvez, cast a set of Malayan Tamil characters in 1577. He had joined the Jesuit Society in 1555 and published several books before his death in 1579. The first book ever printed in India from his press was entitled, *The Rudiments of Catholic Faith.*

14. H. N. Brailsford, *Subject India,* p. 97.

Bibliography

Abnan, Soheil M. *Avicenna, His Life and Works*. London: 1958.

Abul-Fazl, Allami. *Ain-i-Akbari*. Edited by Henry Blochmann. Calcutta: 1873.

Acharya, Pasanna K. *Hindu Architecture in India and Abroad*. (Mānsāra Series, Vol. VI.) London: 1946.

Agrawala, Vasudeva S. *India As Known to Pānini*. Lucknow: 1953.

Ainalov, D. V. *The Hellenistic Origins of Byzantine Art*. New Brunswick: 1961.

Aiyangar, K. V. R. *Considerations on Some Aspects of Ancient Indian Polity*. Madras: 1935.

Akhilananda, Swami. *Hindu Psychology*. New York: 1947.

Akurgal, Ekrem. *The Art of the Hittites*. New York: 1962.

Al Attas, Syed Naguib. *Some Aspects of Sufism as Understood and Practiced Among the Malays*. Singapore: 1963.

Al Beruni's India. Translated by Edward C. Sachau. 2 vols. London: 1888.

Ali, Abdullah Yusub (tr.). *The Holy Quran*. 2 vols. New York: 1966.

Ali, Syed Ameer. *The Spirit of Islam*. London: 1965. First published London: 1891.

Alip, Eufronio M. *Political and Cultural History of the Philippines*. 2 vols. Manila: 1950–1952.

———. *Tagalog Literature*. Manila: 1930.

Allbutt, T. C. (ed.). *A System of Medicine*. London: 1896.

Allen, G. F. *The Buddha's Philosophy*. London: 1959.

Altekar, A. S. *State and Government in Ancient India*. Banaras: 1949.

Andrae, Tor. *Mohammed, The Man and His Faith*. London: 1936.

Anesaki, Masaharu. *Buddhist Art*. Boston: 1915.

———. *History of Japanese Religion*. Tokyo: 1963. First published London: 1930.

———. *Nichiren, The Buddhist Prophet*. Cambridge, Mass.: 1949.

Angus, S. *The Environment of Early Christianity*. London: 1931. First published 1914.

Anthropological Society of Washington. *Evolution and Anthropology*. Washington: 1959.

Anuruddha, R. P. *An Introduction into Lamaism*. Hosiarpur: 1959.

Arberry, A. J. *Aspects of Islamic Civilization*. London: 1964.

———. *Classical Persian Literature*. London: 1958.

331

—— (ed.). *The Legacy of Persia.* Oxford: 1953.

——. *Oriental Essays.* London: 1960.

——. *Revelation and Reason in Islam.* London: 1957.

——. *Sufism.* London: 1956.

Ardeshir, B., and P. Nanavutty (trs.). *Gathas.* London: 1952.

Armstrong, A. H. (ed.). *Plotinus.* London: 1953. (A volume of selections in a new English translation.)

—— (ed.). *The Cambridge History of Later Greek and Early Medieval Philosophy.* Cambridge: 1967.

Arnold, Channing, and Frederick J. Tabor Frost. *The American Egypt.* New York: 1909.

Arnold, Sir Thomas Walker. *The Caliphate.* Oxford: 1926.

—— and Alfred Guillaume (eds.). *The Legacy of Islam.* London: 1952. First published 1931.

Aronson, Alex. *Europe Looks at India.* Bombay: 1946.

——. *Rabindranath Through Western Eyes.* Allahabad: 1943.

Arrian, F. *History of Alexander; and Indica.* Translated by E. I. Robson. 2 vols. London: 1893.

Ashraf, K. M. *Life and Conditions of the People of Hindustan.* Delhi: 1959. First published 1935.

Aston, W. G. *Shinto: The Way of the Gods.* London: 1905.

Atiya, Aziz S. *Crusade, Commerce and Culture.* Bloomington, Ind.: 1962.

Atiyah, Edward. *The Arabs.* London: 1958. First published 1955.

Auboyer, Jeannine. *Daily Life in Ancient India.* London: 1961.

Badian, E. *Studies in Greek and Roman History.* Oxford: 1964.

Bagchi, Prabodha Chandra. *India and Central Asia.* Calcutta: 1955.

——. *India and China.* 2nd ed.; New York: 1951. First published Calcutta: 1927.

Bailey, Cyril (ed.). *The Legacy of Rome.* Oxford: 1951. First published 1923.

Bailey, H. W. *Indo-Scythian Studies.* Vol. IV. Cambridge: 1961–1963.

Ballantyne, J. R. *A Synopsis of Science from the Standpoint of the Nyaya Philosophy.* Vol. I. Mirzapore: 1852.

Bancroft, Hubert Howe. *The Native Races of the Pacific States of North America.* 5 vols. London: 1875–1876.

Banerjea, Jitendra Nath. *The Development of Hindu Iconography.* 2nd ed.; Calcutta: 1956. First published 1941.

Banerjee, G. N. *Hellenism in Ancient India.* 3rd ed.; Delhi: 1961.

Bapat, P. V. (ed.). *2500 Years of Buddhism.* Dehli: 1956.

Barber, C. L. *The Story of Language.* London: 1964.

Barker, Sir Ernest. *The Politics of Aristotle.* Oxford: 1948.

——, Sir George Clark, and P. Vaucher (eds.). *The European Inheritance.* Vols. I, II, and III. Oxford: 1954.

Barnes, E. W. *The Rise of Christianity*. London: 1948.

Barnett, L. D. *Alphabetic Guide to Sinhalese Folklore from Ballad Sources*. Bombay: 1917.

———— (tr.). *Sañtideva*. London: 1947.

Barrau, J. *Plants and the Migrations of Pacific Peoples: A Symposium*. Honolulu: 1961.

Barrere, Albert, and Charles G. Leland (eds.). *A Dictionary of Slang, Jargon and Cant*. London: 1889.

Barthold, V. V. *Four Studies on the History of Central Asia*. Translated from the Russian by V. Minorsky and T. Minorsky. Leiden: 1956–1962.

————. *Le decouverte de L'Aise; histoire de l'orientalisme en Europe et en Russie*. Paris: 1947.

Barua, Benimadhab. *A History of Pre-Buddhist Philosophy*. Calcutta: 1921.

Basham, A. L. *The Wonder That Was India*. London: 1954.

Baynes, Cary F. (tr.). *The I Ching or Book of Changes*. 2 vols. New York: 1950. (The Richard Wilhelm translations rendered into English.)

Baynes, Norman H. *Byzantine Studies and other Essays*. London: 1955.

Beal, Samuel. *Buddhism in China*. London: 1884.

———— (tr.). *Si-Yu-ki: Buddhist Records of the Western World*. 2 vols. London: 1884. (From the Chinese of Hiven Tsiang, A.D. 629.)

————. *Travels of Hiven Tsiang*. Vols. I–IV. Calcutta: 1911.

Beaufort, Duke of, and Alfred E. T. Watson (eds.). *The Badminton Library of Sports and Pastime*. (Volume on Dancing by Lilly Grove). London: 1895.

Bell, Sir Charles. *The Religion of Tibet*. London: 1931.

Bell, Richard. *Introduction to the Quran*. Edinburgh: 1953.

Benfey, T. *Geschichte der Sprachwissenschaft*. Munich: 1869.

————. *Pantschatantra: Fünf Bücher Indischer Fablen, Märchen und Erzählungen*. 2 vols. Leipzig: 1859.

Benitez, Conrado. *The Old Philippine Industrial Development*. Manila: 1916.

Bernal, Ignacio. *Mexico Before Cortez: Art, History and Legend*. New York: 1963.

Bernal, J. D. *Science in History*. London: 1954.

Bernier, Francois. *Travels in the Mogol Empire: A.D. 1656–1668*. Translated by A. Constable. London: 1891.

Berque, Jacques. *The Arabs, Their History and Future*. Translated by Jean Stewart. London: 1964.

Bevan, E. R. *A History of Egypt Under the Ptolemaic Dynasty*. London: 1927.

————. *Later Greek Religion*. London: 1927.

————. *Stoics and Sceptics*. Oxford: 1913.

———— and C. Singer (eds.). *The Legacy of Israel*. Oxford: 1927.

Beveridge, A. S. (tr.). *Tue Babar-nama*. London: 1921.

Beyer, H. O., and Jaime C. de Veyra. *Philippine Saga*. Manila: 1952.

Bhargava, K. D. *A Survey of Islamic Culture and Institutions*. Allahabad: 1961.

Bhatia, Balmokand. *Famines in India*. Bombay: 1963.

Bhatt, V. V. *Aspects of Economic Change and Policy in India 1800–1960*. New Delhi: 1963.

Bhattacharya, Benoytosh Vinayanosha. *The Indian Buddhist Iconography*. 2nd ed.; Calcutta: 1956. First published London: 1924.

Bhattachayya, H. (ed.). *Cultural Heritage of India*. Vols. I–IV. 2nd ed.; Calcutta: 1953–1958.

Bible. (Conpateruiz Version). New York: 1957.

Bible. (King James Version). Garden City: 1940.

Bible. (Old Testament). Philadelphia: 1955.

Bible. (Revised Standard Version containing Old and New Testaments). New York: 1952.

Bingham, H. *Lost City of the Incas*. London: 1951.

Birnbaum, Henrik, and Jaan Puhvel. *Ancient Indo-European Dialects*. California: 1965.

Black, G. F. *A Gypsy Bibliography*. Edinburgh: 1909.

Bloch, Jules. *Les Tsiganes*. Paris: 1953.

Block, Martin (tr.). *Gypsies*. London: 1938. (The English translation of *Zigeuner: ihr Leben und ihre Seele*. Leipzig: 1936.)

Blofeld, J. E. C. *The Jewel in the Lotus: An Outline of Present-day Buddhism in China*. London: 1948.

Bloomfield, M. *The Religion of the Veda, the Ancient Religion of India*. London: 1908.

Boas, Franz. *Mind of Primitive Man*. New York: 1911. Rev. ed. 1938.

Bode, M. H. *The Pali Literature of Burma*. London: 1959.

Bohtlingt, Otto von, and R. Roth. *Sanskrit-German Dictionary*. 7 vols. St. Petersburg: 1852–1875.

Bopp, Franz. *A Comparative Grammar of the Sanskrit, Zend, Greek, Latin, Lithuanian, Gothic, German and Slavonic Languages*. 3 vols. London: 1845–1850.

———. *Glossarium Sañscritum*. Berolini: 1830.

Borrow, G. *The Bible in Spain*. 3 vols. London: 1843.

———. *The Gypsies of Spain*. London: 1907. First published in two volumes in 1841.

———. *Lavengro*. 3 vols. London: 1851.

———. *Ramano Lavo-Lil*. London: 1919. First published 1874.

———. *The Romany Rye*. 2 vols. London: 1857.

———. *The Zincali*. 2 vols. London: 1841.

Bosanquet, Bernard. *Science and Philosophy*. London: 1927.

Bosch, F. D. K. *Selected Studies in Indonesian Archaeology*. Translated by S. Lewis. The Hague: 1961.

Boss, Medard. *A Psychiatrist Discovers India.* Translated by Henry A. Frey. London: 1965.

Bouquet, A. C. *The Christian Faith and Non-Christian Religions.* Welwyn: 1958.

Bowers, Faubion. *Japanese Theatre.* New York: 1952.

Bowle, John. *A New Outline of World History.* London: 1962.

———. *Western Political Thought.* London: 1961. First published 1947.

Bowra, C. M. *The Greek Experience.* London: 1957.

Boxer, C. R. *The Christian Century in Japan 1549–1650.* Berkeley, Los Angeles, and London: 1951.

Boyer, A. M., E. J. Rapson, and E. Senart (trs. and eds.). *Kharoshthi Inscriptions Discovered by Sir Aurel Stein.* Oxford: 1920–1927.

Braddell, Roland. *Study of Ancient Times in the Malay Peninsula. J. R. A. S.* (M. B.) Vols. XIV, XV, XVII.

Brennan, Louis A. *No Stone Unturned.* New York: 1959.

Briggs, L. P. *The Ancient Khmer Empire.* Philadelphia: 1951.

Brinkley, Captain F., and Baron Kikuchi. *A History of the Japanese People.* New York and London: 1912, 1914, 1915.

Brinkley, Frank. *Japan—Its History, Arts and Literature.* 8 vols. Boston and Tokyo: 1901–1902.

Brion, Marcel. *The World of Archaeology: Central Asia, Africa and the Near East.* Translated by Neil Mann. London: 1962.

———. *The World of Archaeology: India, China and America.* Translated by Miriam and Lionel Kochan. London and New York: 1961.

British Broadcasting Corporation (compiled by). *The Western Tradition.* London: 1949.

Brown, Irving. *Deep Song.* New York and London: 1929.

Brown, L. W. *The Indian Christians of St. Thomas.* Cambridge: 1956.

Brown, Percy. *Indian Architecture.* Bombay: 1962.

———. *Indian Painting Under the Mughals.* Oxford: 1924.

Brown, T. Burton. *Excavations in Azarbaijan 1948.* London: 1951.

Brown, W. Norman (ed.). *India, Pakistan, Ceylon.* New York: 1950.

——— (ed. and tr.). *The Saundarya lahari* (by Sankaracarya). Cambridge, Mass.: 1958.

Browne, Edward G. A. *A Literary History of Persia.* 4 vols. Cambridge: 1928.

Bruce, Joseph Percy. *Chu Hsi and His Masters.* London: 1923.

Brunton, Paul. *The Hidden Teaching Beyond Yoga.* London: 1962. First published 1941.

———. *Indian Philosophy and Modern Culture.* London: 1937.

Buck, Peter H. *Vikings of the Pacific.* Chicago: 1959.

Bühler, G. *Encylopaedia of Indo-Aryan Research.* Strasbourg: 1896.

———. *Indian Palaeography.* (An appendix to the Indian Antiquary, Vol. XXXIII.) Bombay: 1904.

Bultmann, Rudolf. *Primitive Christianity.* London and New York: 1956.

Burckhardt, Jacob. *History of Greek Culture*. Translated by Palmer Hilty. London: 1964.

Burke, Edmund. *Works*. 16 vols. London: 1803–1827.

Burke, Marie Louise. *Swami Vivekananda in America: New Discoveries*. Calcutta: 1958.

Burland, C. A. *Art and Life in Ancient Mexico*. Oxford: 1948.

Burlingame, E. W. (tr.). *Buddhist Parables*. New Haven: 1922.

Burma. Fiftieth Anniversary Publications. Vol. II. Rangoon: 1960.

Burrows, Millar. *More Light on the Dead Sea Scrolls*. London: 1958.

Burton, Sir Richard. *The Book of Thousand Nights and a Night*. 12 vols. London: 1897. First published Banares: 1885.

——— and F. F. Arbuthnot (trs.). *The Kama-sutra of Vatsyayana*. London: 1963.

Bushnell, G. H. D. *Peru*. London: 1956.

Butler, A. J. *The Arab Conquest of Egypt*. Oxford: 1902.

Cajori, Florian. *A History of Mathematics*. New York and London: 1894. 2nd ed.; New York: 1919.

Calder, Ritchie. *The Inheritors*. London: 1961.

———. *Medicine and Man*. London: 1958.

The Cambridge Ancient History. Vols. I–XII. London: 1923–1939.

Cannon, Garland, H. *Oriental Jones*. New Delhi and New York: 1964.

Carmichael, Joel. *The Death of Jesus*. London: 1963.

Carpenter, Frederic I. *Emerson and Asia*. Cambridge: 1930.

Carpentier, J. E. *Theism in Medieval India*. Lectures delivered in Essex Hall, London, October–December 1919. London: 1921.

Carter, G. F. "Disharmony between Asiatic Flower-Birds and American Bird-Flowers." *Amer. Antiquity*, XX, No. 2 (1954), 176–177.

———. "Plant Evidence for Early Contacts with America." *Southwest. J. Anthrop.*, VI (1950), 161–182.

———. "Plants across the Pacific." *Amer. Antiquity* (Mem.), XVIII, No. 3, Pt. 2 (1953), 62–71.

Carter, Thomas Francis. *The Invention of Printing in China and its Spread Westwards*. Revised by L. Carrington Goodrich. New York: 1955. First published 1925.

Cary, M. *A History of the Greek World from 323 to 146 B.C.* 2nd ed.; London: 1951. First published 1932.

——— and T. J. Harrhoff. *Life and Thought in the Greek and Roman World*. London: 1957.

Cazamian, Louis Francois. *A History of French Literature*. Oxford: 1955.

Chai, Ch'u, and Chai Winberg. *The Changing Society of China*. New York: 1962.

Chakravarti, Chandra. *An Interpretation of Ancient Hindu Medicine*. Calcutta: 1923.

Chakravarti, Chintaharan. *Tantras: Studies on their Religion and Literature.* Calcutta: 1963.

Chan, Wing Tsit. *Religious Trends in Modern China.* Columbia: 1953.

Chand, Tara. *History of the Freedom Movement in India.* Vol. I. Delhi: 1961.

———. *Influence of Islam on Indian Culture.* Allahabad: 1936.

Chang, Chia-Sen (Dr. Carsun). *China and Gandhian India.* Calcutta: 1956.

———. *The Development of Neo-Confucian Thought.* London: 1958.

Charlesworth, M. P. *Trade-Routes and Commerce of the Roman Empire.* Cambridge: 1924.

Chaterjee, Ashkok Kumar. *The Yogacara Idealism.* Varanasi: 1962.

Chatterjee, B. R. *India and Java.* 2nd ed. revised and enlarged (parts 1 and 2); Calcutta: 1933.

———. *Indian Cultural Influence in Cambodia.* Calcutta: 1928.

Chatterji, A. C. *India's Struggle for Freedom.* Calcutta: 1947.

Chattopadhyaya, Debiprasad. *Lokayata.* New Delhi: 1959.

Chaudhari, Haridas, and Frederick Spiegelberg (eds.). *The Integral Philosophy of Sri Aurobindo.* London: 1960.

Chen, Kenneth K. S. *Buddhism in China.* Princeton: 1964.

Chen, Shou-Yi. *Chinese Literature.* New York: 1961.

Chhabra, B. Chi. *Expansion of Indo-Aryan Culture.* Delhi: 1965.

Chiang-Kunag, Chou. *Mahayana Buddhism in China.* Allahabad: 1960.

Childe, V. Gordon. *The Aryans—A Study of Indo-European Origins.* London: 1926.

———. *The Dawn of European Civilization.* London: 1961. First published 1925.

———. *New Light on the Most Ancient East.* 4th ed.; London: 1952. First published 1934.

———. *Social Evolution.* London: 1951.

———. *What Happened in History.* London: 1954.

Choksi, K. M. *Dentistry in Ancient India.* Bombay: 1953.

Chhabra, B. Chi. *Expansion of Indo-Aryan Culture.* Delhi: 1965.

Chou Hsiang-Kuang. *The History of Chinese Culture.* Allahabad: 1958.

Christy, Arthur C. *The Orient in American Transendentalism.* New York: 1932.

Cipolla, Carol M. *Guns and Sails in the Early Phase of European Expansion, 1400–1700.* London: 1964.

Clebert, Jean Paul. *The Gypsies.* Translated by Charles Duff. London: 1963.

Clements, E. *Introduction to the Study of Indian Music.* London: 1913.

Coe, Michael D. *Mexico.* London: 1962.

Coedés, G. *Les Peuples de la Peninsule Indochinoise.* Dunod, Paris: 1962.

———. *The Making of South East Asia.* California: 1966.

——— and E. de Boccard. *Les États Hindoisés d'Indochine et d'Indonèsie.* Paris: 1948.

Cole, Sonia Mary. *Races of Man.* London: 1963.

Colebrooke, H. T. *Algebra, with Arithmetic and Mensuration from the Sanskrit of Brahmagupta and Bhascara.* 2nd ed.; Calcutta: 1927.

———. *Essays on the Religion and Philosophy of the Hindus.* London: 1927.

Colum, Padraic. *Orpheus. Myths of the World.* New York: 1930.

Congress Commemoration Volume. *To the Gates of Liberty.* Calcutta: 1948.

Conze, Edward. *Buddhism: Its Essence and Development.* Oxford: 1951.

——— (selected and tr.). *Buddhist Scriptures.* London: 1959.

———. *Buddhist Texts Through the Ages.* Oxford: 1955.

———. *Buddhist Thought in India.* London: 1962.

Cook, Arthur B. *Zeus—A Study in Ancient Religion.* 3 vols. Cambridge: 1914–1940.

Cook, O. F. "The Origin and Distribution of the Cocoa Palm." *Contr. U.S. National Herbarium* (Washington), VII, No. 2 (1901), 257–293.

Coomaraswamy, A. K. *The Arts and Crafts of India and Ceylon.* New York: 1964.

———. *Buddha and the Gospel of Buddhism.* Bombay: 1956. First published 1916.

———. *Ceylon Bronzes Chiefly in the Colombo Museum.* Colombo: 1914.

———. *The Dance of Shiva.* New York: 1959. First published in revised form, 1947.

———. *Hinduism and Buddhism.* New York: 1943.

———. *History of Indian and Indonesian Art.* London: 1927. New York: 1965.

———. *Medieval Sinhalese Art.* New York: 1956. First published 1908.

———. *The Origins of the Buddha Image.* New York: 1927.

———. *The Transformation of Nature in Art.* New York: 1934, 1956.

——— and Sister Nivedita (Margaret E. Noble). *The Myths of the Hindus and Buddhists.* London: 1916.

Coulborn, Rushton. *The Origin of Civilized Societies.* Oxford and Princeton: 1959.

Couling, S. *The Encyclopedia Sinica.* London: 1917.

Cowell, E. B. *The Buddha-Charita of Aśvaghosha.* London: 1893.

——— (ed.). *The Jataka.* Vols. I–VI. London: 1957. First published 1895–1913.

Cowley, A. E. *The Hittites.* London: 1920.

Cox, G. W. *Introduction to the Science of Comparative Mythology and Folklore.* London: 1881.

———. *Mythology of the Aryan Nations.* 2 vols. London: 1870.

Cox, M. E. R. *Cinderella.* London: 1893.

Craveri, Marcello. *The Life of Jesus.* Translated from Italian by Charles L. Harkmann. New York: 1967.

Crawfurd, John. *History of Indian Archipelago.* 3 vols. Edinburgh: 1820.

Creel, H. G. *Chinese Thought*. Chicago: 1953.

———. *Confucius, The Man and the Myth*. New York: 1949.

Cresson, Andre. *The Essence of Ancient Philosophy*. Translated by Veronica Hull. New York: 1963.

Croce, Benedetto. *History of Europe in the Nineteenth Century*. Translated by Henry Furst. London: 1965. First published 1934.

Crombie, A. C. (ed.). *Scientific Change*. London: 1963.

Crombie, I. M. *An Examination of Plato's Doctrines*. London: 1962–1963.

Crooke, W. *The Popular Religion and Folklore of Northern India*. 2 vols. London: 1896.

Culin, R. Stewart. *Chess and Playing Cards*. Washington: 1898.

———. *Games of the North American Indians*. Washington: 1907.

———. *Games of the Orient*. Rutland, Vt.: 1958. (First published under title *Korean Games*.)

Cumont, Franz Valery Marie. *The Oriental Religions in Roman Paganism*. New York: 1956. First published 1911.

Cunningham, A. *Ancient Geography of India*. Calcutta: 1924.

Cunningham, J. D. *A History of the Sikhs*. Oxford: 1918.

Dabbs, Jack A. *History of the Discovery and Exploration of Chinese Turkestan*. The Hague: 1963.

Dahlquist, Allan. *Megasthenes and Indian Religion*. Stockholm: 1962.

Dani, A. H. *Prehistory and Protohistory of Eastern India*. Calcutta: 1960.

Daniel, Norman. *Islam and the West*. Edinburgh: 1960.

Danielou, Alain. *Introduction to the Study of Musical Scales*. London: 1943.

———. *Northern Indian Music*. Vols. I and II. London and Calcutta: 1949.

———. *Yoga: The Method of Re-integration*. New York: 1956.

Danvers, F. C. *The Portuguese in India*. 2 vols. London: 1894.

Das, M. N. *The Political Philosophy of Jawaharlal Nehru*. New York and London: 1961.

Dasgupta, R. P. *A Study of Hindu and European Political Systems*. Calcutta: 1958.

Dasgupta, S. B. *An Introduction to Tantric Buddhism*. Calcutta: 1950.

Dasgupta, S. N. (ed.). *A History of Sanskrit Literature*. Vol. I. Calcutta: 1962.

Dasgupta, Surama. *Development of Moral Philosophy in India*. Calcutta: 1961.

———. *Indian Idealism*. Cambridge: 1933.

Dasgupta, Surendranath. *A History of Indian Philosophy*. Vols. I–V. Cambridge: 1952–1957. First published 1922.

Datta, B. Vibhuti. *The Science of the Sulba, A Study in Early Hindu Geometry*. Calcutta: 1932.

Datta, K. K. *Dawn of Renascent India*. Nagpur: 1950.

Davar, Firoz C. *Iran and India Through the Ages*. Bombay and New York: 1963.

Davids, T. W. Rhys. *History and Literature of Buddhism*. 4th ed.; Calcutta: 1952. First published London: 1918.

———— (tr.). *The Questions of King Milinda*. 2 parts. New York: 1963.

Davidson, J. Leroy. *The Lotus Sutra in Chinese Art*. New Haven: 1954.

Davies, A. P. *The First Christian*. New York: 1957.

————. *The Meaning of the Dead Sea Scrolls*. New York: 1960.

Davis, Simon. *Race-Relations in Ancient Egypt*. London: 1951.

Dawson, Christopher Henry. *The Making of Europe*. London: 1946.

Dawson, Raymond (ed.). *The Legacy of China*. Oxford: 1964 .

Dayal, Har. *The Bodhisattva Doctrine in Buddhist Sanskrit Literature*. London: 1932.

De Bary, Wm. Theodore. *Sources of Indian Tradition*. New York: 1958.

————. *Sources of the Japanese Tradition*. New York: 1958.

———— *et al.* (eds.). *Sources of Chinese Tradition*. New York: 1960.

De Burgh, W. G. *The Legacy of the Ancient World*. Vols. I and II. London: 1953. First published 1924.

Defréniery, C., B. R. Sanguinetti, and H. A. R. Gibb (eds. and trs.). *Travels of Ibn Battuta*. Cambridge: 1958.

De Gokuldas. *Democracy in Early Buddhist Samgha*. Calcutta: 1955.

————. *Significance and Importance of Jatakas*. Calcutta: 1951.

De Meester, Marie E. *Oriental Influences in the English Literature of the Nineteenth Century*. Heidelberg: 1915.

Deraniyagala, P. E. P. "Human and Animal Motif in Sinhalese Art." *J.R.A.S. (C.B.)*, IV, Pt. 1.

Desai, A. R. *Recent Trends in Indian Nationalism*. Bombay: 1960.

————. *Social Background of Indian Nationalism*. Bombay: 1948.

Deussen, Paul. *Outline of Indian Philosophy*. Berlin: 1907.

————. *Outline of the Vedanta System of Philosophy*. Berlin: 1907.

————. *The Philsophy of the Upanishads*. Edinburgh: 1906.

Devandra, D. T. *Classical Sinhalese Sculpture*. London: 1958.

Devahuti, D. *India and Ancient Malaya*. Singapore: 1965.

————. *Harsha. A Political Study*. Oxford: in Press.

De Visser, M. W. *Ancient Buddhism in Japan*. 2 vols. Leiden: 1925–1935.

Dey, N. L. *Geographical Dictionary of Ancient and Medieval India*. London: 1927.

Dhalla, Maneckji Nusservanji. *Zoroastrian Civilization*. New York: 1922.

Diaz, Bernal. *The Conquest of New Spain*. Translated by J. M. Bohen. London: 1963. First published in Spanish 1632.

Dictionary of National Biography. Edited by Leslie Stephen. London: 1885.

Dixon, Roland B. *The Mythology of all Races: Oceania*. Edited by Louis Herbert Gray. Boston: 1916. (Vol. IX of the thirteen-volume series on world mythology.)

Dobie, M. R. *Ancient Persia and Iranian Civilization*. London: 1927.

Doblhofer, Ernst. *Voices in Stone*. Translated by Mervyn Savill. London: 1961.

Dodd, C. H. *The Parables of the Kingdom*. London: 1956. First published 1935.

Dodds, E. R. *The Greeks and the Irrational*. Berkeley: 1951, 1956.

Dowson, John. *A Classical Dictionary of Hindu Mythology and Religion, Geography, History, and Literature*. London: 1879.

Dreyer, J. L. E. *A History of Astronomy from Thales to Kepler*. Cambridge: 1953.

Driver, Harold E. *Indians of North America*. Chicago: 1961.

Duchesne, Guillemin J. *The Western Response to Zoroaster*. Oxford: 1958.

Duff, Charles (St. Lawrence). *A Mysterious People*. London: 1965.

Dumoulin, Heinrich. *The Development of Chinese Zen*. New York: 1953.

Durant, Will. *The Story of Civilization*. 6 vols. New York: 1942.

———. *The Age of Faith*. New York: 1950.

———. *Caesar and Christ*. New York: 1944.

———. *The Life of Greece*. New York: 1939.

———. *Our Oriental Heritage*. New York: 1942.

———. *The Reformation*. New York: 1957.

———. *The Renaissance*. New York: 1953.

Dutt, Nalinaksha. *Early Monastic Buddhism*. 2 vols. Calcutta: 1941.

Dutt, Romesh Chunder. *The Early Hindu Civilization*. London: 1888. Calcutta: 1908.

———. *The Economic History of India*. 2 vols. London: 1902.

Dutt, R. Palme. *India Today*. London: 1940.

Dutt, Sukumar. *Buddhist Monks and Monasteries of India*. London: 1962.

Eberhard, Wolfram (tr.). *Chinese Fairy Tales and Folk Tales*. London: 1937.

———. *History of China*. 3rd ed.; London: 1955.

Eckardt, A. *A History of Korean Art*. London: 1929.

Edgerton, Franklin. *The Bhagavad Gita*. Cambridge, Mass.: 1966.

——— (ed. and tr.). *The Panchatantra*. London: 1965.

———. *Panchatantra Reconstructed*. 2 vols. New Haven: 1924.

Edmunds, A. J., and M. Anesaki. *The Buddhist and Christian Gospels*. 4th ed.; Philadelphia: 1935.

Edwards, C. R. "Sailing Rafts of Sechura-History and Problems of Origin." *Southwest. J. Anthrop.*, XVI (1960), 368–391.

Edwards, E. D. *Chinese Prose Literature of the Tang Period*. 2 vols. London: 1937–1938.

Ehrenberg, Victor. *The Greek State*. Oxford: 1960.

Ekholm, Gordon F. "A Possible Focus of Asiatic Influence in the Late Classic Cultures of Meso America." *Amer. Antiquity*, XVIII, No. 3, Pt. 2 (1953), 72–89.

———. "A Possible Focus of Asiatic Influence in the Late Classic Culture of Mexico." *Mem. Soc. Amer. Arch.*, 9, 1953.

Eliade, Mircea. *Yoga: Immortality and Freedom.* Princeton: 1958.

Eliot, Sir Charles N. E. *Japanese Buddhism.* London: 1935, 1959.

———. *Hinduism and Buddhism.* 3 vols. London: 1954.

Ellis, William. *Polynesian Researches.* 4 vols. 2nd ed.; London: 1832–1834.

El Mansouri, S. M. *Art Culture of India and Egypt.* Calcutta: 1959.

Elsee, C. *Neoplatonism in Relation to Christianity.* Cambridge: 1908.

Encyclopaedia Britannica. Chicago: 1964.

Encyclopaedia of Islam. Leiden and London: 1960. First published 1911–1938.

Encyclopaedia of Religion and Ethics, 1908–1926. 13 vols. Edinburgh.

Enslin, M. *Christian Beginnings.* New York: 1956. First published 1938.

Epstein, I. (ed. and tr.). *The Babylonian Talmud.* 5 vols. London: 1935–1952.

Ernst, Earle. *The Kabuki Theatre.* Oxford: 1956.

Evans-Wentz, W. Y. *The Tibetan Book of the Dead.* London: 1927.

———. *The Tibetan Book of the Great Liberation.* London: 1954. (With psychological commentary by C. G. Jung.)

———. *Tibetan Yoga and Secret Doctrines.* London: 1935.

———. *Tibet's Great Yogi Milarepa.* London: 1951.

Fabri, Charles Louis. *An Introduction to Indian Architecture.* London and Bombay: 1963.

Fairbank, John K. (ed.). *Chinese Thought and Institutions.* 2nd ed.; Chicago: 1959.

Fairbank, J. K., E. O. Reischauer, and A. M. Craig. *A History of East Asian Civilization.* 2 vols. London: 1960.

Faris, Nabih Amin (ed.). *The Arab Heritage.* Princeton: 1944.

Farnell, Lewis Richard. *Greek Hero Cults Ideas of Immortality.* Oxford: 1921.

Farquhar, J. N. *Modern Religious Movements in India.* London: 1915.

———. *An Outline of the Religious Literature of India.* London: 1920.

Faruqi, Ziya-ul-Hasan. *The Deobund School and the Demand for Pakistan.* London and Bombay: 1963.

Figgis, John Neville. *The Divine Rights of Kings.* New York: 1965. (Introduction by G. R. Elton.) First published 1896.

Filliozat, Jean. *The Classical Doctrine of Indian Medicine.* Delhi: 1966. First published in French in 1949.

———. *India.* Translated from French by Margaret Ledesert. London: 1962.

———. *Political History of India.* Translated from French by Philip Spratt. Calcutta: 1957.

Finkelstein, Louis. *The Jews: Their History, Culture and Religion.* 2 vols. New York: 1955.

Fisher, C. A. *South East Asia.* London: 1964.

Fiske, John. *Myths and Myth-makers*. Boston: 1873.

Fleet, J. F. (ed.). *Corpus Inscriptionum Indicarum, Gupta Inscriptions*. Vol. III. Calcutta: 1888.

Forbes, Charles. *Oriental Essays*. London: 1813.

Ford, Boris (ed.). *From Blake to Byron*. London: 1957.

Forke, A. *The World Conception of the Chinese*. London: 1925.

Fosberg, F. Raymond. "The American Element in the Flora of Hawaii." *Pacific Science*, V (1951), 204–206.

Fox-Strangways, A. H. *The Music of Hindostan*. Oxford: 1914.

Fradier, Georges. *East and West*. Paris: 1959.

Framjee, Firoze. *English Text Book on Theory and Practice of Indian Music*. Pona: 1938.

Francisco, Juan R. *Indian Influences in the Philippines*. Quezon City: 1964.

Frank, Tenney. *Aspects of Social Behavior in Ancient Rome*. Cambridge, Mass.: 1932.

Frazer, Sir James George. *The Golden Bough*. 12 vols. London: 1911–1927.

Friedrich, R. *The Civilization and Culture of Bali*. Edited by E. R. Rost. Calcutta: 1959. First published 1887.

Furtado, R. de L. *Three Painters: Amrita Sher-Gil, George Keyt and M. F. Hussain*. New Delhi: 1960.

Gallenkamp, Charles. *Maya*. New York: 1959.

Gamio, Manuel. *Cultural Evolution in Guatemala and its Geographic and Historic Handicaps*. Translated from the Spanish by Arthur Stanley Riggs. Washington: 1926.

Gandhi, M. K. *Autobiography*. Washington: 1948.

Gangoly, O. C. *Landscape in Indian Literature and Art*. Lucknow: 1964.

Garbe, Richard (ed.). *The Samkhya-pravacana-bhasya*. Cambridge, Mass.: 1895.

Gard, Richard A. *Buddhist Influences on the Political Thought and Institutions of India and Japan*. Claremont, Calif.: 1949.

Gardiner, Patrick. *Schopenhauer*. London: 1963.

Garratt, G. T. (ed.). *The Legacy of India*. Oxford: 1937.

Garrison, F. H. *An Introduction to the History of Medicine*. Philadelphia: 1961. First published 1913.

Garstang, John. *The Hittite Empire*. London: 1929.

Gaudefroy-Demombynes, Maurice. *Muslim Institutions*. London: 1950.

Geertz, Clifford (ed.). *Old Societies and New States*. New York: 1963.

Geiger, W. *The Mahavamsa*. Vols. I and II. London: 1912.

Getty, Alice. *The Gods of Northern Buddhism*. Tokyo: 1962. First published Oxford: 1914.

Gheerbrant, Alain. *The Incas*. New York: 1961.

———— (ed.). *The Incas: The Royal Commentaries of the Inca, Garcilaso de la Vega, 1539–1616*. Translated by Maria Jolas. London: 1963.

Ghirshman, Roman. *Iran: Parthians and Sassanians*. Translated by Stuart Gilbert and James Emmons. London: 1962.

Ghosh, Manomohan. *A History of Cambodia*. Saigon: 1960.

Ghosh, P. C. *The Development of the Indian National Congress 1892–1909*. Calcutta: 1960.

Ghoshal, U. N. *A History of Indian Political Ideas*. Bombay: 1959.

Gibb, H. A. R. *Arabic Literature, an Introduction*. London: 1926.

————. *Mohammedanism: An Historical Survey*. New York: 1955.

————. *Studies on the Civilization of Islam*. London: 1962.

———— and Harold Bowen. *Islamic Society and the West*. 2 vols. London: 1950, 1957.

Gibbon, E. *The Decline and Fall of the Roman Empire*. Edited by J. B. Bury. Vols. I–VII. London: 1909–1914. First published 1776–1788.

————. *The Decline and Fall of the Roman Empire*. London: 1960. (An abridgement by D. M. Low.)

Giles, H. A. *Confucianism and Its Rivals*. London: 1915.

———— (ed.). *Gems of Chinese Literature*. New York: 1965. First published 1923 in two volumes.

————. *A History of Chinese Literature*. New York: 1958. First published 1901.

————. *Religions of Ancient China*. London: 1918.

Giles, L. (tr.). *The Book of Mencius*. London: 1942.

———— (tr.). *Lao Tzu*. London: 1926.

———— (tr.). *Tao Tē Ching*. London: 1954.

Gilkes, A. N. *The Impact of the Dead Sea Scrolls*. London: 1962.

Gladwin, H. S. *Men out of Asia*. New York: 1947.

Glanville, S. R. K. (ed.). *The Legacy of Egypt*. Oxford: 1953.

Glassenapp, Helmuth von. *Kant and the Religions of the East*. Germany: 1954.

Gokhale, B. G. *Asoka Maurya*. New York: 1966.

————. *Buddhism and Asoka*. Baroda: 1948.

Goldenveizer, Aleksandr. *History, Psychology and Culture*. New York: 1933.

Goldin, Judah (tr.). *The Living Talmud*. New York: 1957.

Goldstucker, Theodore. *Sanskrit and Culture*. Calcutta: 1955.

Goldziher, I. *The Influence of Buddhism Upon Islam*. English translation by T. Duka in the *Journal of Royal Asiatic Society*, January 1904, pp. 125–141.

Gomperz, Theodor. *Greek Thinkers*. Vols. I–II translated by Laurie Magnus; Vol. IV, by G. G. Berry. London: 1901–1912.

Gonda, J. *Sanskrit in Indonesia*. Nagpur: 1952.

Gordon, Antoinette, K. *The Iconography of Tibetan Lamaism*. New York: 1939. 2nd rev. ed.; Tokyo: 1959.

Gorer, Geoffrey. *Exploring English Character*. London: 1955.

Gosvami, O. *The Story of Indian Music*. Bombay: 1957.

Govinda (Lama) Angārika B. *The Psychological Attitude of Early Buddhist Philosophy*. London: 1961.

Granet, Marcel. *Chinese Civilization*. 3rd printing; New York: 1960. First published London: 1930.

Grant, Michael. *Myths of the Greeks and Romans*. London: 1962.

Grant, R. M. (ed.). *Gnosticism: An Anthology*. London: 1961.

———. *Gnosticism and Early Christianity*. New York: 1959.

Grattan, C. Hartley. *The South West Pacific to 1900*. Ann Arbor, Mich.: 1963.

Gray, Basil. *Buddhist Cave Paintings at Tun-Huang*. Chicago: 1959.

Gray, Denis. *Spencer Perceval*. Manchester: 1963.

Gregg, Richard B. *The Power of Non-Violence*. Philadelphia: 1934.

Grellmann, Heinrich. *Dissertation on the Gipsies*. London: 1787.

Griffis, William Elliot. *Corea: The Hermit Nation*. 6th ed.; New York: 1897. First published London: 1882.

Griffiths, Sir Percival Joseph. *The British Impact on India*. London: 1952.

Grimal, Pierre. *The Civilization of Rome*. Translated by W. S. Maguinness. London: 1963.

Grimm, Jacob L. C., and Wilhelm C. Grimm. *German Folk Tales*. Translated by V. P. Magoun Jr. and A. H. Krappe. Carbondale, Ill.: 1960.

Griswold, A. B. *Burma, Korea, Tibet*. London: 1964.

Groenveldt, W. P. *Historical Notes on Indonesia and Malaya*. Djakarta: 1960. (Compiled from Chinese Sources). The reprint of an article published in 1880.

Groome, F. H. *Gypsy Folk Tales*. London: 1889.

———. *In Gypsy Tents*. Edinburgh: 1880.

Groslier, Bernard Philippe. *Indochina*. Translated by George Lawrence. London: 1962.

Grote, George. *Plato and the Other Companions of Sokrates*. 3 vols. London: 1875.

Grousset, René. *Chinese Art and Culture*. Translated from the French by Haakon Chevalier. London: 1959.

———. *The Civilization of India*. Translated from the French by Catherine Alison Phillip. Delhi: 1964.

———. *In the Footsteps of the Buddha*. London: 1932.

———. *Introduction to the Study of Hindu Doctrines*. London: 1945.

———. *The Rise and Splendour of the Chinese Empire*. Translated from the French by A. Watson Gandy. California: 1953.

Grunebaum, G. E. Von. *Islam*. 2nd ed.; London: 1961. First published 1955.

———. *Medieval Islam: A Study in Cultural Orientation*. Chicago: 1953.

———. *Modern Islam: The Search for Cultural Identity*. Berkeley: 1962.

——— (ed.). *Unity and Variety in Muslim Civilization*. Chicago: 1955.

Gubernatis, Angelo de. *Zoological Mythology*. London: 1872.

Gulabkunyerba Ayurvedic Soc., Shree. *The Caraka Sammita.* 6 vols. Jamnagar: 1949.

Gulik, Sidney Lewis. *The East and the West.* Rutland, Vt.: 1963.

Gurjar, L. V. *Ancient Indian Mathematics and Veda.* Poona: 1947.

Guthrie, W. K. C. *The Greek Philosophers from Thales to Aristotle.* London: 1956.

————. *A History of Greek Philosophy.* Vol. I. Cambridge: 1962.

————. *Orpheus and Greek Religion.* 2nd ed.; London: 1952.

Guy, Basil. *The French Image of China Before and After Voltaire.* Geneva: 1963.

Hackin, J. *et al. Asiatic Mythology.* London: 1963. First published 1932.

Haeckel, Ernst H. P. A. *Monism: As Connecting Religion and Science.* Translated by J. Gilchrist. London: 1894.

Hagen, Victor Wolfgang Von. *The Ancient Sun Kingdoms.* Cleveland: 1961.

————. *The Desert Kingdoms of Peru.* London: 1965.

Hall, D. G. E. (ed.). *Historians of South East Asia.* London: 1961.

————. *A History of South-East Asia.* London: 1955.

Hamilton, Angus, *Korea.* 2nd ed.; London: 1904.

Hamilton, Clarence M. *Buddhism, A Religion of Infinite Compassion.* New York: 1952.

Hanayama, Shinsho. *A History of Japanese Buddhism.* Tokyo: 1960.

Hans, H. *Bibliographie Zur Frage nach den Wechselbeziehung Zurschen Buddhismus und Christianismus.* Leipzig: 1922.

Happold, F. C. *Mysticism.* Hammondsworth: 1963.

Harden, Donald. *The Phoenicians.* London: 1962.

Hardie, J. Keir. *India.* London: 1909.

Harper, G. M. *The Neoplatonism of William Blake.* Chapel Hill: 1961.

Hartland, E. S. *Science of Fairy Tales.* London: 1889.

Harvey, G. E. *History of Burma.* London: 1925.

Haskins, Charles Homes. *Studies in the History of Mediaeval Science.* New York: 1960. First published 1924.

Hatt, Gudmund. "Asiatic Influences in America Folklore." *Det. Kgl. Danske Videnskabernes Selskab, Historisk-Filoogiske meddelelser,* XXXI, No. 6 (1949), 1–122.

————. "The Corn Mother in America and in Indonesia." *Anthropos.,* XLVI (1951), 853–914.

————. "Early Intrusion of Agriculture in the North Atlantic Subarctic Region." *Univ. Alaska Anthrop. Pap.,* II, No. 1 (1953), 51–107.

Havell, E. B. *The Art Heritage of India.* London: 1964.

————. *The History of Aryan Rule in India.* London: 1918.

Hazrat, Bikrama Jit. *Dara Shikuh: Life and Works.* Visvabharati: 1953.

Heath, Sir Thomas L. *Diophantos of Alexandria.* Cambridge: 1885.

Hedin, Sven. *Scientific Results of a Journey in Central Asia 1899–1902.* 6 vols. Stockholm: 1904–1907.

———. *Southern Tibet.* 13 vols. Stockholm: 1916–1922.

Heimann, Betty. *Facets of Indian Thought.* London: 1964.

———. *Indian and Western Philosophy.* London: 1937.

Heimsath, Charles H. *Indian Nationalism and Hindu Social Reform.* Princeton: 1964.

Heine-Geldern, Robert. "Asiatische Herkunft der Sudamerikanischen Metalitechnik." *Paideuma,* V (1954), 347–423.

———. "Heyerdahl's Hypothesis of Polynesian Origins: A Criticism." *Royal Geographic Society Journal,* CXVI (1950), 183–192.

Hell, Joseph, *The Arab Civilization.* Cambridge: 1926.

Henke, Frederick Goodrich (tr. and ed.). *The Philosophy of Wang-Yang-Ming.* 2nd ed.; New York: 1964. First published 1916.

Henriques, Fernando. *Prostitution and Society.* 2 vols. London: 1962–1963.

Hermann, A. *Historical Atlas of China.* Cambridge, Mass.: 1935.

Hertel, Johannes. *Das Pancatantra Seine Geschichte und seine Verbreitung.* Leipzig and Berlin: 1914.

Hervieux, Leopold. *Les Fabulistes Latins depuis Le siècle d'Auguste jusqu'à la fin du moyen age.* 5 vols. Paris: 1893–1899.

Heyden, A., A. M. Van Der, and H. A. Schullard. *Atlas of the Classical World.* London: 1963.

Heyerdahl, Thor. *The Kon-Tiki Expedition.* London: 1950.

Hicks, R. D. *Stoic and Epicurean.* London: 1910.

Hiriyanna, M. *The Essentials of Indian Philosophy.* London: 1949.

———. *Outlines of Indian Philosophy.* London: 1932.

Hirst, Désirée. *Hidden Riches. Traditional Symbolism from the Renaissance to Blake.* London: 1964.

Hitti, Philip K. *History of the Arabs.* London: 1956.

———. *Islam and the West.* Princeton: 1962.

Hobson, J. A. *Imperialism: A Study.* London: 1902.

Hocart, A. M. *Kingship.* London: 1941.

Hodgen, Margaret T. *Early Anthropology in the 16th and 17th Centuries.* Pennsylvania: 1964.

Hodous, Lewis. *Buddhism and Buddhists in China.* New York: 1924.

Hoernle, A. F. R. *Manuscript Remains of Buddhist Literature.* Oxford: 1916.

———. *Studies in the Medicine of Ancient India.* Oxford: 1907.

Holtom, D. C. *Modern Japan and Shinto Nationalism.* 2nd ed.; Chicago: 1947.

———. *The National Faith of Japan: A Study in Modern Shinto.* London: 1938.

Honore, Pierre. *In Quest of the White God.* London: 1963.

Hopkins, E. Washburn. *Epic Mythology.* Strasbourg: 1915.

———. *Ethics of India.* New Haven: 1924.

Hottinger, Arnold. *The Arabs*. London: 1963.

Hourani, G. F. *Arab Seafaring in the Indian Ocean in Ancient and Early Medieval Times*. Princeton: 1951.

Hoyland, John. *A Historical Survey of the Customs, Habits and Present State of the Gypsies*. New York: 1816.

Hoyle, Fred. *The Nature of the Universe*. Oxford: 1950.

Hui-li. *The Life of Hsuan-Tsang*. Peking: 1959.

Huizinga, Johan. *Men and Ideas*. Translated by James S. Holmes and Hans van Marle. New York: 1959.

Hull, Denison B. (tr.). *Aesop's Fables*. Chicago: 1960.

Hultzsch, E. (ed.). *Corpus Inscriptionum Indicarum, Inscriptions of Asoka*. Vol. I. Oxford: 1925.

Humboldt, Alexander Von. *Researches Concerning the Institutions and Monuments of the Ancient Inhabitants of America*. London: 1814.

―――― and Aimé Bonpland. *Personal Narrative of Travels to the Equinoctial Regions of the New Continent during the Years 1799–1804*. Translated by Helen Maria Williams. London: 1814–1829.

Hume, R. E. *The Thirteen Principal Upanishads*. London: 1934.

Humphreys, Christmas. *Buddhism*. London: 1951.

Hurvitz, Leon (tr.). *Wei Shou: Treatise on Buddhism and Taoism*. Kyoh: 1956.

Hu Shih. *The Chinese Renaissance*. New York: 1965.

Hutchinson, J. B., R. A. Silow, and S. G. Stephens. *The Evolution of Gossypium*. London: 1947.

Hutchinson, Sir Joseph. "The History and Relationship of the World's Cottons." *Endeavour*, XXI (1962).

Hutchinson, Lester. *European Freebooters in Mughal India*. Bombay: 1964.

Hutton, J. H. *Caste in India*. Cambridge: 1946.

Huxley, Aldous. *The Perennial Philosophy*. London: 1946.

Ikram, S. M. *Muslim Civilization in India*. New York and London: 1964.

Indian Council for Cultural Relations. *Indian Shidis Abroad*. Bombay: 1964.

Indica: The Indian Historical Research Institute Silver Jubilee Commemoration Volume. Bombay: 1954.

Inge, W. R. *Mysticism in Religion*. London: 1947.

――――. *The Platonic Tradition in English Religious Thought*. London: 1926.

――――, L. P. Jacks, M. Hiriyama, and D. T. Raju (eds.). *Radhakrishnan: Comparative Studies in Philosophy*. New York: 1951.

International Congress of Americanists. *The Civilization of Ancient America*. Chicago: 1951.

Irani, D. J. *Gathas*. London: 1924.

Isherwood, Christopher. *Ramakrishna and His Disciples*. London: 1965.

―――― (ed.). *Vedanta for Modern Man*. London: 1952.

————. *Vedanta for the Western World*. London: 1948.

I-tsing. *A Record of the Buddhist Religion as Practised in India and the Malay Archipelago*. Translated by J. Takakausu. Oxford: 1896.

Iyengar, K. R. Srinivasa. *Indian Writing in English*. New York: 1962.

Iyer, Raghavan (ed.). *South Asian Affairs*. No. 1. London: 1960.

Jacobs, Hans. *Western Psychotherapy and Hindu Sadhana*. London: 1961.

Jaffar, S. M. *Some Cultural Aspects of Muslim Rule in India*. Peshawar: 1939.

Jairazbhoy, R. A. *Foreign Influences in Ancient India*. London: 1963.

Jameson, R. D. *Three Lectures on Chinese Folklore*. Peiping: 1932.

Janse, Olov R. T. *Archaeological Research in Indo-China*. Vols. I and II. Cambridge, Mass.: 1947.

Japanese National Commission for UNESCO. *Theatre in Japan*. Japan: 1963.

Jeans, Sir James. *The Mysterious Universe*. Cambridge: 1948.

The Jewish Encyclopedia. 12 vols. London: 1901–1906.

Johnson, A. H. *Whitehead's Philosophy of Civilization*. Boston: 1950.

Johnson, F. *Hitopadesa*. Revised by L. Barnett. London: 1928.

Johnston, E. H. *Early Samkhya; An Essay on Historical Development*. London: 1937.

Johnston, R. F. *Buddhist China*. London: 1913.

Jolly, Julius. *Indian Medicine*. Translated by C. G. Kashikar. Poona: 1951.

Jones, A. M. *Africa and Indonesia*. Leiden: 1964.

Jones, H. L. (tr.). *The Geography of Strabo*. 8 vols. London: 1917–1954.

Jones, Sir William, and Willard N. Augustus. *Music of India*. 2nd rev. ed.; Calcutta: 1962. First published 1793.

Joseph, John. *The Nestorians and Their Muslim Neighbours*. Princeton: 1961.

Journal of the American Oriental Society.

Journal of the Gypsy Lore Society. Old series, 3 vols., Edinburgh: 1888–1892. New series, 9 vols., Liverpool: 1907–1916. Third series, Edinburgh: 1922 to date.

Journal of Hellenic Studies. London.

Journal of the History of Ideas. Pennsylvania.

Journal of Indian History. Travancore.

Journal of the Royal Asiatic Society. London.

Journal of World History. UNESCO. Paris.

Kabir, Humayun. *The Indian Heritage*. Bombay: 1955.

———— (ed.). *Maulana Abul Kalam Azad*. Bombay: 1959. (A memorial volume.)

Kalhana. *Rjatarangini: A Chronicle of the Kings of Kasmir*. Translated by M. A. Stein. London: 1900.

Kālidāsa. *The Megha-Duta*. Edited by S. K. De. New Delhi: 1959. First published Bombay: 1916.

Kamath, M. A. *Hinduism and Modern Science*. Bangalore: 1947. (Foreword by Kunhan Raja.)

Kane, Pandurang Vaman. *History of Dharmasastra*. 5 vols. Poona: 1930–1962.

Kanga, D. D. *Where Theosophy and Science Meet*. 2 vols. Adyar: 1938–1939.

Kañgle, R. P. (ed.). *The Kantilya-Arthasastra*. Parts 1 and 2. Bombay: 1960–1963.

Karambelkar, V. W. *The Athar-veda and the Ayur-veda*. Nagpur: 1961.

Karlgren, Bernard. *The Chinese Language, an Essay on its Nature and History*. New York: 1949.

——— (tr.). *Shih Ching: The Book of Odes*. Stockholm: 1950.

Kato, Genchi. *A Study of Shinto*. Tokyo: 1926.

Kaul, Gwasha Lal. *Kashmir Through the Ages: 5000 B.C. to 1960 A.D.* Srinagar: 1960.

Kaye, G. R. *Indian Mathematics*. Calcutta and Simla: 1915.

Keay, Frank E. *A History of Hindi Literature*. 3rd ed.; Calcutta: 1920.

Keith, A. B. *A History of Sanskrit Literature*. Oxford: 1928.

———. *Indian Logic and Atomism*. Oxford: 1921.

———. *Sanskrit Drama*. Oxford: 1924.

Kern, H. (ed.). *The Jataka-Mala, by Arya Sura*. Cambridge, Mass.: 1914.

Kessel, Joseph. *Afghanistan*. Translated from the French by Bernadette Folliot. London: 1959.

Kielhorn, F. (ed.). *Mahabhashya* (by Pasañjab). 3 vols. Bombay: 1892–1909.

Kimura, Ryokan. *A Historical Study of the Terms Hinayana and Mahayana and the Origin of Mahayana Buddhism*. Calcutta: 1927.

King, C. T. *The Gnostics and Their Remains*. London: 1864.

King, E. (Viscount Kingsborough.) *Antiquities of Mexico*. London: 1831–1848.

King, Martin Luther. *Why We Can't Wait*. London: 1964.

King, Winston L. *Buddhism and Christianity*. London: 1963.

Kitto, H. D. F. *The Greeks*. London: 1960.

Knight, Richard Payne. *The Symbological Language of Ancient Art and Mythology*. New York: 1892.

Kochanowski, Jan. *Gypsy Studies*. Parts 1 and 2. New Delhi: 1963.

Koebner, R., and H. D. Schmidt. *Imperialism*. Cambridge: 1964.

Kondapi, C. *Indians Overseas (1838–1949)*. New Delhi: 1951.

Kosambi, D. D. *The Culture and Civilization of Ancient India in Historical Outline*. London: 1965.

———. *An Introduction to the Study of Indian History*. Bombay: 1956.

Kraemer, Hendrik, *World Cultures and World Religions*. London: 1960.

Kripalani, Krishna. *Rabindranath Tagore*. London: 1962.

Krishna, Isvara. *Sankhya Karika: A Commentary of Gaurapada*. Translated by H. T. Colebrooke and H. H. Wilson. Bombay: 1924.

Kroeber, A. L. *Anthropology*. London: 1924.

———. *The History of Philippine Civilization as Reflected in Religious Nomenclature*. New York: 1923.

———. *Peoples of the Philippines*. New York: 1928.

———. *Peruvian Archaeology*. New York: 1954.

——— et al. *Anthropology Today*. Chicago: 1953.

Krom, N. J. *Hindoe-Javaansche Geschiedenis*. *(Hindu-Javanese History.)* S'Gravenbadge: 1931.

Lach, Donald F. *Asia in the Making of Europe*. Vol. I, Books 1 and 2. Chicago: 1964.

La Fontaine, Jean de. *The Fables*. Translated by Walter Thornbury. London, Paris, and New York: 1867–1870.

La Fontaine, Jean de. *Fables Choisies Mises En Vers*. Paris: 1962.

Lahovary, N. *Dravidian Origins and the West*. Bombay: 1963.

Lal, Chaman. *Gypsies*. Delhi: 1962.

———. *Hindu America*. Bombay, 1960.

———. *India and Japan: Friends of Fourteen Centuries*. Hoshiarpur: 1959.

La Motte, Etienne. *Histoire du Bouddhisme Indien*. Louvain: 1958.

Landau, Rom. *Islam and the Arabs*. London: 1958.

Landon, Kenneth Perry. *South East Asia, Crossroad of Religions*. Chicago: 1949.

Lane, Edward W. *The Thousand and One Nights*. London: 1839–1841.

Lang, Andrew. *Custom and Myth*. London: 1910. First published 1884.

Lang, D. M. *The Wisdom of Balahvar*. London: 1957.

Lang, John Dunmore. *Origins and Migrations of the Polynesian Nations*. 2nd ed.; Sydney: 1877. First published 1834.

Langdon-Davies, John. *A Short History of Woman*. London: 1928.

Latourette, K. S. *The Chinese: Their History and Culture*. London: 1946.

La Vallée Poussin, L. de. *Dynasties et Histoire de l'Inde depuis Kanishka jusqu'aux invasions Musulmanes*. Paris: 1935.

———. *The Way to Nirvana*. Cambridge: 1917.

Law, B. C. *The Historical Geography of Ancient India*. Paris: 1954.

Law, N. N. *Promotion of Learning in India During Muhammadan Rule*. London: 1916.

Lecky, W. E. H. *A History of European Morals*. 2 vols. London: 1869.

Lee, Samuel. *The Travels of Ibn Batuta*. London: 1829.

Leeming, Joseph. *Yoga and the Bible*. London: 1963.

Leeuwen, Arend Th. van. *Christianity and World History*. Edinburgh: 1964.

Legge, J. *The Chinese Classics*. 5 vols. Oxford and London: 1871–1895.

——— (tr.). *A Record of Buddhistic Kingdoms*. Oxford: 1886. (An account of Fa-hien's travels in India.)

———. *Travels of Fa-hien*. Oxford: 1886.

Legouis, Emile. *A Short History of English Literature*. Oxford: 1934.

Leland, C. G. *The English Gypsies and Their Language*. London: 1873.

———. *The Gypsies*. Boston: 1924. First published 1882.

———. *Gypsy Sorcery and Fortune Telling*. London: 1891.

Le May, Reginald. *Buddhist Art in Siam*. Tokyo: 1963. First published Cambridge: 1938.

———. *The Culture of South-East Asia*. London: 1956.

Leon-Portilla, Miguel (ed.). *The Broken Spears: The Aztec Account of the Conquest of Mexico*. Boston: 1962.

Le Strange, Guy. *Baghdad during the Abbasid Caliphate from Contemporary Arabic and Persian Sources*. Oxford: 1924.

———. *The Lands of the Eastern Caliphate; Mesopotamia, Persia, and Central Asia*. Cambridge: 1905.

Leur, J. C. van. *Indonesian Trade and Society*. 2nd ed.; Sumur Bandung: 1960.

Lévi, S. *Le Nepal*. 2 vols. Paris: 1905–1908.

Levy, Reuben (tr.). *The Epic of Kings*. Shahnama by Ferdowsi. Chicago: 1967.

Lewis, A. R. *Naval Power and Trade in the Mediterranean (500–1100)*. Princeton: 1951.

Lewis, Bernard. *The Arabs in History*. London: 1962.

Lewis, H. Spencer. *The Mystical Life of Jesus*. 15th ed.; California: 1962. First published 1929.

Libby, Willard F. *Radio Carbon Dating*. Chicago: 1965.

Lillie, A. *India in Primitive Christianity*. London: 1909.

Lindsay, A. D. (tr.). *The Republic of Plato*. New York: 1950.

Lings, Martin. *A Moslem Saint of the Twentieth Century*. London: 1961.

Littmann. *Tausendundeine Nacht in der Arabischen Literatur*. Tubingen: 1923.

Liu, Wu-chi. *Introduction to Chinese Literature*. London: 1966.

Livingstone, R. W. (ed.). *The Legacy of Greece*. Oxford: 1921.

Lloyd-Jones, H. (ed.). *The Greeks*. London: 1962.

Loeb, Edwin M. and Robert Heine-Geldern. *Sumatra*. Vienna: 1935.

Loenen, J. H. M. M. *Parmenides, Melissus, Gorgias*. Asen, Netherlands: 1959.

Lombard, F. A. *An Outline History of the Japanese Drama*. London: 1928.

Lovejoy, Arthur O. *The Great Chain of Being*. Cambridge, Mass.: 1953.

Lowie, Robert. *The History of Ethnological Theory*. London: 1937.

———. "Some Problems of Geographical Distribution." *Sudseestudien*, pp. 11–26. Basel: 1951.

Macaulay, Thomas Babington. *Critical and Historical Essays*. 2 vols. London: 1951.

Macauliffe, M. A. *The Sikh Religion*. 6 vols. Oxford: 1909.

McCrindle, J. W. *Ancient India as Described by Megasthenes and Arrian.* Calcutta: 1960. First published London: 1901.

────── (tr.), and S. N. Majundar (ed.). *Ancient India as Described by Ptolemy.* Calcutta: 1927.

MacCulloch, J. A. *The Childhood of Fiction.* London: 1905.

Macdonald, J. Ramsay. *The Awakening of India.* London: 1910.

Macdonell, A. A. and A. B. Keith. *Vedic Index of Names and Subjects.* London: 1912.

Macdonell, Arthur A. *A History of Sanskrit Literature.* London: 1905.

──────. *India's Past.* Oxford: 1927.

──────. *Vedic Mythology.* Strasbourg: 1897.

Macdowell, Edward. *Critical and Historical Essays.* Boston: 1912.

McEwan, C. W. *The Oriental Origin of Hellenistic Kingship.* Chicago: 1939.

MacGowan, Kenneth. *Early Man in the New World.* New York: 1950.

Mackay, E. J. H. *Further Excavations at Mohenjo-Daro.* Delhi: 1938.

MacKenzie, Donald A. *Myths of Pre-Columbian America.* London: 1923.

Mckenzie, J. *Hindu Ethics.* London: 1922.

McNickle, D'Arcy. *They Came Here First.* Philadelphia: 1949.

Macnicol, N. (ed.). *Hindu Scriptures.* London: 1938.

──────. *The Making of Modern India.* London: 1934.

Mactie, J. N. *Myths and Legends of India.* Edinburgh: 1929.

Mahmud, Syed. *Hindu Muslim Cultural Accord.* Bombay: 1949.

Maitra, Susila Kumara. *The Ethics of the Hindus.* Calcutta: 1958.

Majumdar, R. C. *Ancient Indian Colonization in South-East Asia.* Baroda: 1963.

────── (ed.). *The Classical Accounts of India.* Calcutta: 1960.

──────. *Hindu Colonies in the Far East.* Calcutta: 1963.

────── and A. D. Pusalker (eds.). *History and Culture of the Indian People.* Vols. I–VI. London: 1951.

Malalasekera, G. P. *The Pali Literature of Ceylon.* London: 1928.

Mangelsdorf, Paul C. "Ancester of Corn." *Science,* CXXVIII, No. 3335 (28 November 1958).

Mansel, H. L. *The Gnostic Heresies of the First and Second Centuries.* London: 1875.

Markham, C. R. *The Incas of Peru.* London: 1910.

Marlow, A. N. *Radhakrishnan.* London: 1962.

Marshall, John H. *Guide to Taxila.* 4th ed.; London: 1960. First published Calcutta: 1918.

Marshall, John, and Alfred Foucher. *The Monuments of Sāñchi.* Calcutta: 1947.

Martin, P. S. *Indians Before Columbus.* Chicago: 1947.

Mason, John Alden. *The Ancient Civilizations of Peru.* London: 1957.

Maspero, Henri. *Le Chine Antique*. Paris: 1955.

Mattingly, Harold. *Roman Imperial Civilization*. London: 1959.

Maude, Aylmer. *The Life of Tolstoy*. London: 1953. First published 1908–1910.

Maximoff, Matéo. *Savina*. Paris: 1956.

Mayer, J. P. *Political Thought. The European Tradition*. London: 1939.

Means, P. A. *Ancient Civilizations of the Andes*. New York: 1931.

Meester, Maria E. de. *Oriental Influences in the English Literature of the Nineteenth Century*. Heidelberg: 1915.

Mehta, Dharam Dev. *Some Positive Sciences in the Vedas*. New Delhi: 1959.

Mendis, G. C. *Early History of Ceylon*. Calcutta: 1940.

Menon, V. K. *The Development of W. B. Yeats*. Edinburgh: 1960.

Menon, V. Laxmi. *Ruskin and Gandhi*. Varanasi: 1965.

Merrill, Elmer Drew. "The Botany of Cook's Voyages, and Its Unexpected Significance in Relation to Anthropology, Biogeography and History." *Chronica Bontanica*, XIV (1954), 161–384.

Metraux, Guy S., and Francois Crouzet (eds.). *The Evolution of Science*. New York: 1963.

Miller, Robert James. *Monasteries and Culture Change in Inner Mongolia*. Wiesbaden: 1960.

Miller, William Robert. *Non-Violence. A Christian Interpretation*. London: 1964.

Ming, Lai. *A History of Chinese Literature*. London: 1964.

Mirza, M. W. *The Life and Works of Amir Khusrau*. Lahore: 1935.

Mitra, Sisirkumar. *Resurgent India*. Bombay: 1963.

Mizuno, Seiichi. *Chinese Stone Sculpture*. Tokyo: 1950.

Mode, Heinz. *The Harappa Culture and the West*. Calcutta: 1961.

Momigliano, Arnaldo (ed.). *The Conflict Between Paganism and Christianity*. Oxford: 1963.

Monier-Williams, M. *Hinduism*. Calcutta: 1951.

———. *Indian Wisdom*. 3rd ed.; London: 1876.

———. *Sakuntala by Kalidasa*. 2nd ed.; Oxford: 1876.

———. *A Sanskrit-English Dictionary*. Oxford: 1872, 1899.

Mookerji, R. K. *Indian Shipping and Maritime Activity*. London: 1910.

Moore, Charles A. (ed.). *Essays in East-West Philosophy*. Hawaii: 1951.

Moorhead, J. H., and S. Radhakrishnan (eds.). *Contemporary Indian Philosophy*. Rev. ed.; London: 1952.

Moraes, George. *A History of Christianity in India*. Vol. I. Bombay: 1964.

Morgan, Kenneth W. (ed.). *Islam: the Straight Path*. New York: 1958.

——— (ed.). *The Path of the Buddha*. New York: 1956.

Morley, S. G. *The Correlation of Maya and Christian Chronology*. Washington: 1910.

———. *Guide Book to the Ruins of Quirigua*. Washington: 1935.

————. *The Religion of the Hindus.* New York: 1953.

Morton, A. Q., and James McLeman. *Christianity and the Computer.* London: 1964.

Moscati, Sabatino. *Ancient Semitic Civilizations.* London: 1957.

————. *The Face of the Ancient Orient.* Chicago: 1960.

Mukerjee, Radhakamal. *The Culture and Art of India.* London: 1959.

Mukherji, Probhat K. *Indian Literature in China and the Far East.* Calcutta: 1932.

Müller, F. Max. *Chips from a German Workshop.* 4 vols. London: 1867–1875.

————. *Collected Works of F. Max Müller.* London: 1898.

————. *Comparative Mythology.* London: 1856.

————. *History of Ancient Sanskrit Literature.* Varanasi: 1964. First published London: 1859.

————. *India, what can it teach us.* London: 1883.

————. *Lectures on the Origin and Growth of Religion.* London: 1891. First published 1878.

————. *Ramakrishna: His Life and Sayings.* London: 1898.

————. *Ram Mohan to Ramakrishna.* Calcutta: 1952.

———— (ed.). *Sacred Books of the East.* 50 vols. Oxford: 1879–1910.
Vedic Hymns, by F. Max Müller and H. Oldenberg (2 vols.).
Hymns of the Atharva-Veda, by M. Bloomfield (1 vol.).
The Satapatha-Brahmana, by J. Eggeling (5 vols.).
The Grihya Sutras, by H. Oldenberg (2 vols.).
The Upanishads, by F. Max Müller (2 vols.).
The Bhagavad gita, by K. Trimbak Telang (1 vol.).
The Vedanta Sutras, by G. Thibut (3 vols.).
The Sacred Laws of the Aryas, by G. Bühler (2 vols.).
The Institutes of Vishnu, by J. Jolly (1 vol.).
The Minor Law Books, by J. Jolly (1 vol.).
Manu, by G. Bühler (1 vol.).
The Gaina-Sutras, by H. Jacobi (1 vol.).
The Saddharma-pundarîka, by H. Kern (1 vol.).
Mahayana Texts, by E. B. Cowell, F. Max Müller, and J. Takakusu (1 vol.).
The Dhammapada and Sutta-Nipâta, by F. Max Müller and V. Fausböll (1 vol.).
Buddhist Suttas, by T. W. Rhys Davids (1 vol.).
Vinaya Texts, by T. W. Rhys Davids and H. Oldenberg (3 vols.).
The Questions of King Milinda, by T. W. Rhys Davids (2 vols.).
The Fo-sho-hing-tsan-king, from the Chinese translation of the Sanskrit, by S. Beal (1 vol.).
The Zend-Avesta, by J. Darmesteter and L. H. Mills (3 vols.).
Pahlavi Texts, by E. W. West (5 vols.).
The Quran, by E. H. Palmer (2 vols.).
Texts of Confucianism, by J. Legge (4 vols.).

355

Texts of Taoism, by J. Legge (2 vols.).

Analytical Index of Names and Subjects, by M. Winternitz (1 vol.).

————. *On Sanskrit Texts Discovered in Japan*. London: 1880.

————. *The Six Systems of Indian Philosophy*. London: 1899.

Murdoch, James. *History of Japan*. 3 vols. London: 1926.

Murray, Gilbert. *Five Stages of Greek Religion*. London: 1946.

————. *Hellenism and the Modern World*. London: 1953.

Murray, H. J. R. *A History of Chess*. Oxford: 1913.

————. *A History of Board-Games other than Chess*. Oxford: 1952.

Murray, M. A. *The Splendour That Was Egypt*. London: 1954.

Murti, T. R. V. *The Central Philosophy of Buddhism*. London: 1955.

Muzumdar, A. M. *Social Welfare in India*. Bombay: 1964.

Mylonas, George E. *Eleusis and the Eleusinian Mysteries*. Princeton: 1961.

Nag, Kilidas. *Discovery of Asia*. Calcutta: 1958.

————. *Greater India*. Calcutta: 1960.

————. *India and the Middle East*. Calcutta: 1954.

Nagarajan, S. "Arnold and the Bhagavad Gita: A Reinterpretation of 'Empedocles on Etna.' " *Comparative Literature*, XII (Fall 1960), 335–347.

Nakamura, Hajime. *Japan and Indian Asia*. Calcutta: 1961.

————. *The Ways of Thinking of Eastern Peoples*. Rev. ed.; Honolulu: 1964.

Nanda, B. R. *Mahatma Gandhi*. Boston: 1958.

Narain, A. K. *The Indo-Greeks*. Oxford: 1957.

Naravane, V. S. *Modern Indian Thought*. Bombay: 1964.

Natarajan, S. *A Century of Social Reform in India*. London: 1959.

Natwar, Singh K. (ed.). *E. M. Forster. A Tribute*. New York: 1964.

Needham, J. (ed.). *Science, Religion and Reality*. London: 1926.

Needham, Joseph. *Science and Civilization in China*. Vols. I–IV. Cambridge: 1954–1962.

Nef, John U. *Cultural Foundations of Industrial Civilization*. Cambridge: 1958.

Nehru, Jawaharlal. *The Discovery of India*. New York: 1946.

————, Arnold Toynbee, and C. R. Attlee, *India and the World*. New Delhi: 1962.

Neill, Stephen C. *The Christian Society*. London: 1952.

Nethercot, Arthur H. *The First Five Lives of Annie Besant*. Chicago: 1960.

————. *The Last Four Lives of Annie Besant*. London: 1963.

Neuburger, M. *History of Medicine*. Translated by E. Playfair. London: 1910.

Neugebauer, O. *The Exact Sciences in Antiquity*. 2nd ed.; Providence, R. I.: 1957.

New Oxford History of Music. Edited by D. A. Hughes and G. Abraham. Oxford: 1960.

Nicholson, R. A. *A Literary History of the Arabs*. London: 1898.
——. *The Mystics of Islam*. London: 1914.
—— (tr.). *Rumi, Poet and Mystic*. London: 1950.
——. *Studies of Islamic Mysticism*. London: 1921.
Niebuhr, Reinhold. *Faith and History*. London: 1949.
Nikhilananda, Swami. *The Bhagavad Gita*. New York: 1944.
—— (tr.). *The Gospel of Sri Ramakrishna*. Madras: 1964.
——. *Upanishads*. New York: 1949.
Nilsson, M. P. *Greek Piety*. Oxford: 1948.
Nivisin, D. S., and A. F. Wright (ed.). *Confucianism in Action*. Stanford: 1959.
Nizami, K. A. *Some Aspects of Religion and Politics in India During the Thirteenth Century*. Aligarh: 1961.
——. *Studies in Medieval Indian History and Culture*. Allahabad: 1966.
Nobel, Johannes. *Central Asia: The Connecting Link Between East and West*. Nagpur: 1952.
Nock, A. D. *Early Gentile Christianity and its Hellenistic Background*. New York: 1964. First published 1928.
Nordenskjold, N. E. H. *Origin of the Indian Civilization in South America*. Gothenburg: 1931.
Norman, Dorothy (ed.). *Nehru: the First Sixty Years*. 2 vols. London: 1965.
Nutt, Alfred. *The Voyage of Bran*. 2 vols. London: 1895.
Nuttall, Zelia. *The Island of Sacrifice*. Lancaster: 1910.
Nyanatiloka. *Buddhist Dictionary*. Colombo: 1950.

Ojha, G. H. *Bharatiya Prachina Lipi-male*. Ajmer: 1918.
Oldenberg, Hermann. *Buddha; His Life, His Doctrine, His Order*. Translated by William Hoey. London and Edinburgh: 1882.
O'Leary, De Lacy. *How Greek Science Passed to the Arabs*. London: 1957.
Olmstead, A. T. *History of the Persian Empire*. Chicago: 1948.
O'Malley, L. S. S. (ed.). *Modern India and the West*. London: 1941.
Oman, J. C. *The Brahmans, Theists and Muslims of India*. London: 1907.
Orientalia Neerlandica. Leiden: 1948.
Osborne, Arthur. *Buddhism and Christianity in the Light of Hinduism*. London: 1959.
Otto, Rudolf. *The Kingdom of God and the Son of Man*. London: 1951.
Owen, Sidney J. *India on the Eve of the British Conquest*. Calcutta: 1954. First published London: 1872.

Pali Texts Society Translation Series. 13 vols. London: 1909–1925.
    I. *Psalms of the Early Buddhists*. Translated by Mrs. Rhys Davids. 1909.
    II. *A Compendium of Philosophy*. Translated, with introductory essay and notes, by Shwe Zan Aung and Mrs. Rhys Davids. 1910.

III. *The Mahāvamsa or Great Chronicle of Ceylon.* Translated by W. Geiger, assisted by M. Hayes-Bodes. 1912.

IV. *Psalms of the Early Buddhists.* Translated by Mrs. Rhys Davids. 1913.

V. *Points of Controversy or Subjects of Discourse.* Translation of the Kathā-Vatthu from the Adhidhamma-Pitaka by Shwe Zan Aung and Mrs. Rhys Davids. 1916.

VI. *Manual of a Mystic.* Translation from the Pali and Sinhalese work entitled the Yogāvachara's Manual by F. L. Woodword. Edited, with introductory essay, by Mrs. Rhys Davids. 1917.

VII. *The Book of the Kindred Sayings (Sanyutta-Nikāya) or Grouped Suttas. Part I. Kindred Sayings with Verses (Sagāthā-Vagga).* Translated by Mrs. Rhys Davids. 1917.

VIII–IX *The Expositor (Atthasālini): Buddhaghosa's Commentary on the Dhammasanganī, the First Book of the Abhidhamma Pitaka.* Translated by Maung Tin, edited and revised by Mrs. Rhys Davids. Vol. I, 1920. Vol. II, 1921.

X. *The Book of the Kindred Sayings (Sanyutta-Nikāya) or Grouped Suttas. Part II. The Nidāna Book (Nidāna-Vagga).* Translated by Mrs. Rhys Davids, assisted by F. L. Woodward. 1922.

XI. *The Path of Purity.* Translation of Buddhaghosa's Visuddhimagga by Pe Maung Tin. 1923.

XII. *Designation of Human Types (Puggala-Paññatti).* Translated by Bimala Charan Law. 1924.

XIII. *The Book of the Kindred Sayings (Sanyutta-Nikāya) or Grouped Suttas.* Translated by F. L. Woodward, edited by Mrs. Rhys Davids. 1925.

Panikkar, K. M. *Asia and Western Dominance.* London: 1953.

Panikkar, Raymond. *The Foundations of New India.* London: 1963.

——. *The Unknown Christ of Hinduism.* London: 1964.

Panini. *The Ashtadhyayi of Panini.* Edited and translated by S. C. Vasu. 2 vols. Delhi: 1962. First published Allahabad: 1891.

Pan Ku. *The History of the Former Han Dynasty.* (The Imperial Annals.) Translated and edited by Homer H. Dubs. Vols. I and II. Baltimore: 1938, 1955.

Park, No-Yong. *Retreat of the West.* Boston and New York: 1937.

Parker, E. H. *Burma with Special Reference to her Relations with China.* Rangoon: 1893.

Parrinder, E. Geoffrey. *Comparative Religion.* London: 1962.

Parsons, E. A. *The Alexandrian Library.* London: 1952.

Partridge, Burgo. *A History of Orgies.* London: 1964.

Patterson, L. *Mithraism and Christianity.* Cambridge: 1921.

Payne, G. H. (ed.). *Akbar and the Jesuits.* London: 1926.

Pennell, Elizabeth Robins. *Charles Godfrey Leland, A Biography.* London: 1906.

Perry, Ben E. *Studies in the Text History of the Life and Fables of Aesop.* Haverford: 1961.

Petech, L. *Medieval History of Nepal.* Rowe: 1958.

———— (ed.). *Northern India According to the Shui Ching Chu.* Rome: 1950.

Peterson, Peter (ed.). *Hitopadesa by Narayana.* Bombay: 1887.

Philips, C. H. (ed.). *Handbook of Oriental History.* London: 1951.

———— (ed.). *Historians of India, Pakistan and Ceylon.* London: 1961.

Philostratus. *The Life of Appollonius of Tyana.* Translated by F. C. Conybeare. London: 1912.

Piggott, Stuart. *Prehistoric India.* London: 1961.

Pirenne, Jacques. *The Tides of History.* Vols. I and II. London: 1962.

Pischel, Richard (ed.). *Kalidasa's Sakuntala.* 2nd ed.; Cambridge, Mass.: 1922.

Plamenatz, John. *On Alien Rule and Self-Government.* London: 1960.

Plowman, Max (ed.). *Poems and Prophecies.* London: 1959.

Pococke, E. (ed.). *India in Greece.* London: 1852.

Poindexter, M. *The Ayar-Incas.* 2 vols. New York: 1930.

Polo, Marco. *The Travels of Marco Polo.* London: 1926. (Introduction by John Masefield.)

Pope, G. U. *The Sacred Kurral.* London: 1886.

Popley, H. A. *The Music of India.* Calcutta: 1950. First published 1921.

Post, L. A., and E. H. Warmington (ed.). *The Leob Classical Library Latin and Greek Volumes.* Cambridge, Mass. and London: 1964.

Pothan, S. G. *The Syrian Christians of Kerala.* Bombay: 1963.

Pound, Ezra (tr.). *Confucian Analects.* London: 1956.

Prakash, Buddha. *India and the World.* Hoshiarpur: 1964.

Prakash, Satya. *Founders of Sciences in Ancient India.* New Delhi: 1965.

Prasad, Beni. *The Hindu-Muslim Question.* Allahabad: 1961.

————. *History of Jahangir.* London: 1922.

Prasad, Isvari. *History of Medieval India.* Allahabad: 1925.

Prasad, Rajendra. *India Divided.* 3rd rev. ed.; Bombay: 1947.

Prescott. W. H. *The Conquest of Mexico.* 2 vols. London: 1913. First published in 3 volumes in 1843.

————. *The Conquest of Peru.* 2 vols. London: 1847.

Press, John (ed.). *Commonwealth Literature.* London: 1965.

Priaulx, Osmund de Beauvoir. *The Indian Travels of Appollonius of Tyana and the Indian Embassies to Rome.* London: 1873.

Price, A. F. (tr.). *The Diamond Sutra.* London: 1955.

Prinsep, James. *Essays on Indian Antiquities.* London: 1858.

Prip-møller, J. *Chinese Buddhist Monasteries.* Copenhagen: 1937.

Pritchard, James B. (ed.). *The Ancient Near East.* Princeton: 1950.

Przyluski, J. *La Légende de l'Empereur Asoka.* Paris: 1923.

————. (Tr. into English by D. K. Biswas). *The Legend of Emperor Asoka.* Calcutta: 1967.

Rackham, H., and N. H. S. Jones (trs.). *Natural History* (Plinus Secundus). 11 vols. London: 1945.

Radhakrishnan, S. *The Bhagavad Gita*. New York: 1948.

———. *The Dhammapada*. London: 1950.

———. *Eastern Religions and Western Thought*. Oxford: 1939.

———. *Hindu View of Life*. London: 1927.

——— (ed.). *History of Philosophy, Eastern and Western*. 2 vols. London: 1952.

———. *India and China*. 3rd ed.; Bombay: 1954.

———. *Indian Philosophy*. 2 vols. London: 1948.

———. *The Principal Upanishads*. London: 1953.

———. *Religion in East and West*. London: 1933.

——— and Charles A. Moore. *A Source Book in Indian Philosophy*. Princeton: 1957.

Radin, Paul. *The Method and Theory of Ethnology*. New York: 1933.

———. *The Story of the American Indian*. London: 1928.

Raghavan, M. D. *India in Ceylonese History, Society and Culture*. New Delhi: 1964.

Raghavan, V. *The Indian Heritage*. Bangalore: 1956.

———. *Prayers, Praises and Psalms*. Madras: 1938.

———. *Sanskrit and Allied Indological Studies in Europe*. Madras: 1956.

Raghu Vira (ed.). *Ramayana*. Lahore: 1938.

Raghu Vira and Lokeschandra. *Gilgit Buddhist Manuscripts*. New Delhi: 1959.

Rahula, Walpola. *History of Buddhism in Ceylon*. Colombo: 1956.

Ralston, W. R. S. *Russian Folk-Tales*. London: 1873.

Ramachandra Rao, S. K. *Development of Psychological Thought in India*. Mysore: 1962.

Randhawa, M. S. *Kangra Valley Painting*. Bombay: 1964.

Rao, M. V. Ramana. *A Short History of the Indian National Congress*. Delhi: 1959.

Rao, R. P. *Portuguese Rule in Goa 1510–1961*. Bombay: 1963.

Rapson, E. J. *Ancient India*. Cambridge: 1914.

Rau, G. Subba. *Indian Words in English*. Oxford: 1954.

Rawlinson, H. G. *India: A Short Cultural History*. Rev. ed.; London: 1952.

———. *Indian Historical Studies*. London: 1913.

———. *Intercourse between India and the Western World*. 2nd ed.; Cambridge: 1926.

Ray, H. C. *History of Ceylon*. Vol. I. Colombo: 1957.

Ray, Nihar Ranjan. *Introduction to the Study of Theravada: Theravada Buddhism in Burma*. Calcutta: 1946.

Ray, P. (ed.). *History of Chemistry in Ancient and Medieval India*. Calcutta: 1956.

Ray, Sunil Chandra. *Early History and Culture of Kashmir*. Calcutta: 1957.

BIBLIOGRAPHY

Raychaudhuri, Hemachandra. *Political History of Ancient India*. Calcutta: 1953.

———. *Studies in India Antiquities*. Calcutta: 1958.

Raychaudhuri, Tapan. *Contributions to Indian Economic History*. Vol. I. Calcutta: 1960.

Reed, Howard S. *A Short History of the Plant Sciences*. Waltham, Mass.: 1942.

Regmi, D. R. *Ancient Nepal*. Calcutta: 1961.

Reichelt, Karl Ludwig. *Religion in Chinese Garment*. New York: 1951.

———. *Truth and Traditions in Chinese Buddhism*. Shanghai: 1927.

Reischauer, A. R. *Studies in Japanese Buddhism*. New York: 1917.

Reischauer, Edwin O. *Ennin's Travels in T'ang China*. New York: 1955.

———. *Japan: Past and Present*. 2nd ed.; Tokyo: 1962.

Renou, Louis. *Religions of Ancient India*. London: 1953.

———. *Vedic India*. Translated by Philip Spratt. Calcutta: 1957.

Rhys, Ernest (Intro.). Aesop's *Fables* (and others). New York: 1913.

Ridley, Michael. *The Seal of Aetea and the Minoan Scripts*. Calcutta: 1963.

Riepe, Dale. *The Naturalistic Tradition in Indian Thought*. Seattle: 1961.

Ritchie, D. G. *Plato*. Edinburgh: 1902.

Rizvi, Saiyid Athar Abbas. *Muslim Revivalist Movements in Northern India in the Sixteenth and Seventeenth Centuries*. Agra: 1965.

——— and Lal Bhargava Moti. *Freedom Struggle in Uttar Pradesh*. Lucknow: 1962.

Roberts, Samuel. *The Gypsies*. London: 1836.

Robertson, William. *An Historical Disquisition Concerning the Knowledge which the Ancients Had of India*. London: 1791.

Robinson, John A. T. *Honest to God*. London: 1963.

Rogers, Millard B. "An Archeological Pilgrimage to Santiago de Compostela." *Science*, CXXXI, No. 3408 (22 April 1960).

Rolland, Romain. *The Life of Ramakrishna*. Translated by E. F. Malcolm-Smith. 6th ed.; Calcutta: 1960.

———. *Prophets of the New India*. Translated by E. F. Malcolm-Smith. New York: 1930.

Rosen, F. *The Algebra of Mohammed ben Musa*. London: 1831.

Rosenthal, Ethel. *The Story of Indian Music and its Instruments*. London: 1929.

Ross, Floyd H. *The Meaning of Life in Hinduism and Buddhism*. London: 1952.

Rostovtzeff, M. *Caravan Cities*. Oxford: 1932.

———. *History of the Ancient World*. Vols. I and II. Oxford: 1926.

———. *Social and Economic History of the Roman Empire*. Oxford: 1926.

Roth, Cecil. *The Historical Background of the Dead Sea Scrolls*. Oxford: 1958.

———. *The Jewish Contribution to Civilization*. Oxford: 1943.

————. *A Short History of the Jewish People*. London: 1936.

Rowe, J. Howland. *Inca Culture at the Time of Spanish Conquest*. Washington: 1946.

Rowland, Benjamin. *The Wall Paintings of India, Central Asia and Ceylon*. Boston: 1938.

Roy, Dhirendra N. *The Philippines and India*. Manila: 1930.

Royle, J. F. *Antiquity of Hindoo Medicine*. London: 1887.

————. *The Arts and Manufactures of India*. London: 1852.

————. *An Essay on the Antiquity of Hindoo Medicine*. London: 1837.

Rustum, A. J. and C. K. Zurayk (eds.). *History of the Arabs and Arabic Culture*. Beirut: 1940.

Ryder, A. W. *The Little Clay Cart*. Cambridge, Mass.: 1905.

———— (tr.). *The Panchatantra*. Chicago: 1925.

Sachs, Curt. *The Rise of Music in the Ancient World*. London: 1944.

Sakasena, Rama Babu. *A History of Urdu Literature*. Allahabad: 1927.

Sale, George (tr.). *The Koran*. London and New York: 1888.

Saleeby, Najeeb M. *The Origins of Malayan Filipinos*. Manila: 1911.

Saletore, B. A. *Ancient Indian Political Thought and Institutions*. London: 1963.

————. *India's Diplomatic Relations with the West*. Bombay: 1958.

Salmony, A. *Sculpture in Siam*. London: 1925.

Sambamoorthy, P. *History of Indian Music*. Madras: 1960.

————. *South Indian Music*. 3rd ed.; Madras: 1933.

Sampson, John. *The Dialect of the Gypsies of Wales*. Oxford: 1926.

Samuel, Viscount, and Herbert Dingle. *A Threefold Cord*. London: 1961.

Sanderson, Gorham D. *India and British Imperialism*. New York: 1951.

Sankalia, H. D. *Indian Archaeology Today*. Bombay: 1962.

————. *Prehistory and Protohistory in India and Pakistan*. Bombay: 1963.

————. *The University of Nalanda*. Madras: 1934.

Sankarananda, Swami. *Hindu States of Sumeria*. Calcutta: 1962.

Sansom, Sir George. *Japan: A Short Cultural History*. Rev. ed.; New York: 1943.

Saraswati, S. K. *A Survey of Indian Sculpture*. Calcutta: 1957.

Sarkar, Benoy K. *Hindu Achievements in Exact Science*. London: 1918.

Sarkar, H. B. *Indian Influences on the Literature of Java and Bali*. Calcutta: 1934.

Sarkar, Sasanka S. *Ancient Races of Baluchistan, Panjab and Sind*. Calcutta: 1964.

Sarma, D. S. *The Renaissance of Hinduism*. Banaras: 1944.

————. *What is Hinduism?* Madras: 1945.

Sarton, George. *A History of Science*. Vols I and II. Cambridge, Mass.: 1959.

————. *The History of Science and New Humanism*. New York: 1931.

————. *Introduction to the History of Science.* Vols. I–III. Baltimore: 1953. First published Washington: 1927.

————. *The Life of Science.* New York: 1948.

Sarup, L. *The Nighantu and the Nirukta.* London: 1920.

Sastri, K. A. Nilakanta (ed.). *Age of the Nandas and Mauryas.* Banaras: 1952.

———— (ed.). *A Comprehensive History of India.* Vol. II. Bombay: 1957.

————. *History of Sri Vijaya.* Madras: 1949.

————. *South Indian Influences in the Far East.* Bombay: 1949.

Sastri, Subrahmanya, and R. Bhat (trs. and eds.). *Brihak-Samhitā* (by Varaha-mihira). 2 vols. Banglore: 1947.

Satomi, Kishio. *Japanese Civilization.* London: 1923.

Sauer, J. D. "The Grain Amaranths: A Survey of their History and Classification." *Annals Missouri Botan. Garden.,* XXXVII (1950), 561–632.

Saunders, E. Dale. *Buddhism in Japan (with an outline of its origins in India).* Philadelphia: 1964.

Saunders, J. H. *The Wild Species of Gossypium and their Evolutionary History.* London: 1961.

Saunders, J. J. *A History of Medieval Islam.* London: 1965.

Schilling, Harold K. *Science and Religion.* New York: 1962.

Schilpp, Paul Arthur (ed.). *The Philosophy of Sarvepalli Radhakrishnan.* New York: 1952.

Schlegel, Frederick. *Lectures on the History of Literature Ancient and Modern.* London: 1818.

————. *Uber die Sprache und Weisheit der Inder.* Heidelberg: 1808.

Schopenhauer, Arthur. *The World as Will and Idea.* Translated and edited by R. B. Haldane and J. Kemp. 3 vols. London: 1883.

Schrödinger, Erwin. *Nature and the Greeks.* Cambridge: 1954.

Schwab, Raymond. *La Renaissance Orientale.* Paris: 1950.

Schweitzer, Albert. *The Quest for the Historical Jesus.* London: 1910.

Seckel, Dietrich. *The Art of Buddhism.* London: 1964.

Séjourné, Laurette. *Burning Water. Thought and Religion in Ancient Mexico.* New York: 1956.

Selincourt, Aubrey de (tr.). *Arrian's Life of Alexander the Great.* London: 1962.

————. *Herodotus, the Histories.* London: 1954.

Sen, Surendra Natha (ed.). *Indian Travels of Thevenot and Careri.* New Delhi: 1949.

Sencourt, Robert. *India in English Literature.* London: 1925.

Sewell, Robert. *A Forgotten Empire.* London: 1900.

Shah, C. L. J. *Jainism in Northern India.* London: 1932.

Sharif, M. M. (ed.). *A History of Muslim Philosophy.* 2 vols. Wiesbaden: 1963 and 1966.

Sharma, Bishan Sarup. *Gandhi As A Political Thinker.* Allahabad: 1956.

Sharma, Chandraddhar. *A Critical Survey of Indian Philosophy*. London: 1960.

Sharma, Dashratha. *Early Chauhan Dynasties*. Delhi: 1959.

Sharma, S. R. *The Crescent in India*. Bombay: 1937.

Sharp, Andrew. *Ancient Voyagers in the Pacific*. Wellington: 1956.

————. *Ancient Voyagers in Polynesia*. Auckland and Hamilton: 1963.

Shastri, D. *A Short History of Indian Materialism and Hedonism*. Calcutta: 1930.

Sherrard, Philip. *The Pursuit of Greece*. London: 1964.

Shinn, Roger L. *Christianity and the Problem of History*. New York: 1933.

Shorey, Paul. *Platonism Ancient and Modern*. California: 1938.

Shoso-In Gyobotsu Zuroku. Pictures of the Imperial properties in the Shoso-in, Nara. 18 vols. Tokyo: 1951.

Shukla, P. N. *Vastu-Sastra: Vol. I. Hindu Science of Architecture*. Lucknow: 1960.

————. *Vastu-Sastra: Vol. II. Hindu Canons of Iconography and Painting*. Lucknow: 1960.

Sila, Brajendranath. *The Positive Sciences of the Ancient Hindus*. Delhi: 1958. First published London: 1915.

Singerist, H. E. *A History of Medicine*. London: 1951.

Singh, A. N., and B. Dutta. *The History of Hindu Mathematics*. Lahore: 1935.

Singh, Karan. *Prophet of Indian Nationalism*. London: 1963.

Singh, Rajendra (Brig.). *History of Indian Army*. New Delhi: 1963.

Singhal, D. P. *Nationalism in India and other Historical Essays*. Delhi: 1967.

Sircar, D. C. *Select Inscriptions bearing on Indian History and Civilization*. Calcutta: 1942.

Siren, O. *Chinese Painting. Leading Masters and Principles*. 7 vols. New York: 1956.

————. *Chinese Sculpture*. London: 1925.

————. *A History of Early Chinese Art*. 4 vols. London: 1929.

Smith, D. E., and L. C. Karpinski. *The Hindu Arabic Numerals*. Boston and London: 1911.

Smith, G. E. *Elephants and Ethnologists*. New York: 1924.

Smith, Stephenson Percy. *Hawaika: The Original Home of the Maori*. Christchurch, New Zealand: 1904.

Smith, Vincent, A. *A History of Fine Art in India and Ceylon*. Oxford: 1911.

————. *A History of Fine Art in India and Ceylon*. Revised and enlarged by Karl Khandalwala. 3rd ed.; Bombay.

Smith, Wilfred Cantwell. *Islam in Modern History*. Princeton: 1957.

————. *Modern Islam in India*. London: 1946.

Society of Antiquarians. *Archaeologia*. Vol. XCVII. Oxford: 1959.

————. *Miscellaneous Tracts Relating to Antiquity*. London: 1785.

Somadeva Bhatta. *Katha Sarit Sagara*. English translation entitled *The Ocean of Story* by C. H. Tawney in ten volumes, edited by N. M. Penzer. London: 1927.

Soothill, W. E. (tr.). *Saddharmapundarika*. Oxford: 1930.

———. *The Three Religions of China*. London: 1913.

Sorabji, Kaikhusrau. *Around Music*. London: 1932.

———. *Mi Contra Fa*. London: 1947.

Soustelle, Jacques. *The Daily Life of the Aztecs*. Translated by Patrick O'Brian. London: 1955.

Spargo, J. W. *Linguistic Science in the Nineteenth Century*. Cambridge, Mass.: 1931.

Spence, Lewis. *The Myths of Mexico and Peru*. London: 1913.

———. *The Myths of the North American Indians*. London: 1914.

Spengler, Oswald. *The Decline of the West*. Translated by Charles F. Atkinson. 2 vols. New York: 1957.

Spinden, H. J. *Ancient Civilizations of Mexico and Central America*. New York: 1917.

———. *Maya Art and Civilization*. Colorado: 1957.

———. *Maya Dates and What They Reveal*. Brooklyn: 1930.

Sridharan, L. *A Maritime History of India*. Delhi: 1965.

Starkie, Walter. *Raggle-Taggle*. London: 1964. First published 1933.

———. *Scholars and Gypsies*. London: 1963.

Stcherbatsky, Th. *Central Concepts of Buddhism*. London: 1924.

———. *The Conception of Buddhist Nirvana*. Leningrad: 1927.

Steiger, G. N., H. O. Beyer, and C. Benitez. *A History of the Orient*. Boston: 1926.

Stein, Sir Mark Aurel. *Ancient Khotan*. 2 vols. Oxford: 1907.

———. *Innermost Asia*. Oxford: 1928.

———. *Memoirs on Maps of Chinese Turkestan and Kansu*. Dehradun: 1923.

——— (tr.). *Rejatarangini*. London: 1900.

———. *Ruins of Desert Cathay*. 2 vols. London: 1912.

———. *Sand-Buried Ruins of Khotan*. London: 1903.

———. *Serindia*. 5 vols. Oxford: 1921.

———. *Wall Paintings from Ancient Shrines in Central Asia*. Vols. I and II. Delhi: 1933.

Steinilber-Oberlin, E. *The Buddhist Sects of Japan*. London: 1938.

Sternbach, Ludwik. *The Hitopadesa and its Sources*. New Haven: 1960.

Stevens, Halsey. *The Life and Music of Bela Bartok*. New York: 1953.

Stevenson, S. *The Heart of Jainism*. London and New York: 1915.

Steward, Julian H. (ed.). *Handbook of South American Indians*. Vols. I–VII. Washington: 1946–1959.

Stobart, J. C. *The Glory That Was Greece*. 3rd ed.; London: 1960. First published 1911.

Stockley, V. *German Literature as Known in England: 1750–1830.* London: 1929.

Stokes, Eric. *The English Utilitarians and India.* Oxford: 1959.

Stonor, C. R., and E. Anderson. "Maize among the Hill Peoples of Assam." *Annals Missouri Botan. Garden.,* XXXVI (1949), 355–396.

Stutfield, H. E. M. *Mysticism and Catholicism.* London: 1925.

Stutterheim, W. F. *Studies in Indonesian Archaeology.* The Hague: 1956.

Subrahmanya, Aiyyar. *The Grammar of South Indian Music.* Bombay: 1939.

Sukthankar, V. S., *et al.* (ed.). *Mahabharata.* Poona: 1933–1958.

Sutherland, Lucy S. *The East India Company in Eighteenth Century Politics.* Oxford: 1952.

Suzuki, Beatrice Lane. *Mahayana Buddhism.* London: 1948.

Suzuki, D. T. *A Brief History of Early Chinese Philosophy.* London: 1914.

————. *Essays in Zen Buddhism.* 3 vols. London: 1934–1949.

————. *An Introduction to Zen Buddhism.* New York: 1949.

————. *Living by Zen.* Tokyo: 1949.

————. *A Miscellany on the Shin Teaching of Buddhism.* Kyoto: 1949.

————. *Studies in Zen.* New York: 1955.

————. *Zen Buddhism and its Influence on Japanese Culture.* Kyoto: 1938.

————. *The Zen Doctrine of No-Mind.* London: 1949.

————, Erich Fromm, and Richard de Martino. *Zen Buddhism and Psychoanalysis.* London: 1960.

Swain, Joseph Ward. *The Ancient World.* 2 vols. New York: 1950.

Swamikannu, Pillai. *An Indian Ephermeris.* 7 vols. Madras: 1952.

Sydow, C. W. V. *Selected Papers on Folklore.* Copenhagen: 1948.

Symonds, J. A. *Studies of the Greek Poets.* 3rd ed.; London: 1920. First published 1873.

Tachibana, S. *The Ethics of Buddhism.* London: 1926.

Tagore, Avanindranath, and Stella Kramrisch. *A. D. Coomaraswamy Commemoration Volume.* Calcutta: 1961.

Tagore, Rabindranath. *Drawings and Paintings.* Calcutta: 1961.

Takakusu, Junjiro. *The Essentials of Buddhist Philosophy.* Bombay: 1956.

————. *A Record of the Buddhist Religion as Practised in India and the Malay Archipelago.* Oxford: 1896.

Tarn, W. W. *Alexander the Great* (Narrative). Cambridge: 1948.

————. *Alexander the Great* (Sources and Studies). Cambridge: 1958.

————. *The Greeks in Bactria and India.* 2nd ed.; Cambridge: 1951.

————. *Hellenistic Civilization.* London: 1927.

Taton, Rene (ed.). *History of Science: Vol. I. Ancient and Medieval Science.* London: 1963.

———— (ed.). *History of Science: Vol. II. The Beginnings of Modern Science.* London: 1964.

Tattwananda, Swami. *Ancient Indian Culture at a Glance.* Calcutta: 1962.

Taylor, F. Sherwood. *Science: Past and Present.* London: 1958.

Taylor, Lily Ross. *The Divinity of the Roman Emperor.* Middletown, Conn.: 1931.

Taylor, Thomas (tr.). *Porphyry on Abstinence from Animal Food.* London: 1823.

Tax, Sol, and W. C. Bennet (ed.). *The Civilizations of Ancient America.* (Selected papers of the XXIX International Congress of Americanists.) Chicago: 1952.

Tello, J. *Andean Civilizations.* Edited by Julian H. Steward. New York: 1930.

Thapar, Romila. *Asoka.* Oxford: 1961.

Thomas, Edward J. *Early Buddhist Scriptures.* London: 1935.

————. *The History of Buddhist Thought.* 2nd ed.; New York: 1951.

————. *The Life of Buddha as Legend and History.* London: 1949.

Thomas, P. *The Story of the Cultural Empire of India.* Ernakulam: 1959.

Thompson, Edward. *Suttee.* London: 1928.

Thompson, John E. S. *The Rise and Fall of the Maya Civilization.* London: 1956.

Thompson, Stith. *The Folktale.* New York: 1946.

Thornbury, George Walter. *Life in Spain: Past and Present.* 2 vols. London: 1859.

Thornton, A. P. *The Imperial Idea and its Enemies.* London: 1959.

Tilak, B. G. *The Orion, or Researches into the Antiquity of the Vedas.* Bombay: 1893.

Titus, Murray T. *Islam in India and Pakistan.* Calcutta. 1959. First published 1930.

Tod, James. *Annals and Antiquities of Rajasthan.* 2 vols. London: 1829–1832.

Toynbee, Arnold. *An Historian's Approach to Religion.* New York: 1956.

————. *A Study of History.* 12 vols. London: 1934–1959.

Trevelyan, G. M. *English Social History.* 3rd ed.; London: 1955.

Tripathi, Rama Kanta. *Spinoza in the Light of the Vedanta.* Banaras: 1957.

Tripathi, R. P. *The Rise and Fall of the Mughal Empire.* Allahabad: 1960.

Tritton, A. S. *Islam: Beliefs and Practices.* London: 1951.

Trivedi, D. S. *Indian Chronology.* Bombay: 1959.

Tucci, Giuseppe. *Minor Buddhist Texts.* Rome: 1956.

————. *Preliminary Report on Two Scientific Expeditions in Nepal.* Rome: 1956.

————. *The Tombs of the Tibetan Kings.* Rome: 1950.

Turner, R. L. *The Position of Romani in Indo-Aryan.* Edinburgh: 1927. (Gypsy Lore Society Monograph No. 4.)

Tweedie, M. W. F. *Prehistoric Malaya.* Rev. ed.; Singapore: 1955.

Tylor, Edward B. *Anthropology.* London: 1881.

————. *Primitive Culture.* 2 vols. London: 1871.

————. *Researches into the Early History of Mankind and the Development of Civilization*. London: 1865.

Tzu, Lao. *The Way of Life*. London: 1946.

UNESCO. *Humanism and Education in East and West*. Paris: 1953.

Urwick, E. J. *The Message of Plato*. London: 1920.

Vacherot, M. *Histoire Critique de l'école d'Alexandrie*. Paris: 1846.

Vahir, Syed Abdul. *Iqbal. His Art and Thought*. London: 1959.

Varma, V. P. *The Political Philosophy of Sri Aurobindo*. Bombay: 1960.

Vatsyayana. *Kamasutra*. Bombay: 1905.

Vermaseren, M. J. *Mithras, the Secret God*. London: 1963.

Verrill, A. Hyatt. *Old Civilizations of the New World*. Indianapolis: 1929.

Vesey-Fitzgerald, Brian. *Gypsies in Britain*. London: 1944.

————. *Gypsy Borrow*. London: 1953.

Vidler, A. R., et al. *Objections to Christian Belief*. London: 1963.

Vidyarthi, Mohan, Lal Venkateswana, and S. Vaidyanatha. *India's Culture through the Ages*. Bombay: 1928–1932.

Visser, M. W. De. *The Dragon in China and Japan*. Amsterdam: 1913. First published 1858.

Vlekke, Bernard H. M. *Nusantara*. Cambridge, Mass.: 1944.

Waddell, L. Austine. *The Buddhism of Tibet*. Cambridge: 1959.

————. *The Buddhism of Tibet or Lamaism*. Cambridge: 1959.

Wagner, Richard. *My Life*. London: 1963.

Wales, H. G. Quaritch. *The Making of Greater India*. 2nd ed.; London: 1961.

————. *Prehistory and Religion in South-east Asia*. London: 1957.

————. *Siamese State Ceremonies*. London: 1931.

Waley, Arthur (tr.). *The Analects of Confucius*. London: 1956.

————. *Ballads and Stories from Tun-Huang*. London: 1960.

———— (tr.). *The Book of Songs*. London: 1954.

————. *An Introduction to Chinese Painting*. London: 1923.

————. *Monkey*. London: 1942.

————. *The No Plays of Japan*. London: 1921.

————. *The Real Tripitaka*. New York and London: 1952.

————. *Three Ways of Thought in Ancient China*. London: 1939.

————. *The Way and Its Power*. London: 1942.

Walzer, Richard. *Greek into Arabic*. Oxford: 1962.

Wang, Kung-hsing. *The Chinese Mind*. New York: 1946.

Warmington, E. H. *The Commerce Between the Roman Empire and India*. Cambridge: 1928.

Warner, Langdon. *The Enduring Art of Japan*. Cambridge, Mass.: 1952.

Warren, Henry Clarke. *Buddhism in Translations*. Cambridge, Mass.: 1922.

Watson, Burton. *Early Chinese Literature*. New York and London: 1962.

———. *Records of the Grand Historian of China*. Translated from the *Shih-Chi* of Ssu-Ma Ch'ien. Vols. I and II. New York and London: 1961.

———. *Ssu-Ma Ch'ien Grand Historian of China*. New York and London: 1963.

Watt, W. Montgomery (tr.). *Al-Ghazali. The Faith and Practice of al-Ghazali*. London: 1953.

———. *Islam and the Integration of Society*. Evanston, Ill.: 1961.

Watters, Thomas. *On Yuan Chwang's Travels in India*. Delhi: 1961. First published London: 1904.

Watts, Alan W. *The Legacy of Asia and Western Man*. London: 1937.

———. *Psychotherapy, East and West*. New York: 1961.

Wauchope, Robert. *Lost Tribes and Sunken Continents*. Chicago and London: 1962.

Waxman, Meyer. *A History of Jewish Literature*. 4 vols. New York: 1938–1947.

Webb, G. C. E. *Gypsies: The Secret People*. London: 1960.

Weber, Albrecht. *The History of Indian Literature*. Translated by John Mann and Theodor Zachariae. 6th ed.; Varanasi: 1961. First published 1878.

Webster, T. B. L. *From Mycenae to Homer*. London: 1960.

Weigall, Arthur. *The Paganism in our Christianity*. London: 1928.

Welch, Holmes. *The Parting of the Way*. Boston: 1957.

Wells, H. G. *The Outline of History*. London: 1925.

Wells, Henry W. *The Classical Drama of India*. London: 1963.

Wells, Kenneth E. *Thai Buddhism: Its Rites and Activities*. Bangkok: 1934.

Wertheim, W. F. *Bali-Studies in Life, Thought, and Ritual*. The Hague and Bandung: 1960.

Westcott, G. H. *Kabir and the Kabir Panth*. Cawnpore: 1907.

Wheatley, Paul. *The Golden Khersonese*. Kuala Lumpur: 1961.

Wheeler, J. A. *Geometrodinamica*. New York and London: 1962.

Wheeler, J. T., and M. Macmillan. *European Travellers in India*. Calcutta: 1956.

Wheeler, Sir Mortimer. *The Indus Civilization*. Cambridge: 1953.

Wheeler, Post (ed. and tr.). *The Sacred Scriptures of the Japanese*. London: 1952.

Whitehead, Alfred N. *Adventures of Ideas*. New York: 1959. First published Cambridge: 1933.

———. *Science and the Modern World*. New York: 1959. First published 1926.

Whittaker, Thomas. *The Neo-Platonists: A Study in the History of Hellenism*. Cambridge: 1901.

Wichmann, Hans, and Siegfried Wichmann. *Chess: The Story of Chesspieces from Antiquity to Modern Times*. London: 1964.

Wickramasinghe, Martin. *Landmarks of Sinhalese Literature*. Colombo: 1963.

Wiener, Philip P., and A. Noland (eds.). "Ideas in Cultural Perspective." *Journal of the History of Ideas*. New Brunswick, N.J.: 1962.

Wilhelm, R. *A Short History of Chinese Civilization*. London: 1929.

Wilke, G. *Kulturbeziehungen Zwischen Indien, Orient and Europa*. 2nd ed.; Leipzig: 1923.

Wilkins, H. T. *Secret Cities of Old South America*. London: 1950.

Willetts, William. *Chinese Art*. 2 vols. London: 1958.

Willey, Gordon R. "New World Prehistory." *Science*, CXXXI, No. 3393 (8 January 1960).

Williams, Raymond. *Culture and Society, 1780–1950*. London: 1958.

Willson, A. Leslie. *A Mythical Image: The Ideal of India in German Romanticism*. Durham, N.C.: 1964.

Wilson, Anne C. *A Short Account of the Hindu System of Music*. London: 1904.

Wilson, Edmund. *The Scrolls from the Dead Sea*. London: 1955.

Wilson, Horace H. *Works*. 12 vols. London: 1862–1871.

Winstedt, Richard. *The Malays: A Cultural History*. 5th ed.; London: 1958.

Winter, H. J. J. *Eastern Science*. London: 1952.

Winternitz, M. *A History of Indian Literature*. Translated by S. Ketkar. Vol. I. 2nd ed.; Calcutta: 1927.

Wood, W. A. R. *A History of Siam*. London: 1926.

Woodcock, George. *The Greeks in India*. London: 1966.

Woods, J. H. (tr.). *The Yoga-System of Patañjali*. Cambridge, Mass.: 1914.

Woodward, F. L. *Some Sayings of the Buddha*. London: 1925.

Woolley, Sir Charles Leonard. *Mesopotamia and the Middle East*. London: 1961.

Wormington, H. M. *Ancient Man in North America*. 4th ed.; Denver: 1939.

Wright, Arthur F. *Buddhism in Chinese History*. Stanford: 1959.

——— (ed.). *Studies in Chinese Thought*. Chicago: 1953.

——— and Denis Twitchett (eds.). *Confucian Personalities*. Stanford: 1962.

Wright, Daniel. *History of Nepal*. Calcutta: 1877.

Wright, Elizar Jr. (tr.). *Fables of La Fontaine*. 2 vols. New York: 1841.

Yang, C. K. *Religion in Chinese Society*. Berkeley: 1961.

Yates, D. E. (ed.). *A Book of Gypsy Folk-Tales*. New York and London: 1948.

Yeats, W. B. *Autobiography*. London: 1926.

Yesudian, Selvarajan, and Elisabeth Haich. *Yoga: Uniting East and West*. London: 1956.

Yi-Pao Mei (tr.). *The Ethical and Political Works of Motse*. London: 1929.

Young, T. C. (ed.). *Near Eastern Culture and Society*. Princeton: 1951.

Yu-Lan Fung (tr.). *Chuang Tzu*. Shanghai: 1933.

———. *A History of Chinese Philosophy*. Translated by Derk Bodde. Vols. I–III. Princeton. 1956.

———. *A Short History of Chinese Philosophy*. London: 1948.

———. *The Spirit of Chinese Philosophy*. London: 1947.

Yutang, Lin (ed.). *The Wisdom of China and India*. New York: 1942.

———. *The Wisdom of Laotse*. New York: 1948.

Zaehner, R. C. *Hindu and Muslim Mysticism*. London: 1960.

———. *The Teachings of the Magi*. London: 1956.

Zaide, Gregario F. *Philippine Political and Cultural History*. Vols. I and II. Rev. ed.; Manila: 1957.

Zeller, Eduard. *Outlines of the History of Greek Philosophy*. New York: 1960.

Zimmer, Heinrich R., and J. Campbell. *The Art of Indian Asia*. 2 vols. New York: 1955.

Zimmer, Henry R. *Hindu Medicine*. Baltimore: 1948.

———. *Myths and Symbols in Indian Art and Civilization*. New York: 1953.

———. *Philosophies of India*. New York: 1951.

Zoete, Beryl D. E. *Dance and Magic Drama in Ceylon*. London: 1957.

———. *The Other Mind*. London: 1953.

Zürcher, E. *The Buddhist Conquest of China*. 2 vols. of text and notes respectively. Leiden: 1959.

INDEX

Abel-Rémusat: translator of Fa-hsien, 212

Akbar: Mughal Emperor, 167; patronizes painting, 175-76

al-Arabi, Muhi al-Din ibn: complete monism of, 188

Al Biruni: on stagnation of Hindus, 158-159

al-Ghazali, Imam, 188

America: Atlantic voyages to claimed, 317n2; early migrants to, 35; first cultivation in, 35; probable course to from Asia, 320n37. *See also* Mexico; South America

Amerinds. *See* Asiomericans

Amitabha, the Compassionate Buddha: cults of in Japan, 16

Anawartha, Pagan king, 109

Angkor Thom: design of, 129; stimulus for, 128; symbolism of, 128-29

Angkor Wat, 129-30

Anglo–Oriental College (Aligarh): rivalry with Deoband School, 290-91

Annam, 120

Arabs: attitudes toward India, 161-62; first conquests in India, 161-62, 216-217; opinions of India, 161; in Sind, adopt local customs, 162; trade destroyed by Europeans, 195; trade spreads Islam, 162-63. *See also* Muslims, in India

Architecture: in Bali, Hindu, 154; in Burma, Buddhist, 109-10; in Cambodia, religious, 127-31 *passim*; in Ceylon, Buddhist, 102-03; in Ceylon, Hindu, 103; in India, attempts to blend East and West, 297; in India, European-style, 296; in Indonesia,

religious, 151-54 *passim*; Islamic, 176-177, 177; Islamic, compared to Hindu, 177; Islamic, contributions to India, 179; Islamic, Hindu contributions to, 179; Islamic, in India, 177-83; Islamic, in India, compared to Hindu, 179; in Japan, Buddhist influence on, 27-29 *passim*; in Japan, temples, 10, 11; in Korea, Buddhist, 5-6; in Java, Buddhist, 151-52; in Java, Hindu, 153; Mughal, buildings listed, 176; Mughal, early, 177; Mughal, Indian elements in, 180, 181; Mughal, Iranian influence on, 180; Mughal, under Akbar, 180-81; Mughal, under Jahangir, 181-82; under Shahjahan, 182; under Suri Dynasty, 179-80

Art: in Borneo, Indian influence on, 153-54; Buddhist, routes to Indo-China, 322n32; in Ceylon, Indian influence on, 103-04; in Champa, 124-25; in Funan, Indian influence on, 123; in India, modern, 296; in India, reaction against European, 296-97; in Kedah, Indian influence on, 135-36; in Japan, Buddhist influence on, 24, 27-29 *passim*; in Khmer Kingdom, Indian influence on, 127; Mayan, elephant in, 65; Mayan, evolution of lotus motif, 57; Mayan, makara motif in, 57, 60; Mayan, naga in, 319n24; Mayan, similarities to Asian, 55-60; in Siam, Buddhist, 119. *See also* Painting

Arya Samaj: advocates social reform, 285-86; founded, 285; spreads English education, 286; weaknesses of, 286

Coomaraswamy, Ananda: researches of, 265-66; wish of for India, 266
Cotton: first used in India, 69-70; found at Huaca Prieta, 70; genetics of, 70-71, 319n31, 33; hybrid, theories of origin of, 71-72, 319n33
Cultural diffusion. *See* Diffusionist theory
Cultural Evolutionism: applied to America, arguments against, 52-53; decline of, 52; in England, 52; effect of Darwin on, 51; early proponents, 51-52; suppositions of, 50, 51
Cunningham, Alexander, 227
Czechoslovakia: Indian studies in, 222-223

Dara Shikoh: Mughal Emperor, 167; and religion, 193
Davids, T. W. Rhys: founder of Pali Text Society, 250
de Körös, Alexander Csoma: first Hungarian Orientalist, 223
De Quincey, Thomas: knowledge of India, 244-45
Deguignes, Joseph: determines Indian chronology, 210; shows wide influence of Buddhism, 209-10
Deoband School: purpose of, 289; rivalry with Anglo–Oriental College, 290-91
Deussen, Paul: attracted to Vedanta philosophy, 236-37
Devanagari Script: introduced into Indonesia, 146
Deva Raja, cult of: in Cambodia, 127; in Cambodia, encourages religious building, 128; similar to Javanese cult, 127
Diffusionist theory: suppositions of, 50-51
Dihlawi, Shah Walli Allah: inspires Deoband doctrines, 289
Dogen: philosophy of, 16-17
Dong-son culture: bronzes of, 96; defined, 96; in Funan, 121; navigation in, 96; period developed, 121; theory of origin, 96
du Perron, Anquétil: discovers *Avesta*, 210; studies Persian, 210; translates Upanishads, 210, 211
Dubois, Abbé, 202

East India Company: corruption of, 204; founded, 196-97; lack of social services by, 298-99; resists missionaries to India, 279. *See also* Britain,

Indian rule of; England, early Indian administration of
École des Hautes Études: centre of Indology, 213-14
Eddy, Mary Baker: founder of Christian Science, 256
Education, in India: ancient, 297-98; by Christian missionaries, 299; effect of Western, 299-301; English, reaction against, 301; mediaeval, 298; Ram Mohan Roy's efforts, 299; under British, 299; under East India Company, 298-99; under Muslims, 298
Egypt: theory of American influence on, 36
Eliot, T. S.: Indian themes in poetry, 264
Emerson, Ralph Waldo: influence of Indian thought on, 253-54
Eminescu, Mihai: Indian themes in poetry of, 252
England: commercial expansion of, 196-97; decline of Indian studies in, 208-09; early Indian administration of, 242; early writings on India in, 242. *See also* Britain; East India Company; Indology, British
English (language): Indian words in, 250-51
Equatorial Counter-current: aids Pacific crossings, 77
Europe: in Age of Enlightenment, 276-277; Catholic–Protestant rivalry in, 196; early universities of, 197; in late eighteenth century, 228; mediaeval, Indian influence on literature, 194-95; mediaeval, knowledge of India in, 194; reactions to Indian thought, 270; responses to Indian thought, 228-29, 270. *See also* Britain; England; Europeans; France; Germany; Indology; Portugal; West, the
Europeans: attitudes toward Hinduism, 200-01; early studies of India by, 199; in India, misconceptions of travelers, 200; in India, motives of, 200. *See also* Europe; Indology
Evangelicalism: seeks conversion of Indians, 276. *See also* Missionaries, Christian
Evolutionist Theory. *See* Cultural Evolutionism

Filipinos: suggest related to Indians, 323n61. *See also* Philippines, the
Filliozat, Jean: Indologist, 216

49216

ST. MARY'S COLLEGE OF MARYLAND
ST. MARY'S CITY, MARYLAND